Wege aus dem Krieg

TRANSFORMATIONEN - DIFFERENZIERUNGEN - PERSPEKTIVEN

MAINZER STUDIEN ZUR NEUZEIT

Herausgegeben von Michael Kißener,
Jan Kusber, Andreas Rödder und
Matthias Schnettger

BAND 13

PETER LANG

Berlin - Bruxelles - Chennai - Lausanne - New York - Oxford

Svetlana Bogojavlenska / Benjamin Conrad /
Jan Kusber (Hrsg.)

Wege aus dem Krieg

Auf der Suche nach Frieden und Stabilität in Nordosteuropa nach 1918

PETER LANG

Berlin - Bruxelles - Chennai - Lausanne - New York - Oxford

Bibliografische Information der Deutschen Nationalbibliothek
Die Deutsche Nationalbibliothek verzeichnet diese Publikation in der Deutschen Nationalbibliografie; detaillierte bibliografische Daten sind im Internet über http://dnb.d-nb.de abrufbar.

Umschlagabbildung:

gemeinfrei, Original bei der Lettischen Nationalbibliothek:
https://kartes.lndb.lv/viewer/image-map?h=34232

ISSN 2566-6215
ISBN 978-3-631-90774-0 (Print)
E-ISBN 978-3-631-91503-5 (E-PDF)
E-ISBN 978-3-631-91504-2 (E-PUB)
DOI 10.3726/b21580

Verlegt durch:
Peter Lang GmbH, Berlin, Deutschland

info@peterlang.com http: www.peterlang.com

Diese Publikation wurde begutachtet.

Inhaltsverzeichnis

Svetlana Bogojavlenska / Benjamin Conrad / Jan Kusber

Einführung

In den letzten zwei Jahrzehnten ist das östliche Europa ab dem Ersten Weltkrieg durch Historiker wie Jörg Baberowski und Timothy Snyder als Gewaltraum konzeptualisiert worden.[1] Fragile Gesellschaften in der Zwischenkriegszeit sowie die Herausforderungen multinationaler Gesellschaften, die durch das Pariser System keinesfalls abgemildert wurden, führten zu Gewaltbereitschaft in den Staaten und zwischen den Staaten. Der nachgelagerte Zweite Weltkrieg prägt dabei den Blick auf die Zwischenkriegszeit. Von 2024 aus gesehen, insbesondere vor dem Hintergrund des seit 2022 andauernden russischen Angriffskrieges gegen die Ukraine, ist es schwer, sich von dem ebenso essentialistischen wie einprägsamen Bild der „Bloodlands" zu lösen. In der Tat entstand die neue Staatenwelt im Nordosten Europas im Ersten Weltkrieg und in seinen Nachfolgekriegen auf den Trümmern der Imperien. Die Friedensschlüsse der neuen Staaten insbesondere mit dem sowjetischen Nachbarn, bedeuteten zunächst nur die Abwesenheit von Krieg.

Der Erste Weltkrieg schuf dabei die Voraussetzungen für eine Nachkriegsgewalt, war aber natürlich nicht allein deren Ursache. Diese lag vielmehr in der Verknüpfung von Niederlagen, Revolutionen, Konterrevolutionen und imperialem Zerfall. Dass sich in den Bruchzonen der alten Reiche und in der Phase der Staatsneugründungen besonders viele und heftige Gewaltexzesse abspielten, ist seit längerem Gegenstand intensiver Forschungen. Dabei ist unter anderem gefragt worden, ob man, wie das für Deutschland getan worden ist, von einer Nachkriegsgewalt sprechen kann, oder ob man nicht von einem Krieg sprechen müsse, der in Nordosteuropa den Großen Krieg, Bürgerkrieg und Unabhängigkeitskriege zusammendenkt, in dem paramilitärische Gewalt, Vertreibung und Zwangsmigration sowie Pogrome eingewoben waren.[2] Die analytische Trennung

---

1 Dietrich Beyrau Schlachtfeld der Diktatoren. Osteuropa im Schatten von Hitler und Stalin, Göttingen 2000. = Kleine Reihe V & R.; 4021; Jörg Baberowski Der rote Terror. Die Geschichte des Stalinismus, München 2003; Timothy Snyder Bloodlands. Bloodlands. Europa zwischen Hitler und Stalin, München 2011.

2 Jan Kusber Wegscheide Krieg. Defekte Imperien, defekte Nationalstaaten, in: Osteuropa 64 (2014), Nr. 2–4, S. 233-246; Joshua Sanborn Imperial Apocalypse: The Great War and the Destruction of the Russian Empire, Oxford 2014; Martin Aust Die Russische Revolution. Vom Zarenreich zum Sowjetimperium, München 2017;

der Historikerinnen und Historiker ging keinesfalls immer mit der lebensweltlichen Erfahrung der Menschen einher.

Doch lässt sich hieraus folgern, Frieden, Sicherheit und zivilgesellschaftliche Entwicklungen hätten in der sogenannten Zwischenkriegszeit keine Chance gehabt? Robert Gerwarth jedenfalls hat in seinem Buch „Die Besiegten. Das blutige Erbe des Ersten Weltkrieges“ davor gewarnt, die jeweiligen Kriegserfahrungen als Grund für die anhaltende Brutalisierung der Nachkriegsjahre zu überschätzen.[3]

Der vorliegende Band will die Konzeptualisierung von Gewalträumen und dem daraus abgeleiteten Narrativ von dysfunktionalen Staaten und Gesellschaften umdrehen und fragen, welche Wege aus dem Krieg zur friedlichen Entwicklung von Staaten und ihrer multiethnischen Gesellschaften sowie zur friedlichen Absicherung staatlicher Existenz gesucht wurden. Die Imperien, die ja in der „New Imperial History“ mit Blick auf die Möglichkeiten eines multinationalen und multireligiösen Staates überschätzt wurden, boten immerhin die Möglichkeiten eines wenn auch nicht immer gedeihlichen Miteianders, so doch eines Nebeneinanders.[4] Wie sah dies aus in den neuen Staaten aus, die den Anspruch erhoben, Nationalstaaten zu sein und damit diesbezügliche Prozesse von Inklusion und Exklusion strukturierten, die die gesellschaftliche Teilhabe bedingten oder verweigerten? Wie sah dies auf der Ebene der internationalen Beziehungen aus? Bekannt ist, dass führende Vertreter des British Foreign Office beispielsweise die baltischen Staaten als ökonomisch und politisch nicht lebensfähig ansahen.

Die neue Weltordnung, die in Paris ausgehandelt und in seinen Vororten unterzeichnet wurde,[5] entstand unter Einflussnahme oder versuchter Einflussnahme von 10.000 Personen als Sachverständige und Berater. Diese tagten in 50 Kommission und Ausschüssen sowie mit über 1.000 Delegierten in der

---

Jeffrey Veidlinger Mitten im zivilisierten Europa. Die Pogrome von 1918 bis 1921 und die Vorgeschichte des Holocaust, München 2022.

3 Robert Gerwarth Die Besiegten. Das blutige Erbe des Ersten Weltkrieges, München 2017.

4 Jane Burbank/Frederick Cooper, Empires in World History: Power and the Politics of Difference, Princeton 2010; Jane Burbank Empires after 1919. Old, new transformed, in: International Affairs 95 (2019), Nr. 1, S. 81-100.

5 Zum weiteren Kontext umfassend: Jörn Leonhard Der überforderte Frieden. Versailles und die Welt 1918-1923, München 2018; Eckart Conze Die große Illusion. Versailles 1919 und die Neuordnung der Welt, München 2018.

Vollversammlung.[6] Keinesfalls aber waren alle Interessierten gleichberechtigt, von der von vornherein vorgesehenen Ungleichbehandlungen von Sieger und Besiegten einmal abgesehen. So konnten sich die baltischen Regierungen ebenso wie finnische Repräsentanten ganz anders als Polen auf der Konferenz kaum Gehör verschaffen. Zudem blieb aufgrund des Bürgerkriegs Russland, in welcher Gestalt und Vertretung auch immer, „the missing party" (Zara Steiner).[7]

Boris Barth hat in seinem Buch „Europa nach dem Großen Krieg. Die Krise der europäischen Demokratie" eine Krise ausgemacht, die natürlich nicht nur für Nordosteuropa Geltung beansprucht. Eine Stärke von Traditionsbeständen, die zumeist eben nicht demokratisch war, eine Verbindung einer Nationsvorstellung, die an eine essentialistisch gedachte Vorstellung der Ethnie gedacht war, vor allem aber die labile ökonomische Entwicklung, machten seiner und nicht nur seiner Auffassung nach die Krise der Demokratie aus.[8] Diesen Ansatz soll in diesem Buch mittels Aufsätzen mit jeweils unterschiedlichen Zugriffen hinterfragt werden. Manche schauen die Forschung zu ihrem Thema zusammen, andere arbeiten mit neuem archivalischen Material. Vollständigkeit kann und soll nicht erreicht werden, aber es soll ein vertiefter Blick auf jene Staaten im Ostseeraum geworfen werden, die aus den monarchischen Landimperien entstanden und sich nun zwischen Deutschland und Sowjetrussland bzw. der Sowjetunion befanden. Wenn im Titel vom Ostseeraum die Rede ist, so werden Dänemark und Schweden aus dem naheliegenden Grund ausgelassen, dass beide Staaten im Ersten Weltkrieg neutral geblieben waren, mithin keinen Weg aus dem Krieg zurückzulegen hatten. Alle anderen Staaten finden Berücksichtigung.

Im ersten Teil des vorliegenden Buches, „Frieden und gelingende Gesellschaften", wird in die neuen Staaten hineingeschaut werden, dies von Norden nach Süden. Marko Tikka setzt in seinem Beitrag dabei den Schwerpunkt auf die Betrachtung der sozialen Gruppen unmittelbar nach Finnlands Unabhängigkeit. Karsten Brüggemann schaut auf das Wechselspiel zwischen Politik, Militär und Gesellschaft während und unmittelbar nach dem Estnischen Unabhängigkeitskrieg. Svetlana Bogojavlenska nimmt in ihrem Beitrag die demokratische Periode im Lettland der Zwischenkriegszeit bis 1934 aus Perspektive der nationalen

6 Boris Barth Europa nach dem Großen Krieg Die Krise der Demokratie in der Zwischenkriegszeit 1918–1938, Frankfurt am Main/New York 2016, S. 26.

7 Zara Steiner The lights that failed. European international history 1919-1933, Oxford 2005, S. 131.

8 Barth, Europa nach dem Großen Krieg, S. 294-296.

Minderheiten ins Visier. Mathias Niendorf schlägt einen noch weiteren Bogen von der Proklamation der Unabhängigkeit Litauens 1918 bis zum Beginn des Zweiten Weltkriegs 1939. Werner Benecke schließt den ersten Teil des Bandes mit einer Betrachtung des nordöstlichen Teils der Zweiten Polnischen Republik mit einem Schwerpunkt in den 1920er Jahren ab.

Im zweiten Teil des Buches, „Friedensordnungen in Nordosteuropa", wird auf die internationale Dimension eingegangen. Hierbei werden Deutschland und (Sowjet)-Russland, aber auch internationale Arenen mit einbezogen und chronologisch vorgegangen. Christian Müller beschäftigt sich unmittelbar nach dem Ende des Ersten Weltkriegs mit den Diskussionen und Vorbereitungen einer Friedenskonferenz für den russischen Raum auf der Insel Prinkipo (Prinzeninsel) vor Konstantinopel, die nicht einberufen werden konnte. Benjamin Conrad widmet sich der innerpolnischen Forschungsdiskussion, ob sich eine stärkere Berücksichtigung der Friedenskonferenz von Riga zwischen Polen und den Sowjets in dem Begriff einer „Paris-Rigaer Friedensordnung" für die Zwischenkriegszeit niederschlagen sollte. Timo Nahler betrachtet die US-amerikanische Botschaft in Riga während der demokratischen Periode Lettlands bis 1934, die eine weit über das Baltikum hinausreichende Rolle für den Ostseeraum einnahm. Jan Kusber beschließt den Band mit einem übergreifenden Beitrag zu bi- und multilateralen Sicherungsmaßnahmen der Zwischenkriegszeit im östlichen Ostseeraum.

Nicht nur Wege aus dem Krieg können, wie in dem vorliegenden Band dargelegt, mehrjährig, windungsreich und langwierig sein. Auch ungleich unwichtigere Vorhaben wie ein Sammelband nehmen mitunter solche Wege. Dieses Buch basiert auf Referaten des 70. Baltischen Historikertreffen, das im Juni 2017 in der Universität Göttingen auf Einladung der Baltischen Historischen Kommission und der Johannes Gutenberg-Universität Mainz als Mitveranstalter stattfand. Anders als der für die Produktion typische Bearbeitungszeitraum von zwei oder drei Jahren vergingen bis zur Drucklegung sechs Jahre. Ein Publikationsstau, der in den Geisteswissenschaften häufiger als wünschenswert auftritt, gepaart mit der Bewältigung der Corona-Pandemie ab 2020 führten wieder und wieder zu Verzögerungen. Das Werk erschien schließlich 2024 unter für die Region Ost- und Ostmitteleuropa völlig veränderten Rahmenbedingungen: Am 24. Februar 2022 schlug Russlands Präsident Vladimir Putin den Weg in den Krieg ein, in dem er dem Nachbarland Ukraine einen unprovozierten Angriffskrieg aufzwang – ein Krieg, der europa- und weltweit für schwere Verwerfungen und Veränderungen sorgte und noch sorgen wird. Die Betrachtung von historischen Wegen aus dem Krieg erhielt durch diese jüngsten Ereignisse eine nochmals höhere Bedeutung.

Die Herausgeber danken den Autoren der Beiträge für ihre Werke sowie ihre Geduld und die Bereitschaft, alle Windungen klaglos hinzunehmen. Semjon Kaul, Anna Rammonat, Ronja Ringleben-Fricke und Caroline Schmidt halfen eifrig bei der Herstellung des Bandes. Der Peter Lang Verlag ermöglichte die Aufnahme der Publikation in der Reihe „Transformationen – Differenzierungen – Perspektive. Mainzer Studien zur Neuzeit".

Marko Tikka

After the Finnish Apocalypse: The social groups in Finland after the Civil War of 1918

The well-known Finnish historian Jaakko Paavolainen finished his classic book "*Valkoinen terrori*", 1967, on the violent events of Finland's Civil War with the words: "against the backdrop of the violence during the spring of 1918, the unified domestic front in Finland in the Winter War was not just a miracle; it was the miracle of all miracles."[1] What did he mean by this?

Finland's Civil War in the winter of 1918 was, in proportion to the country's population, one of Europe's most destructive internal conflicts of the 20th century.[2] In a war that lasted only for three and a half months, the acts of terror and the prison camps took the lives of more than one per cent of Finland's 3,5 million population at the time, some 36.400 Finns. As a consequence of the Civil War, Finland got politically divided into two: the Finland of the vanquished Reds and the Finland of the victorious Whites. It is difficult to believe that a country so severely sundered could present a unified front against the attack of the Soviet Union in the fall of 1939 after the start of WW2. The national integration called the "miracle of the Winter War" was indeed like a miracle especially to the Finnish right wing that had during the 1920s and 1930s mainly striven to exclude the left wing, the losers of 1918, from the society. Those aspirations did not succeed, and that failure had a decisive impact on Finland's development after the Civil War.

Finland had detached from Russia after the Russian Revolution of 1917. The country's Civil War was the first European conflict in which national revolutionary and conservative forces confronted each other. The war fought between two paramilitary political armies, Finland's Reds and Whites, became brutal particularly as regards acts of terror. 11,000 Finns lost their lives to terror. The legacy of the war was gigantic humanitarian suffering and destruction, after

1 PAAVOLAINEN, Poliittiset väkivaltaisuudet Suomessa 1918, p. 418.

2 On Finland's Civil War in English e. g. TEPORA/ROSELIUS, The Finnish Civil War; ALAPURO, State and Revolution; HAAPALA/HOPPU, Tampere 1918; GERWARTH/HORNE, War in Peace.

which one could have imagined it impossible to make peace between the social groups which had been killing each other *en masse* in the winter of 1918 for decades to come. For the Finns, the war was an internal power struggle, but for the troops of Russia and especially imperial Germany that were involved it was a part of WW1. When Finland had declared independence and been liberated in November 1918 and imperial Germany had lost the war also as regards the German troops in Finland, the construction of the independent Republic of Finland could commence.

After the world war and the civil war, the development during the post-war years was nothing short of astonishing. Already in the following year Finland became a parliamentary republic as one of the first among the new European states; a representative democracy governed by political parties.

Parliamentary election was arranged only half a year after the Civil War, and representatives of the losing side could also participate. Only a few months after the end of the war Finland adopted municipal suffrage, and as the result, municipalities and towns switched to universal suffrage from the earlier voting right based on property. As a consequence of the election reform, Social Democrats, that is the losing Red side in the Civil War, gained the majority in the councils in several municipalities, among them Finland's second largest city of Tampere.

After the Civil War, free formation of political parties was allowed in Finland, although the activities of both fascists and Communists were restricted during the time between the world wars. In a European context, it was exceptional that fascist movements did not grow into a significant political factor.

Although political extreme factions were discriminated, for the most of the population the 1920s and 1930s meant an improvement in social circumstances: universal compulsory education, freedom of religion, significant improvements to the rights of farmers, workers, and women.

How was all this possible only after a few years after the Civil War? In recent years, this historical period has been studied in Finnish historical research in the wake of the Civil War history. The research has been constructing an idea of strongly divided cultures, looking at the ideology and construction of the so-called White Finland, but also sketching the crucial role of the Social Democrats in the detente politics following the Civil War.[3]

---

3 On the division and mental atmosphere e. g. KAARTINEN ET AL., Maamme; on White Finland SIIRONEN, Valkoiset and SIIRONEN, Mustan lipun alla; also SORMUNEN, Sivistäviä seuroja; on the importance of Social Democrats KANNISTO, Vaaleanpunainen

This article will look at Finland's exceptional path after the Civil War. The following describes those social groups, reforms, and solutions which had a crucial impact on Finland's political and social development during the time between the world wars.

The region of Southern Karelia in Southern Finland[4] is used in this article as a regional example of the post-war development. The region, located near Vyborg, reflects the development of Finland extremely well. In the beginning of the 20th century, Southern Karelia was like a miniature of Finland: a combination of industrialized southern population centers and rural municipalities almost entirely dependent on agriculture. The region boasted three strongly industrialized parishes of Lappee, Ruokolahti ja Jääski and one town, Lappeenranta; the rest of the municipalities were countryside. The population of Southern Karelia (125,000 inhabitants in 1930) made up some 3.5% of the total population of Finland (some 3,6 million.)[5]

1. After the Civil War: Two different Finlands?

The three-month-long Civil War ended in May 1918. After the battles were over, there were dozens of prison camps in the country with some 80,000 Reds and their supporters held in them. April and May of 1918 were a time of cleansings by the winning side, later described as the White Terror. While the rebels were being convicted in official trials, the so-called state crime courts, most of the camp prisoners were being released.

In addition to the civil war in Russia, Finland's situation was also affected by the presence of Imperial German troops in the country. The so-called Baltic Sea Division and Detachment Brandenstein boasted a total of 14.500 soldiers. The Germans had made a contract with the Finnish Whites and remained in the country in order to secure the position of the Central powers in the Baltic Sea region, the Baltic states, and Finland. The pact with Finland's White government gave Finland's foreign trade and among others the organizing of the army to the hands of imperial Germany.[6] German troops did not leave the country until

tasavalta. The author has also looked at the tensions created by White Finland's key element, the civil guards, in local communities, see TIKKA, Valkoisen hämärän maa.

4 Statistical data and research results are based on the author's research for Southern Karelian history 1913-1936 TIKKA, Maailmansodan, laman ja kasvun vuodet. Between the world wars Souther Karelia was called "region of Southern Saimaa".

5 SVT 1930 population statistics. Southern Karelia had 125,601 inhabitants in 1930, with the national population of 3,6 million.

6 See HENTILÄ/HENTILÄ, Saksalainen Suomi; RAUTKALLIO, Kaupantekoa.

November 1918 after Germany had lost the World War.[7] Regulations on political freedoms and individual security stayed in effect until the spring of 1919.

The unrest of 1917-1918 had divided the people in two, and the same happened to political parties. After the Civil War the parties regrouped, as the conservatives formed the National Coalition Party and the town bourgeoisie formed the Progress Party. The biggest old political parties were the farmers' Agrarian Party, the workers' Social Democrat Party, and the conservative Swedish Folk Party of the Finnish-Swedish populace, all formed in the beginning of the 20th century. A Finnish Communist Party had also been founded in Moscow in 1918; because it was prohibited in Finland, Finland's Socialist Workers' Party (SSTP) was founded in 1920 to operate as its Finnish version. The late 1920s also witnessed the rise of the first Finnish fascist movements. The biggest change in the field of politics happened in the labour movement – from which the movement detached itself – and the conservatives who divided into three groups: traditional conservatives, liberal urban bourgeoisie, and fascist movements of the extreme right wing. The birth of the extreme left wing and the extreme right wing was directly linked to the final outcome of the war of 1918.When everyday life returned back to normal after the Civil War, many economic and cultural institutions seemed to divide into movements of the war's Reds and Whites, the working class and the bourgeoisie.

There were sufficient grounds to speak of two Finlands; the "White Finland" of the winners and the "Red Finland" of the losing side.[8] The key manifestation of White Finland in every Finnish town and municipality in the 1920s and 1930s were the civil guards. As a part of the winners' voluntary army the civil guards continued their operation after the war. A law on civil guards passed in August 1918 legalized voluntary civil guard troops and appointed them various tasks of official nature.

A large share of the people integrated to the Whites joined the White Finland of the civil guards; land-owning farmers, local businessmen, leaders of industry, and most of the establishment of the state, the towns, and the municipalities. The Reds actively involved in the war or those that belonged to their circle, agrarian and urban labour, seemed to be excluded from that Finland.

---

7 See HENTILÄ/HENTILÄ, Saksalainen Suomi.

8 White Finland as a local phenomenon has been studied by SIIRONEN, Valkoiset and SORMUNEN, Sivistäviä seuroja, repiviä riitoja, vahvoja vaikuttajia. On conflicts between social groups, TIKKA, Valkoisen hämärän maa.

For a brief period of time, the shadow of the Civil War also reflected on social rights and social security. The suffrage of those on the Red side in the war was restricted in state and municipal elections. The Red widows and orphans had to seek shelter from poor relief, whereas White widows and orphans received state subsidies.[9]

The division of Finnish association activities and enterprise apparently linked to the Civil War, however, had a long history which the events of 1918 ultimately only accelerated. Ever since the 1890s, there had in fact been many different varieties of Finland: that of the landowners, the bourgeoisie, the upper class, the agrarian and industrial labour, and the landless. This division only got more concrete after the Civil War.

After the Civil War the cooperative retail society SOK, Finland's largest retail chain, divided into workers' retail shops and the bourgeois cooperative retail society. In practice the division had actually taken place already in 1916-1917, when the workers' retail shops generally split from SOK due to differences of opinion concerning the prices of the goods and formed their own central organization: Cooperative Retail Central Society OTK.[10]

One of the most concrete divisions created by the Civil War happened in sports fields: as a consequence of the war, Finland's Gymnastics and Sports Union (SVUL) fired workers' sports clubs which had participated in the war from the national union, because the view was that they had taken part in revolutionary activities as clubs. Workers' clubs formed their own Workers' Sports Union (TUL). This division could be seen in the Finnish sports of the 1920s and 1930s. The SVUL athletes competed in their own national events and the Olympic Games while the TUL athletes competed in their own sports events and among others the Spartakiads.[11]

In association activities the division of the citizens had happened during 1917 at the latest, as part of the Red and White mobilization. The biggest cultural movement of the Finnish countryside, the youth associations, had changed openly bourgeois, while working class youth distanced themselves from the youth associations during the autumn of 1917. The youth associations were the most significant foundation for local White civil guards.[12]

9 Herranen, Yhdessä eteenpäin, p. 78-87; locally Kaarninen, Aatteesta kaupaksi, p. 65-68.

10 Kaarninen, Aatteesta kaupaksi, p. 65-67.

11 Hentilä, Suomen Työläisurheilun historia, p. 66-73.

12 Numminen, Yhteisön voima 2, p. 104-130, citation: p. 117.

Also, the social division of association activities, mainly between the landowning population of the countryside and the working class, had also begun much earlier. The youth associations in the Finnish countryside were formed in the last decades of the 19th century as movements led by the educated classes with the intention to activate the rural youth to take up good hobbies and at the same time to strengthen their nationalistic sentiments.[13] Already towards the end of the 19th century, workers' associations and trade union activities based on the theory of socialism had started to appear alongside the youth associations. In the beginning of the 20th century, the labour movement had the most comprehensive network of associations in Finland, which served its part in the birth of the labour movements' political spearhead, the Social Democratic Party, and the rapid growth of the party's support.[14]

The working population had gained suffrage in state elections in the parliamentary reform of 1906, and the Social Democrats got more than one third of the votes in all national elections held before Finland became independent. In addition to workers' associations and trade associations, the labour movement had their own newspapers which grew into a national newspaper network right at the turn of the century.

Political activity was also for its part constructing the workers' own cultural activities that had often mainly been created separately from other social groups, such as workers' theatre groups, brass bands, libraries, and reading rooms. Ultimately the Civil War only emphasized their social separation from the society surrounding them.

Although the country had divided into "Red Finland" and "White Finland", there were also many factors forcing people to work together. Attempts to build a bridge between the two had started already during the war.

A prominent liberal politician, Kaarlo J. Ståhlberg of the Progress Party, was constructing guidelines for the stabilization of the society already during the Civil War. The outset of his essay "Guidelines for the future" was that the rebels who had lost the war should not be turned into a pariah class; instead, they should be returned their social rights and obligations as quickly as possible.[15]

---

13 Widely on the birth of the youth club movement, Numminen, Yhteisön voima 2; The ideological side in particular, Rantanen, Laulun mahti ja sivistynyt kansalainen, p. 78-94, 257-277.

14 Numminen, Yhteisön voima. SDP temperance movement on Sulkunen, Raittius kansalaisuskontona, p. 260-278.

15 Blomstedt, K. J. Ståhlberg, p. 352–356.

Many of the social policy reforms that had troubled Finnish society and been delayed because of the World War were now realized at a quick pace in the early 1920s. Ståhlberg's views were reasonably acceptable to the key political groups, and as the result, the Civil War was followed by several social reforms, most of which had been discussed in the parliament already before the Civil War but had been left to wait for their passing due to the World War.[16]

The key reforms dealt with a worker's rights and position. In the agricultural Finland, there were several attempts to remedy the faults linked to land ownership through giving leaseholders rights to purchase the leased farms for themselves. Social injustices were being corrected with the adoption of compulsory education and reforms stressing individual status, such as freedom of religion. The most notable reforms included new municipal laws which made decision-making more socially equal especially in the countryside.

2. The silent revolution in the countryside

More than four fifths of Finns (83.9%) lived in the countryside in the beginning of the 1920s.[17] Finland was not only an agricultural country, but one strongly based on land ownership. The farmers owned their lands and forests and were free to trade their products. The number of farms had doubled during the last 20 years of Finland's Grand Duchy era between 1895-1917, and one fifth of even the very smallest farms were independent.[18] In 1920 there were 182,000 independent farms, in other words 72.7% of all cultivated lands in Finland.[19]

From the point of view of the structure of the Finnish society this was a decisive structural difference to e. g. Western Russia, where the peasants were mainly leaseholders. Unlike in many West European countries, grand scale land ownership and manors did not – apart from individual regions in Western Finland – have much significance in terms of the social structure in the Finnish countryside.[20]

Although it has been shown that farmer-owned lands and forests brought a small economy like the Grand Duchy of Finland and Finnish agriculture within the sphere of world trade economic fluctuations, it on the other hand gave the

16 Generally on this, Haapala, Kun yhteiskunta hajosi.

17 E. g. II Väestö SVT 1927, p. 36.

18 Haapala, Kun yhteiskunta hajosi, p. 79f.

19 Peltonen et al., Maatalous II, table 5.

20 Haapala, Kun yhteiskunta hajosi, p. 84-86.

farmers security and stability.[21] Most of the landowners owned farms of under ten hectares of pasture, forest and a few live cattle. The farms were so small that the income of most farmers equaled that of a well-paid industrial worker. The real income of the farmers did not start to rise until 1917-1918.[22] This situation also saw the rise of the first major rift between the agricultural population, that is the providers of goods, and the industrial labour, that is the consumers, in 1916-1917, when the supply of provisions in the Grand Duchy of Finland stopped functioning, like elsewhere in Europe at war.[23]

The farmers' private land ownership created a large rural middle class into Finnish society. Particularly the smallholders could identify with the demands of the working population, in part perhaps easier than with the suspicious policy of the conservatives, which still divided everything in the society into Red and White. What was also decisive was the nature of both Social Democrats and the Agrarian Party as young "class parties": they were political movements that had emerged in the beginning of the 20th century and found their supporters from a population group that had formed distinctively on a social basis.

Although universal suffrage in state elections had been achieved in the Grand Duchy of Finland already in 1906, the right to local decision-making was in the hands of individuals who owned the land or had assets. When this was seen as a clear discrepancy in municipalities that had grown quickly due to industrialization, there were attempts to gradually extend local-level municipal power also to "lower population classes" in the beginning of the 20th century.

When it became possible to elect municipal councils based on universal suffrage after the passing of the new municipal law in the autumn of 1918, a kind of revolution took place in local decision-making. Before this, the local decision-making power had been in the hands of a narrow elite. This power was now being transferred from the local establishment and the richest farmers to small or medium-sized farm-owners and the working population. Municipal power also got more politicized as the freeholders widely started to support the Agrarian Party (ML) during the 1920s while the working population divided to support the Social Democrats and the small Communist Party (STTP) that had been founded after the Civil War. In this situation, the number of conservative representatives in local councils gradually dwindled to one or two.[24] While the most affluent freeholders and the most important

---

21 Kuisma, Metsäteollisuuden maa, p. 382f.

22 Haapala, Kun yhteiskunta hajosi, p. 109f. and table 6.

23 Nyström, Poikkeusajan kaupunkielämäkerta, p. 336-344.

24 This can be seen well e. g. in local history research.

local merchants and entrepreneurs in practice held their presence in the municipal councils, the change of atmosphere in local decision-making was an important one.

In the first municipal election of 1918 the left got one fifth (19%) of the votes. The number was significant in that 68,000 working class individuals had temporarily lost their voting rights due to prison sentences for acting on the Red side in the Civil War and some 27,000 people on the Red side had died in the war. Already in the second municipal election in 1919 the support for the left wing nearly doubled to 36%, while conservative parties got a total of 63% of the votes.[25] In the municipal election of 1922 the left wing reached absolute majority in more than every fourth municipal counties in 161 councils.[26] Only after a year after the Civil War, a former Red, a Social Democrat, became the chairman of the council in Tampere, the biggest industrial town in Finland.[27] While it has been commented that the voters were not particularly active in this election, the political positions changed decisively in the countryside.[28]

The support for the left wing was strong throughout the period between the wars especially in the countryside, where left wing parties got more than one third of the votes in the municipal elections in the countryside. This is explained by the fact that industrial population centers were often located in the countryside. In Finland the local power was divided between the Agrarian Party and the Social Democrat Party during the 1920s. In most rural councils these two parties seized local power, while the conservatives and the Communists got only a few seats.

The following example illuminates this development. Southern Karelia, a region in Eastern Finland with some 125,000 inhabitants, 16 rural communes and one town, had divided strongly into Reds and Whites in the 1918 war. The war's front line went through the region, and the devastation of war was severe. As a consequence of the Civil War, more than 1500 people lost their lives in Southern Karelia communes. 570 casualties were victims of terror,

25 SVT Municipal elections in 1918-1922, p. 28.

26 HENTILÄ, Pitkät varjot, p. 115–116. There were 588 municipalities: i.e. towns, densely populated communities, market towns, and rural communes in Finland in the 1920s; of this, 161 is 27.4%.

27 KANNISTO, Vaaleanpunainen tasavalta, p. 246-256; HENTILÄ, Pitkät varjot, p. 113-116.

28 HENTILÄ, Pitkät varjot, p. 116.

which corresponds with the national percentage of one third of the victims.[29] After the war, the political bisection in Southern Karelia was severe, and in the 1920s and 1930s there was both underground Communist activities and extreme right activity in the area. However, neither of the two grew into an important political force in Southern Karelia.

After the municipal law reform of fall 1918, municipal councils were elected annually, and after 1924 for three years at a time. In the table, nearly all of the communes with working class (Social Democrat) representatives had got the first left wing representative into the council already in the early 1920s.

Table 1: Southern Karelia municipal councils' political distribution 1930.

Municipality	SDP	NCP.PP	AP	total
Joutseno	6	1	12	19
Jääski	11	8	10	29
Lappee	13	7	15	35
Lappeenranta	5	18	0	23
Lemi*	0	0	17	17
Luumäki	0	12	7	19
Nuijamaa*	3	0	14	17
Parikkala	0	0	20	20
Rautjärvi	2	0	16	18
Ruokolahti	11	5	14	30
Saari	0	0	16	16
Savitaipale*	4	0	19	23
Simpele	4	2	9	15

29 Statistical data is based on SVT Population statistics, SSSP 1914-1922, forthcoming separate research on Southern Karelia county 1913-1936, TIKKA: Maailmansodan, laman ja kasvun vuodet.

Suomenniemi	0	15	0	15
Taipalsaari*	3	0	14	17
Uukuniemi	2	0	22	24
Ylämaa*	3	0	12	15
Altogether	67	68	217	352

*so-called village list, mainly farmer population.

Tikka, Maailmansodan, laman ja kasvun vuodet.

The table above shows the political distribution of Southern Karelia municipal councils in 1930, the same year the fascist *Lapua* movement was at its strongest and Communist council members (altogether 20 in Southern Karelia) had been expelled from the councils as a result of the so-called Communist laws.[30] In other words, the situation represents a certain kind of state of emergency from the point of view of municipal democracy: the number of the political left wing members was at its smallest. The setting was perplexing, however. There was a total of 67 representatives (19.1%) of the labour movement (SDP) in Southern Karelian municipal councils. The conservatives (NCP, PP) had nearly as many seats (19.3%) and the Agrarian Party (AP) had all the rest (61.6%).

The conservative group consisted of the members of the National Coalition Party, the liberal Progress Party, and the Swedish Party in the municipalities. In some municipalities, local circumstances created some special groups: there was a big garrison in Lappeenranta, and cavalry officers had their representatives in the town council.[31]

In five municipalities, the councils were formed on the basis of the so-called village lists. The council members were elected from every village, and nearly all of the elected represented the Agrarian Party. Although only the local

30 The *Lapua* movement of the late 1920s pressured in 1929-1930 the government to pass the so-called Communist laws which were meant to prevent Communists' political influence in the decision-making. The government bent under pressure and the laws were passed in the autumn of 1930. See e. g. Siltala, Lapuan liike ja kyyditykset, p. 124f., 183f.; Silvennoinen et al., Suomalaiset fasistit, p. 152-165, 189-197.

31 Antikainen et al., Lappeenrannan kaupungin historia, p. 255-263. The officers are included in the conservatives in the table.

distribution of the council seats had significance, the total number represents the political distribution of the councils quite accurately.

Political middle-of-the-road groups (Agrarian Party, Social Democrat Party) had two thirds of the council seats or, alternately, right wing groups (Agrarian Party, Coalition Party, Progress Party and others). The role of the conservatives was strong mainly in the only town in the region (Lappeenranta) and the significant industrial municipalities of Ruokolahti, Jääski, and Lappee. One of the biggest pulp mills in the country was being built in Jääski in the 1920, Ruokolahti became more and more industrialized throughout the 1920s and 1930s with several factories, and in Lappee a privately owned wood processing industry group, Kaukas Oy, had been in operation since the turn of the 20th century.

The only exceptions to this were the rural communities of Luumäki and Suomenniemi, due to local structures – in Luumäki the politics of White Finland were strengthened by the memory of extremely severe Red terror experienced during the Civil War, and in Suomenniemi the central establishment in the municipality was politically concentrated in conservative parties.[32]

In Southern Karelia local decision-making was largely in the hands of two population groups: independent farmers and industrial workers with permanent jobs. In terms of economy, both groups were relatively well-off. They were also strong in terms of social structure: the people in these population groups represented two political movements – the Agrarian Party and the Social Democrat Party. In the background of these two groups there was long-term and steady association activity – the workers had their workers' associations, the farmers their associations specialized in agriculture and cattle breeding.

In the background of both population groups there was also the retail trade, the cooperative retail society of farmers and workers. Thus, the Agrarian Party and the Social Democrats were locally in many ways closer to each other than the conservatives were – the latter represented in the local councils often by private entrepreneurs, officials, the clergy, and other members of the local establishment.[33]

The central factor dividing the farmers and the Social Democrats also on the local level was naturally the war of 1918. The freeholders had formed the backbone of the White army, the civil guards, while agricultural and industrial workers had formed the Red guards. In the early 1920s, the Agrarian Party's

---

32 Tikka, Maailmansodan, laman ja kasvun vuodet, p. 253–258.

33 The interpretation is based on statistical data and an extensive analysis of Southern Karelia local history researches.

policy aimed at closing the gap created by the Civil War. This was partly due to the election victory of the Agrarian Party in the parliamentary election of 1919: many of their votes came from the countryside from smallholders and leaseholders who had previously voted for Social Democrats.[34]

Although the Agrarian Party supported the structures of White Finland, it did not completely subscribe to the White ideology. The central rift in national politics took place in 1919, when the dispute concerning Finland's form of government drove the center parties and the conservatives into different camps. The Agrarian Party representatives also had a key role in preventing Mannerheim, the White army general, from being elected President of Finland. Central White Finland activists wanted Mannerheim for president and urged the civil guards to support the general. In the political center, this created suspicion and fear of a right-wing coup.[35]

The representatives of the Agrarian Party and the Social Democrat Party also often thought along the same lines as regards social policy and education. Necessity also became a uniting factor. The great social reforms launched in the beginning of the 1920s, compulsory education being one of the key reforms, forced political groups to cooperate with each other. In the end, cooperation was not even all that difficult. The biggest reform, the building of elementary schools in the countryside, was in the interests of all social groups. When this reform was largely funded by the state, there was not much of the usual opposition based on stinginess.

The development of local nursing and poor relief was also in the interest of the political center groups: in the 1920s, the municipalities were obliged to arrange midwife, nursing, and medical services to the residents. The needs of special groups like the handicapped, the mentally ill, and other special groups of social welfare were also to be solved locally. In order to treat these special groups, a joint asylum and a tuberculosis hospital for all the municipalities were founded also in Southern Karelia in the 1920s and 1930s.

So, political cooperation between the biggest political groups developed on the local level already in the 1920s. This was also quickly achieved on the national level: already in 1926, there was a government led by Social Democrats, and the center groups – the Agrarian Party and the Social Democrats – followed

34 Mylly, Maalaisliitto-Keskustapuolueen historia 2, p. 68-74.

35 On the form of government as regards the Agrarian party, Mylly, Maalaisliitto-Keskustapuolueen historia 2, p. 80-86. On the threat of a right-wing coup, Ahti, Kaappaus, p. 196-200.

the example of Sweden and set up a government between them in 1936. As the central groups took hold of local power, the conservatives were in many cases left as bystanders.

3. Finnish workers: isolated and divided?

The division of the Finnish labour movement in 1917-1918 followed the European example. The Communist movement separated from the labour movement's Social Democrat policy partly due to the development of Soviet Russia and partly to direct Soviet influence. A part of the Finnish emigrants who had fled to Russia after the lost Civil War set up Finland's Communist Party in Moscow in August 1918.

The birth of Finnish Communism was affected both by the active operation of the emigrants who had fled to Soviet Russia and the experiences of those Reds who remained in Finland. It has been noted that these two, the Communist movement in Finland (STTP) and Finland's Communist Party founded by emigrant Communists did not fuse into a united Finnish Communist movement until 1920.[36]

The difference with the Social Democrat movement was manifest precisely in relation to the events of 1918: the Social Democrats committed themselves to representative democracy on local and national levels and turned their backs on revolutionary ideas. For its part, the Communist movement strove for revolutionary activities and continued the revolution. As a concession to the parliamentary system, the Communists engaged in municipal politics in the beginning of the 1920s and also got into the parliament.[37]

A tiny part of Finnish Social Democrats had not participated in the Civil War at all and regained their political rights quite quickly. The prominent Social Democrat Väinö Tanner, a key figure in the workers' cooperative retail society, became the era's guarantor of the Social Democrats. Under his leadership the Social Democrat movement attempted to get quickly rid of the trauma of 1918, to oppose Communist activities, and to seek cooperation with the political center and right wing.

The activities of the Communists were closely monitored by the state in the 1920s. The army's internal intelligence kept an eye on them, and local civil guards, the police, and county governors regularly reported to the state police (EK) about

---

36 SAARELA, Suomalaisen Kommunismin synty, p. 359-361.

37 SAARELA, Suomalainen kommunismi ja vallankumous, p. 785-787.

Communist activities. Several Communist newspapers were suppressed, and Communist associations dealt with many times after the mid-1920s. The Communists managed to get a foothold in the Social Democrat youth movement and the trade union movement, but their strength was widely suppressed in 1925 in the so-called youth movement affair, where dozens of individuals partaking in Communist activities were tried and convicted.[38]

The trade union central organization SAJ had fallen into Communist hands towards the end of the 1920s and lost its position when the Social Democrats replaced it with SAK, the new trade union central organization.[39] The state authorities had a strong hold of the Communist movement in Finland. As a consequence of these actions it became clear to a large part of Finland's political center and right wing that the standing of the Communists in Finland was weak, in fact almost nonexistent.[40]

Local analysis provides one example of the labour movement's standing after the Civil War. In the region of the Southern Karelia, almost every municipality had a local workers' association in the 1910s. Nearly all had been founded around the first parliamentary election during the wave of political organization in 1905-1907. At the peak in 1916 there were some 2600 members in Southern Karelia workers' associations.[41] Immediately after the Civil War the number had dropped by at least 700, as a significant part of the membership had been killed on the Red side of the Civil War.

Table 2. Southern Karelia workers' association membership 1907-1931

Commune**	founded*	members 1907	1916	1919	1931***
Joutseno	1907	39	179	237	113
Jääski	1902	508	348	278	161

38 Saarela, Suomalainen kommunismi ja vallankumous, p. 401-410, Widely e. g. Björne, Syihin ja lakiin eikä mielivaltaan.

39 More widely: Ala-Kapee et al., Yhdessä elämä turvalliseksi.

40 Silvennoinen et al., Suomalaiset fasistit, p. 18f. Pointing this out – the weakness of the Communist position – in the research caused objections in Finnish media still in 2016.

41 Membership data of a few associations is missing.

Lappee	1902	589	537	239	79
Lappeenranta	1893	387	269	40	75
Lemi	1911	?	27	0	5
Luumäki	1906	81	10	21	0
Nuijamaa	1906	?	53	41	28
Parikkala	1905	116	283	82	14
Rautjärvi	1907	72	0	0	0
Ruokolahti	1899	462	659	748	381
Saari (as part of Parikkalaa)	1906	?	-	-	-
Savitaipale	1909?	0	85	14	0
Simpele	1906	0	?	132	43
Suomenniemi	1905	46	21	?	20
Taipalsaari	1907	62	82	0	0
Uukuniemi	1907	0	0	0	46
Ylämaa (part of Säkkijärvi?)	1906	0	0	0	0
Known membership altogether		2353	2553	1832	965

*earliest founding date stated

**if several associations in commune, membership in all

***members at the end of the year

Source: Suomen sosialidemokraattinen puolue, Tilastoja puolueeseen kuuluvista yhdistyksistä.

More than 1100 people died in the Southern Karelia region on the Red side of the Civil War: most as victims of White terror or in prison camps. Additionally, nearly 900 Reds in the region's prison camps were convicted to prison sentences of different durations in political crime courts.[42]

42 Statistical data gathered in Tikka, Maailmansodan, laman ja kasvun vuodet. According

The impact of the Civil War could be seen the clearest precisely in the workers' association activities. For example, in Southern Karelia, those activities never returned to what they had been, in spite of the initial enthusiasm after the war. By 1930s the number of members in the associations had dropped by a half despite the fact that the number of potential members of association activities, industrial workers in the region, increased strongly with industrialization.

There were several reasons for this. In the post-war era, the contradictions of the labour movement's direction resulted also in workers' associations in lack of new members. The government's grip on Communist activities strengthened during the 1920s, which also reflected on the Social Democrat movement. The state police began to systematically suppress Communist organizations from 1923 on. Is Southern Karelia 29 organizations were suppressed: most of the Communist associations were minute ones consisting of only a couple of individuals, and some apparently existed only on paper.[43]

During the economic depression of 1929-1932 many people failed to pay the membership fees. Also, the industry's employment policy limited participation in associations: industrial employers preferred their workers to join civil guards rather than workers' associations. The share of the working population close to the labour movement was indeed measured mainly in local and national elections.

4. The people of White Finland: captured fatherland?

The political goals of conservatives and the so-called activists who had fought for national independence already before the Civil War crumbled in many ways in 1918-1919. The prospect supported by the conservatives, a German King for Finland, failed after imperial Germany lost the world war. It also seemed that the

to Rättstatistik/Statistisk undersökning över 1918 års statsförbrytare (Statistics research on the 1918 state criminals) (1923), 870 people from the Vyborg county were sentenced for state crimes in the Lappeenranta prison camp where most of the Southern Karelia Reds were collected. Although the number includes some people from elsewhere in Vyborg county than the municipalities of Southern Karelia and some of the Southern Karelia Reds were placed in the Vyborg prison camp, the number of the dead and the sentenced closely corresponds with the numbers of Southern Karelia's Red troops. Accurate municipal numbers of the sentenced in state crime courts in 1918 are not available.

43 Tikka, Maailmansodan, laman ja kasvun vuodet, based on official reports to county of Viborg governor, 1923-1931.

victory of the Whites in the Civil War did not after all result in the total defeat of the Reds; instead, the Reds regained their civil rights rather too quickly for many Whites to stomach.[44]

The movement that organized itself to stand up for national conservative values is now commonly called White Finland. The main values of White Finland were nationalism, civil guard spirit, right wing ideals, and anti-Communism. White Finland attempted to present itself as a unified whole, but in fact it was not politically very unified.[45] This fact, the heterogeneity of White Finland, served its part in the salvation of democratic social development. Ultimately only a part of those supporting White Finland's values were prepared to support them by trampling democracy and the parliamentary rule. This heterogeneity of White Finland is well illustrated for example by the failed coup attempt of the *Lapua* movement, in the Mäntsälä rebellion of 1932: although there were more than 90,000 civil guard members in the country, only some five thousand of them were in the end ready to travel to Mäntsälä to rebel against the nation's government and army.

The civil guards were White Finland's central local manifestation. After the Civil War they stressed the new post-war order and the social structure the winning side hoped for. The civil guard organization was declared a permanent organization by a new law in August 1918. The mere existence of the 90,000-member organization divided the people. From one point of view it fed the division created by 1918, from another it maintained order and monitored the former Reds and other suspicious elements.[46]

The attitude of the civil guards towards the political system and the left wing had been influenced by the post-war era of terror and trials against the Reds. Local civil guards had been responsible for the "purging" of their municipalities in the spring of 1918 and had been guilty of White terror in many places. However, the Civil War did not end for the civil guards just yet: the staff of the local civil guards participated through the summer of 1918 in the official aftermath of the rebellion, i. e. the operation of the so-called state crime courts. The guards identified the key revolutionaries of their municipalities and their actions in the war for the state crime courts. There were hundreds of suspects even in the

---

44 Silvennoinen et al., Suomalaiset fasistit, p. 57-68.

45 See Siironen, Valkoiset, p. 207-216.

46 See widely Selén, Sarkatakkien maa; Pylkkänen, Suojeluskuntalaiset; Tikka, Valkoisen Hämärän maa; Roselius, Kiista eheys unohdus.

smallest of municipalities. This inspection created an atmosphere of suspicion towards the workers and their association activities within the civil guards.[47]

The civil guards organized military exercises and also operated as the localities' sports and culture associations. On the other hand, they also monitored the political trustworthiness of the citizens by giving statements to employers and by choosing the men fit for military service in the army call-ups. The civil guards also acted as police officers, state police, and supervisors of former Reds at the behest of the military intelligence.[48] All of this was prone to divide the society and to maintain suspicions.

Let us use Southern Karelia as an example again. The membership of the region's 21 local civil guards in 1930 – again the time when the right-wing trend in the country was at its strongest – was some 3700 men, in other words 6.8% of the male population. This number means that only a fraction of the so-called White population were members of the most central White Finland organization. On the national level the number was about five per cent of the male population.[49]

The number varied significantly from one municipality to another. Workers were not admitted to civil guards, especially if their families had been active on the Red side in 1918. In densely populated industrial municipalities like Lappee, Ruokolahti, and Jääski, the number of civil guard members was high. This is explained by the factories' recruiting policy. In some industrial facilities the precondition for a job was active participation in the factory-sponsored civil guard activities. The workers that came to work in these industrial plants were freeholder population from the surrounding countryside, for whom joining the civil guards did not pose a problem.

Table 3: Southern Karelia civil guard membership 1930 and its share of the male population.

municipality	civil guards	male popuation	% share
Joutseno	161	3384	4,7

47 TIKKA, Valkoisen hämärän maa, p. 31-36.

48 TIKKA, Valkoisen hämärän maa, p. 36-43, 52-63.

49 In 1920 there were calculated to be 93,000 civil guard men in the country; the male population at the time was 1,660,230 (present and absent) of which the number of civil guard members is 5.6%. In 1930 11.8% of Civil Guard -aged male population (age between 20 and 60 years) were members of the local Civil Guard. TIKKA Maailmansodan, laman ja kasvun vuodet, p. 253–255.

Jääski	458	6363	7,2
Lappee	617	10632	5,8
Lappeenranta	277	1769	15,6
Ilmee	102	1800	5,7
Lemi	139	2308	6
Luumäki	379	3668	10,3
Nuijamaa	167	2112	7,9
Parikkala	157	4774	3,3
Rautjärvi	179	2709	6,6
Ruokolahti	470	7283	6,5
Saari	62	1916	3,2
Savitaipale	178	4019	4,4
Simpele	100	1119	8,9
Taipalsaari	149	1886	7,9
Uukuniemi	90	2781	3,2
Ylämaa	112	1396	8
Altogether	3797	59919	6,776471

TIKKA, Maailmansodan, laman ja kasvun vuodet.[50]

In individual countryside municipalities, for example Taipalsaari, the attendance of the municipality's central elite in the civil guard increased its support.[51] Location of state establishments in the municipality played a role: in Joutseno, all 50 guards of the state prison joined the civil guard on the recommendation of the prison warden. The events of 1918 also affected the local popularity of the

50 Source for this statistic has been collected from Vyborg civil guard district reports 1930, NA.

51 On the relationship between the elite and civil guard in the commune, see KOIVISTO, Elämää maalla ja kaupungissa, p. 50f., 56-60.

civil guards: for example, in Luumäki the civil guard was the biggest in Southern Karelia in relation to the population partly because the strong Red terror in the municipality during the Civil War had created an atmosphere favoring the civil guards.

The central element of civil guard work, political monitoring, regularly called for by the state police and county governors, created conflicts. In the civil guard law of 1918 local civil guards were obliged to provide executive assistance to the police when necessary. In the beginning of the 1920s such executive assistance often meant searching for former Red guard members or people trying to avoid conscription, monitoring different events, or confiscating illegal alcohol (prohibition had been declared in Finland in 1919).[52]

In the municipalities of the examples, conflicts were quite common and the Vyborg civil guard district of which Southern Karelia was a part was one of the most restless ones precisely as regards conflicts created by executive assistance. No less than 38% of the civil guard executive assistance tasks for the police in 1919-1920 happened in the Vyborg district. Also, one third (32.2%) of violent actions resulting in death in connection to the executive assistance in post-civil-war years 1918-1921, a total of 73 casualties, took place in the Vyborg district.[53]

The existence of the civil guards caused conflicts in municipalities, especially if bad deeds had been done on both sides during the 1918 war. On the other hand, the share of the civil guards was limited in local communities, and not all of the White Finland supporters approved of the civil guards' actions.

5. European war veteran experience and Finnish fascists

A part of White veterans of the Civil War and the so-called independence activists separated from the conservative circle in the 1920s to form a group of their own. Gradually this group adopted the thinking and methods of the European extreme right. Towards the end of the 1920s this circle developed into Finland's fascist movement with its war veteran organization and the *Lapua* movement.[54]

Underlying Finnish fascism there was the same European war veteran experience that had given rise also to the other European fascist movements. In

52 Tikka, Valkoisen hämärän maa, p. 111-122.

53 Tikka, Valkoisen hämärän maa, Table 5 and Table 7.

54 Interpretation presented here, see Silvennoinen et al., Suomalaiset fasistit. Earlier interpretations Ekberg, Führerns trogna följeslagare; Siltala, Lapuan liike; Nygård, Suomalainen äärioikeisto.

Finland, the frontline experience stemmed from the Civil War. A part of the White combatants experienced the sacrifices and achievements of the war to be soiled by the politicians, just like their ideological brothers thought in Central Europe. The victory had been soiled by shameful politics.

The Finnish version of the myth of a stab in the back was a counter-reaction to the politics represented by the first president of Finland, K. J. Ståhlberg. Ståhlberg's goal had been to get quickly rid of factors creating social inequality. Those factors were considered to have underlain the Civil War.[55] To a part of the Civil War's White victors, Ståhlberg's "amnesty policy" became a swearword. Amnesting the Red guard members sentenced to prison and reforms with positive effects for the Reds related to land ownership, work conditions, and education were seen in this circle as desecration of the war victory.[56]

Finland's fascist unrest started in November 1929. An incident in Lapua, Southern Osthrobotnia quickly led to the birth of the anti-Communist *Lapua* movement. The "mass meetings" organized by the *Lapua* movement around the country got the support of the political centre and right wing within a few weeks – practically all political groups apart from the Social Democrats and Communists.

The *Lapua* movement considered Communism a threat and demanded laws to ban all Communist activities. Prominent high officers, officials and among others industrial employers and conservative leaders supported the movement for a brief time. It has been noted that the Finnish fascism was almost a more severe threat to democracy than the Red revolutionaries of the Civil War because it, unlike Finnish Communism, stemmed from inside the state: the army, the civil guard organization, even the officialdom.

The downfall of the fascist movement was the result of its incredibility and its resorting to violence. For the majority of the Finnish right wing and center groups it was obvious that the Communist movement was not as big a threat as the fascists tried to make it. The government had already dealt with Communist infiltration effectively by suppressing Communist organizations and newspapers and putting dozens of people suspected of Communist activities to trial.[57]

The violence of the fascist unrest and the Finnish version of the march to Rome, the so-called peasant march in the summer of 1930, pressuring the nation to change its government by excluding the Social Democrats, showed to the

55 Encompassingly of late, e. g. VASLICK/SADLER, The Stab-in-the back Myth.

56 Widely on this e. g. SILVENNOINEN ET AL., Suomalaiset fasistit.

57 See SAARELA, Suomalainen kommunismi ja vallankumous, p. 401-410.

parties of the right wing and center supporting parliamentary rule that the fascist movements posed a serious threat against that rule.[58] Following the example of Italian fascists, the *Lapua* movement started abducting and manhandling the enemies. It actively used the help of local civil guards in the abductions.[59]

The government intervened with the *Lapua* movement violence in 1930 after the movement's forcible ejection of former President Ståhlberg. Those guilty of forcible ejections were brought before court. The so-called Mantsälä rebellion of the early spring of 1932 has also been considered the final strike against Finnish right-wing radicalism. A weakly organized rebellion prospect got a group of civil guard members to some 50 kilometers away from the capital Helsinki. About 5000 of the country's about 90,000 civil guard members participated in the attempt. Eventually the government bloodlessly put down the rebellion attempt. One hundred participants were charged in the Court of Appeal; fifty of them were convicted.[60]

After this the Finnish fascist movement dispersed into small political groups during the 1930s. The biggest of them, the Patriotic People's Movement (IKL) at best gained the support of some 90,000 voters in the parliamentary election. Alongside it in the 1930s operated the veteran organization of the White veterans of 1918, the Union of the Veterans of the War for Freedom (VRL) that later changed from a pressure group for extreme right values into a traditional veteran organization towards the end of the 1930s. At its beginning in 1929 the Union was comparable to European veteran organizations that did not merely promote the veterans' interests, but also pursued active extreme right-wing policy. The leadership included some of the same individuals who were behind the *Lapua* movement.

In Southern Karelia, the fascist unrest was moderate: like elsewhere in Finland, the *Lapua* movement managed to get the center and rightwing groups to join the first mass meetings in the winter of 1929-1930, but the violence of the movement removed the wider support of the movement in the summer of 1930.

---

58 Siltala, Lapuan liike, p. 119-124.

59 On this more widely and in detail, Siltala, Lapuan liike.

60 The Lapua movement tried to gather the country's civil guards to Mäntsälä, a small rural community some 50 km from Helsinki, with the intention to march to the capitol and to seize control of the country's administrative organs. The rebellion withered, as only a few thousands of Lapua movement supporters turned up instead of nearly 100,000 civil guard members. The attempt was considered a rebellion and those guilty of it were sentenced in court. The Lapua movement was discontinued. On this widely, Ahti, Kaappaus; Siltala, Lapuan liike etc.

Support for the *Lapua* movement was visible in Southern Karelia mainly in the industrial areas and, due to individual leaders, in some rural municipalities, but in practice the impact of the movement was negligible. As some kind of measure of the support for fascist movements was the support of IKL in state elections. In the western Vyborg electoral district, the result was high even on national terms, no less than 10.5% in the 1936 parliament election, when it appeared in the election for the only time as an independent party, without an electoral pact. Nationally, the support of IKL was in the neighborhood of 8%.[61]

One indicator for the fascist support were the local sections of VLR, because in many cases they gathered also the supporters of the *Lapua* movement and IKL in addition to the White veterans. VLR managed to form a local section only in eight Southern Karelia municipalities, i. e. half of the municipalities of the region. These VLR local sections boasted a total of some 1000 members, i. e. less than one per cent (0.8%) of the population.[62]

6. Finland 1918-1939: the power and prosperity of center groups

The development of the Finnish society during the era between the world wars is in many respects curious and exceptional. While many Central European countries moved to strong right-wing rule or even right-wing dictatorship in the course of the 1920s, Finland appears as a strange middle-of-the-road nation. There was Communist and fascist unrest in Finland in the 1920s and 1930s, but their support was marginal, and both were controlled and suppressed by the democratic government.

What factors could explain Finland's line? Crucial factors could include the power of political center groups and their ability to make significant political and social reforms. Extensive social and social policy reforms partly explain Finland's development. The 1920s improvements in the situation of workers, leaseholders, and the poor also served to level Finland's development.

One of the key reforms to make Finnish society more equal was the redistribution of municipal power, which just happened to occur precisely during 1918-1919. Due to it, Finnish society's strong political center groups of the Agrarian

---

61 SVT – IKL participated independently (without an electoral pact) only in the parliamentary election of 1936 with support of 8.4%.

62 VRL 1929-1939.

Party and the Social Democrats found each other on the local and national levels alike.

Social policy reforms, first and foremost the construction of the elementary school system and statutory reforms of social welfare and health care, required local cooperation. They were in the interests of two large population groups: the farmers and the workers.

Both the farmer population and the worker population were in many respects solid groups with long traditions of organization. The labour movement as well as the youth associations and other association activities in the countryside had an extensive organizational structure throughout the country already in the first decades of the 20th century. The Civil War had caused a dividing element for a time, but in practice it mainly strengthened the two-way organizational development that had started already in the beginning of the 20th century.

In practice, Finland's Civil War created two political movements, the Red revolutionary movement and the European war veteran spirit, of which the latter divided into the conservative spirit of White Finland and the small fascist movement at its fringes. The Communist movement was born as a subsequent phenomenon of the Russian Revolution. Ultimately both the Communist and the fascist movement remained minor groups in Finnish society. Neither was the standing of White Finland fully legitimate, as the Whites of the Civil War had included not only the conservatives but also bourgeois groups of the political center, farmer population, and urban burghers, who all restrained the creation of political juxtaposition.

Bibliography

AHTI, MARTTI Kaappaus? Suojeluskuntaselkkaus 1921. Fascismin aave 1927. Mäntsälän kapina 1932, Keuruu 1990.

ALA-KAPEE, PIRJO ET AL. Yhdessä elämä turvalliseksi. SAK: laisen ammattiyhdistysliikkeen historia vuoteen 1930, Helsinki 1982.

ALAPURO, RISTO State and Revolution in Finland, Berkeley 1988.

ANTIKAINEN, JYRKI ET AL. Toivanen, Pekka Lappeenrannan kaupungin historia 1917-1966, Ensimmäinen nide, Lappeenrannan kaupunki, Jyväskylä 1988.

BJÖRNE, LARS "Syihin ja lakiin eikä mielivaltaan...". Tutkimus Turun hovioikeuden poliittisista oikeudenkäynneistä 1918-1939, Vammala 1977.

BLOMSTEDT, YRJÖ K. J. Ståhlberg. Valtiomieselämäkerta. Otava, Keuruu 1969.

EKBERG, HENRIK Führerns trogna följeslagare. Den finländska nazismen 1932-1944, Ekenäs 1991.

Gerwarth, Robert/Horne, John (Eds.) War in Peace. Paramilitary Violence in Europe after the Great War, Oxford 2012.

Haapala, Pertti/Hoppu, Tuomas (Eds.) Sisällissodan pikkujättiläinen, Helsinki 2010.

Haapala, Pertti/Hoppu, Tuomas Tampere 1918. A Town in Civil War, Tampere Museums, Tampere 2010.

Haapala, Pertti Kun yhteiskunta hajosi. Suomi 1914-1920, Helsinki 1995.

Hentilä, Marja-Liisa/Hentilä, Seppo Saksalainen Suomi 1918, Helsinki 2016.

Hentilä, Seppo Pitkät varjot. Muistamisen historia ja politiikka, Helsinki 2018.

Hentilä, Seppo Suomen Työläisurheilun historia I, Hämeenlinna 1982.

Herranen, Timo Yhdessä eteenpäin. SOK 100 vuotta, Helsinki 2004.

Kaarninen, Pekka Aatteesta kaupaksi. Osuustoimintaa Pirkanmaalla 1901-1983, Tampere 2012.

Kaartinen, Marjo et al. Maamme. Itsenäisen Suomen kulttuurihistoria, Helsinki 2016.

Kannisto, Niko Vaaleanpunainen tasavalta? SDP, itsenäisyys ja kansallisen yhtenäisyyden kysymys 1918-1924 (Diss.), Tampere 2016.

Koivisto, Hanne Elämää maalla ja kaupungissa, in: Maamme, itsenäisen suomen kulttuurihistoria, Marko Kaartinen et al. (Eds.), Suomalaisen Kirjallisuuden Seura, Porvoo 2016.

Kuisma, Markku Metsäteollisuuden maa. Suomi, metsät ka kansainvälinen järjestelmä 1620-1920, Suomen Historiallinen Seura (SHS), Helsinki 1993.

Mylly, Juhani Maalaisliitto-Keskustapuolueen historia 2. Maalaisliitto 1918-1939, Helsinki 1989.

National Archives, Helsinki: Vyborg Civil Guard district annual reports 1930

Numminen, Jaakko Suomen nuorisoseuraliikkeen historia 1. Vuodet 1881-1905, Helsinki 1961.

Numminen, Jaakko Yhteisön voima 2. Nuorisoseuraliikkeen historia 1906-1944, Helsinki 2011.

Nurmio, Yrjö Suomen itsenäistyminen ja Saksa. Porvoo, Helsinki 1957.

Nygård, Toivo Suomalainen äärioikeisto maailmansotien välillä. Ideologiset juuret, järjestöllinen perusta ja toimintamuodot, Jyväskylän yliopisto, Jyväskylä 1982.

Nyström, Samu Poikkeusajan kaupunkielämäkerta. Helsinki ja helsinkiläiset maailmansodassa 1914-1918 (Diss.), Helsingin yliopisto 2013.

Paavolainen, Jaakko Poliittiset väkivaltaisuudet Suomessa 1918 II "Valkoinen terrori", Helsinki 1967.

PELTONEN, MATTI (Ed.), Suomen maatalouden historia II. Kasvun ja kriisien aika 1870-luvulta 1950-luvulle, Helsinki 2004.

PYLKKÄNEN, ALI Suojeluskuntalaiset – Keitä he olivat? Vapaaehtoisten maanpuolustajien sosiaalinen kerrostuneisuus 1917-1944. (English Summary: The Civil Guard volunteers – Who were they? The social strata of voluntary defenders of the nation 1917-1944), Helsinki 2001.

RANTANEN, SAIJALEENA Laulun mahti ja sivistynyt kansalainen. Musiikki ja kansanvalistus Etelä-Pohjanmaalla 1860-luvulta suurlakkoon (Diss.), Sibelius-Akatemia, Helsinki 2013.

RAUTKALLIO, HANNU Kaupantekoa Suomen itsenäisyydellä. Saksan sodanpäämäärät Suomessa 1917-1918, Helsinki 1977.

ROSELIUS, AAPO Kiista, eheys, unohdus. Vapaussodan muistaminen suojeluskuntien ja veteraaniliikkeen toiminnassa 1918-1944 (Diss.), Societas Scientiarum Fennica, Helsinki 2010.

SAARELA, TAUNO Suomalainen kommunismi ja vallankumous 1923-1930, Helsinki 2008.

SAARELA, TAUNO Suomalaisen Kommunismin synty 1918-1923, Helsinki 1996.

SELÉN, KARI Sarkatakkien maa. Suojeluskuntajärjestö ja yhteiskunta 1918-1944, Juva 2001.

SIIRONEN, MIIKA Mustan lipun alla. Elias Simojoen elämä ja utopia, Jyväskylä 2017.

SIIRONEN, MIIKA Valkoiset. Vapaussodan perintö, Tampere 2012.

SILTALA, JUHA Lapuan liike ja kyyditykset 1930, Helsinki 1985.

SILVENNOINEN, OULA ET AL. Suomalaiset fasistit. Mustan sarastuksen airuet, Helsinki 2016.

SORMUNEN, ESA Sivistäviä seuroja, repiviä riitoja, vahvoja vaikuttajia. Kansalaisyhteiskunta Polvijärvellä 1900-1933 (Diss.), Joensuun yliopisto 2009.

SULKUNEN, IRMA Raittius kansalaisuskontona. Raittiusliike ja järjestäytyminen 1870-luvulta suurlakon jälkeisiin vuosiin, Helsinki 1986.

SUOMEN SOSIALIDEMOKRAATTINEN PUOLUE Tilastoja puolueeseen kuuluvista yhdistyksistä 1930, Sosialidemokraattinen puolue, Helsinki 1936. (SDP organization statistics 1930)

SVT, Rättstatistik 32 / Statistisk undersökning över 1918 års statsförbrytare (Statistics research on the 1918 state criminals), Tilastollinen Päätoimisto, Helsinki 1923.

SVT, 1930 population statistics.

SVT, Municipal elections in 1918-1922.

Tepora, Tuomas/Roselius, Aapo (Eds.), The Finnish Civil War 1918. History, Memory, Legacy, Leiden/Boston 2014.

Tikka, Marko Maailmansodan, laman ja kasvun vuodet, in: Rajamaakunta. Etelä-Karjalan historia II. Edita, ed. by Paaskoski, Jyrki/ Talka, Anu, Helsinki 2019.

Tikka, Marko Valkoisen hämärän maa? Suojeluskunnat, viranomaiset ja kansa 1918-1921, Suomalaisen Kirjallisuuden Seura, Jyväskylä 2006.

Vaslick, George S./Sadler, Mark R. (Eds.) The Stab-in-the-Back Myth and the Fall of the Weimar Republic. A History in Documents and Visual Scources, London 2016.

VRL: Vapaussodan Rintamamiesten Liitto 1929-1939, Tampere 1939.

War Victims in Finland 1914-1922. The Registry of names of the war dead between 1914-1922. (Suomen sotasurmat 1914-1922 –tietokanta), URL: http://vesta.narc.fi/cgi-bin/db2www/sotasurmaetusivu/main?lang=en

Karsten Brüggemann

Estlands Weg zum Staat in Revolution und Krieg: Die Einhegung der Gewalträume

Am formalen Ende der Okkupation des Baltikums durch kaiserliche deutsche Truppen veröffentlichte die bürgerliche Estnische Provisorische Regierung (*Eesti ajutine valitus*, EAV) am 11. November 1918 einen Aufruf „an die Völker Estlands". Aktiv werden konnte diese Exekutive jedoch zunächst nur nach Absprache mit der militärischen Führung der Besatzer unter Generalleutnant Adolf von Seckendorff. Wie eine Regierungssitzung am selben Tag zeigte, hingen nicht nur die Möglichkeiten der EAV, sondern auch die Lebensmittelversorgung und die Verteidigung des Landes von der Kooperationsbereitschaft der Deutschen ab.[1] So war der Aufruf vor allem von symbolischer Bedeutung: Die Esten werden das Machtvakuum nach Abzug der Deutschen zukünftig selbst zu füllen versuchen – mit der Errichtung eines Nationalstaats.

Der Aufruf betonte die Kontinuität und Legitimität der EAV, die sich auf den im Laufe des revolutionären Jahres 1917 indirekt gewählten Provinziallandtag, den *Maapäev* (dt. Landtag, russ. *zemskij sovet*, daher auch die offizielle estnische Bezeichnung *Maanõkogu*), sowie auf ein durch diesen bevollmächtigtes Rettungskomitee berief.[2] Nach der Auflösung des *Maapäev* durch die estnischen Bolschewiki im November 1917 hatte dieses aus drei Männern bestehende Gremium kurz bevor die deutschen Truppen am 24. Februar 1918 in Tallinn einmarschierten, Estland zu einer demokratischen Republik erklärt.[3] Die EAV sah darüber hinaus die im Frühjahr 1918 erlangten De-facto-Anerkennungen Großbritanniens, Frankreichs und Italiens, welche auf Betreiben der vom *Maapäev* entsandten Auslandsdelegation der EAV erteilt worden waren, als weitere Quelle ihrer Autorität an.[4] Somit ist auch das im Text des Aufrufs folgende Versprechen – in „den nächsten Tagen" werde der *Maapäev* wieder zusammenkommen,

---

1 Sitzungsprotokoll der EAV, 11.11.1918, in: RA, ERA fond 31, nimistu 1, säilik 8, Bl. 11. Siehe die Publikation in Pajur, Eesti!, S. 178-189. Siehe Pajur Die Übernahme.

2 Arens, Estonian Maapäev; Arens, Soviets.

3 Pajur, Die Geburt; Tannberg/Pajur, Iseseisvusmanifest.

4 Piip, Tormine aasta; Hovi, Die Orientierung; Kuldkepp, Intriigid. Siehe die Dokumente in: Pajur, Eesti!, S. 171 (Großbritannien, 3.5.1918), 172 (Frankreich, 13.5.1918), 173 (Italien, 29.5.1918).

um seine „Hauptaufgabe" zu erfüllen, die demokratische Wahl der Estnischen Nationalversammlung – vor dem Hintergrund zu sehen, sich durch die Etablierung demokratischer Strukturen die Sympathie der Siegermächte zu erhalten. Schließlich waren die De-facto-Anerkennungen im Frühjahr 1918 in erster Linie als antideutsche Maßnahme im Weltkrieg zu verstehen gewesen. Bis zur Einberufung der Konstituante sollten dem Aufruf zufolge die 1917 gewählten Lokalverwaltungen diejenigen aus der Zeit der deutschen Besatzung ersetzen und auf Anweisungen der „Bevollmächtigten" der EAV warten. Die Bevölkerung wurde aufgerufen, „mit ruhigem Vertrauen" die Regierung zu unterstützen und ordnungswidrige Demonstrationen zu vermeiden, schließlich seien „für den Schutz von Land und Volk Schritte eingeleitet" worden. Der von Außenminister Jaan Poska unterzeichnete Text – der designierte Premier Konstantin Päts war noch nicht aus der deutschen Gefangenschaft heimgekehrt – schloss mit der Hoffnung, dass das „estnische Volk in diesem großen historischen Moment sein Selbstbestimmungsrecht kultiviert nutzen kann".[5] Als nur zwei Tage später die sowjet-russische Regierung den Frieden von Brest-Litovsk aufkündigte[6], stellte sich indes die Frage, ob Estland sein Selbstbestimmungsrecht auch kultiviert würde verteidigen können.

Der vorliegende Beitrag beschäftigt sich mit der so genannten „Februarkrise", einem Konflikt zwischen der EAV, dem *Maapäev*, den Lokalverwaltungen und der estnischen Militärführung zu Beginn des Unabhängigkeitskriegs im Winter 1918/19. Es war ein mehrschichtiger Konflikt, da sich zum einen die Lokalverwaltungen gegen die als Bevormundung angesehenen Direktiven der EAV wandten und gegen die als Anmaßung betrachteten Maßnahmen der Militärs wehrten. Zum anderen sah sich der demokratische Anspruch der Politik und weiter Teile der Öffentlichkeit konfrontiert mit den traditionellen Praktiken der Armee des Russländischen Imperiums, deren Strukturen die estnischen Offiziere ja zumeist durchlaufen hatten.[7] Die Feldgerichte, um deren Machtbefugnisse es vordergründig bei dem Konflikt ging, wurden zum Vehikel einer prinzipiellen Auseinandersetzung zwischen den Vertretern einer revolutionären Politik, die sich selbst in einer militärisch angespannten Situation den Erfordernissen einer militärischen Pragmatik verweigerten und letztlich sogar den Bruch der EAV in Kauf nahmen, und der Militärführung.

---

5 Eesti Ajutine Valitsus Eestimaa rahvastele, 11.11.1918, in: RA, ERA 31/1/8, Bl. 2; Pajur, Eesti!, S. 181.

6 DVP I, Nr. 398, S. 565-567.

7 Kröönström, Eesti sõjaväe juhtivkoosseis.

Das Ziel dieses Beitrags ist es zu zeigen, dass für den weiteren (erfolgreichen) Verlauf des Krieges, aber letztlich auch für den Prozess der Staatsgründung insgesamt dieser Konflikt von einiger Bedeutung war. Die Einführung von Kontrollmechanismen in die Militärgerichtsbarkeit unterwarf die Armee der Regierungskontrolle und erhöhte damit zugleich die demokratische Legitimation der Militärführung. Gerade im Vergleich zu den zahlreichen weiteren Schlachtfeldern des Russischen Bürgerkrieges, in dessen Kontext letztlich auch der estnische Unabhängigkeitskrieg gesehen werden muss, ist dies eine nahezu unikale Erscheinung.[8]

Nach einer knappen Einführung in die Ereignisgeschichte der Staatsgründung wende ich mich der Februarkrise und anschließend konkret dem Problem der Feldgerichte zu, bevor in einem abschließenden Teil die Frage der Einhegung der Gewalträume auf ihre Bedeutung für den „Weg zum Staat" untersucht werden soll. Neben meinen eigenen Untersuchungen über die fragliche Zeit[9] dienen vor allem neuere estnische Studien als Grundlage dieses Beitrags, doch hat sich bislang nur ein Autor speziell mit den Feldgerichten befasst.[10] Dabei geht es mir nicht so sehr um eine Gegenüberstellung oder sogar Aufrechnung der Opfer des „roten" bzw. „weißen" Terrors (hierzu werden auch die von den Feldgerichten Verurteilten gezählt), wie es in letzter Zeit in der estnischen und lettischen Geschichtsschreibung versucht wird.[11] Fragen möchte ich demgegenüber eher nach den Argumenten und Überlegungen, von denen die Kritik an der (militärisch zunehmend erfolgreichen) Armeeführung begleitet wurden. Es

---

8 Siehe die jüngste Gesamtdarstellung des Bürgerkriegs SMELE, The „Russian" Civil Wars; vgl. die letzte größere deutschsprachige Studie KATZER, Die weiße Bewegung. Zur Geschichte eines typischen „Warlord" der Bürgerkriegszeit siehe SUNDERLAND, The Baron's Cloak.

9 BRÜGGEMANN, Die Gründung; BRÜGGEMANN, Foreign Rule; BRÜGGEMANN, The National and Social Revolution.

10 MINNIK, The Establishment. Die Jubiläumsjahre 2018-2020 haben zwei Publikationen hervorgebracht, die den aktuellen Forschungsstand zum Freiheitskrieg zusammenfassen: VAHTRE, Eesti Vabadussõja ajalugu; TANNBERG, Vabadussõja mitu palet. Vgl. dazu die kritischen Anmerkungen von KOPÕTIN/PIIRIMÄE, The Modern History of the Estonian War of Independence. Ebenfalls nach der Göttinger Tagung von 2017, für die dieser Beitrag ursprünglich verfasst wurde, erschien eine ausführliche Darstellung der „Februarkrise": ROSENTHAL, Kord ja kohus, S. 48-112.

11 Siehe MINNIK, Terror; MINNIK, Kontrrevolutsiooni vastu võitlemise komisjonide rollist; MINNIK, The Cycle of Terror; ŠILIŅŠ, Rīgas cietumi un lielinieku terors; ŠILIŅŠ, Sarkanais terors Rīgā.

waren vor allem Vertreter linker Parteien, die sich kritisch z. B. über die Praxis der Feldgerichte, aber auch über die zunehmend als undemokratisch wahrgenommene Tätigkeit der EAV äußerten. Kurz darauf feierten diese sozialistischen Parteien einen überwältigenden Sieg bei den noch unter Kriegsbedingungen durchgeführten Wahlen zur estnischen Verfassunggebenden Versammlung Anfang April 1919. Daraus darf geschlossen werden, dass die Einschränkung der Willkür der militärischen Strukturen, die demokratische Einhegung der Gewalträume, offenbar der Vision eines „kultivierten" Staatsaufbaus entsprach, die von der Mehrheit der Bevölkerung mitgetragen wurde.

1. In Revolution und Krieg: vom russischen Gouvernement zur estnischen Republik

Estlands Weg zum Staat begann nicht erst mit dem eingangs erwähnten Unabhängigkeitsmanifest vom 24. Februar 1918, sondern mit dem nur wenige Wochen nach dem Sturz des Zaren von der Russischen Provisorischen Regierung erlassenen provisorischen Autonomiestatut vom 30. März (12. April) 1917.[12] Damals war freilich noch kein Nationalstaat intendiert, doch erhielt das Gouvernement Estland mit dem *Maapäev* eine Art Vorparlament, das zwar indirekt über Wahlleute, aber doch von Männern wie Frauen über 20 Jahre gewählt wurde.[13] Bereits zuvor war am 5. (18.) März mit dem Bürgermeister Tallinns, Jaan Poska, erstmals ein Este an die Verwaltungsspitze des Gouvernements gesetzt worden, womit die Jahrhunderte währende Dominanz der deutschen Ritterschaften bzw. der russischen Statthalter im Lande endete. Viel wesentlicher noch im Hinblick auf die Zukunft war die territoriale Erweiterung der Provinz, deren Grenzen nun in Folge des Autonomiegesetzes nach ethnographischen Kriterien gezogen wurden. Daher wurden Estland die nördlichen, estnisch besiedelten Kreise des Gouvernements Livland angeschlossen. Damit verfügte das Land über den entscheidenden Vorteil, in der Staatsgründungsphase keine Gebietsansprüche an seine Nachbarn zu hegen. Während ein „Estland" so gebildet wurde, war das zukünftige „Lettland" zum einen von den Deutschen besetzt (Kurland) und gehörte zum anderen zum Gouvernement Vitebsk (Lettgallen), weshalb im Frühjahr 1917 in Petrograd keine Entscheidung getroffen werden konnte. Der litauische Fall lag in dieser Hinsicht noch komplexer, nicht zuletzt wegen der polnischen Ansprüche auf ein Revival des polnisch-litauischen Commonwealth.[14]

---

12 VOSR, Nr. 61, S. 65-67; PAJUR, „Meie riigipoliitiliseks paleuseks on autonoomia".

13 Vremennye pravila.

14 ANGERMANN/BRÜGGEMANN, Geschichte, S. 232-234.

Estland ist ein Kind der russischen Februarrevolution und hätte wohl kaum als unabhängiger Staat überlebt, wenn die Rote Armee im Sommer 1920 Polen geschlagen hätte und womöglich weiter nach Westen marschiert wäre, um die Revolution nach Zentraleuropa zu tragen. Lässt man diese gesamteuropäischen Zusammenhänge beiseite, ergibt sich jedoch ein erstaunlich stringentes Bild der Konsolidierung einer Republik im Krieg: Als am 2. Februar 1920 Poska, nun als Außenminister, seine Unterschrift unter den Friedensvertrag mit Sowjet-Russland setzte, erklärte er diesen Tag zum bedeutendsten in der Geschichte seines Landes, da Estland von nun an sein Schicksal selbst bestimmen könne.[15] Letztlich war dies eine Untertreibung, denn Estland hatte bereits im Frühjahr 1919 eine Nationalversammlung gewählt, aus der Anfang Mai die erste demokratisch legitimierte Regierung hervorgegangen war. Zu den wesentlichen Errungenschaften dieses Parlaments gehörte die im Oktober verabschiedete Agrarreform, durch die (mehrheitlich deutscher) Großgrundbesitz entschädigungslos verstaatlicht, aufgeteilt und umverteilt werden sollte.[16]

Die Radikalität dieser sozial, politisch, aber auch militärisch für die Konsolidierung der Republik wichtigen Reform – im Krieg aktive Soldaten sollten bevorzugt behandelt werden – kam dabei nicht von ungefähr. Von 1917 bis zu den Wahlen zur Nationalversammlung im April 1919 hatten revolutionäre, linke Parteien konstant zwei Drittel bis drei Viertel der Stimmen erhalten. In der internationalen Forschung zu den Revolutionen des Jahres 1917 wird stets auf die Letten verwiesen, die im November 1917 bei den Wahlen zur russischen Nationalversammlung den Bolschewiki mit 72 Prozent der Stimmen ein reichsweit einmaliges Ergebnis beschert hätten. Da jedoch das lettische Siedlungsgebiet seit 1915 durch die Ostfront des Ersten Weltkriegs geteilt war, konnten die Wahlen nur im unbesetzten lettisch besiedelten Livland im frontnahen Hinterland durchgeführt werden. Abgeschnitten vom deutsch besetzten Riga waren viele politische Gruppierungen nur rudimentär organisiert, was die Sozialdemokraten mit ihren weit verzweigten Netzwerken abseits der Metropole begünstigte. In Livland traten diese zudem noch mit einer (bolschewistischen) Einheitsliste an, weshalb sie alle mehr oder weniger revolutionär gesinnten Stimmen auf sich vereinten. In Estland hingegen hatte sich bereits im Mai 1917 eine estnische sozialdemokratische Arbeiterpartei von der imperialen russischen Mutterorganisation abgespalten, hinzu kamen die Estnischen Sozialrevolutionäre und die Estnische Arbeitspartei. Tatsächlich erhielten die Bolschewiki im November

---

15 Piip, Tartu rahu, S. 420.

16 Rosenberg, Agrarfrage; Pajur/Tannberg, Eesti ajalugu VI, S. 58f.

1917 in Estland knapp 40 Prozent der Stimmen, was ihrem Anteil in den Metropolen Moskau und Petrograd nahekam; alle linken, revolutionären Parteien zusammen vereinigten knapp 70 Prozent auf sich. In diesem Licht wirkt das lettische Ergebnis nicht mehr ganz so spektakulär.[17]

Noch die Zusammensetzung der im April 1919 gewählten estnischen Nationalversammlung spiegelte diesen Trend deutlich wider (bei einem Boykott der Bolschewiki). Die Sozialdemokraten, die im Zuge der Debatten um die Machtbefugnisse der Armeeführung, denen dieser Artikel gewidmet ist, aus der EAV austraten, erhielten mehr als ein Drittel der Stimmen und 40 Prozent in der Armee. Mit der Arbeitspartei (25 Prozent) und den Sozialrevolutionären (5,5 Prozent) erhielten die linken Parteien gut zwei Drittel der Stimmen (und fast drei Viertel unter den Soldaten). Bei einer Wahlbeteiligung von 80 Prozent ergab sich aus diesem Ergebnis ein starker Sog in Richtung der Forderungen der Februarrevolution: Land und Frieden. Das radikale Potential, das Ende 1917 noch die Bolschewiki hatten abschöpfen können, wurde nun von einer nationalen revolutionären Vision absorbiert. Die zunächst recht absurd erscheinende Idee der Gründung eines Nationalstaates als letzte Chance, nachdem die Idee eines freien demokratischen Russland durch Lenins Regierung mit der Auflösung der russischen Nationalversammlung Anfang 1918 torpediert worden war, erhielt nun die massive Unterstützung der Wahlberechtigten. Es war allerdings bezeichnend, dass der Bauernbund, die Partei des Ministerpräsidenten der EAV Konstantin Päts, nur 6,5 Prozent erhielt (ca. 4 Prozent in der Armee). In der Regel wird diese Niederlage auf die vermutete Zusammenarbeit mancher Anhänger der Partei mit den deutschen Besatzungsbehörden und auf die moderate Haltung Päts' in der Agrarfrage zurückgeführt, der das ökonomische Potential des (deutschen) Großgrundbesitzes nicht verlieren wollte.[18] Man darf jedoch davon ausgehen, dass mittelbar auch die „Februarkrise" zu dieser Niederlage beigetragen hat.

2. Der Weg in die „Februarkrise"

Im November 1918 unterschätzte die EAV die Dringlichkeit des Aufbaus einer effektiven Armee zunächst.[19] Erst kurz vor Weihnachten war die Struktur gefunden, die bis zum erfolgreichen Abschluss des Freiheitskrieges Bestand haben

---

17 Näher hierzu Brüggemann, Yearning for Social Change, S. 360f.

18 Brüggemann, National and Social Revolution, S. 158; Pajur, Konstantin Päts, S. 164-166.

19 Pajur, Konstantin Päts, S. 111; Pajur Eesti riigikaitse.

sollte: Neben dem von einem Zivilisten geführten Kriegsministerium stand die gleichberechtigte Institution eines Oberkommandierenden. Am 23. Dezember trat der gerade einmal 34-jährige Oberst Johan Laidoner diese Stelle an, dessen Kompetenzen einstweilen mit Hilfe entsprechender russischer Verordnungen festgelegt wurden.[20] Zu diesem Zeitpunkt war die militärische Lage extrem kritisch, da die deutschen Truppen, auf die die EAV zunächst gezählt hatte, im Abzug begriffen waren und Mobilisierungen des eigenen Staatsvolks, sei es auf freiwilliger Basis oder unter Androhung von Straflager, gescheitert waren. Vor der außerordentlichen Sitzung des *Maapäev* am 27. Dezember beschönigte Laidoner nichts: Estland verfüge über keine einsatzbereite Armee. Ohne ausländische Hilfe werde man den „eigenen Freiheitskrieg" nicht siegreich beenden können. Allerdings habe diese Hilfe keinen Sinn, wenn nicht das Land selbst alles zur Verteidigung Notwendige unternimmt: „Wenn die Interessen des Bürgertums in Gefahr sind, dann müssten die bürgerlichen Elemente selbst an die Front gehen."[21] Premier Päts schlug in dieselbe Kerbe, als er die Gymnasiasten lobte, die sich freiwillig gemeldet hatten, sich aber zugleich nicht nur über die Deserteure, sondern auch über diejenigen echauffierte, die friedlich zuhause säßen und auf andere hofften.[22] Schon Anfang Dezember hatte Päts die Spaltung der kriegsmüden Gesellschaft beklagt: Der Bauer sei nicht bereit, für den Städter zu kämpfen.[23] Und die Städter? Generalmajor Aleksander Tõnisson, der seit dem 2. Dezember die 1. Estnische Division an der Narva-Front kommandierte, wunderte sich bei einem Besuch in Tallinn Ende Dezember über die große Anzahl wehrfähiger Männer, welche die Hauptstadt zu einem „Ameisenhaufen" gemacht hätten, während die Front verwaist sei.[24]

Von einem großartigen Aufschwung an patriotischen Gefühlen berichten die Quellen zu diesem Zeitpunkt nichts. Kaum jemand setzte die Hoffnung in einen kleinen, wehrlosen Nationalstaat. Es gehörte mehr als nur eine Prise Optimismus dazu zu erwarten, der junge Staat könne militärisch gegen das große Russland bestehen. Zudem: Hatte man nicht selbst noch bis vor Kurzem in den Reihen der russischen Armee gekämpft? Nach all den Jahren des Krieges und der

---

20 Sitzungsprotokoll der EAV, 23.12.1918, in: RA, ERA 31/1/8, 80r-81; vgl. den entsprechenden Tagesbefehl vom 25.12.1918, in: RA, ERA 2315/1/1, Bl. 11; Sõjavägede Ülemjuhataja võimupiiridest; ROSENTHAL, Kord ja kohus, S. 27-33. Zu Laidoners Werdegang: ROSENTHAL, Laidoner, S. 23-28.

21 MN prot., S. 344.

22 MN prot., S. 347f.

23 EAV-Prot., 3.12.1918, in: RA, ERA 31/1/8, Bl. 51.

24 TÕNISSON, Visked vabadussõja mälestustest, S. 27f., 30.

Revolution war überdies auch in Estland eine pazifistische Grundhaltung verbreitet, denn wie sollte es „Land" ohne „Frieden" geben? Die beiden Parolen des revolutionären Jahres 1917 waren noch nicht verklungen und das ideelle Projekt des Sozialismus hatte Ende 1918 keineswegs seine Attraktivität verloren. Vom Geist der Zeit zeugt auch der Umstand, dass die estnische Armee zunächst auf Titel und Epauletten verzichtete. Allein die Bolschewiki hatten in den wenigen Wochen ihrer Herrschaft im Lande 1917/18 die weit verbreitete Sympathie, die ihnen auch aus Estland entgegengeschlagen war, verspielt.[25] Es war eine diffuse Stimmung, die Ende 1918 herrschte, aber sie schien einem Krieg gegen Sowjet-Russland entgegenzustehen.

Einen Hoffnungsschimmer stellte das von der britischen Regierung in die Ostsee entsandte Geschwader unter Leitung von Admiral Edwyn S. Alexander-Sinclair dar, mit dem sich Laidoner Mitte Dezember in Liepāja getroffen hatte. Auch wenn das britische Geschwader keinen Kampfauftrag erhalten hatte, sondern in erster Linie „die britische Flagge zeigen" sollte, war es bereit, die Rote Flotte im Finnischen Meerbusen zu beobachten.[26] Unter diesem Eindruck bat die EAV im Auftrag des *Maapäev* am 27. Dezember Admiral Sinclair sogar darum, dass die Regierung Ihrer Majestät Estland okkupieren und unter ihren militärischen Schutz stellen möge.[27] Diese verzweifelte Aktion blieb indes – wen wundert's – erfolglos.

Erst langsam setzte ein Stimmungsumschwung ein. Am 20. Dezember 1918 kündigte die EAV an, aktive Soldaten würden bei der bevorstehenden Agrarreform bevorzugt behandelt werden.[28] Zugleich machte sich die Unterstützung aus dem Ausland bemerkbar. Einerseits schützte das britische Geschwader, solange die Navigationsperiode andauerte, die estnischen Küsten. Andererseits trafen um die Jahreswende die ersten finnischen Freiwilligen ein.[29] Trotzdem stand die Rote Armee zur Jahreswende nur noch gut 30 Kilometer vor Tallinn.

---

25 Pajur, Konstantin Päts, S. 110f.; Vahtre, Eesti Vabadussõja ajalugu I, S. 171f.; Brüggemann, Foreign Rule.

26 Oll, Suurbritannia seisukohad.

27 MN prot. S. 346 (Lisa 1); Brüggemann, Die Gründung, S. 113; Pajur, Konstantin Päts, S. 139-141 (mit Faksimile des entsprechenden englischsprachigen Dokuments).

28 Siehe den Beschluss der EAV vom 20.12.19, in: Pajur, Eesti!, S. 219.

29 Siehe Brüggemann, Die Gründung, S. 97-106. Zu den finnischen Freiwilligen sei angemerkt, dass selbst Päts, der sich sehr für den Einsatz der Finnen stark gemacht hatte, am 30.4.1919 vor der Verfassunggebenden Versammlung erklärte, die finnische Hilfe habe in erster Linie in dem „Begreifen, dem Gefühl" bestanden, „dass das Brudervolk an unserer Seite steht, dass wir nicht allein sind". AK prot. I, Sp. 210f.

Allerdings konzentrierte sich deren Angriff Richtung Westen auf die Einnahme Rigas, das am 2. Januar 1919 erobert wurde. In Estland machten sich demgegenüber Nachschubprobleme bemerkbar, die zum Teil dadurch bedingt waren, dass das britische Geschwader eine Eisenbahnbrücke bei Narva zerstört hatte. Nachdem Laidoner am 6. Januar einen Gegenangriff gestartet hatte, wurden am 9. Januar der wichtige Eisenbahnknotenpunkt Tapa, am 14. Januar Tartu und am 19. Januar Narva zurückerobert. Die militärische Initiative ging nun von den Esten aus. Nur im Süden des Landes kam es weiterhin zu erbitterten Kämpfen. Mit der Eroberung des lettischen Alūksne am 21. Februar war schließlich der erste Höhepunkt von Laidoners „aktivem Verteidigungskrieg"[30] erreicht: Zum ersten Jahrestag der Unabhängigkeitserklärung am 24. Februar war der Feind weitgehend aus dem von der EAV beanspruchten Gebiet vertrieben. Zwar waren die militärischen Auseinandersetzungen – auch auf eigenem Territorium – damit noch nicht beendet, doch lieferte der Kriegsverlauf der EAV nun die Möglichkeit, auf befreitem Staatsgebiet die Wahlen zur Verfassunggebenden Versammlung durchzuführen.

Bewusst war die EAV eine Koalitionsregierung, die aus Vertretern aller größeren Parteien vom konservativen Bauernbund bis zu den estnischen Sozialdemokraten bestand. Unter den im *Maapäev* vertretenen Parteien – die 1917 gewählten Bolschewiki hatten ihre Mitarbeit aufgekündigt – blieben nur die Sozialrevolutionäre in der Opposition. Es gehört zur Vorgeschichte der Februarkrise, dass der *Maapäev* Ende November 1918 beschloss, der EAV weitreichende Vollmachten auch hinsichtlich der Legislative zu erteilen. Die Abgeordneten selbst wollten sich auf die Organisation der Wahlen zur Nationalversammlung konzentrieren und bis auf Weiteres nicht mehr zusammenkommen. Der anvisierte Wahltermin am 20. Februar 1919 musste jedoch bald aufgrund der Kriegssituation auf unbestimmte Zeit verschoben werden. Damit stellte sich in der Sicht mancher Abgeordneter die Frage der parlamentarischen Kontrolle der EAV neu, schließlich verlängerte sich damit auch die Zeit, in der die Minister ihre außerordentlichen Vollmachten ausschöpfen konnten.[31]

30 Dieses Konzept sah vor, die eigenen Grenzen auf fremden Gebiet von russischen und lettischen Einheiten verteidigen zu lassen. Zum Teil war dies eine Reaktion auf die Abneigung der estnischen Soldaten, über die eigenen Grenzen hinaus militärisch aktiv zu sein. Zusammenfassend: Brüggemann, Die Gründung, S. 106-108; ausführlich Rosenthal, Laidoner, S. 112-130.

31 MN prot. S. 337f.; Eesti ajalugu VI, S. 47f.; Pajur, Eesti riigikaitsepoliitika, S. 48.

Dabei darf nicht übersehen werden, dass sich die kritische Situation im Lande nicht nur aus dem Angriff der Roten Armee ergab, sondern auch mit den Aktivitäten der estnischen Kommunisten zu tun hatte. Seit Ende November 1918 existierte eine Gegenregierung zur EAV, die von Moskau unterstützte „Estnische Arbeiterkommune" (*Eesti töörahva kommuun*) unter Leitung Jaan Anvelts.[32] Abgesehen von durchaus erfolgreichen Streikaufrufen seit Mitte November machten die Kommunisten mit Putschgerüchten auf sich aufmerksam, die sich schließlich dahingehend verdichteten, dass sie am 17. Dezember die Macht übernehmen würden. Letztlich behielt die EAV jedoch die Lage auch an diesem Tag unter Kontrolle. Aber nach dem Vorbild der entsprechenden Anordnungen der deutschen Besatzungsmacht wurden nun die Versammlungs- und Bewegungsfreiheit eingeschränkt.[33] Hiermit jedoch wurden augenscheinlich die Errungenschaften der Februarrevolution in Frage gestellt. Aber waren die Volksvertreter nicht 1917 angetreten, genau diese Rechte für Estland zu sichern?

Die EAV nutzte ihre Vollmachten weidlich aus – angesichts der Situation blieb ihr auch kaum etwas Anderes übrig. So setzte sie in den Regionen die im Manifest vom 11. November angekündigten „Bevollmächtigten" ein, die nun als Regierungskommissare auftraten und das Recht hatten, sich in die Belange der Lokalverwaltungen einzumischen. Die Praxis der Feldgerichte, die durchaus auch abseits der unmittelbaren Frontregion aktiv wurden, stand genauso unter Kritik wie der Umstand, dass die Regierungskommissare Vertreter der Lokalverwaltungen vor diese unkontrollierten und von juristischer Kompetenz freien Militärorgane bringen konnten. Auch die Armee insgesamt schränkte die Befugnisse der Lokalverwaltungen z. B. durch Mobilisierungen und Requisitionen ein. Nun waren aber, wie gesehen, die 1917 gewählten lokalen Vertreter wiedereingesetzt worden, deren „überdemokratische Mentalität" (Ago Pajur) in all diesen Maßnahmen antidemokratische Willkür erblickte. Die Bezirksverwaltung von Viljandi z. B. beschwerte sich über den Stadtkommandanten, der mit der Erschießung von „Staatsfeinden" ohne Gerichtsverhandlung drohte, sollte es in der Stadt zu Unruhen kommen. Eine solche Drohung sei „roh und wild" und würde „uns in den Augen der Kulturvölker erniedrigen", hieß es in der Beschwerde.[34] Der *Maapäev* erhielt zahlreiche ähnliche Klagen über das Verhalten der zivilen und militärischen Organe, darunter auch über Verhaftungen aus politischen Gründen („kommunistische Gesinnung"), weshalb die bereits

32 Hierzu ausführlich: BRÜGGEMANN, Foreign Rule.

33 PAJUR, Konstantin Päts, S. 132-135.

34 Zit. n. ROSENTHAL, Kord ja kohus, S. 50. Die Beschwerde stammte vom 4.1.1919.

erwähnte außerordentliche Sitzung des *Maapäav* am 27. Dezember einberufen wurde.[35] Dies beflügelte wiederum ein zunehmendes Misstrauen der bürgerlichen Politiker wie der Militärführung gegenüber den Lokalverwaltungen.[36] Angesichts der nach innen wie nach außen angespannten Situation wurde der Konflikt, der sich auf mehreren Ebenen abzeichnete – Zivileinrichtungen vs. Armee, Lokalverwaltungen vs. EAV –, einstweilen noch nicht ausgetragen.

Wiederaufgenommen wurde er anderthalb Wochen später – von der EAV selbst. Am 7. Januar 1919, d. h. am Tag nach dem Beginn des estnischen Gegenangriffs, bewog der parteilose Innenminister August Peet die EAV dazu, Laidoner zu verpflichten, in Zukunft alle Maßnahmen, die nicht rein militärischer Natur waren, „sondern das bürgerliche Leben regeln", ihr zum Entscheid vorzulegen. Zugleich forderte Finanzminister Juhan Kukk von der Arbeitspartei Laidoner auf, seine finanziellen Forderungen zu spezifizieren, schließlich „pumpe" der Krieg die Kassen leer, und man wolle wissen, wofür man zahle.[37] Eine Woche später beschloss das Kabinett, „zur Vermeidung von Konflikten" eine Kommission mit der Ausarbeitung eines Gesetzes zu beauftragen, das die Machtgrenzen des Oberkommandierenden festlegen sollte. Es wurde nach der Februarkrise am 25. Februar beschlossen.[38]

Vor allem die Vertreter linker Parteien, darunter auch die Minister, sparten nicht mit Kritik, sprachen – mit Verweis auf die Feldgerichte – vom „weißen Terror" und sahen die Gefahr eines Bürgerkriegs wie in Finnland heraufziehen. Auf einer zur Klärung einberufenen gemeinsamen Sitzung der EAV und des Ältestenrates des *Maapäev* am 15. Januar fragte der Sozialdemokrat und Sozialminister Karl Ast polemisch, ob man noch für die Einberufung der Nationalversammlung oder „für die Interessen einer gewissen Gruppe" kämpfe und malte das Gespenst eines bevorstehenden rechten Staatsstreiches aus.[39] Ein Artikel im „Sotsiaaldemokraat", in dem der stellvertretende Ministerpräsident August Rei den „weißen Terror" in Finnland heftig kritisierte, führte aufgrund eines finnischen Protestes am 24. Januar zu dessen Absetzung, schließlich war Tallinn auf die Hilfe Helsinkis angewiesen.[40] Die Kritiker der EAV forderten die stärkere

35 Eesti ajalugu VI, S. 48; Pajur, Eesti riigikaitsepoliitika, S. 48f.

36 Rosenthal, Kord ja kohus, S. 46; hier auch (S. 50-80) ausführlich zu den vorgebrachten Klagen und einzelnen Konflikten aus dem Dezember und Januar.

37 EAV-Prot., 7.1.1919, in: RA, ERA 31/1/13, Bl. 12-14.

38 EAV-Prot., 14.1.1919, in: RA, ERA 31/1/13, Bl. 31r-32; Rosenthal, Kord ja kohus, S. 33. Zu dem Gesetz vom 25.2.1919 siehe unten.

39 Pajur, Konstantin Päts, S. 142f.; Graf, Eesti rahvusriik, S. 268; Rosenthal, Kord ja kohus, S. 61-64.

40 Ant, August Rei, S. 70f.; vgl. Rei, Mälestusi, S. 231.

Kontrolle der Feldgerichte und der Willkür der Militärs sowie die Erweiterung der Rechte der Lokalverwaltungen im Interesse der Vertiefung der Demokratie. In dieser Situation und aufgrund zahlreicher weiterer Klagen[41] beschloss der Ältestenrat des *Maapäev* am 21. Januar, gegen den Willen der EAV eine außerordentliche Sitzungsperiode zum 1. Februar einzuberufen.[42]

Das noch fragile Konstrukt der Machtaufteilung zwischen zivilen und militärischen Strukturen implodierte, als der gerade erst zum Generalmajor beförderte Laidoner am 24. Januar, wenige Tage nach der Befreiung Narvas, um seine Entlassung bat. In seinem äußerst knappen Gesuch verwies er auf „Reibereien" mit den lokalen Selbstverwaltungsorganen, die seine Arbeit derartig behinderten, dass an eine sachgemäße Führung der Streitkräfte nicht mehr zu denken sei.[43] Erwartungsgemäß lehnte die EAV zwar ab. Nun lief aber in der Tat alles auf den Showdown im *Maapäev* hin.

In seiner Eröffnungsansprache am 1. Februar betonte der Vorsitzende des *Maapäev*, Ado Birk von der liberalen Volkspartei, ostentativ die von den Siegermächten anerkannte Funktion dieses Gremiums als „Träger der höchsten Macht".[44] Es war deutlich, dass sich viele Abgeordnete von der EAV übergangen fühlten und aufgrund der Regierungspraxis fürchteten, ihre Kontrollfunktion nicht mehr ausüben zu könnten. Nicht die vom Volk gewählten Lokalverwaltungen, sondern die Regierungskommissare und Militärs seien die eigentlichen Herren im Lande. Karl Ast verstieg sich in der Debatte gar zu der Andeutung, dass nach den Absetzungen von manchen Vertretern der Lokalverwaltungen bald auch die Reihe an Abgeordneten des *Maapäev* sein könnte. Neben den Sozialdemokraten und Sozialrevolutionären griffen auch Vertreter der Arbeitspartei die EAV und die Militärführung scharf an: Aleksander Veiler zufolge verfahre die Armee schlimmer mit dem Land als eine Besatzungsarmee und die Gefängnisse seien voller als zu Zarenzeiten. Der Vorschlag, ein Gesetz auszuarbeiten, das all diesen Vorwürfen Rechnung getragen und zu einer schärferen Kontrolle von Regierung und Armee geführt hätte, wurde indes mit deutlicher Mehrheit abgelehnt. Päts zufolge würde ein solches Gesetz das Land in die Hände der Kommunisten treiben.[45] Am Ende beschloss die Versammlung bei aller Kritik

41 Siehe MN prot., S. 359-364; Pajur, Konstantin Päts, S. 142-144.

42 Graf, Eesti rahvusriik, S. 268.

43 Laidoners Gesuch, 24.1.1919, in: RA, ERA 2124/1/4 Bl. 278; Sitzungsprotokoll der EAV, 24.1.1919, in: 31/1/13, Bl. 46f.

44 MN prot., S. 357f.

45 MN prot. S. 357-364; Graf, Eesti rahvusriik, S. 269. Der *Maapäev* hatte keine deutliche sozialistische Mehrheit: Unter den 62 Abgeordneten im Oktober 1917 vertraten

einstimmig, der Armeeführung, den Soldaten und den ausländischen Freiwilligen zu danken.

Trotz dieser Geste der Versöhnung plante Laidoner erneut seinen Rücktritt. Es habe zu viel Kritik an der Armee gegeben, schreib er dem Kommandeur der II. Division, Viktor Puskar, nach Tartu.[46] In der Nacht auf den 2. Februar kam es dann aber fast zur Eskalation, als Puskar sich daraufhin anschickte, Truppen aus Tartu nach Tallinn zu schicken, um den *Maapäev* zu „beeinflussen" und zu „befrieden". Die Militärs drohten damit, die Waffen an der Front niederzulegen, sollten die Anschuldigungen gegen den Oberkommandierenden und die Armee nicht zurückgenommen werden. Damit stand die junge Republik nach den Worten Pajurs „wenn nicht vor der Gefahr eines Bürgerkriegs oder eines Soldatenaufstands, aber doch zumindest vor dem ernsthaften Versuch der Einmischung in die Angelegenheiten der Zivilbehörden" seitens der Armee.[47] Vereitelt wurde diese Aktion durch die Absage der I. Division unter General Aleksander Tõnisson, sich an ihr zu beteiligen – man verteidige schließlich das Land gegen den äußeren Feind und verurteile „jeglichen Bürgerkrieg".[48] Auch Laidoner wurde Puskar gegenüber deutlich: Die am 1. Februar von den Abgeordneten erhobenen Anschuldigungen dürften in keinem Falle dazu führen, die Lage an der Front zu verändern. Er erlaube keine Einmischung der Armee in die Innenpolitik, denn die Entscheidung über die Staatsform obliege der Nationalversammlung. Bis zu deren Zusammenkunft „müssen wir den *Maapäev* und die Provisorische Regierung als höchste Macht im Staat anerkennen".[49]

---

13 den Bauernbund, 11 die spätere Volkspartei, 11 die Arbeitspartei, 9 die estnischen Sozialdemokraten, 8 die Sozialrevolutionäre, 5 die Bolschewiki (die seit Ende 1918 nicht mehr an den Sitzungen teilnahmen). BRÜGGEMANN, Die Gründung, S. 56.

46 ROSENTHAL, Kord ja kohus, S. 83.

47 PAJUR, Eesti riigikaitsepoliitika, S. 52f. (Zitat auf S. 53); PAJUR, Konstantin Päts, S. 145; Puskars Memoiren ist zu entnehmen, dass die Putschisten planten, die Wahlen zur Verfassunggebenden Versammlung auf die Zeit nach Kriegsende zu verschieben und bis dahin Laidoner die Macht zu übergeben. Ein Szenario der Militärdiktatur, dass im Kontext des Russischen Bürgerkriegs durchaus bekannt vorkommt. PUSKAR, Mälestusi, S. 1565.

48 General Tõnissons Resolution, 2.2.1919, in: RA, ERA 515/1/634, Bl. 67; ROSENTHAL, Kord ja kohus, S. 84.

49 Laidoner an die II. Division, 2.2.1919, in: RA, ERA 495/10/39, Bl. 24; PAJUR, Eesti riigikaitsepoliitika, S. 53. Puskar schrieb 1933, es sei noch zu früh zu entscheiden, ob Laidoners Eingriff „gut oder schlecht" gewesen sei. PUSKAR, Mälestusi, S. 1566.

In die Nachrichten dieses Tages platzte auch Laidoners Rücktrittsgesuch, das wohl eher als Protest gegen die seiner Ansicht nach übertriebenen Anschuldigungen zu werten ist. Er dürfte von seiner Unersetzlichkeit ausgegangen sein und wollte wohl vor allem Druck auf die EAV ausüben.[50] Allerdings erklärte auch die Regierung an diesem Tag ihren Rücktritt, da ihrer Meinung nach der *Maapäev* seine Kompetenzen überschritten hatte.[51] Den Vorschlag an Ado Birk, seinen Posten abzugeben, hatte dieser zunächst abgelehnt, weshalb nun die EAV mit ihrem Rücktritt Druck auf die *Maapäev*-Führung ausüben wollte. Erst jetzt trat Birk dann tatsächlich zurück.[52] Die sozialdemokratischen Minister indes hatten sich der Rücktrittsdrohung nicht angeschlossen. Die Gräben zwischen linksdemokratischen und gemäßigten Kräften wurden so deutlich sichtbar.

Die aufgrund dieser dramatischen Ereignisse auf den 3. Februar verschobene nächste Sitzung des *Maapäev* setzte ein mit einer emphatischen Dankadresse an Laidoner und die Armee – schließlich wollte niemand die militärischen Erfolge gefährden. Der Konflikt mit der Militärführung und Laidoners Rücktritt waren damit einstweilen ad acta gelegt.[53] Im Anschluss verkündeten Birk und drei weitere Männer aus der *Maapäev*-Führung nun auch offiziell ihre Amtsniederlegung: Birk erklärte später, man habe damit „die Lösung der Krise erleichtern" wollen; die Kontinuität blieb jedoch gewahrt, denn Birks Posten übernahm dessen Parteifreund Kaarel Parts.[54]

Regierung und Militärführung hatten mit ihren Rücktrittsdrohungen zu einer spürbaren Mäßigung der Kritik seitens der Abgeordneten beigetragen. Tatsächlich wurde am 4. Februar mehrheitlich eine Resolution der Volkspartei angenommen, in der der EAV das Vertrauen ausgesprochen wurde.[55] In einer Regierungserklärung hatte Päts am Tag zuvor den Grundstein für eine gütliche Einigung gelegt, indem er eigene Fehler eingestand. Zugleich bat er um Verständnis für die jungen und unerfahrenen Bediensteten seiner Regierung. Wie die Militärbehörden seien auch sie von keinem anderen Ziel geleitet worden als

---

50 Laidoners Gesuch, 2.2.1919, in: RA, ERA 495/10/39, Bl. 20; Rosenthal, Kord ja kohus, S. 85f.

51 MN prot., S. 366.

52 Rosenthal, Kord ja kohus, S. 87.

53 MN prot., S. 365; Laidoner antwortete am Tag darauf im Namen der Armee, er sei sich sicher, dass Letztere wie ehedem das Land und die demokratische Ordnung verteidigen werde. MN prot., S. 374.

54 MN prot. S. 365f., 368.

55 MN prot., S. 378.

dem Bemühen um die demokratische Ordnung.[56] Der parteilose Innenminister Peet verteidigte die heftig kritisierten Regierungskommissare, die in den Verwaltungsbezirken mit außerordentlichen Vollmachten ausgestattet waren. Zwar könne man einzelne Personen mit Recht kritisieren, doch garantierten sie als Vertreter der Regierung die demokratische Ordnung. Bevollmächtige man hingegen die Selbstverwaltungsorgane, sei dies gefährlich nahe an sowjetischer Machtausübung. Am 4. Februar kam schließlich auch eine speziell eingesetzte juristische Kommission zu der Erkenntnis, dass es keinen Grund gebe, die EAV in ihren Kompetenzen zu beschneiden: Der *Maapäev* sei ja berechtigt, alle Beschlüsse der Exekutive zu kontrollieren, wenn auch nur zeitversetzt. Diese Entscheidung wurde bemerkenswerterweise einstimmig, selbst von den Sozialdemokraten und Sozialrevolutionären, verabschiedet.[57] Demgegenüber enthielten sich die Sozialdemokraten bei der Abstimmung über die Vertrauenserklärung an die EAV (nur die Sozialrevolutionäre votierten dagegen) und traten am 5. Februar aus der Regierung aus. Nun hatten sie freie Hand zur Kritik an der Regierung. Ihrem späteren Wahlerfolg war dies sicher nicht abträglich.[58]

Nach Ansicht von Ago Pajur und Reigo Rosenthal erreichte die Opposition während der „Februarkrise" nicht allzu viel. Die Vollmachten der Regierungskommissare wurden eingeschränkt und man habe anerkannt, dass diejenigen der Feldgerichte präzisiert werden mussten. Das von der EAV bereits vor der Krise anvisierte Gesetz über die Machtbefugnisse des Oberkommandierenden, das am 25. Februar angenommen wurde, änderte aber kaum etwas am Status quo. Immerhin wurde geklärt, dass nur Vertreter der Lokalverwaltungen auf Gemeindeebene von den Kommandanturen abgesetzt werden durften; Vertreter der übergeordneten Lokalverwaltungen durften nur auf Befehl des Oberkommandierenden ihres Postens enthoben werden.[59] Schon dies regulierte aber die kritisierte Willkür im Verhältnis zwischen Armee und Zivilverwaltung. Später schränkte Laidoner die Kompetenzen der Kommandanturen noch weiter ein.[60] Wie abschließend gezeigt werden soll, gab es auch im Falle der Feldgerichte durchaus regulative Einschränkungen.

56 MN prot., S. 367f.

57 MN prot., S. 367, 369. Vgl. Brüggemann, Die Gründung, S. 116-118.

58 MN prot., S. 378; zum Austritt aus der Regierung siehe Graf, Parteid Eesti Vabariigis, S. 130f.

59 Pajur, Eesti riigikaitsepoliitika, S. 53f.; Rosenthal, Kord ja kohus, S. 96.

60 Rosenthal, Kord ja kohus, S. 105f.

3. Die Feldgerichte

Die EAV sanktionierte die Einrichtung der Feldgerichte am 5. Dezember 1918. Die niedrigste Ebene, auf der dieses Sanktionsinstrument installiert werden sollte, war das Regiment. Die Entscheidung, gegen wen vorgegangen werden sollte, lag entsprechend beim Regimentskommandeur. Zwar sollten die Urteile eigentlich vom Kriegsminister (Päts) bestätigt werden, doch blieb es in der Praxis bei einer Bestätigung des Regimentskommandeurs. Am 18. Dezember legte der Militärstaatsanwalt die Zusammensetzung der Feldgerichte fest: Sie bestanden aus fünf Offizieren, für deren Ernennung ebenfalls der Regimentskommandeur verantwortlich war. Das Urteil musste innerhalb von zwei Tagen mit einfacher Mehrheit gefällt und dann innerhalb von 24 Stunden vollzogen werden. Sollte der Regimentskommandeur das Urteil nicht bestätigen, kam der Fall vor das Militärgericht in Tallinn. Eine Anfechtung des Urteils seitens der Beschuldigten war nicht vorgesehen. Laut den Instruktionen konnte jedermann vor Gericht gestellt werden, der gegen die Republik Estland arbeite, mit ihren Feinden kollaboriere oder kommuniziere, die Armee behindere oder subversive Gerüchte verbreite. Ende Dezember wurde zudem festgelegt, dass, wie erwähnt, die Regierungskommissare Vertreter der Lokalverwaltungen vor die Feldgerichte bringen konnten. Als juristische Grundlage für die Einrichtung der Feldgerichte verwies die EAV Anfang Januar 1919 auf die Militärgesetzgebung des Russländischen Reiches.[61] Unreguliert blieb dabei aber das Strafmaß.[62]

Generalmajor Aleksander Tõnisson äußerte sich in seinen Erinnerungen militärisch knapp über die Effektivität der Feldgerichte: „Zuvor waren viele Desertionen vorgekommen. Manchmal blieben in manchen Rotten weniger Soldaten als Offiziere übrig. Dann setzten wir ein außerordentliches Hilfsmittel in Gang: die Feldgerichte. Deren Einfluss war mit den bloßen Augen zu sehen. Die Desertionsgefahr war vorbei."[63] In seiner Regierungserklärung vor dem *Maapäev* am 3. Februar 1919 wollte Päts die Feldgerichte, welche die Gemüter so erhitzt hatten, zwar nicht in Schutz nehmen. Immerhin, so der Ministerpräsident der EAV, verringere dieses unzulängliche Institut die Zahl der eigenen Opfer und schütze die Grenzen; es werde ohnehin nur im Frontstreifen eingesetzt.[64] Selbst der Sozialdemokrat Ast ruderte an diesem Tag der allgemeinen Versöhnung zurück,

---

61 Ajutise Valitsuse määrus välikohtute asutamise kohta; Minnik, The Establishment, S. 101f.; Minnik, Terror, S. 134f.; Rosenthal, Kord ja kohus, S. 35.

62 Rosenthal, Kord ja kohus, S. 76.

63 Tõnisson, Visked vabadussõja mälestustest, S. 34.

64 MN prot., S. 367f.

indem er im Namen seiner Partei nun zugab, „dass es ohne Feldgerichte in den Kampfgebieten nicht geht". Man fordere nur deren Einschränkung, d. h. Kontrolle.[65] Der „weiße Terror" blieb jedoch dessen ungeachtet einer der wichtigsten Aspekte im Wahlkampf von Asts Partei, die sich ja nun ihrer Mitverantwortung in der Regierung entledigt hatte. Es steht zu vermuten, dass die EAV dadurch unter Zugzwang gesetzt wurde.

In der Tat ist es im Einflussbereich der Feldgerichte der estnischen Armee im Winter 1918/19 zu willkürlichen Exekutionen ohne jegliche juristische Basis gekommen. Betroffen waren vor allem Esten, die in der Roten Armee kämpften, niedrige bolschewistische Funktionäre und „Sympathisanten" des Feindes, die meist denunziert worden waren und ohne viel Federlesens erschossen wurden. Neben den zahlreichen, eher zufälligen Opfern – der 14-jährige Ivan Osipov, ein Flötist der Roten Armee, oder Anette Abel, die Freundin eines estnischen Rotarmisten, die wegen „Kommunikation mit dem Feind" zum Tode verurteilt wurde – sei auf die Hinrichtung von knapp 30 Kriegsgefangenen verwiesen, die just an den Tagen der *Maapäev*-Sitzungen Anfang Februar exekutiert wurden.[66] Sie gehörten zu den Mannschaften der sowjetischen Zerstörer „Avtoril" und „Spartak", die im Dezember 1918 vom britischen Geschwader aufgebracht und den Esten übergeben worden waren.[67] Ihnen wurden von einem Feldgericht Aktionen gegen die EAV oder ihre Mitgliedschaft in der Parteizelle der Schiffe vorgeworfen, die vier Esten unter ihnen wurden des Verrats beschuldigt.[68] Die größte Opferzahl in Zusammenhang mit dem Einsatz von Feldgerichten verlangte der durch den Widerstand gegen die drohende Mobilisierung ausgelöste Aufstand auf der Insel Saaremaa Mitte Februar 1919 (also nach der Febrauarkrise). Nach dessen Niederschlagung ließ ein Feldgericht Anfang März 68 Personen hinrichten.[69]

Minnik zufolge hat es insgesamt knapp 300 Opfer der Feldgerichte gegeben, wobei eine annähernd große Zahl an Menschen von der estnischen Armee und

---

65 MN prot., S. 377. August Rei, der damals als scharfer Kritiker der Feldgerichte auftrat, konnte sich später nicht mehr daran erinnern, ob diese Instanzen überhaupt Todesurteile gefällt hatten. Rei, Mälestusi, S. 255.

66 Minnik, The Establishment, S. 102, 104f.

67 Es waren jedoch insgesamt knapp 250 Kriegsgefangene, von denen viele in der estnischen Marine weiterbeschäftigt wurden. Oll, Eesti merevägi, S. 153-156; vgl. Bennett, Cowan's War, S. 39-46; EV I, S. 289-293.

68 Minnik, The Establishment, S. 105.

69 Die Zahl ist umstritten, wird aber bestätigt bei Hiie, 1919. aasta mäss, S. 93-96; und Minnik, The Establishment, S. 105f.

ihren Verbündeten exekutiert wurde, ohne dass diese Instanz überhaupt aktiviert worden sei. Die überwiegende Mehrheit der in diese Statistik eingegangenen Todesurteile fiel in die Zeit von Ende 1918 bis März 1919: 234.[70] Eine Übersicht aller im Jahr 1919 aus politischen Gründen (kommunistische Aktivität, staatsfeindliche Agitation etc.) vor die Feldgerichte gebrauchten Personen zeigt jedoch auch, dass bei 554 Angeklagten immerhin 199 (35%) freigesprochen, 144 (26%) verhaftet und 214 (39%) hingerichtet wurden. Tatsächlich traten Anfang April neue Regelungen für die Feldgerichte in Kraft, welche die EAV, offenbar angesichts der Proteste im *Maapäev* und wohl auch des Wahlkampfes, am 25. März beschlossen hatte. Von nun an wurden die Verfahren der Feldgerichte vom estnischen Militärstaatsanwalt kontrolliert, weshalb sie nun auch zwingend protokolliert werden mussten. Todesurteile mussten seither vom Kriegsminister bzw. einem Armeekommandeur bestätigt werden. Schließlich erhielten die Beschuldigten auch das Recht auf Verteidigung und, wenn notwendig, einen Dolmetscher. Das genaue Strafmaß blieb jedoch weiterhin unbestimmt und eine räumliche Beschränkung auf das unmittelbare Frontgebiet unterblieb. Immerhin wurde das quantitative Ausmaß an Verfahren vor den Feldgerichten eingeschränkt. Während sich von Januar bis März 1919 970 Personen vor ihnen verantworten mussten, kam es in der Zeit von April bis Dezember „nur" noch zu 691 Verfahren, von denen allein 460 Deserteure betrafen.[71]

Im weiteren Verlauf des Krieges wurde das Verfahren indes weiter reglementiert. Die Nationalversammlung wies denjenigen, die von den Feldgerichten zu Haft oder Strafarbeit verurteilt worden waren, das Recht auf Revision zu und amnestierte zugleich Deserteure.[72] Dass dieses Gesetz bereits am 3. Mai in dritter Lesung noch vor der Wahl einer neuen Regierung auf der insgesamt erst neunten Sitzung der Nationalversammlung beschlossen wurde, zeigt erneut, wie wichtig den Abgeordneten die Demokratisierung dieser Einrichtung der Kriegszeit war – sie fühlten sich offenbar auch ihren Wählern gegenüber in der Bringschuld. Zwar wäre es wohl ohnehin in friedlicheren Zeiten zu einer solchen gesetzlichen Einhegung der Willkür gekommen. Zu konstatieren bleibt, dass der

70 MINNIK, The Establishment, S. 103; MINNIK, Terror, S. 138. Notorisch unter den „Verbündeten" war in erster Linie Rittmeister Stanislav Bulak-Balachovič (*Stanisław Bułak-Bałachowicz*), der im Mai/Juni 1919 in Pskov zahlreiche standrechtliche Erschießungen und Hinrichtungen vornehmen ließ. BRÜGGEMANN, Die Gründung, S. 234-238.

71 Eesti Vabariigi ajutised sõjakohtud ja nendele alluvad süüteod. Vgl. ebenso Määrus välikohtute üle. MINNIK, The Establishment, S. 106f.; ROSENTHAL, Kord ja kohus, S. 96-101.

72 AK prot., S. 289-297.

Krieg im Mai bei Weitem noch nicht vorbei war, auch wenn er sich in die Grenzregionen des Landes verlagert hatte. Die Politik sicherte sich so Schritt für Schritt mehr Kontrolle über den Krieg. Nach allem, was wir wissen, trug Laidoner diese Eingriffe in die traditionelle Praxis der Armee loyal mit.

Mit den Sozialdemokraten und der Arbeitspartei, die zusammen 71 der 120 Abgeordneten der Konstituante stellten, führte nun eine politische Richtung die Staatsgeschäfte, die sich einer raschen Beendigung des Krieges verschrieben hatte. Es war bezeichnend für die politische Stimmung, dass sich der mit 100 gegen 14 Stimmen zum Vorsitzenden der Konstituante gewählte August Rei bei seiner Eröffnungsansprache am 23. April Verdächtigungen glaubte entgegenstellen zu müssen, seine Partei sei halbbolschewistisch. Als er ausrief, dass „imperialistische Landgier" noch nie so offen und zynisch zu Politik gemacht worden sei wie von Moskau im November 1918, legte er ein klares antibolschewistisches Bekenntnis ab. Es folgte ein Loblied auf die Armee, das von stürmischem Applaus und Ausrufen „Es lebe Laidoner!" unterbrochen wurde. Über die Beendigung des Krieges, eine der wesentlichen sozialdemokratischen Forderungen des Wahlkampfes, verlor Rei in dieser Stunde kein Wort. Demgegenüber betonte er das zweite wichtige Thema des Wahlkampfes seiner Partei: Der junge estnische Staat stehe und falle mit der Lösung der Landfrage. Seinem Aufruf, den Soldaten das Recht auf eigenes Land zu sichern, spendeten auch die Abgeordneten von Päts' Bauernpartei Applaus – bei allen war die Erinnerung an das Jahr 1917, als die Soldaten der Zarenarmee die Schützengräben eigenmächtig verließen, um bei der erhofften Landverteilung nicht zu spät zu kommen, noch lebendig. Als zweite wesentliche Zukunftsaufgabe benannte Rei die dringend notwendige Stabilisierung der demokratischen Strukturen. Bei dieser Gelegenheit kam er auch auf die Feldgerichte zu sprechen. Er forderte, dass dieses Instrument auf das unmittelbare Frontgebiet beschränkt bleiben sollte und die Urteile gegebenenfalls einer Sonderkommission zur Überprüfung vorgelegt werden müssten.[73] Bei der Debatte um das Amnestiegesetz am 3. Mai wurde Reis Fraktionskollege Ast deutlicher, indem er beklagte, dass die Neuregelung der Feldgerichte vom 25. März nichts an der Praxis geändert habe.[74] Den Versuch der Regelung begrüßte indes auch Ast. Somit waren die Feldgerichte tatsächlich zu einer Art Lackmustest für die Ernsthaftigkeit des demokratischen Anspruchs der Staatsführung geworden, zu einem Faktor, an dem sich – je nach Standpunkt – zeigte, wie „kultiviert" die junge Republik ihre Freiheit zu verteidigen imstande war.

---

73 AK prot. I, Sp. 5-12; Rei, Mälestusi, S. 249-254.

74 AK prot. I, Sp. 280f.

4. Zusammenfassung

Bemerkenswerterweise waren während der Februarkrise alle Seiten zu Zugeständnissen bereit, was mit Sicherheit auch daran lag, dass sich die Sicherheitslage etwas entspannt hatte. So hatte nicht nur Päts vor dem *Maapäev*, sondern schon Laidoner in seiner Rücktrittserklärung vom 2. Februar um Verständnis für die Fehler der eigenen Leute gebeten. Dies erscheint umso bemerkenswerter, als dass Laidoner später zu bedenken gab, die EAV habe dem *Maapäev* gegenüber viel zu stark zum Nachgeben tendiert. Hätte dieses Gremium das alleinige Sagen gehabt, hätte es seiner Ansicht nach das „Ende" bedeutet. Demgegenüber hatte er am 19. Februar in einem Tagesbefehl, der sich explizit nicht nur an die Armee, sondern auch an die Lokalverwaltungen im Frontgebiet richtete, nicht nur die Kompetenzen der Kommandanturen beschränkt, sondern auch erklärt, dass das gemeinsame Ziel der Schaffung einer „unabhängigen demokratischen Republik Estland (...) nur mit gemeinsamer Arbeit" zu erreichen sei.[75] Letztlich hatte der Oberbefehlshaber aber auch ein gutes Gespür für die Stimmung in der Armee. Die Männer hätten einige Revolutionen erlebt und wüssten, wofür sie kämpften, schrieb er seinem Stabschef Jaan Soots am 5. Februar. Wer Sozialist war, sei es weiterhin, und wer den Bauernbund unterstützt, kämpfe eben für sein Land. Seine Überzeugung, die Wahlen zur Konstituante so schnell wie möglich noch während des Krieges durchzuführen, rührte damit auch von der Sorge um die Motivation der Soldaten her. Nur die Nationalversammlung konnte schließlich das Agrargesetz verabschieden.[76]

Sieht man die „Februarkrise" als Bewährungsprobe für die demokratischen Institutionen der jungen Republik, so muss man feststellen, dass diese eher noch gefestigt werden konnten. An der Notwendigkeit der Einberufung der Konstituante kam kein Zweifel auf.[77] Der im November 1918 vom *Maapäev* festgelegte und im Dezember auf unbestimmte Zeit verschobene Wahltermin musste trotz des Krieges nur um anderthalb Monate verlegt werden. Sowohl die EAV als auch der *Maapäev* betrachteten demokratische Wahlen als Ziel und Legitimation für die eigene Arbeit. Laidoner selbst war es, der der EAV den Rat gab, die Wahlen ungeachtet des noch nicht entschiedenen Krieges schnellstmöglich durchzuführen.[78] Kompetenzstreitigkeiten zwischen Exekutive und der selbstentmachteten

---

75 Zit. n. ROSENTHAL, Kord ja kohus, S. 87, 106.

76 ROSENTHAL, Kord ja kohus, S. 73, 94.

77 Derartige Zweifel kennt man aus der Rhetorik der weißen Bewegung, für die die Berufung auf die Nationalversammlung im Laufe des Bürgerkriegs immer mehr dazu diente, Entscheidungen zu vertagen. KATZER, Die weiße Bewegung, S. 134-138.

78 REI, Mälestusi, S. 243.

Legislative können nicht überraschen, wenn man sich die aufgrund der äußeren und inneren Bedrohung schwierige Situation des Landes vor Augen führt. Überraschen kann höchstens die Konsequenz, mit der sich auch der Oberkommandierende den demokratischen Spielregeln unterwarf. Der nicht unberechtigte Einwand, Laidoners Rücktrittsgesuch sei zu einer Zeit erfolgt, in der die estnische Armee ihre ersten Erfolge erzielte, weshalb ihm die EAV hätte kaum etwas abschlagen können, mindert die Relevanz dieses Befundes keineswegs. Laidoner war klar, dass in dem Bekenntnis zur Verfassunggebenden Versammlung, von der sich die Bevölkerung in erster Linie eine radikale Landreform versprach, zum einen der Schlüssel für das Vertrauen und die Opferbereitschaft der Soldaten lag. Zum anderen hatte er bzw. die EAV hiermit eine propagandistische Waffe gegen die Agitation der Bolschewiki in der Hand, der zufolge das Volk nichts von der von den „baltischen Baronen" resp. den „englischen Kapitalisten" gekauften „weißen Regierung" in Tallinn zu erwarten hätte.[79] Demokratische Wahlen waren in jedem Fall auch als außenpolitisches Signal gedacht; schließlich hing nach wie vor das Schicksal Estlands auch militärisch ganz entscheidend von der Haltung der Entente ab.

Kriegsführung nach internationalen Regeln war sicher ein weiterer Aspekt, den die estnische Regierung daher beachten musste, zumal sie durch die im Laufe des Frühjahrs entsendeten alliierten Missionen unter stärkerer Beobachtung stand. Auch in dieser Hinsicht war die Kontrolle über die Feldgerichte wesentlich. Es kam zwar auch weiterhin zu zweifelhaften Exekutionen. Der spektakulärste Fall ereignete sich Mitte Juli 1919, als 22 Soldaten von einem Feldgerichtsurteil im Reservebataillon Tartu wegen Befehlsverweigerung erschossen wurden. Sofort wurde daraufhin jedoch eine Sonderkommission der Konstituante eingesetzt, ganz wie Rei es angekündigt hatte, deren Bericht zwei Monate später vorlag und von regelmäßiger Gewaltanwendung gegenüber den Soldaten sprach. Die Nationalversammlung forderte daher die Armeeführung auf, gegen derartige Misshandlungen energisch vorzugehen.[80] Nach den regulierenden Eingriffen der EAV und der Konstituante in die Praxis der Feldgerichte konnte von einer willkürlichen Ausübung von Terror keine Rede mehr sein.

In einem Rückblick auf die „Krisen des Oberbefehlshabers" schrieb Laidoners Stabschef Jaan Soots Anfang 1934, die Linken hätten im Januar 1919, als die unmittelbare Gefahr für Tallinn abgewendet worden sei, sich jeder starken

---

79 Rei, Mälestusi, S. 243f.

80 AK prot. Sp. 1326-1337; Minnik, The Establishment, S. 107.

Macht widersetzen wollen, um zu den Freiheiten der Kerenskij-Zeit zurückzukehren.[81] Nun konnte sich kein vernünftiger Mensch damals wünschen, die Situation der russischen Provisorischen Regierung im Herbst 1917 wiederauferstehen zu lassen, als Aleksandr Kerenskij Ministerpräsident war. Soots' Vergleich zwischen Kerenskij als Inbegriff des Chaos und dem zum Vertreter der Ordnung stilisierten Laidoner ist auch vor dem Hintergrund der angespannten Situation in Estland unmittelbar vor dem Staatsstreich von Päts und Laidoner im März 1934 zu sehen. Vielleicht spielte Soots aber auch darauf an, dass Kerenskij im Frühjahr 1917 in Estland ein revolutionärer Held gewesen war. Dies hatte nicht zuletzt der triumphale Empfang gezeigt, den die Estnische Arbeitspartei ihrem parteipolitischen Cousin, der der Gruppierung der *Trudoviki* angehörte, Anfang April bereitete.[82] Damals hatte die Provisorische Regierung in Petrograd gerade der Bildung von estnischen Einheiten in der Armee des Zarenreichs zugestimmt. Wie kein anderer verkörperte Kerenskij als Projektionsfläche für viele Visionen zunächst auch die Hoffnungen der Esten auf eine Demokratie westlichen Typus als Garantin der bürgerlichen Freiheiten.[83] Diesem Bild aus dem Frühjahr 1917 folgten die estnischen linksorientierten Parteien in der Tat auch Anfang 1919 noch – allerdings im Rahmen des Nationalstaats.

Die Leidenschaft, mit der die Vertreter des linken Parteienspektrums damals um die Stärkung der demokratischen Institute – ist bemerkenswert. Ging es ihnen um die Rettung der Revolution oder – mitten im Krieg – um Gestaltungsmacht nach dem baldigst erwarteten Friedensschluss? Reis und Asts Chargieren zwischen revolutionärer Agitation und staatsmännischer Ratio ist wohl symptomatisch für einen Anpassungsprozess, den gerade sozialdemokratische Politiker in der neuen Situation zu leisten hatten. In ihrer Agitation oft noch vom Klassenkampf ausgehend, mussten sie im Rahmen des Nationalstaats sich eher um einen Ausgleich der Klasseninteressen bemühen. Die Erkenntnis, dass es in Kriegen ohne außerordentliche Gerichte nicht geht, war bei Rei schon Ausdruck des Verständnisses, dass der Impuls, Entwicklungen nach Klassenperspektive zu beurteilen, dann nicht mehr weiterführte, wenn es um das Überleben eines Nationalstaates ging, in dessen Kontext die „bürgerlichen Interessen" auf einmal den „eigenen" glich.

81 Hier zit. n. Pajur, Riigikaitsepoliitika, S. 47.

82 Päälinna külalised Tallinnas, S. 3.

83 Vgl. zu Kerenskij als Projektionsfläche vieler Sehnsüchte die neue Studie: Kolonickij, Kerenskij.

Es sei daran erinnert, dass die Februarrevolution 1917 auch in Petrograd eine kurzfristige Koalition zwischen „bürgerlicher" und „sozialistischer" Revolution evoziert hatte. Im estnischen Kontext waren sich „Sozialisten" und „Nationalisten" bereits während der Revolution von 1905 nähergekommen[84], nicht zuletzt weil beide von der zarischen Regierung verfolgt wurden. Das Ende des Revolutionsjahres 1917 hatte diese „Einheitsfront" (Mart Kuldkepp) wieder zusammengeführt, als beide Seiten mit den Bolschewiki buchstäblich keinen Staat mehr machen wollten. Die Realisierung der Ideale der Februarrevolution im nationalen Rahmen war die Formel, auf die sich das estnische politische Spektrum 1918/19 einigen konnte. Damit die revolutionären Parteien mitzogen, war eine Einhegung der Gewalträume an den Fronten des Unabhängigkeitskrieges notwendig. Die Stärkung des Primats der Politik auch in der Armee war eine Forderung der revolutionären Kräfte, was dann aber von der bürgerlichen EAV (die sozialdemokratischen Minister waren ja ausgetreten) realisiert wurde. Das Tüpfelchen auf das *I* setzte jedoch der Oberkommandierende, der einer drohenden Einmischung seiner Armee den Riegel vorschob und der unter seinen Offizieren kursierenden Idee einer Militärdiktatur resolut Einhalt gebot. Alle drei Seiten zogen damals letztlich an dem Strang der Demokratisierung einer Gesellschaft mitten im Krieg, welche formal durch die erfolgreiche Wahl der Nationalversammlung symbolisiert wurde. Auch diese war ein Kind der Februarrevolution, doch war sie im russischen Kontext von den Bolschewiki entmachtet worden. Unter estnischen Bedingungen brachte sie schließlich den Sieg der nationalorientierten sozialen Revolutionäre. Zwar wurde der Krieg nicht sogleich beendet, denn es war klar, dass die eigenen Ideale unter bolschewistischer Herrschaft keine Chance gehabt hätten; dafür aber sollten mit der Stärkung der Demokratie die Interessen möglichst Vieler gewahrt bleiben und die Erniedrigung Estlands in den „Augen der Kulturvölker" vermieden werden. Während die Formel der Stärkung der Demokratie für alle Seiten akzeptabel war, mussten auch die konservativen Gruppen ein Opfer bringen, wollten sie den prekären Zusammenhalt der Nation nicht gefährden: Was der Linken die Fortführung des Krieges war – eine Aufweichung der eigenen Wahlversprechen – war der Rechten die radikale Agrarreform.

---

84 Kuldkepp, 1905. aasta revolutsioonist.

Literaturverzeichnis

Ajutise Valitsuse määrus välikohtute asutamise kohta, in: Riigi Teataja 1918, Nr. 6 (11.12.1918).

Angermann, Norbert/Brüggemann, Karsten Geschichte der baltischen Länder, Stuttgart 2018.

Ant, Jüri August Rei. Eesti riigimees, poliitik, diplomaat, Tartu 2012.

AK prot. = Asutava Kogu I istungjärk. Protokollid Nr. 1-27; II istungjärk. Protokollid Nr. 28-97. Tallinn [1919].

Arens, Olavi The Estonian Maapäev During 1917, in: The Baltic States in Peace and War, hg. von V. Stanley Vardys/Romuald J. Misiunas, University Park 1978, S. 19-30.

Arens, Olavi Soviets in Estonia 1917/18, in: Die baltischen Provinzen Rußlands zwischen den Revolutionen von 1905 und 1917, hg. von Andrew Ezergailis/Gert von Pistohlkors, Köln/Wien 1982, S. 295-314. = Quellen und Studien zur baltischen Geschichte; 4.

Bennett, Geoffrey M. Cowan's War. The Story of British Naval Operations in the Baltic, 1918-1920, London 1964.

Brüggemann, Karsten „Foreign Rule" during the Estonian War of Independence 1918–1920: The Bolshevik Experiment of the „Estonian Workers' Commune", in: Journal of Baltic Studies 37 (2006), Nr. 2, S. 210-226 (https://doi.org/10.1080/01629770608628880).

Brüggemann, Karsten Die Gründung der Republik Estland und das Ende des „Einen und Unteilbaren Rußland". Die Petrograder Front des Russischen Bürgerkriegs 1918-1920, Wiesbaden 2002. = Forschungen zum Ostseeraum; 6.

Brüggemann, Karsten National and Social Revolution in the Empire's West. Estonian Independence and the Russian Civil War, 1917-20, in: Russia's Home Front in War and Revolution 1914-22. Vol. 1, Russia's Revolution in Regional Perspective, hg. von Sarah Badcock u. a., Bloomington 2015, S. 143-174.

Brüggemann, Karsten Yearning for Social Change. The Russian Revolution in the Baltic Provinces, in: Studies in Ethnicity and Nationalism 17 (2017), Nr. 3, S. 358-368 (https://doi.org/10.1111/sena.12254).

DVP I = Dokumenty vnešnej politiki SSSR. T. 1: 7 nojabrja 1917 g. – 31 dekabrja 1918 g, Moskva 1957.

Eesti Vabariigi ajutised sõjakohtud ja nendele alluvad süüteod, in: Riigi Teataja 1919, Nr. 21 (5.4.1919).

EV = Eesti Vabadussõda 1918-1920, Vabadussõja Ajaloo Komitee populaarteaduslik väljaanne, 2 Bde., Tallinn 1937-1939; Neuauflage Tallinn 1996-1997.

Graf, Mati Eesti rahvusriik. Ideed ja lahendused: Ärkamisajast Eesti Vabariigi sünnini, Tallinn 1993.

Graf, Mati Parteid Eesti Vabariigis 1918-1934 koos eellooga 1905-1917 ja järellooga 1934-1940, Tallinn 2000.

Hiie, Piret 1919. aasta mäss Muhu- ja Saaremaal, Kuressaare 2010.

Hovi, Kalervo Die Orientierung der estnischen Auslandsdelegation im Frühjahr 1918, Turku 1973.

Katzer, Nikolaus Die weiße Bewegung in Russland. Herrschaftsbildung, praktische Politik und politische Programmatik im Bürgerkrieg, Köln u. a. 1999. = Beiträge zur Geschichte Osteuropas; 28.

Kolonickij, Boris I. „Tovarišč Kerenskij". Antimonarchičeskaja revoljucija i formirovanie kul'ty „voždja naroda": mart-ijun' 1917 goda, Moskva 2017.

Kopõtin, Igor/Piirimäe, Kaarel The Modern History of the Estonian War of Independence or How Military History is Written in Estonia, in: FzbG 17 (2022), S. 188-199 (https://doi.org/10.30965/9783657790364_010).

Kröönström, Mati Eesti sõjaväe juhtivkoosseis Vabadussõjas 1918-1920 [Die Zusammensetzung der Führung des estnischen Militärs im Freiheitskrieg 1918-1920], Tartu 2008. = Dissertationes historiae Universitatis Tartuensis; 16.

Kuldkepp, Mart Intriigid, provokatsioonid ja iseseisvuse sünd. Eesti välisdelegatsioon ja Aleksander Kesküla, in: Ajalooline Ajakiri (2013), Nr. 3, S. 321-374 (https://doi.org/10.12697/AA.2013.3.03).

Kuldkepp, Mart 1905. aasta revolutsioonist Eestis ja Soomes. Rahvuslaste ja sotsialistide ühisrinded, in: Vikerkaar (2015), Nr. 7-8, S. 111-121.

MN prot. = Maanõukogu protokollid. 1. koosolekust 1. juulil 1917 78. koosolekuni 6 veebruaril 1919. 1917-1919, Tallinn 1935.

Määrus välikohtute üle, in: Riigi Teataja 1919, Nr. 19 (29.3.1919).

Minnik, Taavi The Cycle of Terror in Estonia, 1917-1919. On its Preconditions and Major Stages, in: Journal of Baltic Studies 46 (2015), Nr. 1, S. 35-47 (https://doi.org/10.1080/01629778.2015.1009688).

Minnik, Taavi The Establishment of „drumhead" Courts Martial and Their Actions in the Estonian War of Independence 1918-1919, in: Juridiskā zinātne / Law. Journal of the University of Latvia (2015), S. 99-110.

Minnik, Taavi Kontrrevolutsiooni vastu võitlemise komisjonide rollist enamlaste terroripoliitika täide viimisel Eestis 1918-1919, in: Acta Historica Tallinnensia 21 (2015), S. 51-68 (https://doi.org/10.3176/hist.2015.1.03).

Minnik, Taavi Der Teufelskreis der Gewalt: Terror und Repressionen in Estland 1917-1919, in: FzbG 6 (2011), S. 120-141.

OLL, ARTO Eesti merevägi Vabadussõjas 1918-1920 Phil. Diss. Universität Tallinn 2018 = Tallinna ülikool: Humanitaarteaduste dissertatsioonid; 42.

OLL, ARTO Suurbritannia seisukohad Eesti suhtes ja Briti eskaadri tegevus Soome lahel 1918-1919, in: Vabadussõja mitu palet. Sõda ja ühiskond aastatel 1918-1920, hg. von TÕNU TANNBERG, Tartu 2019, S. 185-234. = Rahvusarhiivi toimetised; 3 [34].

PAJUR, AGO Eesti riigikaitsepoliitika 1918-1936 Tallinn 1999. = Uurimusi ja allikmaterjale sõjaajaloost; 2.

PAJUR, AGO Die Geburt des estnischen Unabhängigkeitsmanifests 1918, in: FzbG 6 (2011), S. 136-163.

PAJUR, AGO Die Übernahme Estlands von der deutschen Besatzungsmacht im November 1918, in: FzbG 15 (2020), S. 142-168 (https://doi.org/10.30965/9783657760237_007).

PAJUR, AGO Eesti riigikaitse korraldamine Vabadussõja eel, in: Vabadussõja mitu palet. Sõda ja ühiskond aastatel 1918-1920, hg. von TÕNU TANNBERG, Tartu 2019, S. 9-118. = Rahvusarhiivi toimetised; 3 [34].

PAJUR, AGO Konstantin Päts. Poliitiline biograafia. II osa: riigimees (1917-1956), Tartu 2018.

PAJUR, AGO „Meie riigipoliitiliseks paleuseks on autonoomia". 30. märtsi 1917. aasta määrus Eestimaa ajutise valitsemiskorra kohta, in: Eesti ja Esimene maailmasõda, hg. von TÕNU TANNBERG, Tartu 2014, S. 217-269. = Eesti Ajalooarhiivi toimetised; 22 [29].

PAJUR, AGO (Hg.) Eesti! Sa seisad lootusrikka tuleviku lävel, kus sa vabalt ja iseseisvalt oma saatust määrata ja juhtida void. Eesti riikluse alusdokumendid 1917-1920, Tartu 2008.

PAJUR, AGO/TANNBERG, TÕNU (Hg.) Eesti ajalulgu VI. Vabadussõjast taasiseseisvumiseni, Tartu 2005.

Päälinna külalised Tallinnas, in: Postimees (10.4.1917).

PIIP, ANTS Tartu Rahu [Der Frieden von Tartu], in: Mälestused iseseisvuse võitluspäevilt, Bd. 2: Vabadussõda 1918-1920, Tallinn 1930, S. 351-420.

PIIP, ANTS Tormine aasta: ülevaade Eesti välispoliitika esiajast 1917-1918. aastal dokumentides ja mälestusis, Stockholm 1966.

PUSKAR, VIKTOR Mälestusi Eesti Vabariigi alguspäevilt, in: Sõdur (1933), Nr. 50-52, S. 1563-1566.

RA, ERA = Riigiarhiiv, Eesti Riigiarhiiv, Tallinn und Tartu.

REI, AUGUST Mälestusi tormiselt teelt, Stockholm 1961.

ROSENBERG, TIIT Agrarfrage und Agrarreform in Estland 1919. Ursachen und Folgen, in: The Independence of the Baltic States. Origins, Causes, and

Consequences. A Comparison of the Crucial Years 1918-1919 and 1990-1991, hg. von Eberhard Demm u. a., Chicago 1996, S. 87-95.

Rosenthal, Reigo Kord ja kohus. Eesti sõjaväejuhtkond Vabadusõja-aegses sisepoliitikas, Tallinn 2019.

Rosenthal, Reigo Laidoner – väejuht. Johan Laidoner kõrgema operatiivjuhi ja strateegia kujundajana Eesti Vabadussõjas, Tallinn 2008.

Šiliņš, Jānis Rīgas cietumi un lielinieku terors, 1919. gada janvāris - maijs, in: Latvijas Vēstures Institūta Žurnāls (2009), Nr. 3, S. 119-137.

Šiliņš, Jānis Sarkanais terors Rīgā 1919. gadā, in: Latvijas Arhīvi (2014), Nr. 1/2, S. 101-118.

Smele, Jonathan D. The „Russian" Civil Wars 1916-1926. Ten Years That Shook the World, London 2015.

Sõjavägede Ülemjuhataja võimupiiridest, in: Sõdur (1919), Nr. 1, S. 3f.

Sunderland, Willard The Baron's Cloak. A History of the Russian Empire in War and Revolution, Ithaca 2014.

Tannberg, Tõnu/Pajur, Ago (Hg.) Iseseisvusmanifest. Artikleid, dokumente ja mälestusi, Tartu 2014.

Tannberg, Tõnu (Hg.) Vabadussõja mitu palet. Sõda ja ühiskond aastatel 1918-1920, Tartu 2019. = Rahvusarhiivi toimetised; 3 [34].

Tõnisson, Aleksander Visked vabadussõja mälestustest, in: Mälestused iseseisvuse võitluspäevilt, Bd. 2: Vabadussõda 1918-1920, Tallinn 1930, S. 21-63.

Vahtre, Lauri (Hg.) Eesti Vabadussõja ajalugu. 2 Bde. Tallinn 2020.

VOSR = Velikaja Oktjabr'skaja Socialističeskaja revoljucija v Ėstonii: Sbornik dokumentov i materialov, Tallinn 1958.

Vremennye pravila o proizvodstve vyborov členov uezdnych izbiratel'nych cobranij, in: Ėstljandskie Gubernskie Vedomosti (Osoboe priloženie), Nr. 17, 29.04.1917.

Svetlana Bogojavlenska

Auf dem Weg zur „Staatsgemeinschaft": Kulturelle Autonomie der Minderheiten in Lettland 1919-1934

Mums vēl nav vispār lietojama vārda šiem līdziemītniekiem, kuri, kaut gan nav latvieši, bet ir Latvijas pilsoņi – latvijieši.
Wir haben noch keine allgemeingültige Bezeichnung für diese Mitbewohner, die, auch wenn sie keine Letten sind, doch Bürger Lettlands sind – die Lettländer (latvijieši).
Jānis Rainis, Vorwort zum Werk „Septiņi malēnieši" (1928)[1]

Die Gründung des lettischen Staates am 18. November 1918 schaffte eine vollständig neue Situation für alle auf dem Territorium von Lettland lebende Gruppen. Während die Letten zur tragenden politischen Kraft wurden und die Juden in dem neugegründeten Staat zum ersten Mal in ihrer Geschichte auf diesem Territorium vollständige Gleichberechtigung als Bürger erhielten, mussten Russen und Deutsche sich mit der Situation arrangieren, in der sie nicht nur zahlenmäßig, sondern auch politisch zu Minderheiten wurden.[2] Sie mussten den Übergang von der politischen Elite zur ethnischen Minderheit in einem neuen Staat zuerst verarbeiten und neue Wege der Koexistenz mit der Mehrheitsgesellschaft finden. Der neue Staat befand sich in den ersten zwei Jahren in einer schwierigen politischen und militärischen Lage. Außerdem war der Volksrat[3] mit verschiedenen Loyalitäten der Minderheiten konfrontiert, von denen die meisten Bedenken die deutsche und die russische hervorrief. Die Abgeordneten der

1 Raiņa priekšvārdi savu darbu izdevumiem.

2 1925 betrug die Einwohnerzahl Lettlands 1.354.126, darunter 193.648 (10,5%) Russen, 95.675 (5,2%) Juden und 70.964 (3,9%) Deutsche. Skujenieks, Trešā tautas skaitīšana, S. 63. Zum Problemfeld „Mehrheit-Minderheit" in der Umbruchszeit in Europa vgl. Hint, Mehrheit und Minderheit; Weilemann, Schwierigkeit.

3 Der Volksrat Lettlands (Latvijas Tautas padome) wurde von den lettischen Politikern im November 1918 als Vertretung der lettischen politischen Parteien und ethnischer Minderheiten ins Leben gerufen und erfüllte bis zu den Wahlen der Verfassunggebenden Versammlung (Satversmes sapulce) 1920 Parlamentsfunktionen. Vgl. Krūmiņš, Deviņu vīru spēks, S. 15.

russischen und jüdischen Minderheiten kündigten jedoch in der ersten Sitzung, die nach der Rückkehr des Volksrates aus Liepāja nach Riga am 13. Juli 1919 abgehalten wurde, ihre Loyalität der Republik Lettland gegenüber im Namen der russischen und jüdischen Minderheiten an. Die deutschen Abgeordneten schlossen sich spontan dieser Erklärung an.[4] Wegen der Konflikte der Letten mit den Deutschbalten während der ganzen parlamentarischen Phase, gelang es den Deutschbalten jedoch nicht, sich vollumfänglich mit dem Lettischen Staat zu identifizieren. Als Ersatzkonstrukt wurde von ihrer Seite der Heimatgedanke ausgebaut.[5]

Der neue Staat stand vor vielen Herausforderungen, eine davon war, wenn nicht eine politische Nation aus allen in Lettland lebenden Nationalitäten herauszubilden, dann wenigstens die Minderheiten, von denen zwei die Stellung der Führungselite eingebüßt haben, nicht in die Opposition zu drängen. Deshalb war schon in der politischen Plattform, die einen Tag vor der Gründung der Republik angenommen wurde und am 18. November 1918 mit der Regierungsdeklaration bestätigt wurde, das Thema des Umgangs des neuen Staates mit den Minderheiten präsent.[6] Im Abschnitt vier der Regierungsdeklaration, welcher die Rechte der Minderheiten regelte, wurde den ethnischen Minderheiten das uneingeschränkte Recht eingeräumt, sich politisch zu betätigen (Teilnahme an den Wahlen zur Konstituante, Teilnahme an der Regierungsarbeit). Außerdem wurde in der Deklaration die Absicht verfestigt, die kulturellen und nationalen Minderheitenrechte im Grundgesetz (Lett. *pamata likumos*) zu verankern.[7] Die von dem lettischen Bauernbund herausgegebene nationalliberale lettische Zeitung „*Līdums*" (Rodung) kommentierte am 22. November 1918 die Bedenken der konservativen Deutschen gegenüber dem neuen Staatsgebilde mit der Aussage, dass das neu gegründete Lettland keine Absicht habe die nationalen Minderheiten zu bedrängen. Das lettische Volk, das selbst Jahrhunderte

4 Zur Zusammenarbeit der russischen und deutschen Abgeordneten näher: Bogojavlenska, Deutsche und russische Parlamentarier, S. 83-98.

5 Dazu, wie auch zur Arbeit der deutschbaltischen Parlamentarier in Lettland hat Benjamin Conrad geforscht. Deswegen wird in diesem Beitrag nicht auf die Einzelheiten der Wechselbeziehungen der Deutschbalten mit dem lettischen Staat eingegangen. Vgl. Conrad, Loyalitäten.

6 Auch Erwin Oberländer sieht in der Einbindung der Minderheiten in die Arbeit des Volksrates und in der Verabschiedung des Schulgesetzes am 8. Dezember 1919 den Versuch, die ethnischen Minderheiten dem neuen Staat gegenüber loyal einzustimmen. Vgl. Oberländer, Stärken und Schwächen, S. 29f.

7 Cittautiešu tiesības, S. 6.

lang diskriminiert worden sei, wisse am besten, was Diskriminierung bedeute. Daher spreche die Regierungsdeklaration auch nicht von „Fremdstämmigen“ (Lett. *sveštautuieši*), sondern von nationalen Minderheiten, die gleichberechtigt seien. Alle Minderheiten seien dazu eingeladen, den neuen Staat mitzugestalten. Ein Lettland der Fremdstämmigen werde es nicht geben. Der neue Staat werde demokratisch sein. Es soll politisch und sozial gerecht werden.[8]

Eines der ersten Gesetze, das vom Volksrat verabschiedet wurde, war das Gesetz über die Bildungsanstalten Lettlands. Dieser wurde an gleichem Tag mit dem Gesetz über die Selbstverwaltung der Minderheitenschulen, am 8. Dezember 1919, verabschiedet. Mit diesem Gesetz erhielten fünf in Lettland lebende Minderheiten – die deutsche, russische, jüdische, polnische und weißrussische – eine weitgehende Schulautonomie, die den Minderheiten den staatlich geförderten obligatorischen Schulunterricht in der jeweiligen Muttersprache des Kindes garantierte. Im Rahmen dieses Gesetzes wurde auch auf die freie Verwaltung des kulturellen Lebens der Minderheiten durch die entsprechenden Minoritäten-Abteilungen des Bildungsministeriums hingewiesen, die später zur kulturellen Autonomie ausgebaut werden sollte.[9] Das Gesetz schrieb die allgemeine Schulpflicht für Kinder im Alter von acht bis 16 Jahren vor. Es sicherte staatliche Finanzierung für obligatorische Schulen und räumte das Recht auf Unterricht in der Muttersprache des Kindes ein, welche unabhängig von der ethnischen Zugehörigkeit gewählt werden konnte. Dies schuf Bedingungen für multiethnische Schulen und ermöglichte der jüdischen Bevölkerung Gründung jüdischer Schulen mit verschiedenen Unterrichtssprachen. Das Gesetz sah vor, dass die Minderheiten ihre Schulen selbst kontrollieren. Es wurde jedoch vorgeschrieben, dass das Unterrichtsprogramm in den Minderheitenschulen so zu gestalten sei, dass es den Anforderungen vergleichbarer lettischer Schulen entspreche. Die Ausarbeitung der Lehrpläne wurde den Schulabteilungen der Minderheiten bei dem Bildungsministerium übertragen, die schon im Januar 1920 ihre Arbeit aufnahmen.[10] Außerdem gehörte zu den Aufgaben und Rechten der Abteilungen die Verwaltung und Inspektion der Schulen, Einsetzung der Lehrer, Unterstützung der Minderheitenkultur, Mitspracherecht im Ministerkabinett bei allen Fragen, die die Kultur der Minderheit betrafen. Die Verwaltung der eigenen

8 Nacionalo minoritāšu jautājumā, S. 6.
9 LVVA, 2125, 1, 1, Bl. 2-8.
10 Fejgmane, Russkie v dovoennoj Latvii, S. 20; LVVA, 2125, 1, 1, Bl. 1.

Schulen war für die Minderheiten jedoch eindeutig das wichtigste Instrument der Aufrechterhaltung und Verbreitung der eigenen Kultur.[11]

Der jüdische Jurist und Parlamentsabgeordnete Paul Mintz bewertete 1929 das Gesetz von 1919 als „Heldentat der staatlichen Weisheit", denn der Volksrat habe „in der Morgenröte des selbstständigen Daseins des Landes" verstanden, dass das Minderheitenrecht eines der Prinzipien des demokratischen Staates sei. Daher habe der Volksrat in Zusammenarbeit mit den Abgeordneten der Minderheiten, „ohne jeglichen Druck von außen", das Gesetz verabschiedet, welches die Zukunft der Minderheitenrechte in Lettland vorzeichnete.[12]

Vergleicht man den Wortlaut der erwähnten Gesetze mit den ähnlichen Schulgesetzen in Europa, die nach dem 28. Juni 1919 verabschiedet wurden, so wird deutlich, dass sowohl das Gesetz über die Minderheiten-Schulen, als auch der vierte Teil der Unabhängigkeitsdeklaration des Volksrates Ähnlichkeiten mit den entsprechenden legislativen Akten anderer europäischer Staaten aufweisen. Die neuen Staaten räumten den Minderheiten das Recht auf Staatsangehörigkeit, auf die Bewahrung und Nutzung der eigenen Sprache, politische Partizipation und staatlich finanzierte obligatorische Schulen in den Minderheitensprachen ein.[13] Dies bedeutet, dass die Gesetze in Lettland, auch wenn sie ohne ersichtlichen Druck von außen entstanden waren, so doch im Kontext der Entwicklungen in den neuen Staaten zu sehen sind, die auf den Territorien der ehemaligen multiethnischen Reiche entstanden.

Das Gesetz über die Verwaltung der Minderheitenschulen war als erster Schritt in Richtung Kulturautonomie gedacht. Bei der Ausarbeitung der Verfassung (Satversme) in der Verfassunggebenden Versammlung zwischen 1920 und 1922 wurde vorgesehen, dass die Rechte der Minderheiten auf kulturelle Autonomie, wie in der Unabhängigkeitsdeklaration vom November 1918 festgelegt, zusammen mit den Grundrechten und Pflichten der Bürger im zweiten Teil des Grundgesetzes Lettlands verankert werden sollten. Der Versuch, den zweiten Teil der Satversme zu verabschieden scheiterte jedoch. Daher blieb das Gesetz über die Minderheitenschulen die einzige gesetzliche Grundlage für die autonome Kulturarbeit der Minderheiten bis zum Ende des Parlamentarismus in Lettland 1934, weshalb es für ethnische Gruppen so wichtig war, die Rechte,

---

11 Dies wird von der minderheitenspezifischen Forschungsliteratur ebenfalls so gesehen, vgl. z. B. zum deutschen Schulwesen: Wachtsmuth, Autonome deutsche Schule.

12 Minc, Men'šinstvennaja problema v Latvii, S. 7.

13 Vgl. Vediščeva, Mazākumtautību pamatizglītība, S. 21f.

die ihnen mit dem Gesetz über die Schulen versprochen wurden, auch durchzusetzen und dafür zu sorgen, dass diese nicht beschnitten wurden.

Am 22. September 1921 wurde Lettland in den Völkerbund aufgenommen und musste die Mindestanforderungen des Völkerbundes in Bezug auf Minderheitenrechte einhalten. Über den entsprechenden Vertrag verhandelten die Vertreter Lettlands zwei Jahre lang. In der Forschungsliteratur herrscht die Meinung vor, dass Lettland am 7. Juli 1923 die Verhandlungen mit dem Völkerbund mit der Abgabe der sogenannten einseitigen „Minderheitenschutz“-Erklärung gegenüber dem Völkerbund beendete. Dies bedeutete, dass Lettland sich verpflichtete, die vom Völkerbund garantierten Minderheitenschutzverträge einzuhalten.[14] Juris Goldmanis vermerkte jedoch, dass Lettland die Beendigung der Verhandlungen dem Völkerbund abnötigte. Allerdings ging er nicht näher auf den Inhalt der abgegebenen Deklaration ein.[15] John Hiden hingegen vermerkte, Lettland habe sich wegen der schon fortgeschrittenen Gesetzgebung im Land im Betreff auf Minderheiten aus der Verpflichtung gegenüber dem Völkerbund rausgehalten, signalisierte jedoch die Bereitschaft, die Prinzipien des Minderheitenrechts des Völkerbundes zu achten.[16] In der Tat gab Lettland im Juli 1923 gegenüber dem Völkerbund eine Deklaration ab, die äußerst schwammig formuliert war. Darin bot Lettland an, die Verhandlungen zu beenden, denn die Bestimmung der Rechte der Minderheiten in Lettland unterliege dem souveränen Recht Lettlands und werde den sozialen Gegebenheiten im Land angepasst. Die Regierung werde die Frage des Minderheitenschutzes in Lettland prüfen. Sollte der Völkerbund es für nötig halten, können die Verhandlungen wieder aufgenommen werden. Bis dahin verpflichte sich der Völkerbund, alle Beschwerden von Seiten der Minderheiten Lettlands an die lettische Regierung zurück zu schicken, um diese dort der Prüfung zu unterziehen. Im Falle einer berechtigten Klage wurde dem Völkerbund das Recht eingeräumt, über die weitere Vorgehensweise von Seiten Lettlands informiert zu werden.[17] Da der Völkerbund über keine Kontrollmechanismen verfügte und keine Strafmaßnahmen im Falle der Nichtbeachtung der Minderheitenrechte in den einzelnen Mitgliedstaaten vorgesehen hatte, war

---

14 Vgl. Dribins, Etniskās un nacionālās minoritātes, S. 43f; Michaelsen, Der Europäische Nationalitäten-Kongress, S. 43; Loeber, Minderheitenschutzverträge, S. 189-200; Vedīščeva, Mazākumtautību pamatizglītība, S. 22.

15 Goldmanis, Vopros o nacional'no-kul'turnoj avtonomii evreev, S. 271.

16 Hiden, Defender of Minorities, S. 118.

17 Latvju delegācija minoritāšu jautājumā, S. 3.

diese Bekundung nichts weiter als ein symbolischer Akt, mit dem von der lettischen Seite keine Verpflichtungen aufgenommen wurden.[18]

Um die gesetzlichen Grundlagen für die freie Entfaltung ihrer Schulen und Kultur zu festigen, ging nach dem Ende der Verfassungsgebenden Versammlung der Kampf der Minderheitenabgeordneten um die kulturelle Autonomie in der ersten Saeima (1922-1925) weiter. Maksim Ganfman, selbst russischakkulturierter jüdischer Journalist und Herausgeber der russischen Zeitung *Segodnja* („Heute") postulierte 1922:

> „In einem demokratischen Staat (…) sei es normal, dass alle Wähler sich nach dem politisch-sozialen Prinzip aufteilen. (…) das Wesen (…der Demokratischen) Ideologie fordert auf, dass die Bürger aller Nationalitäten bei der Beteiligung am politischen Leben des Staates ganz unabhängig von ihrer Volkszugehörigkeit den gemeinsamen politischen Gruppierungen und Parteien beitreten würden. Und wir würden eine solche Erscheinung in unserem Land willkommen heißen, denn diese würde bezeugen, dass die nationalen Rechte der Minderheiten in dem Maße verwirklicht sind, in dem Maße sich im Alltag etablierten, dass man sich nicht darum kümmern muss, nicht dafür kämpfen muss (…)."[19]

Da die Situation jedoch anders aussehe und die Minderheiten Rechte noch nicht gesichert seien, waren die Minderheiten darum bemüht, diese Rechtssicherheit zu schaffen.

> „Man darf nicht denken, dass diese Tätigkeit im Widerspruch zur Staatsbildung steht (*obščegosudarstvennoj rabotoj*). Im Wesentlichen ist bei der Bildung eines demokratischen Staates die Festigung der Rechte der Minderheiten ebenso notwendig, wie die Festigung anderer Grundlagen des Staatswesens."[20]

Auch für den deutschbaltischen Parlamentsabgeordneten Paul Schiemann bestand im Kampf für die Autonomie der Minderheiten in Lettland kein Widerspruch zur Bildung einer Staatsgemeinschaft aus allen in Lettland lebenden Ethnien. Er war der Meinung, die von ihm später auch auf dem Nationalitäten-Kongress[21] in Genf vertreten wurde, dass die Befreiung des Staates von

---

18 Über die Machtlosigkeit des Völkerbundes betreffend Minderheitenschutz vgl. z. B. Bamberger-Stemmann, Der Europäische Nationalitätenkongress, S. 53-55.

19 Ganfman, Pered vyborami, S. 1.

20 Ganfman, Pered vyborami, S. 1.

21 Der Nationalitäten-Kongress wurde im Herbst 1925 einberufen. Bei der ersten Konferenz in Genf nahmen Vertreter von 34 Minderheiten aus 17 europäischen Staaten teil. Smith/Hiden, Ethnic Diversity, S. 70-91. Mehr dazu: Bamberger-Stemmann, Der Europäische Nationalitätenkongress.

nationalkulturellen Aufgaben zu Gunsten der Volksgemeinschaften, die als Körperschaft des öffentlichen Rechts anerkannt sind, die endgültige Lösung des Minderheitenproblems sein könnte. Die Volksgemeinschaften, nicht nur der Minderheiten, sondern auch der Mehrheit, aber auch religiöse Gemeinschaften und sogar die Gemeinschaften, die eine gemeinsame Weltanschauung vertreten, hätten für die Belange ihrer Kultur selbst sorgen müssen. Für ihn war das der einzig richtige Weg zur Konsolidierung der Gesellschaft und zur Bildung der Staatsgemeinschaft, in der die Volksangehörigkeit keine Rolle spielen würde.[22] Daher wurde die Einreichung der Autonomieprojekte der Minderheiten von ihm und der ganzen deutschen Fraktion ebenfalls unterstützt.

1922, am Ende der Arbeit der Verfassungsgebenden Versammlung, hatte die jüdische Minderheit ihr Autonomieprojekt eingereicht. Dieses war jedoch nicht mehr von der Versammlung bearbeitet worden. Im Dezember 1923 wurde das „Gesetzesprojekt über die nationalkulturelle Selbstverwaltung der deutschen Volksgemeinschaft und den Gebrauch der deutschen Sprache in Lettland“ in die öffentlich-rechtliche Kommission der ersten Saeima eingereicht worden.[23] Im März 1924 folgte das polnische Projekt. Im Januar 1925 reichten die jüdischen abgeordneten ihr Autonomieprojekt zum zweiten Mal ein. Am 6. Februar 1925 haben schließlich die russischen Abgeordneten ihr Projekt eingereicht.[24] Das jüdische Projekt wurde auch von Paul Schiemann mitunterzeichnet, was im Angesicht der Spannungen zwischen den deutschen Abgeordneten und den lettischen Parteien kein kluger Zug seitens der Juden war und später, nach dem Scheitern aller Autonomie-Anträge, von Seiten der jüdischen Gesellschaft als eines der Gründe für den Misserfolg gedeutet wurde.[25] Es gab auch mehrere Versuche seitens der russischen und jüdischen Abgeordneten, ein gemeinsames Autonomieprojekt für alle vier Minderheiten auszuarbeiten.[26] Diese Idee scheiterten jedoch an den deutschen Parlamentariern.[27]

Vergleicht man alle Projekte, so wird klar, dass die Entwürfe anderer Minderheiten in manchen Paragraphen wortwörtlich aus dem deutschen Projekt

---

22 Schiemann, Staatsgemeinschaft und Volksgemeinschaft, S. 1f. Mehr zum Konzept Schiemanns: Hiden, Defender of Minorities, S. 142-146.

23 Gesetzesprojekt über die nationalkulturelle Selbstverwaltung der deutschen Volksgemeinschaft und den Gebrauch der deutschen Sprache in Lettland, S. 1891-1893.

24 V sejm vnesjon proekt russkoj avtonomii, S. 2; Projekt russkoj i evrejskoj avtonomii, S. 6; Projekt russkoj avtonomii (okončanie), S. 7.

25 Stranga, Ebreji un diktatūras, S. 113f.

26 Edinyj zakon ob avtonomii men'šinstv otvergnut, S. 3.

27 Vgl. dazu Smith/Hiden, Ethnic Diversity, S. 44.

übernommen worden waren.[28] So wurde in den Paragraphen 9-18 des russischen Entwurfs, in denen die Rede von den Bildungsangelegenheiten der Minderheit ist, nur das Wort „deutsch" durch die entsprechende Bezeichnung ersetzt. Auch die sonstigen Paragraphen, in denen beispielsweise die Zahlen der Schüler oder Einwohner der Minderheit, die als Voraussetzung für die Eröffnung der getrennten Schulen und für die Benutzung der Minderheitensprache in kommunalen Einrichtungen und im Gericht gelten sollten reglementiert wurden, waren kaum verändert übernommen worden.[29]

Die nationalkulturelle Selbstverwaltung sollte folgendermaßen aussehen. Jeder Bürger Lettlands, der sich zu einer ethnischen bzw. kulturellen Gemeinschaft angehörig fühlte, sollte sich in einem Kataster registrieren, um offiziell als angehöriger dieser Gruppe betrachtet zu werden. Bei den Juden wurde die Registrierung an den Passeintrag gekoppelt: nur diejenigen, die laut Pass als Juden galten, konnten sich dann im jüdischen Kataster registrieren lassen. Beim Verlassen des Katasters sollte der Passeintrag auch abgeändert werden. Darüber hinaus sollte die ethnische Zugehörigkeit zum Judentum durch die Religion und nicht durch die kulturelle o. ä. Identifikation bestimmt werden.[30] Dieser Vorschlag traf nicht bei allen jüdischen Gruppen auf Zustimmung, denn er widersprach erstens dem Geist der Freiwilligkeit des Beitritts und schloss zweitens all die Gruppen aus dem Judentum aus, die säkular waren.[31]

Die im Kataster registrierten Bürger im wahlfähigen Alter sollten dann einen zentralen Volksrat wählen, der sich um die Belange der Gruppe als eine Art Regierung kümmern sollte. Offiziell wurde diese Aufgabe vom Staat mit

28 Goldmanis, Vopros o nacional'no-kul'turnoj avtonomii evreev, S. 270.

29 Vgl. Gesetzesprojekt über die nationalkulturelle Selbstverwaltung der deutschen Volksgemeinschaft und den Gebrauch der deutschen Sprache in Lettland; Proekt russkoj avtonomii; Proekt zakona o nacional'no-kul'turnom samoupravlenii.

30 Vgl. Gesetzesprojekt der jüdischen Minderheit, § 2: „Zur jüdischen Nationalität gehören die lettländischen Staatsbürger, die in ihren Pässen oder anderen Dokumenten als Juden bezeichnet werden. Sie sind in das nationale Kataster eingetragen. Die staatlichen Behörden sind verpflichtet auf Wunsch des Inhabers im Passe die Bezeichnung seiner Nationalität entsprechend seiner Angabe vorzunehmen. Scheidet jemand aus dem Kataster aus, so muss dieses Zwecks entsprechender Änderung im Passe der zuständigen Behörde zur Kenntnis gebracht werden. Anmerkung. Die Änderung der religiösen Zugehörigkeit zieht nach sich auf jeden Fall den Ausschluss aus dem Kataster." Proekt zakona o nacional'no-kul'turnom samoupravlenii, S. 5.

31 Auf politischer Ebene waren es der jüdische Bund und die Folkspartai. Vgl. Goldmanis, Vopros nacional'no-kul'turnoj avtonomii evreev, S. 271.

dem Schulgesetz von 1919 vorübergehend, d. h. bis die Autonomie gewährt werden sollte, den Leitern der jeweiligen Schulabteilungen zugewiesen. Inoffiziell hatten Minderheiten in Lettland ihre eigenen Vertretungen: bei den Russen waren es – als Vereine registriert – die Russische nationale Union und die Russische nationale Vereinigung. Beide Vereine gingen 1924 aus der Nationaldemokratischen Union russischer Bürger heraus. Die Vereinigung sollte für das kulturelle Leben der russischen Bevölkerung Lettlands stehen und bündelte zeitweise bis zu 29 russische Kulturvereine. Die Union sollte den politischen Teil des russischen gesellschaftlichen Lebens regeln.[32] Bei den Deutschen galt der Verband des Bildungswesens und die 1923 als Verein registrierte Deutschbaltische Volksgemeinschaft als offizielle Vertretung. Die Katasterlisten sollten in erster Linie zum Zweck der Besteuerung der Volksgruppe dienen. Die Steuereinnahmen sollten für die Finanzierung des kulturellen Lebens der Gruppe ausgegeben werden, vor allem für die Schulen und die Arbeit der Kulturvereine. Bei der jüdischen Minderheit sollte Religionsausübung ebenfalls aus diesen Mitteln finanziert werden, was jedoch auf Proteste der jüdischen linken Vereinigungen und offen areligiöser Kreise stieß. Auch die öffentlich-rechtliche Kommission der Saeima sprach die Verwaltung des religiösen Lebens der Minderheiten den Autonomiestrukturen ab.[33]

Die Projekte beinhalteten außerdem die Forderung nach der Nutzung der Sprache der jeweiligen Gruppe als Amtssprache in den Gegenden Lettlands, wo diese bestimmte prozentuale Anzahl der Einwohner erreichte: bei den Deutschen 30%, bei den Russen 15%, bei den Juden 20%.

Somit wurde in die Gesetzesprojekte das Gedankengut der Theoretiker der national-kulturellen Autonomie eingearbeitet. Diese Theorien aus der Zeit vor dem Ersten Weltkrieg, erarbeitet in Österreich-Ungarn von Otto Bauer und Karl Renner[34] sahen vor, dass die Minderheiten ihre Kultur selbst verwalten und finanzieren sollten, um den Kampf um die Ressourcen der Staaten zu vermeiden. Die Einführung des nationalen Katasters und die Freiwilligkeit der Aufnahme in diesen waren die Grundlagen des Konzeptes der exterritorialen Kulturautonomie der Minderheiten, das innerhalb der Sozialdemokratie auch in Lettland einen breiten Konsens gefunden hat. Die Lettische Sozialdemokratische Arbeiterpartei (LSDSP) forderte schon in ihrem Programm, welches vor dem Volksrat

32 LVVA 5645,1,3, Bl. 42, 77; LVVA 5645,1,14.

33 Vgl. Goldmanis, Vopros nacional'no-kul'turnoj avtonomii evreev, S. 274.

34 Vgl. z. B. Bauer, Nationalitätenfrage und die Sozialdemokratie; Renner, Politische Demokratie.

am 17. November 1918 vorgetragen wurde, die kulturelle Autonomie der Minderheiten in Lettland im Gesetz zu verankern.[35]

Die erste Saeima verabschiedete jedoch keines der Projekte. Es kam zu hitzigen Debatten in der Presse. Die Presse der Minderheiten verteidigte das Vorhaben als Fortschritt in Richtung Staatskonsolidierung, denn die Autonomie wurde als Ersatz des nicht angenommenen zweiten Teils der Verfassung, der die Rechte der Minderheiten hätte garantieren sollen, empfunden. Die lettische Presse sprach dagegen von der „deutschen" und „jüdischen" Bedrohung für den lettischen Staat, von der Schaffung eines Staates im Staat. In seiner Broschüre „Über die Autonomie der Minderheiten" sprach der lettische Publizist Kroders davon, dass die Autonomie der Minderheiten nur in einem multiethnischen Staat durchführbar sei, nicht jedoch in einem Staat, der sich als lettischer Nationalstaat, d. h. Nationalstaat der Letten, definiert und versteht.[36]

Hier muss auf die Tatsache hingewiesen werden, die den Vertretern der Minderheiten sehr wichtig war (und immer noch in den heutigen politischen Debatten in Lettland wichtig ist): Der zweite Punkt der Verfassung der Republik Lettlands von 1922 sagt folgendes: Die souveräne Gewalt des Staates Lettland gehört dem Volke Lettlands. (*Latvijas valsts suverēnā vara pieder Latvijas tautai.*)[37]

Entgegen der Behauptung vieler lettischer Nationalisten, die den Staat Lettland als einen reinen Nationalstaat der Letten sahen, wurde hier postuliert, dass die Macht im Staate allen dort lebenden Ethnien gleichermaßen zusteht. Deshalb drehten sich die Diskussionen von Seiten der Minderheiten auch darum, dass auch sie am Aufbau des Staates mitwirken, und da sie ein Teil dieses Staatsgebildes seien, ihre Rechte auf freie Entwicklung ihrer Kultur vom Staat garantiert kriegen sollten. Nur dann wäre die Integration der Minderheiten in den Staat vollständig.

Schon im Mai 1925 sagte Paul Schiemann jedoch in einer Rede im Parlament, dass die Idee der Autonomie in dieser Saeima „begraben" worden sei.[38] Die Mehrheit der Abgeordneten war dagegen, die Autonomie der Minderheiten nach dem estnischen Muster zu verabschieden.[39] Die zweite Saeima, die im

35 Latwijas Tautas Padomes sēdes, Nr. 1, S. 10.

36 Kroders, Par minoritātu autonomiju, S. 26-33.

37 Latvijas republikas Satversme.

38 Rede Paul Schiemanns am 06.05.1925, Spalte 352.

39 Das Gesetz über die Kulturautonomie der Minderheiten wurde in Estland am 5. Februar 1925 verabschiedet. Mehr dazu Smith/Hiden, Ethnic Diversity, S. 31.

Herbst 1925 gewählt wurde, kam nicht mehr auf die Projekte zurück. So blieb das Vorhaben, das schon im Volksrat diskutiert wurde, den Minderheiten volle Autonomie zu gewähren, in Lettland nicht verwirklicht.

Häufig wird das Scheitern der Beantragung der Autonomie in Lettland als das große Problem und Versagen sowohl der lettischen Regierung als auch der Minderheiten selbst betrachtet. Nach der Beschäftigung mit der Geschichte der Minderheiten in Lettland und der Analyse der Wortlaute der einzelnen Projekte muss man jedoch zur Überzeugung kommen, dass dieses Scheitern kaum als Niederlage im Kampf um die Rechte der Minderheiten bewertet werden kann und noch weniger als Hindernis zur Bildung einer Staatsgemeinschaft, wie sie von Paul Schiemann und Unterstützern seiner Ideen verstanden wurde. Die Abgeordneten der Minderheiten hätten nach 1925 die Autonomieprojekte wieder einreichen können, es wurde jedoch, wie aus den Quellen ersichtlich, von keinem gemacht. Einerseits wurde im Laufe der Zeit sehr deutlich, dass die russischen, jüdischen und polnischen Minderheiten, ganz zu schweigen von der weißrussischen, die mit der nationalen und sprachlichen Identität haderte, nicht so gut organisiert waren, wie die deutsche, die auch ohne gesetzliche Grundlage einen nationalen Kataster hatte und ihre Mitglieder besteuerte. Wäre die Autonomie in der Form, in der sie in den von den Deutschen vorgegebenen Projekten dargestellt war, gewährt, hätte es mit ziemlicher Gewissheit erhebliche Schwierigkeiten bei der Finanzierung des Bildungssystems gegeben, denn dieses hätte dann aus den Steuermitteln der Minderheiten selbst bestritten werden. Da war es sicherer, sich mit dem weitreichenden Gesetzüber die Schulautonomie, das auch die kulturelle Autonomie beinhaltete, zufrieden zu geben und sich auf staatliche Zuweisungen zu verlassen.

Andererseits rief der Kampf um die kulturelle Autonomie so viel Feindschaft von Seiten der Letten hervor, dass jeder weitere Versuch von Seiten der Minderheiten, diesen zur Sprache zu bringen, auf dem Weg zur Ausbildung einer politischen Nation für alle in Lettland lebende Ethnien, nur als destruktiv betrachtet werden musste. Auch wenn die Minderheiten weiterhin daran hielten, dass die Verteidigung ihrer Rechte auf Entwicklung und Bewahrung ihrer Sprache und Kultur ein organisches Grundrecht der Gesetzgebung der Republik Lettland sei, wurde das Gesetz über die Schulen der Minderheiten von 1919 als Grundlage für die Kulturarbeit genutzt und von den Angriffen Seitens der nationalistisch eingestimmten lettischen Politikern verteidigt.

Die Zeitung *Segodnja* vermerkte anlässlich des zehnjährigen Jubiläums ihrer Herausgabe, das auch mit dem zehnjährigen Bestehen des Schulgesetzes zusammenfiel, dass es die Aufgabe der Zeitung immer gewesen sei, für die Rechte der Minderheiten in Lettland zu kämpfen. Es wurde ebenfalls besonders erwähnt, dass die Minderheitengesetzgebung in Lettland immer häufiger als Beispiel der Errungenschaften der lettischen Politik im Bereich der Staatsbildung auf der europäischen Arena diskutiert wurde, denn dieses garantierte „das zivilisierteste Miteinander der Mehrheit mit den Minderheiten.“[40] Der Herausgeber der Zeitung *Segodnja* bekräftigte in seinem Jubiläumsbeitrag, dass die Minderheiten in Lettland kein fremdes Element, keine *inorodcy* (Lett. *sveštautieši*) sind, sondern gleichberechtigte Bürger Lettlands. Das zehnjährige Bestehen des Gesetzes wurde deswegen auch von allen Minderheiten öffentlich als Grundlage des friedlichen Miteinanders auf der Ebene der Gesetzgebung gefeiert. Auch wenn die Rechte der Minderheiten beispielsweise auf Kontrolle der eigenen Schulen immer wieder von verschiedenen Regierungen Lettlands in Frage gestellt wurden,[41] diente das Gesetz von 1919 doch als unveränderbare Grundlage für die freie Entfaltung ihres Kulturlebens. Sowohl die Russen als auch die Juden akzeptierten das Schulgesetz als Grundlage ihrer Arbeit und als ein Grund mehr, dem Staat loyal zu sein, insbesondere, als 1925 klar wurde, dass keine Kulturautonomien für die Minderheiten gewährt würden. Ganfman rief die Minderheiten auf, nicht nur loyal dem lettischen Staat gegenüber zu sein, sondern sich auch weiterhin an dem Aufbau des Staates in allen Bereichen zu beteiligen.[42]

Während die Deutschbalten versuchten, ihre Differenzen mit der lettischen Regierung vor dem Völkerbund zu klären,[43] betonte der jüdische Parlamentsabgeordnete Paul Mintz deshalb 1929 im Einklang mit den Vertretern anderer Minderheiten außer den Deutschbalten, dass die Minderheitenfrage eine innere Angelegenheit des Staates sei und durch etwaigen Druck des Völkerbundes nicht gelöst werden könne. Das Schulgesetz von 1919 wurde von ihm als „gesunde Lösung“ für die Minderheitenfrage bewertet, denn das Gesetz habe die Minderheiten als „Volkskollektive“ anerkannt und diesen das Recht eingeräumt,

---

40 Ganfman, Desjat' let, S. 1.

41 So z. B. in den Jahren 1923, 1925 und letztlich 1932, als die Stellen der Inspekteure bei den Schulabteilungen der Minderheiten gänzlich gestrichen wurden. LVVA, 7469, 2, 77, Bl. 19.

42 Ganfman, Desjat‘ let, S. 1.

43 1926 reichten die deutschen Abgeordneten beim Völkerbund Beschwerde ein, die Republik Lettland habe ihre Rechte als Minderheit durch die Enteignung während der Landreform von 1920 verletzt, ohne sie dafür zu entschädigen. Der Völkerbund wies die Klage zurück, mit dem Argument, es sei eine politische Maßnahme gewesen, die nicht auf die Beschränkung der Minderheitenrechte abzielte. Vgl. Conrad, Loyalitäten, S. 90.

ihre nationale Kultur frei zu entfalten.[44] Somit wurde Ende der 1920er Jahre die Schulautonomie als Ersatz für die gescheiterte vollständige kulturelle Autonomie deklariert.

Anfang der 1930er Jahre kam es jedoch seitens der Regierung zu mehrfachen Beschneidungen der Schulautonomie,[45] was Proteste der Minderheiten hervorrief. Paul Schiemann war dann einer der federführenden Politiker, die die Forderungen der Minderheiten an den Staat formulierte. 1930 schrieb er in seinem Beitrag „Staat und Nationalität" über die Pflichten des Staates gegenüber Minderheiten, über die Gefahren der nationalistischen Politik und über die Möglichkeiten, doch noch eine Staatsgemeinschaft für alle Bürger Lettlands zu schaffen. Seine Vorstellung von der Autonomie der Minderheiten beinhaltete nicht nur die Rechte der Minderheiten auf die Verwaltung der eigenen Kultur, sondern auch die Pflicht der Minderheitenvertreter, die grundlegenden Gesetze des Heimatlandes zu achten und Bereitschaft, sich als Teil dieses Landes zu fühlen und so zu leben. Vom Staat forderte er Toleranz und Kompromissbereitschaft in der Ethnopolitik.[46] Er prangerte diejenigen an, die der Meinung waren, dass die Bewahrung der Rechte der Minderheiten auf die freie Entwicklung ihrer Kultur nur eine Wohlfahrtstat von Seiten der Mehrheitsbevölkerung sei. „Es muss endlich begriffen werden, dass die Minderheitenfrage eine Frage des Wesens des Staates, eine Frage seiner Rechte und Pflichten ist." „Es handelt sich *vielmehr* um eine Politik, die ganz unmittelbar im Staatsinteresse liegt und alle diejenigen, die dagegen arbeiten [...] arbeiten unmittelbar an der Auflösung des Staates." „Mit der Freigabe der nationalen Kulturentwicklung" wäre die Voraussetzung für die Bildung einer starken und in sich geschlossenen Staatsgemeinschaft geschaffen. „Das Wesen solcher Staatsgemeinschaft im Hinblick auf die Pflichten und Rechte der Volksgemeinschaften zu erkennen, wird nunmehr unsere Aufgabe sein."[47]

Paul Schiemann bestand darauf, dass die Rechte der Minderheiten auf der gesamteuropäischen Ebene zu schützen sind. Er führte aus, dass im Nationalitätenkongress Konsens darüber herrschte, dass der Staat den Minderheiten die Selbstverwaltung überlassen sollte. Jedoch wurden die Forderungen des

---

44 Minc, Men'šinstvennaja problema v Latvii, S. 7.

45 Außer der Abschaffung der internen Inspektion der Minderheiten Schulen wurde 1932 von dem rechtsliberalen Bildungsminister Atis Ķeniņš im Widerspruch zur Schulautonomie z. B. eine bestimmte Anzahl der Stunden für alle Fächer in den Minderheiten Schulen festgelegt. Somit hatten die Schulabteilungen der Minderheiten weniger Spielraum, was den Unterricht der spezifischen „nationalen" Fächer betraf.

46 Vgl. Dribins, Kultūras autonomijas teorija un prakse, S. 2.

47 Schiemann, Staat und Nationalität, S. 2.

Nationalitäten Kongresses und die Problematik der Minderheiten im Baltikum von der Mehrheit der Staaten des Völkerbundes nicht verstanden und daher nicht geteilt.[48]

Paul Schiemann war in diesem Sinne ein Idealist. Weder er noch Vertreter anderer Minderheiten konnten sich dem aufsteigenden Nationalismus in Lettland wirkungsvoll widersetzen. Als Rainis 1928, wie auch kurz vor seinem Tod 1929, wohlbemerkt, in russischer Sprache, den Vorschlag machte, das Wort *latvijieši* oder *latvijcy* als Bezeichnung für alle Bürger Lettlands zu verwenden, schien das den Minderheiten noch möglich. Wie gezeigt war die Bereitschaft da, Lettland als gemeinsamen Staat für alle Bürger Lettlands und sich selbst als *latvijieši* zu sehen. Spätestens nach dem Staatstreich von Karlis Ulmanis im Mai 1934 stand der Vorschlag von Rainis nicht mehr zur Diskussion. Am 12. Juli 1934 wurde das neue Gesetz über die Volksbildung verabschiedet. Mit diesem wurden die Minoritäten-Abteilungen liquidiert. Stattdessen wurden Posten der Minderheitenreferenten im Bildungsministerium geschaffen, die jedoch wenig Spielraum und noch weniger Mittel zur Verwaltung der Schulen und Unterstützung des Kulturlebens der Minderheit hatten. Die Schulen wurden ethnisch homogen organisiert. Die ethnische Zugehörigkeit wurde laut Gesetz nach dem Vater und nicht mehr freiwillig bestimmt. War jedoch ein Elternteil Lette, auch wenn es Mutter war, wurde das Kind als Lette registriert und musste in die lettische Schule gehen, unabhängig von Sprachkenntnissen. Es bestand also keine freie Wahl der Unterrichtssprache mehr und keine freie Wahl der Schule. Somit war auch die Schulautonomie und partielle Kulturautonomie faktisch abgeschafft worden.

Abschließend ist zu vermerken, dass zumindest die russische und jüdische Minderheit von Anfang an dem lettischen Staat gegenüber aufgeschlossen und loyal waren, denn die demokratischen Freiheiten, die sie genossen, und die bestehende Gesetzgebung erlaubten es ihnen ihre Kultur und Sprache frei zu entfalten. Außerdem bestand für diese beiden Minderheiten keine Ausweichmöglichkeit, sie hatten keinen Staat, den sie Eigen nennen konnten. Russland war für sie, wie der Presse entnommen werden kann, verloren. Die Hoffnung auf eine Zukunft ohne die Bolschewiki bestand noch am Anfang der 1920er Jahre. Diese schwand jedoch mit jedem Jahr immer mehr dahin. Auch wenn die vollständige Autonomie nicht gewährt wurde, war doch das Schulgesetz von 1919 für alle Seiten nutzbar und zufriedenstellend. Die Finanzierung der kulturellen Belange der Minderheiten wurde nicht nur aus den Mitteln der Minderheiten

---

48 Mehr dazu: Rimscha, Schiemann als Minderheitenpolitiker, S. 57f.

selbst, sondern durch regelmäßige staatliche Finanzierung gewährleistet. Somit hat sich der Staat willig gezeigt, allen Bürgern ohne Unterschied ethnischer und sozialer Herkunft die kulturelle Selbstbestimmung und Selbstverwaltung zu ermöglichen und dadurch beizutragen, dass sich alle in Lettland lebende als Teil einer Staatsgemeinschaft identifizieren können. Durch den Putsch Ulmanis' 1934 und die folgende Abschaffung der Schulautonomie wurde das geschaffene Gleichgewicht zwischen den Minderheiten und der lettischen Mehrheitsbevölkerung jedoch nachhaltig zerstört.

Literaturverzeichnis

BAMBERGER-STEMMANN, SABINE Der Europäische Nationalitätenkongress 1925-1938. Nationale Minderheiten zwischen Lobbyistentum und Großmachtinteressen. Marburg 2000. = Materialien und Studien zur Ostmitteleuropa-Forschung; 7.

BAUER, OTTO Die Nationalitätenfrage und die Sozialdemokratie, Wien 1907.

BOGOJAVLENSKA, SVETLANA Deutsche und russische Parlamentarier in Kooperation und Konfrontation in Lettland 1919-1927, in: Parlamentarier der deutschen Minderheiten im Europa der Zwischenkriegszeit, hg. von BENJAMIN CONRAD u. a. Düsseldorf 2015, S. 84-98. = Parlamente in Europa; 4.

Cittautiešu tiesības, in: Latwijas Tautas Padomes sēdes, Nr. 1, Riga 1920.

CONRAD, BENJAMIN Loyalitäten, Identitäten und Interessen. Deutsche Parlamentarier im Lettland und Polen der Zwischenkriegszeit, Göttingen 2016.

DRIBINS, LEO Kultūras autonomijas teorija un prakse Latvijā, in: Latvijas vēstnesis, 2000, Nr. 197/200 (2108/2111), URL: www.vestnesis.lv/ta/id/7460, 23.05.2018.

DRIBINS, LEO Etniskās un nacionālās minoritātes Eiropā. Vēsture un mūsdienas, Rīga 2004.

Edinyj zakon ob avtonomii men'šinstv otvergnut, in: Segodnja (1925), Nr. 24, S. 3.

FEJGMANE, TAT'JANA Russkije v dovoennoj Latvii. Na puti k integracii, Riga 2000.

GANFMAN, MAKSIM Desjat' let, in: Segodnja (1929), Nr. 270, S. 1.

GANFMAN, MAKSIM Pered vyborami, in: Segodnja (1922), Nr. 173, S. 1.

GOLDMANIS, JURIS Vopros nacional'no-kul'turnoj avtonomii evreev v parlamente Latvii (1918-1925), in: Evrei v menjajuščemsja mire. Materialy meždunarodnoj konferencii, hg. von GERMAN BRANOVER/FERBER, RUVIM, Bd. 5, Riga 2005, S. 266-281.

Gesetzesprojekt über die nationalkulturelle Selbstverwaltung der deutschen Volksgemeinschaft und den Gebrauch der deutschen Sprache in Lettland, in: Rigasche Rundschau (1924), Nr. 1, S. 1891-1893.

Hiden, John Defender of Minorities. Paul Schiemann, 1876-1944, London 2004.

Hint, Mati Das Problem von Mehrheit und Minderheit im estnischen Kontext, in: Estland und seine Minderheiten. Esten, Deutsche und Russen im 19. und 20. Jahrhundert, hg. von Konrad Maier, Lüneburg 1995, S. 627-633.

Kroders, Arturs Par minoritātu autonomiju, Rīga 1924.

Krūmiņš, Gatis (Hg.) Deviņu vīru spēks. Stāsti par deviņiem ministru prezidentiem (1918-1940), Rīga 2016.

Latwijas Tautas Padomes sēdes, Nr. 1, Riga 1920.

Latvijas valsts vēstures arhīvs (LVVA) Bestand 2125, Findbuch 1, Akte 1; Bestand 5645, Findbuch 1, Akte 3, Akte 14; Bestand 7469, Findbuch 2, Akte 77.

Latvijas republikas satversme, URL: https://likumi.lv/doc.php?id=57980, 29.05.2018.

Latvju delegācija minoritāšu jautājumā, in: Valdības Vēstnesis 153 (1923), S. 3.

Loeber, Dietrich A. Die Minderheitenschutzverträge. Entstehung, Inhalt und Wirkung, in: Ostmitteleuropa zwischen den beiden Weltkriegen (1918-1939). Stärke und Schwäche der neuen Staaten, nationale Minderheiten, hg. von Hans Lemberg, Marburg 1997, S. 189-200.

Minc, Paul Men'šinstvennaja problema v Latvii, in: Segodnja (1929), Nr. 270, S. 7.

Nacionalo minoritāšu jautājumā, in: Līdums (1918), Nr. 221, S. 1.

Oberländer, Erwin Stärken und Schwächen des neuen Staates 1918-1940, in: Lettland 1918-2018. Ein Jahrhundert Staatlichkeit, hg. von Ivars Ījabs u. a., Paderborn 2018, S. 27-41.

Proekt russkoj avtonomii, in: Segodnja (1925), Nr. 30, S. 2.

Projekt russkoj i evejskoj avtonomii, in: Segodnja (1925), Nr. 30, S. 6.

Projekt russkoj avtonomii (okončanie), in: Segodnja (1925), Nr. 31, S. 7.

Proekt zakona o nacional'no-kul'turnom samoupravlenii ob"edinenija evrejskogo naselenija v Latvii, in: Narodnaja Mysl' 01.02.1925, S. 5.

Raiņa priekšvārdi savu darbu izdevumiem, URL: http://www.korpuss.lv/klasika/Senie/Rainis/Raksti/1.htm, 29.05.2018.

Rede Paul Schiemanns am 06.05.1925, in: Latvijas republikas Saeimas stenogrammas. 8. Sesija, Rīga 1925, Spalte 352.

Renner, Karl Politische Demokratie und nationale Autonomie. Rede des Abgeordneten Karl Renner und Debatte auf dem Parteitag der Deutschen Sozialdemokratie in Österreich, zu Wien im Oktober 17, Berlin 1917.

Rimscha, Hans von Paul Schiemann als Minderheitenpolitiker, in: VfZ 4 (1956), Heft 1, S. 43-61.

Schiemann, Paul Staat und Nationalität, in: Rigasche Rundschau (1930), Nr. 38, S. 2.

Schiemann, Paul Staatsgemeinschaft und Volksgemeinschaft, in: Rigasche Rundschau (1927), Nr. 107, S. 1f.

Skujenieks, Marģers (Hg.) Trešā tautas skaitīšana Latvijā. Rīga 1930.

Smith, David J./Hiden, John Ethnic Diversity and the Nation State. National cultural autonomy revisited, London 2012.

Stranga, Aivars Ebreji un diktatūras Baltijā (1926-1940), Rīga 2002.

Vedīščeva, Jeļena Mazākumtautību pamatizglītība Latvijā (1918-1940). Doktorarbeit an der Universität Lettlands, Rīga 2010.

V sejm vnesjon proekt russkoj avtonomii, in: Segodnja (1925), Nr. 30, S. 2.

Wachtsmuth, Wolfgang Die autonome deutsche Schule in Lettland 1920-1934. Mit einem Anhang: Das Herder-Institut zu Riga (Private deutsche Hochschule), Köln 1952. = Von deutscher Arbeit in Lettland 1918-1934; 2.

Weilemann, Peter R., Die Schwierigkeit, mit dem Selbstverständlichen zu leben. Nationen und Nationalismen in Europa, in: Nationalismen im Umbruch. Ethnizität, Staat und Politik im neuen Osteuropa, hg. von Magarditsch A. Hatschikjan/Peter R. Weilemann, Köln 1995, S. 7-11.

Mathias Niendorf

Friede, Freude, Wasserkraft. Litauens Wege aus dem Ersten Weltkrieg und die Stabilität des Provisorischen

Immer schon hatten sie es schwer, als selbständige Akteure wahrgenommen zu werden, die Staaten zwischen Deutschland und (Sowjet-)Russland. Sprach man nach dem Ersten Weltkrieg von „Zwischeneuropa“[1] oder den „Randstaaten“, so werben um die Aufmerksamkeit des Lesers mittlerweile Titel wie „Schlachtfeld der Diktatoren“, „Shatterzones“ oder „Bloodlands“[2]. Nicht mehr Herablassung, sondern Mitgefühl für die Opfer scheint aus solchen Wortschöpfungen zu sprechen. Fortgeschrieben wird damit zugleich jedoch eine Sichtweise, welche die betroffenen Gesellschaften zu Objekten degradiert. Mehr noch, in der gewählten Makroperspektive, verstärkt durch die Fokussierung auf Gewaltgeschichte, erscheint jene Großregion wie schon in der Publizistik der Zwischenkriegszeit als eine im Grunde gestaltlose Masse. Vielfalt und Besonderheiten einzelstaatlicher Entwicklungen drohen dabei zu verschwimmen.

Diese Unschärfe neuerer Gesamtdarstellungen zu benennen, bedeutet noch kein Bekenntnis zu einem Neo-Historismus oder einer Nationalgeschichte herkömmlichen Typs. Die Folgen des Ersten Weltkriegs zu überwinden, war tatsächlich ein transnationales Problem, wurde von Zeitgenossen auch als internationale Herausforderung begriffen, angegangen jedoch überwiegend im nationalen Rahmen.

Wenn es im Folgenden um Litauens Weg aus dem Krieg gehen soll, gilt es also, das Wechselspiel innen- und außenpolitischer Faktoren genauso im Blick zu behalten wie deren Verhältnis zu anthropologischen Kategorien. Ohne an Heidegger und dessen gelehrt-assoziative Etymologien anknüpfen zu wollen, sei doch angemerkt, dass – wenigstens im Deutschen – ‚Friede‘ und ‚Zufriedenheit‘ förmlich miteinander in einem Zusammenhang stehen.[3] Inhaltlich bezeichnen

1 Wirsing, Zwischeneuropa. Ohne Auseinandersetzung mit der problematischen Perspektive trotz ähnlichem Titel Prusin, The lands between.

2 Beyrau, Schlachtfeld der Diktatoren; Bartov, Shatterzones of empires; Snyder, Bloodlands.

3 Vgl. Marten, Bedeutung der Etymologie, v.a. S. 235.

beide einen Zustand, in welchem ein stabiles Gleichgewicht erreicht worden ist: zwischen einem Staatswesen und dessen Nachbarn, aber auch den eigenen Bürgern einerseits, beziehungsweise zwischen einem Individuum mit sich selbst und seiner Umgebung andererseits. Der länger schon etablierten Friedensforschung lässt sich mittlerweile eine moderne, auf empirischer Grundlage arbeitende Glücksforschung an die Seite stellen.[4]

Voraussetzungen und Visionen

Suggestiv beschworen wurde Litauens künftiges Glück in einer ersten Regierungserklärung am 15. November 1918. Vor einem dreiviertel Jahr, am 16. Februar hatte Litauen sich für selbständig erklärt, doch diese Unabhängigkeit bedurfte erst noch ihrer Ausgestaltung. Selbst die Frage der Grenzen war offen. Anders als Estland und Lettland verfügte Litauen über eigenstaatliche Traditionen, doch an das Großfürstentum gleichen Namens wollten die Gründerväter nicht anknüpfen. Wenn sie gleichwohl auf dessen historische Hauptstadt Wilna Anspruch erhoben, eine polnisch-jüdisch Stadt inmitten eines überwiegend weißrussischen Umlandes, so lag hierin ein Widerspruch zum ansonsten verfochtenen ethnischen Prinzip. Dieses wiederum schien die Angliederung litauisch sprachiger Territorien in Ostpreußen zu rechtfertigen. Der Besitz Memels mit seinem Hafen versprach zudem wirtschaftlich und strategisch entscheidende Vorteile. Anders als ihr Umland war die Stadt selbst aber überwiegend deutschsprachig. Ebenso wenig bildete das litauische Kernland eine homogene Einheit. Zwar standen russische Amtsstuben seit längerem leer, doch zwischen litauischen Dörfern lagen nach wie vor polnische Herrenhäuser und jüdische Kleinstädte, die *Schtetl*. Ethnische Argumentation bedeutete in solch einer Lage, sich passend erscheinender Statistiken zu bedienen. Ihre Basis bildeten Volkszählungen, deren Kategorie der Muttersprache schwerlich dem Phänomen von Mehrsprachigkeit gerecht werden konnte, ganz abgesehen von der Frage, inwieweit sich aus dem Sprachgebrauch die Zuschreibung einer bestimmten Identität ableiten ließ. Sowohl das Wilna- wie das Memelgebiet gehörten aber gerade zu den typischen, ethnisch gemischten Grenzregionen des östlichen Europas.

Aus dem Osten der heutigen Republik stammte auch Litauens erster Ministerpräsident. Mit dem Kleinbauernsohn Augustinas Voldemaras (1883-1942) „betrat eine der widerspruchvollsten und umstrittensten Persönlichkeiten die

---

4 Frey, Glücksforschung, S. 17.

politische Bühne des jungen litauischen Staates."[5] Ideologisch vertrat er das nationale, rechte Lager der später so genannten „Tautininkai" um Präsident Antanas Smetona (1874-1944).[6] Dessen Putsch im Dezember 1926 markiert die Zäsur zwischen einer parlamentarischen und einer autoritären Regierungsform. Vor dem Zerwürfnis der beiden im Jahre 1929 gehörte Voldemaras zu Smetonas engsten Gefolgsleuten und bekleidete wiederholt Spitzenämter.

Kaum ein erstes Mal als Regierungschef unmittelbar nach dem Waffenstillstand von Compiègne im Amt, entwarf Voldemaras am 15. November 1918 das Bild eines künftigen Gemeinwesens. Der Staat sei kein Selbstzweck, sondern nur Mittel zum Zweck, damit die Menschen im Leben besser zu Recht kommen und sich glücklich fühlen könnten:[7] „Ja, wir wollen, dass in einem wieder errichteten Litauen alle seine Einwohner, ganz gleich welchen Glaubens oder Sprache, glücklich sind, dass sie alle sagen können: ‚Nur in einem unabhängigen Litauen können wir auch künftig glücklich sein.'"[8] Den Weg dahin skizzierte Voldemaras recht konkret. Er verwies darauf, dass Litauen ein Agrarland sei, was jetzt, nach dem großen Krieg, wo allerorten Hunger herrsche, keine schlechte Ausgangslage bedeute. Litauen könne Lebensmittel ausführen und notwendige Waren dafür einführen:

> „Es stimmt, Kohle haben wir nicht, und eine große Industrie werden wir deshalb nicht auf die Beine stellen, aber wenn wir Energie benötigen, können wir sie aus Wasser gewinnen. Wasser schafft elektrische Energie, für Fabriken, Eisenbahn und Beleuchtung. Was für ein Anblick wird sich uns dann bieten? Litauen wird sich in große Felder und Gärten verwandeln, in schöne Wiesen, dazwischen schöne, von lauter Grün umgebene Bauernhäuser. [...] Und in alle Ecken Litauens gelangt man leicht, schnell und billig. Hier und da steht eine große Fabrik. Aber sie gibt sich nicht etwa schon von weitem durch einen hohen Schornstein mit Rauchwolken zu erkennen. Nein, sie wird

---

5 Rauch, Geschichte der baltischen Staaten, S. 45; vgl. Rudis, Augustinas Voldemaras, sowie als populärwissenschaftlichen Überblick Kaminskas, Voldemaro likimo keliais.

6 Kohrs, Die Litauische Nationale Union.

7 Klimas, Lietuvos dešimtmetis, S. 88-101. Nach dieser Vorlage auch in: Voldemaras, Raštai, S. 65-75; geringfügig abweichende Fassung (mit Datum 14.11.1918) in: Eidintas, Lietuvos Taryba, S. 609-618. – Vgl. Kiaupienė, Lietuvos istorija, Bd. 10, Teil 1, S. 97; Mačiulis, Dvarų kultūrinio palikimo likimas, S. 33 f.

8 Klimas, Lietuvos dešimtmetis, S. 89: „Taip, mes norim, kad atgimstančioj Lietuvos valstybėj visi jos gyventojai, nežiūrint į tai, kurios jie tikybos, kuris kokią kalbą vartoja, būtų laimingi, kad visi sakytų: ‚Tik nepriklausomoj Lietuvoj mes tegalim būti laimingi'."– Übersetzung aller Zitate und Titel durch den Verfasser, der sich für die freundliche Unterstützung sowie manche Anregung bedankt bei Anastasija Kostiučenko (Greifswald).

> mit Strom betrieben, so dass man sie erst aus nächster Nähe ausmachen kann, sobald das fröhliche Summen von Arbeit erklingt. Um sie herum wächst eine Reihe großer und kleiner Städte. Der Unterschied zwischen den Städten ist nicht groß: Alle sind sie sauber, hübsch anzusehen, mit allen Bequemlichkeiten versehen. Überall Strom, überall Kanalisation. Also ist der Unterschied nur ein äußerlicher. Wohin man auch schaut – überall glückliche Menschen mit fröhlichen Gesichtern. Wer nach Litauen kommt, wird sagen können: ‚Dies ist ein Land, wo Glück und Arbeit zu Hause sind.'“[9]

Wie hier einer Versöhnung von Ökonomie und Ökologie das Wort geredet wird, erinnert nicht nur an das *pursuit of happiness* der US-Verfassung oder an Helmut Kohls „blühende Landschaften“, sondern scheint auch schon Kreml-Propaganda vorwegzunehmen. Man könnte meinen, Sowjetlitauen habe sich die Visionen eines Voldemaras zum Vorbild genommen, was die Nutzung von Wasserkraft anbelangt.[10] Den Premier der bourgeoisen Republik auch nur zu erwähnen, verbot sich freilich von selbst. Doch als nach dreijähriger Bauzeit 1959 ein Elektrizitätswerk an der Memel eingeweiht wurde, durfte des Ingenieurs Jonas Smilgevičius (1894 [?]-1984) gedacht werden, als eine Art verkannten Genies, dessen zukunftsweisende Pläne vor Errichtung der Sowjetmacht zwangsläufig hätten auf Unverständnis und Ablehnung stoßen müssen. Dass jener Visionär 1941 nach Sibirien deportiert worden war,[11] erwähnte auch ein Justas Paleckis (1899-1980) nicht, lange Jahre Ministerpräsident von Moskaus Gnaden. Dafür beschrieb der ehemalige Journalist die Feierlichkeiten von 1959 mit einem an

---

9 Klimas, Lietuvos dešimtmetis, S. 90 f.: „Tiesa, anglių mes neturime ir pertat labai plačiai industrijos nesudarysim, bet kiek mums jėgos reikia, galime gauti iš vandens. Vanduo duos elektros jėgą, kurios užteks fabrikams, geležinkeliams ir švietimui. Koks iš tų ypatybių vaizdas išeina? Lietuva pavirsta į didelius laukus ir sodus, gražias pievas, tarp kurių išmėtyti gražūs, paskendę žalumoj ūkinikų namai. [...] Į visas Lietuvos puses lengva ir greita ir pigu nuvažiuoti. Vietomis užeini [sic] didelį fabriką. Bet jo nerodo ištolo aukšti kaminai su dūmų debesiais. Jis elektra varomas, taigi galima pažinti tik arčiau priėjus, kada išgirsti linksmą darbo ūžimą. Aplink juos auga eilė miestų ir miestelių. Skirtumas tarp miestų nedidelis: visi švarūs, visi malonūs, visi gyventi patogūs. Visur elektra, visur kanalizacija. Taigi skirtumas daugiau dėl akių. Kur pažvelgsi, pamatysi sveikus žmones linksmais veidais. Kas pamatys Lietuvą, pasakys: ‚Čia darbo ir laimės šalis'.“ Vgl. die Übersetzung bei Drėmaitė, Das fortschrittliche Litauen, S. 99.

10 Niendorf, Geschichte Litauens, S. 284; vgl. Štanzel, Wasserträume.

11 https://www.vle.lt/Straipsnis/Jonas-Smilgevicius-117893c (4.7.2018).

Voldemaras gemahnenden Vokabular: „und unter Jubelrufen floß das Wasser [...] in ein neues Bett, um Litauen Freude und Licht zu bringen."[12]

Beachtung verdient hier weniger der Versuch, Sowjetherrschaft und eigene Karriere mit Modernisierungserfolgen zu rechtfertigen, als vielmehr die Kontinuität einer Semantik und damit einhergehender Leitvorstellungen. Inwieweit sich tatsächlich ein Zusammenhang zwischen technischem Fortschritt und subjektiven Wohlbefinden nachweisen lässt, muss offenbleiben. Glück (wie im Königreich Bhutan) als Staatsziel zu definieren, stellt in den Augen von Wissenschaftlern jedenfalls keine erfolgversprechende Strategie dar. Einem – nicht im klassischen Sinne als neoliberal zu bezeichnenden – Autor zufolge kommt es vielmehr auf die Sicherung von Rahmenbedingungen an.[13] Hierzu zähle auch ein breites Spektrum politischer Mitsprachemöglichkeiten.[14]

Diesbezüglich fallen die Defizite der Regierungserklärung von November 1918 auf. Bildung wird eher kurz abgehandelt, als notwendig zwar, aber nicht unbedingt als Glücksverheißung. Erwähnung finden noch außenpolitische Lage und Staatsfinanzen, nicht aber die künftige Regierungsform oder politische Kultur des Landes. Dass es sich um ein multiethnisches, multireligiöses Territorium handelt, wird nur indirekt aufgegriffen. Von einer gewaltfreien, gerechten oder gar „gelingenden" Gesellschaft ist keine Rede, dafür auffallend häufig von „Glück" (laimė – als Personifizierung in der Folklore zugleich der Name einer Göttin[15]). Mittels einer solchen ahistorisch verstandenen, quasi anthropologischen Kategorie beschwor Voldemaras eine konfliktlose Gesellschaft. Deren utopischer Charakter wurde nicht erst von einer späteren Glücksforschung kritisiert. Schon frühe Vertreter von Modernisierungstheorien sahen Verbindungen zwischen Konfliktregelung und Moderne.[16] Dass umgekehrt Menschen sich nirgends unglücklicher fühlen als in einer vom Krieg heimgesuchten Region, haben quantitative Erhebungen zur Genüge bestätigt.[17] Für das Baltikum trifft dies lange Jahre zu.

---

12 Paleckis, In zwei Welten, S. 396; Paleckis, Dviejuose pasauliuose, S. 512: „[...] ir džiugesio šūksmams aidint Nemuno vandenys pasuko naująja vaga, nešdami Lietuvai džiaugsmą ir šviesą."

13 Frey, Glücksforschung, S. 33-37.

14 Frey, Glücksforschung, S. 23 f.

15 Vgl. Kerbelytė, Litauische Volksmärchen: Das Glück des Armen (S. 248-251), Das Unglück (S. 251 f.), Der Sohn ohne Glück (S. 253 f.), Giltinė und Laimė (S. 254-257).

16 Mergel, Geht es weiter voran, S. 224.

17 Frey, Glücksforschung, S. 8 f.

Mit dem Waffenstillstand im November 1918 war der Weltkrieg als solcher beendet, nicht jedoch die Kampfhandlungen im östlichen Europa. Auch Litauen blieb ein Schlachtfeld.[18] Die neueste, maßgebliche Gesamtdarstellung datiert – eher mechanistisch – den Unabhängigkeitskrieg vom 1. Februar 1919 bis zum 30. November 1920.[19] Einen Gleichgewichtszustand hatte die junge Republik damit jedoch weder nach außen noch im Innern erreicht.

Symbolhaft steht hierfür ihr Regierungssitz. Nachdem sich Polen im Oktober 1920 den Besitz Wilnas erst militärisch, dann 1923 auch diplomatisch gesichert hatte, wurde Kaunas Litauens „provisorische Hauptstadt".[20] Dass sich das ganze Land in einem Provisorium wähnte, seine Eliten in ständiger Angst vor dem Kommunismus gelebt hätten, stellt indes eine vereinzelte, nachträglich festgehaltene Beobachtung dar – erkennbar verfasst unter dem Eindruck des Zweiten Weltkriegs und des Verlustes staatlicher Unabhängigkeit.[21] Zeitgenössische Quellen vermitteln ein anderes Bild. Demnach muss wohl eher von einer Verfestigung des Vorläufigen ausgegangen werden. Eine frühe Weichenstellung erfolgte 1926, als eine Kirchenprovinz mit Metropolitansitz in Kaunas geschaffen wurde. Diese Regelung, die kirchliche und weltliche Grenzen zur Deckung brachte, bedeutete ein Stück weit eine Anerkennung politischer Realitäten, auch wenn Litauen damit noch keinen förmlichen Verzicht auf Wilna geleistet hatte.[22] Groß angelegte Medienkampagnen im In- und Ausland sollten weiterhin jenen Anspruch untermauern.

Dieser Propaganda fielen letztlich sogar ihre Urheber zum Opfer. Spitzenpolitiker entwarfen 1938 Pläne für eine Exilregierung in der Schweiz, da sie glaubten, sich auf einen – wie man heute weiß: nie beabsichtigten – Einmarsch Warschaus vorbereiten zu müssen.[23] Polnische Parolen wie „Führer, führ uns nach Kaunas!" blieben bloße Drohkulisse.[24] Ihre Wirkung in Litauen verfehlten sie gleichwohl nicht. Selbst auf dem Land, auf den Versammlungen der Tautininkai, beschäftigte die Bauern das Verhältnis zu Polen: Drohte womöglich eine Rückkehr des Gutsherrn?[25] Die Beschwörung einer Gefahr für die Nation, als Kombination von innerer und äußerer Bedrohung, vermochte zu mobilisieren,

---

18 Lesčius, Lietuvos kariuomenė; Balkelis, Demobilisierung.

19 Surgailis, The 1919-1920 Lithuanian War, S. 219.

20 Žepkaitė, Die fehlende Hauptstadt.

21 Mukdoni, A jor, Sp. 1098.

22 Kužulis, Staatskirchenrecht, S. 119-127.

23 Žulys, Polska w polityce zagranicznej Litwy, S. 165.

24 Łossowski, Ultimatum polskie, S. 90: „Prowadź nas Wodzu na Kowno!"

25 Mačiulis, Valstybės kultūros politika, S. 147.

nicht aber vollständig von Alltagsproblemen abzulenken. Auch inmitten der Krise galten die Sorgen der Parteimitglieder den örtlichen Wegeverhältnissen. Ende der 1930er Jahre hatte die Landwirtschaft einen bedeutenden Aufschwung genommen, litt aber nach wie vor unter Mängeln in der Infrastruktur.

Wie es einem Weltkrieg entspricht, waren auch die Schäden, die dieser hinterließ, weltweit zu verzeichnen. In Litauen bezifferte sie eine amtliche Kommission auf umgerechnet 450 Millionen US-Dollar.[26] Weniger leicht lässt sich menschliches Leid in Zahlen fassen. Anfang der 1920er Jahre war nahezu jeder sechste Bewohner Litauens ein – meist aus Russland – zurück gekehrter Flüchtling.[27] Vor allem bei Frauen sind als Reaktionen auf die extremen Belastungen psychische Störungen beobachtet, jedoch kaum professionell diagnostiziert, geschweige denn behandelt worden.[28] In der historischen Forschung findet zunehmendes Interesse das Schicksal der Kinder, der ungezählten Waisen und Halbwaisen.[29] Geht es um Opfer physischer Gewalt, stehen aber nach wie vor Männer im Mittelpunkt. 1.113 Invaliden aus dem Ersten Weltkrieg und 329 aus dem Unabhängigkeitskrieg wurden offiziell als Kriegsbeschädigte anerkannt. „Lebende Monumente der Freiheit" nannte sie Smetona.[30]

Ein Weg aus dem Krieg bestand somit darin, diesen – wenigstens in Teilaspekten – als positive Erinnerung zu beschwören und den erbrachten Opfern einen Sinn zuzuschreiben. Das neu erwachte Interesse an Denkmälern und Gedächtniskultur hat entsprechende Erzählmuster zu Tage gefördert.[31] Eine wichtige Rolle spielten in diesem Zusammenhang „Gewaltgemeinschaften", paramilitärische Verbände als vermittelnden Instanzen zwischen Staat und Gesellschaft, aber auch zwischen den Generationen.[32]

Offenkundig war es nicht der Frieden, welcher die Diskurse der Nachkriegszeit bestimmte.[33] Pazifistische Positionen vertraten weltweit in erster Linie Gruppierungen am linken Rand des politischen Spektrums. Dieser war aber

---

26 Kiaupienė, Lietuvos istorija, Bd. 10, 2, S. 240.

27 Balkelis, War.

28 Griffante, „Irgendetwas in mir ist verhärtet", v.a. S. 203 f.

29 Griffante, Children.

30 Jurevičiūtė, Karo invalidų organizacijos, S. 12: „gyvieji laisvos Lietuvos paminklai". Vgl. auch dessen durch eine Konkordanz erschlossenen „Großen Gedanken": Meškauskas, Antono Smetonos Didžiosios Mintys.

31 Staliūnas, Der Kult des Unbekannten Soldaten; Safronovas, Didysis karas.

32 Petronis, Guarding the honor of the nation; Haslinger / Petronis, Erster Weltkrieg; Jokubauskas, Lietuvos šauliai.

33 Kuodys, Pacifizmo refleksija.

schwach ausgeprägt in einem Land, wo – etwa im Gegensatz zu Lettland – eine Industriearbeiterschaft fehlte. Als Voldemaras selbst einmal eigene Streitkräfte für entbehrlich erklärte, erntete er heftige Kritik.[34] Auch die integrative Kraft des Katholizismus mit seinem Universalanspruch dürfte nicht allzu hoch zu veranschlagen sein. Für Streit sorgte immer wieder die Frage, in welcher Sprache ein Gottesdienst abgehalten werden solle, ob auf Polnisch oder Litauisch. Der Konflikt mit Polen wurde ebenso auf diplomatischer Bühne wie in abgelegenen Dorfkirchen ausgetragen.

Verflechtungen von Innen- und Außenpolitik

Wenn um Wege aus dem Krieg geht, dann scheint Litauen ein Fall eigener Art gewesen zu sein. Das Kriegsrecht blieb hier, von kurzen Unterbrechungen abgesehen, bis 1938 in Kraft. Begründet wurde es zumeist mit einer „polnischen" Gefahr, aufgehoben wurde es dann auf deutschen Druck. Diese enge Verflechtung von Innen- und Außenpolitik gehörte zu den Kennzeichen von Litauens Geschichte in der Zwischenkriegszeit.

Einen förmlichen Friedensvertrag schloss Litauen lediglich mit Sowjetrussland.[35] Seine Unterzeichnung am 12. Juli 1920 fiel in einen Zeitraum, als die Rote Armee im Westen ein Gebiet nach dem anderen eroberte – der Ausbruch der Weltrevolution schien unmittelbar bevorzustehen. Entsprechend großzügig konnte Moskau sich geben, was die Anerkennung litauischer Gebietsansprüche einschließlich Wilnas anbelangt. Eine erfolgreiche polnische Gegenoffensive ließ den Vertrag ohnehin schon bald wie ein Stück Makulatur erscheinen.

Umso länger, bis in die 1990er Jahre, stiftete ein anderes Dokument Unfrieden, nämlich das Abkommen von Suwałki.[36] Die Vereinbarung vom 7. Oktober 1920 wollte auch kein Friedensvertrag sein, sondern legte lediglich eine Demarkationslinie zwischen Polen und Litauen fest; Wilna blieb darin unerwähnt. Vertrug es sich aber mit dem Geist des Abkommens, wenn schon einen Tag später ein polnischer General vorgeblich den Gehorsam aufkündigte und sich mit Tausenden von Getreuen aufmachte, um eben dieses Wilna einzunehmen? Kaunas sah sich mit Warschau sogleich im Kriegszustand. Erst auf polnischen Druck erklärte es ihn Ende 1927 für beendet.[37] Innenpolitisch noch schwerer

---

34 Rudis, Augustinas Voldemaras, S. 22.

35 Laurinavičius, Lietuvos-Sovietų Rusijos Taikos sutartis.

36 Suvalkų sutartis.

37 Sierpowski, Piłsudski w Genewie.

vermittelbar war die Annahme eines Ultimatums, mit dem Warschau – nach Aufbau der oben skizzierten Drohkulisse – 1938 die Aufnahme diplomatischer Beziehungen erzwang.[38]

So wie Litauen sich an seiner Ostgrenze vor vollendete Tatsachen gestellt sah, schuf es selbst solche im Memelgebiet. Voraus gegangen waren geheime Absprachen bzw. Sondierungen mit Berlin und Moskau. Anfang 1923 überschritten notdürftig als Freischärler getarnte litauische Verbände die Grenze und entwaffneten die französische Besatzung. Die Alliierten erkannten jenen Coup an, machten aber die Gewährung weitgehender Autonomierechte zur Bedingung. Um deren Auslegung wurde später auf internationalen Foren gestritten, bis schließlich im März 1939 das nationalsozialistische Deutschland die Rückgabe des Memelgebiets erzwang.[39] Entsprechend kompliziert gestaltete sich Litauens außenpolitischer Lage.[40] Die längste Zeit trat es in einer Doppelrolle auf – als Verteidiger des Status quo im Memelgebiet, als revisionistische Macht in der Wilna-Frage.

Zu einer Zeit, als alle Welt bemüht schien, Lehren aus dem Krieg zu ziehen, Wege aus Imperialismus und Nationalismus zu finden, wirkte die Beharrlichkeit, mit welcher Litauen auf seinen Forderungen gegenüber Polen insistierte, wie aus der Zeit gefallen, wie ein Relikt aus einer längst für überwunden geglaubten Epoche. Auf dem Höhepunkt globaler Konferenzdiplomatie, Ende der 1920er Jahre, wurde Litauen durch Voldemaras vertreten. Hatte der Bauernsohn 1919 in London noch durch seine moderate Haltung beeindruckt,[41] stand er nun im Ruf eines *enfant terrible*. Sein Äußeres schien diesem Klischee zu entsprechen. Klein von Statur, aber mit markantem Kopf und Bürstenhaarschnitt wurde er zu einer beliebten Zielscheibe von Karikaturisten.[42] Sie zeichneten ihn meist als Giftzwerg und unartiges Kind. Voldemaras schien als Person den kleinen Gernegroß, die ganze Unreife eines jungen Staatswesens zu verkörpern. Gefürchtet

---

38 Łossowski, Ultimatum polskie.

39 Tauber, Das Memelgebiet.

40 Žalys, Lietuvos diplomatijos istorija.

41 „Report of a Conversation with Professor Voldemar [sic]" vom 5.2.1919 von Rex Leeper und Lewis Namier, zit. nach Alston, Antonius Piip, S. 59: „He gave us the impression of an intelligent, level-headed and moderate man. Contrary to the usual habit of the small nationalities, he did not unduly exaggerate the size of the ethnic territory of his nation. He admitted that large parts of the Government of Vilna were White Russian and not Lithuanian [...]".

42 Gueslin, La France et les petits États baltes, S. 417 f., 425 f.; Buchowski, Panowie i żmogusy, S. 17 f. (mit Bildbeispielen S. 81-131).

waren seine „professoralen Reden […], die fast jedesmal ‚mit der Erschaffung der Welt und den ersten Litauern im Paradies' […] anfingen".[43]

Die zeitgenössische Wahrnehmung Litauens und seines Regierungschefs als Karikatur eines kleinen Landes sollte nicht ohne weiteres auch die des Historikers sein. Konstruktiv waren Vorstöße und Anregungen zur Fortentwicklung des Minderheiten-, vielleicht auch des Völkerrechts, die – in ganz Ostmitteleuropa – insbesondere von jüdischen Gelehrten ausgingen.[44] Bis heute wirkt hier allerdings die Sprachbarriere nach. Der Staatsrechtler Michał Römer (Mykolas Römeris, 1880-1945), ein adliger Gutsbesitzer polnischer Muttersprache, veröffentlichte seine Werke überwiegend auf Litauisch.[45] Ebenso wenig ein Litauer bäuerlicher Herkunft war der Zionist Jacob Robinson (Jakūbas Robinzonas, 1889-1977).[46] Beide Juristen vertraten wirkungsvoll Litauens Interessen auf internationaler Bühne. Insgesamt wäre der Beitrag Litauens für eine funktionierende Friedensordnung in Europa wohl dennoch nicht allzu hoch zu veranschlagen. Selbst Estland und Lettland wahrten Distanz, wenn Fragen einer engeren Kooperation innerhalb „des" Baltikums anstanden. Sie wollten nicht Gefahr laufen, in Litauens Dauerkonflikt mit Polen hereingezogen zu werden.[47]

Wie es um die beiderseitigen Beziehungen bestellt war, ließ sich an der Grenze studieren, im litauischen Sprachgebrauch ohnehin nur eine Demarkations- oder Verwaltungslinie. Um deren provisorischen Charakter zu unterstreichen, wurde ihr Verlauf gar nicht erst in Stein gemeißelt. Kein dauerhaftes Material markierte die polnisch-litauische Grenze, sondern Holzstangen, an deren oberem Ende Strohbündel befestigt waren. Ein wenig erinnerten sie an Besen, als die sie im Litauischen auch bezeichnet wurden (šluota; im Polnischen meist ‚wiecha': ‚Strohwisch'). Sie eines nicht fernen Tages beseitigen zu können – diese Hoffnung wurde aus Kaunas durch eine Dauerpropaganda genährt. Einstweilen begnügten sich litauische wie polnische Grenzer damit, immer mal wieder Stangen heimlich zu versetzen und so das eigene Staatsgebiet über Nacht um ein paar Quadratmeter zu vergrößern.[48]

---

43 Schmidt, Statist auf diplomatischer Bühne, S. 145. Auswahl positiver, nicht kontextualisierter Würdigungen bei Kaminskas, Voldemaro likimo keliais, S. 58.

44 Bendikaitė, Interwar Lithuania; Müller / Schwarz, Ein übernationales Laboratorium.

45 Motieka, Mykolas Römeris.

46 Bendikaitė, The life, times and work of Jokūbas Robinzonas.

47 Stranga, The destiny of the Baltic Entente.

48 Niendorf, Geschichte Litauens, S. 205.

Um im Herbst 1939, und damit schon wieder am Beginn eines Weltkrieges, endlich seine historische Hauptstadt in Besitz nehmen zu dürfen, hatte es für Litauen einer Niederlage Warschaus und einer scheinbar großzügigen Geste Moskaus bedurft. Ein Jahr später war ganz Litauen sowjetisch, ohne dass man deshalb die Republik insgesamt zu einem Provisorium erklären sollte. Doch etwas fällt auf: In jenem dreiviertel Jahr, von Oktober 1939 bis Juli 1940, weilte Präsident Smetona kein einziges Mal in Wilna; Regierung und Parlament ließen sich mit den Umzugsvorbereitungen Zeit.[49]

Dabei schien Litauen nichts sehnlicher erhofft zu haben als die Wiedergewinnung seiner verfassungsmäßigen Hauptstadt. Vorstöße auf diplomatischem Parkett machten dies glauben, ebenso eine Dauerpropaganda im Innern. Doch nun zeigte sich: Seine Politiker hatten es versäumt, Vorkehrungen für den Ernstfall, sprich Erfolgsfall zu treffen. Längst hatten sie sich in einem Provisorium eingerichtet. Man darf dies durchaus wörtlich verstehen. Auch manche Litauer mokierten sich darüber, wie sehr die Oberschicht des Landes an ihren Häusern in Kaunas hängen würde.[50] Eine reservierte bis ablehnende Haltung der Wilnaer Bevölkerung, die sich von Litauen eher besetzt als befreit fühlte, war wenig dazu angetan, die Umzugsbereitschaft zu fördern.

Wann also endete das Provisorium? Nationalbewusste Litauer würden womöglich das Jahr 1993 nennen.[51] Erst dann nämlich waren drei Voraussetzungen gleichzeitig erfüllt: Sowohl das Wilna- als auch das Memelgebiet waren Bestandteil Litauens, ohne dass dafür Truppen Moskaus im Land standen. Bis zum Abzug der letzten, schon nicht mehr sowjetischen, sondern mittlerweile russländisch gewordenen Soldaten, waren schließlich nie mehr als zwei der drei Bedingungen gegeben.[52] Was bedeutete dies aber für das individuelle Lebensglück?

Indikatoren für Glück und Unglück

Erste Anhaltspunkte ergibt die Statistik. Litauens demographische Entwicklung bis 1940 ist geprägt durch einen Rückgang der Säuglingssterblichkeit und eine Erhöhung der Lebenserwartung. Wenn die Suizidrate auf einem im

---

49 Lewandowska, Losy Wilnian, S. 39 f.

50 Aufzeichnung des sowjetischen Gesandten in Kaunas N. G. Pozdnjakov vom 21.9.1939, in: Komplektov, Polpredy soobščajut, S. 53 f., hier S. 53; Römer, Dzienniki, S. 141; vgl. Paleckis, Dviejuose pasauliuose, S. 324; Paleckis, In zwei Welten, S. 243.

51 Buchowski, Litwa 1993.

52 Surgailis, Rusijos kariuomenės išvedimas.

europäischen Maßstab niedrigen Niveau verharrte (zwischen 1924 und 1939 im Schnitt 8,1 Selbsttötungen auf 100.000 Einwohner), muss dies nicht von Lebenszufriedenheit zeugen. Eher handelt es sich um das Merkmal einer traditionalen, katholisch geprägten Gesellschaft. Litauens Kennziffer lag jedenfalls näher an der polnischen als an der lettischen.[53]

Insgesamt ergibt sich aus der einzigen Volkszählung (von 1923, ohne Memel- und Wilna-Gebiet) das Bild eines Agrarlandes, in welchem fast neun Zehntel aller Bürgerinnen und Bürger auf dem Lande lebten. Bei einer Gesamtbevölkerung von gut zwei Millionen Menschen waren der amtlichen Erhebung zufolge 83,9 % Litauer, 7,6 % Juden, 3,2 % Polen, 2,5 % Russen und 1,4 % Deutsche.[54] Mit dem Memelgebiet übernahm Litauen ein Minderheitenproblem, bei dessen Bewältigung selbst ein international garantiertes Autonomiestatut wenig auszurichten vermochte. Verantwortlich war der Mangel an gutem Willen auf allen Seiten.[55] Nicht auf territorialer, sondern auf personaler Grundlage beruhte eine Autonomieregelung für die zerstreut siedelnde jüdische Bevölkerung. Eine Bewährungsprobe blieb ihr indes versagt; schon 1925 entzogen ihr die erstmals allein regierenden Christdemokraten den rechtlichen Rahmen.[56]

Doch wenn es mentalitätsgeschichtlich um Wege aus dem Krieg geht, verdient durchaus die anfängliche Euphorie Erwähnung, die ebenso große wie unrealistische Erwartung, im jüdisch-litauischen Verhältnis an vormoderne Formen der Selbstverwaltung anknüpfen zu können. Immerhin erleichterte es die Autonomie, Verbindungen zu jüdischen Organisationen im Ausland zu knüpfen, deren Hilfsleistungen wiederum dem Aufbau des Landes zugutekamen.

Was blieb, war ein im außersowjetischen Osteuropa einzigartiges, großzügig vom Staat finanziertes Minderheitenschulwesen.[57] Freilich sind hier auch Unterschiede nicht zu übersehen. Während die Zahl polnischer Schüler an polnischen Grundschulen bis zum Ende der Zwischenkriegszeit geradezu dramatisch zurückging (von 3.336 auf 266), konnten jüdische Einrichtungen sogar noch einen Zuwachs verzeichnen (von 10.845 auf 14.009 Schüler), obwohl die Gesamtstärke jener Bevölkerungsgruppe im Abnehmen begriffen war.[58] Nicht

53 Gailienė, Ką jie mums padarė, S. 173 f.; Gailienė, Why are suicides so widespread.
54 Niendorf, Geschichte Litauens, S. 193.
55 Žalys, Ringen um Identität.
56 Liekis, "A state within a state?".
57 Vgl. Mendelsohn, The Jews of East Central Europe, S. 234.
58 Kaubrys, Lietuvos mokykla, S. 46.

nur Litauern, sondern auch Juden gegenüber fühlten sich Polen häufig wie Bürger zweiter Klasse.[59]

Eine tiefe Zäsur bedeutete die Agrarreform von 1922. Landbesitz über 80 ha (der sich fast ausnahmslos in polnischer Hand befand) wurde enteignet und unter der landlosen und landarmen Bevölkerung verteilt.[60] Die Gutsbesitzer erhielten – anders als in Lettland – eine zumindest symbolische Entschädigung. Im Vergleich zu anderen Staaten Osteuropas fiel die litauische Agrarreform moderat aus. Das Angebot an Land konnte hier nie mit der Nachfrage schritthalten. Dabei nimmt sich das Ergebnis immer noch imposant aus: 40.000 landwirtschaftliche Betriebe wurden neu geschaffen; weitere 90.000 erhielten zusätzlich Land.[61]

Folge war ein sozialer Wandel, und zwar sowohl am Sockel wie an der Spitze der Pyramide. Die seit Jahrhunderten prägende Gestalt des Gutsherrn trat praktisch nicht mehr in Erscheinung. Dafür sank im Agrarsektor der Arbeiteranteil von 21,3 % im Jahre 1923 bis 1940 auf 13,8 %.[62] Wenn damit auch noch keine Aussagen über Lebensstandard und Lebensqualität möglich sind, deuten diese Zahlen doch auf eine stärker nivellierte, egalitäre Gesellschaft. Im Europa von heute fördern derartige Entwicklungen die Lebenszufriedenheit.[63]

In eine gegenläufige Richtung wies dafür der Verlauf sozialer Kontakte; Häufigkeit und Intensität nahmen ab.[64] Verantwortlich war die Flurbereinigung, welche mit der Agrarreform einherging. Gewachsene Dorfsiedlungen wurden aufgelöst; an ihre Stelle traten weit auseinander liegende Einzelhöfe. Die Gebäude befanden sich nun inmitten der bäuerlichen Besitzungen, und damit, ganz wie ein Voldemaras es wollte, im Grünen. Was die beschworenen „schönen" Wiesen anbelangt, so werden sie derartigen Ansprüchen in ästhetischer und ökologischer Hinsicht entsprochen haben. Ungünstiger fiel die ökonomische Bilanz aus. Eine Ertragssteigerung hätte im regenreichen Litauen systematische Entwässerungsmaßnahmen erfordert, für die es jedoch an Mitteln fehlte.

Alles in allem gelang die Umstrukturierung der Landwirtschaft, nicht zuletzt deren Umstellung auf den Export. Dies machte Kaunas wiederum abhängig von seinen wichtigsten Abnehmern, Großbritannien und dem Deutschen Reich.

---

59 Vgl. Paszkiewicz, Pod znakiem „Omegi", S. 80, 166.

60 Vgl. Buchowski, Polacy w niepodległym państwie litewskim, S. 25.

61 Penkaitis, Agrarentwicklung, S. 45 f.

62 Norkus, Du nepriklausomybės dvidešimtmečiai, S. 500.

63 Frey, Glücksforschung, S. 17.

64 Niendorf, Geschichte Litauens, S. 198-201.

Ungeachtet schwieriger Marktzugänge und Absatzkrisen stieg das Bruttoinlandsprodukt (BIP).[65] Neuesten Untersuchungen zufolge verzeichnete Litauen zwischen 1924-1938 ein Wachstum um real 113,3 % bzw. einen jährlichen Zuwachs um durchschnittlich 4,3 %. Bezogen auf eine ebenfalls wachsende Bevölkerung bedeutete dies einen pro-Kopf-Anstieg um 80,4 %. Wie sich dieser Durchschnittswert konkret verteilte, wer wie stark vom Wachstum profitierte und wer weniger oder gar nicht, wurde bisher weder untersucht noch als Forschungsfrage formuliert.

Lediglich eine – mit Unsicherheiten behaftete – Pauschalberechnung liegt vor: 1924 entfielen etwa 27-29 % des Nationaleinkommens auf die jüdische Bevölkerung; 1938/39 belief sich dieser Anteil auf nur noch 22-25 %.[66] Er wäre damit stärker als die absolute Größe jener Minderheit zurückgegangen, deren Zahl von 153.000 auf rund 140.000 Personen sank.

Dass steigende Einkommen die Zufriedenheit steigern, während Arbeitslosigkeit sie gefährdet, gehört zu den unmittelbar einsichtigen Ergebnissen einer mit empirischem Anspruch auftretenden Glücksforschung.[67] 1930, als die Weltwirtschaftskrise in Litauen ihren Höhepunkt noch nicht erreicht hatte, soll es auf dem Land eine Viertelmillion unterbeschäftigter Menschen gegeben haben – zusätzlich zu 50-60.000 Arbeitslosen in der Stadt. Einem jährlichen Bevölkerungszuwachs von bis zu 26.000 Menschen standen in den 1930er Jahren weder ausreichend Arbeitsplätze im Land noch Möglichkeiten einer Erwerbsmigration offen. Von den rund 100.000 offiziell erfassten Auswanderern bis 1940 hatten 90 % das Land bereits in der ersten Hälfte der Zwischenkriegszeit verlassen. In Litauens Industrie waren zwischen 1930 und 1939 gerade einmal 16.000 neue Arbeitsplätze entstanden. Im öffentlichen Dienst gehörten 1934 über zwei Drittel aller Beschäftigten der Altersgruppe zwischen 25 und 40 Jahren an; die Fünfzig erreicht oder überschritten hatte nur etwa jeder zehnte. Entsprechend schlecht fielen dort die Aussichten für Schulabgänger wie Hochschulabsolventen aus.[68]

Anders als es ein Voldemaras voraussah, war das Litauen der 1930er Jahre also schwerlich ein Land, in dem die „Arbeit zu Hause" war. Zivilisatorisch dagegen näherte es sich dessen Vision an. In der Innenstadt von Kaunas verfügten die meisten Gebäude bereits über fließendes Wasser und einen Anschluss an die

65 Norkus, Kas turtėjo greičiausiai?, S. 19-21. Kritik hierzu, ohne diese im Detail zu begründen: Mertelsmann [Rez.], S. 324.

66 Vaskela, Tautiniai aspektai, S. 136.

67 Frey, Glücksforschung, S. 38.

68 Niendorf, Geschichte Litauens, S. 200.

Kanalisation. Dies war das Ergebnis einer großen Kraftanstrengung aller Bürger, von Juden wie von Christen. Anders sah es in kleineren Ortschaften aus, und um 1930 lag landesweit der Stromverbrauch pro Kopf bei einem Prozent des deutschen Wertes.[69]

Schwachstellen bei der Energieversorgung entsprachen dem Kalkül einer etatistischen Wirtschaftspolitik: Zuerst sollte Litauens Landwirtschaft Unterstützung erfahren, dann mit ihr verbundene, agrarnahe Unternehmen, und erst am Schluss sonstige Fabrikbetriebe. Phase eins und zwei konnten bis zum Ende der Zwischenkriegszeit als nahezu abgeschlossen gelten; Planungen für die dritte und letzte Phase waren bereits weit gediehen. Zu ihren vorrangigen Zielen gehörte der Ausbau des Elektrizitätsnetzes.[70]

An Plänen hatte es schon zuvor nicht gefehlt. Ältere Überlegungen sowie erste Voruntersuchungen gingen bis auf russische Zeiten bzw. die deutsche Besetzung im Ersten Weltkrieg zurück. Vergeblich bemühte sich Litauen, Einsicht in die Unterlagen zu erhalten. Wenn das Thema Elektrifizierung dennoch nicht aus der Öffentlichkeit verschwand, war dies vor allem privater Initiative zu verdanken.[71]

Eine Aktiengesellschaft namens „Galybė (Kraft)" warnte bereits 1923: Litauen müsse lernen, seine natürlichen Reichtümer selbst zu nutzen, bevor andere ihm zuvorkämen. Seite für Seite führte jene Werbebroschüre Berechnungen an. Zum Schluss aber geriet ihr Autor, ein eher nüchterner Ingenieur, doch noch ins Schwärmen. Fast so, als wollte er an Voldemaras anknüpfen (den er unerwähnt ließ), sah er im Bau von Wasserkraftwerken den Weg „in eine lichte Zukunft Litauens (į šviesią Lietuvos ateitį)".[72]

Seine Begeisterung für die „Weiße Kohle" stellte nicht etwa eine landestypische Eigenheit dar.[73] Der Enthusiasmus einzelner Ingenieure war älter als Lenins Parole von der Elektrifizierung des gesamten Landes, speiste sich aber teilweise aus denselben Quellen.[74] Litauens führender Hydrologe Steponas Kolupaila (1892-1964) hatte in Moskau bei Viktor Grigor'evič Gluškov (1883-1939)

---

69 Polkaitė-Petkevičienė / Černiauskas, Urbanizacija, S. 180-184; Kulikauskas, Lietuvio kodas, S. 270-273.

70 Norkus, Du nepriklausomybės dvidešimtmečiai, S. 241 f.; Vaskela, Lietuva 1939-1940, S. 135; Mažeika, Danijos santykiai su Lietuva, S. 231-233, 248 f.

71 Cholševnikov, Neman; Smilgevičius, Nemuno hidroelektros stotis.

72 Pauliukonas, Kur Lietuvos ateitis?, S. 26.

73 Maier, „Weiße Kohle" versus Schwarze Kohle.

74 Coopersmith, The electrification of Russia; Schlögel, Jenseits des Großen Oktober, S. 272-313.

studiert, einem der Wegbereiter der unionsweiten Elektrifizierung,[75] sein Kollege Smilgevičius in Deutschland.

Anders als in der Sowjetunion verbanden sich in Litauen keine gesellschaftlichen Visionen mit der Nutzung von Wasserkraft. Als saubere Energieform schien sie Fortschritt ohne soziale Verwerfungen zu garantieren, sich in eine organische Entwicklung des Landes einzufügen. Kolupaila beschwor sogar eine Art Synergieeffekt, wenn er für einen Kraftwerksbau mit den Worten warb, der vorgesehene Standort befände sich „in aussergewöhnlich reizvoller Landschaft". Ökonomie und Ökologie schienen kein Widerspruch, sondern sogar eine fruchtbare Verbindung mit dem Fremdenverkehr eingehen zu können.[76] Darüber hinaus versprach die Nutzung heimischer Ressourcen wirtschaftliche Unabhängigkeit. Das patriotische Argument der Autarkie hätte sich allerdings in sein Gegenteil verkehrt, wäre die Elektrifizierung das Werk ausländischer Investoren geworden. Litauen selbst fehlte es vorerst noch an Kapital.

1927 betrug die Leistung aller Wasserkraftwerke (einschließlich umgebauter Mühlen) gerade einmal 7.900 Pferdestärken, wo nach Ansicht von Experten ohne weiteres 200.000 PS möglich gewesen wären.[77] Anfang der 1930er Jahre konkretisierten sich Pläne für ein System von Kraftwerken entlang der Memel. Dänische und vor allem schwedische Unternehmen, die dabei waren, ein ähnliches Projekt im lettischen Ķegums (dt. Keggum) an der Düna umzusetzen, zeigten sich interessiert. Allerdings waren die Zeiten inmitten der Weltwirtschaftskrise ungünstig.[78] 1935 stammten lediglich 2,5 % der litauischen Energieerzeugung aus Wasserkraft.[79] Kolupaila wurde deshalb nicht müde, seinen Landsleuten die Nachbarn im Norden als Vorbild nahe zu legen.[80] Inwieweit sich die mit Elektrizität besser versorgten Letten deswegen auch glücklicher fühlten, entzieht sich einer Nachprüfung.

75 Gluškov, Voprosy teorii i metody gidrologičeskich issledovanij.

76 Kolupaila, Die hydrometrischen Arbeiten, S. 32.

77 Kolupaila, Die hydrometrischen Arbeiten, S. 27.

78 Nordlund, Temporary partners or permanent connections, S. 241; Karnups, Ulmaņa autoritārā režima valdišanas laiks, S. 140-142; Latvenergo, Ķeguma hidroelektrostacija.

79 Meškauskas, Lietuvos pramonė, S. 415.

80 Kolupaila, Latvija ruošiasi elektrifikacijai; Gimbutas / Danys, Steponas Kolupaila, S. 91.

Momente von Glück und Unglück

Glück zu messen, fällt Sozialwissenschaftlern leichter als dem Historiker, der selten über genügend Zahlenmaterial verfügt. Ersatzweise ließe sich herkömmlich nach Beschreibungen von Glück und Unglück suchen. Ohne Anspruch auf strenge Repräsentativität sollen im Folgenden die quantitativen Analysen um solche qualitativen Charakters ergänzt bzw. die Makro- mit der Mikroebene konfrontiert werden. Die Frage, ob in Litauen „Glück und Arbeit zu Hause waren", ist eine Frage sowohl des Zeitpunkts, als auch eine des Ortes. Ihr wird im Folgenden in vier Zeitschritten nachgegangen, wobei unterschiedliche Lebenswelten im Fokus stehen werden: Zunächst ein idealtypischer Gutshof im Jahre 1927, dann reale *Schtetl* zu Beginn und Dörfer gegen Ende der Weltwirtschaftskrise sowie schließlich die provisorische Hauptstadt in der zweiten Hälfte der 1930er Jahre.

Eine erste Bilanz litauischer Unabhängigkeit zog 1927 der Poet und Publizist Kazys Binkis (1893-1942). Eine Wochenzeitung veröffentlichte dessen gereimte Rückschau unter dem Titel „Früher und heute": Der Gutshof, wo die eigenen Vorfahren nicht nur Fronarbeit leisten mussten, sondern ihnen auch noch Prügel drohte, falls sie nicht sogleich auf Polnisch reagierten, befindet sich nun in Bauernhand. Auch der „Russki mit der Knute (ruskis su bizūnu)" kann nicht mehr schrecken. Alle, vom alten Adel bis zum letzten Knecht, müssen heute Litauisch reden.[81] Nationale Emanzipation erscheint hier als Erfahrung sozialer Gerechtigkeit. Wo früher Hunger herrschte, kommt jetzt sogar Schweinefleisch auf den Tisch. Und statt den sauer ersparten Groschen zum Juden zu bringen, geht jeder in seine eigene Genossenschaft. Zum materiellen Wohlstand gesellt sich die Verbreitung von Bildung: Erschwingliche Bücher, erschwinglicher Braten stehen so für die Fortschritte des neuen Litauens.

Was der spätere Smetona-Biograph Binkis hier als Idyll zeichnete, war sicherlich eine Verdichtung, aber nicht unbedingt eine Verzerrung der Wirklichkeit. Die Anfangsjahre des autoritären Regimes fielen mit einer Hochkonjunktur zusammen. Dies ist bei der Diskussion um Erfolg oder Misserfolg der Agrarreform ebenso zu berücksichtigen wie die Krisenstimmung des Jahres 1938, als sich Angst vor einer Rückkehr des polnischen Gutsherrn breit machte. Ob sie ihr Leben als Provisorium empfanden oder nicht, die Siedler glaubten, etwas zu verlieren zu haben.

81 Binkis, Seniau ir dabar: „Dabar šlėkta ir burliokas / Mūsiškai kalbėti mokos".

Ein ideologisch unverdächtiges Zeugnis stammt aus einer jüdischen Kleinstadt Mitte der 1930er Jahre. Ein Einwohner wusste von frohem Gesang („frejleche klangen") zu berichten, welcher an Sommerabenden von ehemaligem Gutsland herüberdrang. Es waren litauische Volkslieder, angestimmt von den Neusiedlern – für den jüdischen Ohrenzeugen Ausdruck der Freude über ein Leben in Freiheit und voll erfüllter Arbeit.[82] Ihn selbst erfüllte diese Aufbruchsstimmung eher mit Wehmut, da er nur umso deutlicher den Niedergang seines *Schtetls* empfand. Damit stimmte der Korrespondent zugleich in den pessimistischen Grundton ein, welcher damals die jüdische Literatur bestimmte.[83]

Den Folgen der Weltwirtschaftskrise vermochte sich letztlich ebenso wenig die christliche Bevölkerung zu entziehen. Der von Binkis beschworene Schweinebraten drohte wieder zu einem Luxusgut zu werden.[84] Sie müsse lernen, den Geschmack von Fleisch zu vergessen, antwortete die Arbeiterin einer Schuhfabrik auf die Frage, welche Erwartungen sie mit dem Jahreswechsel 1930/31 verbinden würde. Dabei hatte sie noch das Glück, nicht von Entlassung, sondern „nur" von Kurzarbeit betroffen zu sein.[85] Bei einem Teil der Bevölkerung kam Schweinefleisch ohnehin nie auf den Tisch – Litauens Juden hielten sich in der Regel an die Speisevorschriften. Der Gegensatz war mehr als ein rein gastronomischer. Binkis hatte den wirtschaftlichen Hintergrund angedeutet: Genossenschaften sollten den jüdischen Zwischenhandel überflüssig machen, zu dem seit jeher auch das eine oder andere Bankgeschäft gehörte.

Spätestens, als Bürger unfreiwillig zu Vegetariern wurden, hatten Ausläufer des „Schwarzen Freitags" an der New Yorker Börse auch Litauen erreicht.[86] Extrem betroffen waren die *Schtetl* im Norden. Ein in die USA ausgewanderter Bundist, der zu Besuch in der alten Heimat weilte, fühlte sich wie in Geisterstädten. Alles Leben schien erloschen, Handel und Gewerbe völlig zum Erliegen gekommen. Wäre er länger geblieben, bemerkte der Autor trocken, wäre er womöglich noch Zionist geworden.[87] Andere beschrieben das Leben der Ladeninhaber als ein Leben im Wartestand – Warten auf Kundschaft, Warten auf die nächste Hilfssendung. Kam neben kleinen Geldbeträgen aus den USA oder Südafrika gar noch

82 L. B. E., Anišok (Anušišok), Sp. 1624.

83 Volbikaitė, Maža pakraščio šalies sostinė; Grigoravičiūtė, Jidiš literatūra.

84 Vgl. zum sozial gestaffelten Konsumverhalten Daniliauskas, Lietuvos miesto gyventojų materialinė kultūra, S. 84.

85 Černiauskas, Nedarbas Lietuvoje, S. 256.

86 Kiaupienė, Lietuvos istorija, Bd. 10, 2, S. 290-294; Kohrs, Die Litauische Nationale Union, S. 190 f.

87 Zivion, Mejne cvej bazuchn, Sp. 1301.

ein Päckchen mit gebrauchter Kleidung, waren sie „gliklech".[88] Das Warten auf Ausreisemöglichkeiten dagegen stellte immer weniger eine realistische Perspektive dar. Besonders die Jugend empfand ihre Lage als ausweglos.[89]

Den Städten fehlte die Kundschaft vom Land. 1935 brachen im Süden Litauens Unruhen aus.[90] Zu den treibenden Kräften gehörten Hofbesitzer, die in ihre Betriebe investiert und sich dafür verschuldet hatten. Dass bald darauf, im Zuge der Weltwirtschaftskrise, die Erzeugerpreise für landwirtschaftliche Produkte stark zurückgehen würden, war nicht einkalkuliert. Industriewaren und Verbrauchsgüter wie Zucker, Salz und Petroleum verbilligten sich zwar ebenfalls, aber in weit geringerem Umfang. Dafür verharrten Zinsen und Kreditgebühren auf alter Höhe, des gleichen Steuern und Abgaben. Um Forderungen nach einem Ausgleich Nachdruck zu verleihen, stellten Bauern nicht nur die Zahlungen an öffentliche Kassen, sondern auch die Belieferung von Märkten und Genossenschaften ein. Bei den anfangs friedlichen, später eskalierenden Protesten verliefen die Fronten zwischen verzweifelten Landwirten und dem Staat, manchmal auch zwischen den Aufständischen und einzelnen als besonders regimetreu geltenden Bauern. Letztlich sahen sich Litauens Politiker zum Einlenken gezwungen, auch wenn sie den Aufstand selbst mit drakonischen Mitteln beendeten. Der euphemistische Begriff der Pazifizierung erscheint hier angebracht. Von antisemitischen Ausschreitungen ist in diesem Zusammenhang dagegen nichts bekannt.

Jüdische Feiertage galt es im Gedächtnis zu behalten. Andernfalls riskierte man, vor verschlossenen Ladentüren zu stehen. Tadeusz Katelbach (1897-1977), dem aus der polnischen Hauptstadt entsandten Korrespondenten, muss dies mehr als einmal passiert sein. Den Lesern zu Hause glaubte er damit etwas Besonderes mitteilen zu dürfen.[91] Dabei besaß Warschau die seiner Zeit größte jüdische Gemeinde Europas. Nicht dort, wohl aber in Litauens provisorischer Hauptstadt konnten sich Geschäftsleute eine Einhaltung der Feiertagsruhe leisten. Katelbach vergaß nicht hinzuzufügen, dass sich hinter den Fassaden

---

88 Ril, Plungian, hier v.a. Sp. 1593; vgl. Tarulis, Die Juden im Wirtschaftsleben, S. 388.

89 Dan, Lazdej, Sp. 1598.

90 Leonavičius / Maksimavičius, Valstiečių streikas.

91 Katelbach, Za litewskim murem, S. 90 f. Schon Anfang der 1920er Jahre überraschte diese Sabbatheiligung Auswärtige; s. Senn, Lithuania in my life, S. 24; Hermann, Lietuviškai vokiškų pasikalbėjimų knygelė, S. 141; vgl. Bendikaitė, Zwischen Anspruch und Wirklichkeit, S. 115 f.

gleichwohl ein stiller Kampf zwischen Litauern und Juden um ihren Platz im Wirtschaftsleben abspielte.

Das Problem antisemitischer Radikalisierung bis zu den Pogromen von 1941 führt über den zeitlichen Rahmen dieses Beitrags hinaus. Doch wirft es einen Schatten auf die Zwischenkriegszeit. Was die Mitwirkung von Litauern an der Ermordung von Juden betrifft, fällt es jedenfalls schwer, die Bedeutung zweier aufeinander folgender Diktaturen, der ersten Sowjetherrschaft von 1940/41 und der anschließenden deutschen Besetzung, zu übersehen.[92]

Zuvor jedoch ist der soziale Frieden überraschend selten aus dem Gleichgewicht geraten, selbst wenn es sich um ein labiles gehandelt haben mag. Das unter Smetona autoritär regierte Litauen stützte sich auf Militär und Polizei, ohne damit schon einen Polizeistaat darzustellen. Die Möglichkeiten des Regimes, mit repressiven Maßnahmen Unruhen im Vorfeld zu unterdrücken, sollten nicht überschätzt werden.

Doch gegen Ausschreitungen wurde eingeschritten. Dies galt auch bei antisemitisch motivierten Vorfällen.[93] Ein Überlebender des Ghettos von Kaunas, dessen Blick auf Litauen von den Erfahrungen des Zweiten Weltkriegs geprägt war, glaubte rückblickend festhalten zu müssen: „We were thankful for the school system Lithuania let us have and for the protection we had from the government against hooligans." Stärker religiös geprägte Juden hätten zusätzlich wohl noch die Freiheit der Glaubensausübung angeführt.[94]

Litauen – eine Insel der Glückseligen?

Der Wunsch eines Voldemaras, dass Litauens „Einwohner, ganz gleich welchen Glaubens oder Sprache, glücklich" seien, ging allenfalls zum Teil in Erfüllung. Während Wachstumsraten eine Zunahme des Wohlbefindens hätten erwarten lassen, sprechen Momentaufnahmen mitunter eine andere Sprache. Diese Eindrücke korrelieren wiederum mit den Arbeitsmarktzahlen. Auch in Litauen führte die Weltwirtschaftskrise zu massiven Beeinträchtigungen der individuellen Zufriedenheit. Stärker noch als die christliche war die jüdische Bevölkerung betroffen. Dies gilt nicht zuletzt für die Jugendarbeitslosigkeit in den 1930er Jahren. Aber auch der Titularnation gelang es nicht, Prinzipien der Generationengerechtigkeit zu verwirklichen. In Verbindung mit einer martialischen

---

92 Dieckmann, Deutsche Besatzungspolitik in Litauen.

93 Truska, Lietuviai ir žydai.

94 Mishell, Kaddish for Kovno, S. 7; Matz, Mejn geburtštat kalvarie, Sp. 1512.

Propaganda, der Beschwörung traditionell männlicher Tugenden, drohte sich ein Gewaltpotenzial aufzubauen.

Litauens Weg aus dem Krieg war außenpolitisch ein langer und schwieriger. Der Konflikt mit Polen engte den Handlungsspielraum eines kleinen, wirtschaftlich schwachen Landes zusätzlich ein. Innenpolitisch förderte ein solches Feindbild womöglich die nationale Konsolidierung, weniger jedoch die Identifikation mit einem Staat, der sich gemessen an seiner Rhetorik als wenig prinzipienfest erwies. Dabei konnte Litauens Erste Republik objektiv Erfolge vorweisen, ohne dass diese subjektiv immer als solche wahrgenommen wurden. Sie wirken unspektakulär, waren aber aus eigener Kraft erreicht worden (auch ohne Wasserkraft). Es klingt trivial, ist jedoch festzuhalten: Litauens Weg aus dem Krieg vollzog sich über wachsenden Wohlstand und sozialen Ausgleich. Seine Minderheitenpolitik war, obschon nicht frei von Schikanen, insbesondere nicht Polen gegenüber, ein Teil davon. Den Alltag interethnischer Beziehungen kennzeichnete ohnehin ein gewisser Pragmatismus.

Der erwähnte Steponas Kolupaila darf als ein Beispiel gelungener Integration gelten. Polnischsprachig aufgewachsen, hatte er sich das Litauische angeeignet, um Vorlesungen in der Landessprache halten zu können. Dabei blieb der Professor souverän genug, dem politischen Klima zum Trotz auch Fachliteratur in polnischer Sprache zu empfehlen.[95] Unter Studierenden trug er den Spitznamen „Hydropaila". Durchaus respektvoll klangen darin große Namen der Geschichte Litauens an, und sei es nur derjenige des Großfürsten Švitrigaila (poln. Świdrygiełło, um 1370-1452). Vor allem aber handelte es sich um eine Anspielung auf Kolupailas Lebensthema, die Nutzung von Wasserkraft.

Als Ende 1939, nach Beginn des Zweiten Weltkriegs, ganze Dörfer im Dunkeln lagen, weil es an Petroleum für die Lampen mangelte, ließ sich Litauens führender Hydrologe diese Gelegenheit nicht entgehen. In der Oppositionspresse ergriff er das Wort. Ein letztes Mal vor Verlust der Unabhängigkeit warb Kolupaila für die Elektrifizierung. Wenn er entschiedene Schritte „in eine lichte Zukunft (į šviesią Lietuvos ateitį)" anmahnte, gebrauchte er die gleichen Worte wie anderthalb Jahrzehnte vor ihm ein Kollege. Doch bevor Kolupaila diese Vision mit einem an Voldemaras gemahnenden Pathos skizzierte, versuchte er sich an einer Gegenwartsanalyse. Auch inhaltlich schien sie auf die Regierungserklärung von November 1918 Bezug nehmen zu wollen. Geblieben war die Frage nach dem Glück, verschoben hatten sich die Maßstäbe.

95 Paszkiewicz, Pod znakiem „Omegi", S. 168.

Kopailas mit „Weihnachtsgedanken zum Licht“ überschriebene Glosse trug einen längeren Untertitel, eingeleitet von der Frage: „Warum sind wir glücklicher als andere?“ Die Antwort des Autors mag naiv wirken, von mangelnder politischer Weitsicht zeugen, empirisch nicht genügend abgesichert oder schlicht falsch sein. Doch verdient sie Beachtung, weil sich hier der Blick des Ingenieurs vom technischen Fortschritt auf die Gesellschaft weitet. Kolupaila beschwor ein Bild des Glücks im Unglück: dass Litauen vom Krieg verschont geblieben sei, dass hier die Klassengegensätze, die Unterschiede zwischen arm und reich weniger stark ausfallen würden als anderswo. Gleiches gelte für die Diskrepanz zwischen Stadt und Land, zwischen Intellektuellen und Bauern. Ohne Hitlerdeutschland oder die UdSSR namentlich zu erwähnen, hatte der Hydrologe diese Diktaturen vor Augen, wenn er – das immer noch autoritär regierte – Litauen als „demokratischer“ bezeichnete. Deshalb, so sein Fazit, das mit dem Forschungsstand von heute nicht gänzlich unvereinbar erscheint, „fühlen wir uns glücklicher als unsere Nachbarn“.[96]

Literaturverzeichnis

ALSTON, CHARLOTTE Antonius Piip, Zigfrīds Meierovics and Augustinas Voldemaras. The Baltic states, London 2010.

BALKELIS, TOMAS War, revolution and nation making in Lithuania, 1914–1923, Oxford 2018.

BARTOV, OMER / WEITZ, ERIC D. (Hg.) Shatterzones of empires. Coexistence and violence in the German, Habsburg, Russian, and Ottoman borderlands, Bloomington, Indianapolis 2013.

BAUER, GERHARD / KLEIN, MANFRED Das alte Litauen. Dörfliches Leben zwischen 1861 und 1914, Köln, Weimar, Wien 1998.

BENDIKAITĖ, EGLĖ Interwar Lithuania as a laboratory of international law, in: Jus Gentium. Journal of International Legal History 2 (2017), Nr. 2, S. 555-580.

BENDIKAITĖ, EGLĖ / HAUPT, DIRK ROLAND (Hg.) The life, times and work of Jokūbas Robinzonas – Jacob Robinson, Sankt Augustin 2015.

BENDIKAITĖ, EGLĖ Zwischen Anspruch und Wirklichkeit. Die Politik gegenüber den Juden in Litauen in der Zwischenkriegszeit, in: Zwischen großen Erwartungen und bösem Erwachen. Juden, Politik und Antisemitismus in Ost- und

96 KOLUPAILA, Kalėdinės mintys apie šviesą: „jaučiames laimingesni kaip mūsų kaimynai“ [Hervorhebung im Original]. Zur Rezeptionsgeschichte der Regierungserklärung vgl. SKIPITIS, Nepriklausoma Lietuva, S. 297, 301 f.

Südosteuropa 1918-1945, hg. von Dittmar Dahlmann und Anke Hilbrenner, Paderborn u.a. 2007, S. 101-120.

Beyrau, Dietrich Schlachtfeld der Diktatoren. Osteuropa im Schatten von Hitler und Stalin, Göttingen 2000.

Binkis, Kazys Seniau ir dabar, in: Ders. Poezija, hg. von Adolfas Juršėnas, Vilnius 1999, S. 248 f. = Raštai; 1.

Buchowski, Krzysztof Litwa 1993: kluczowy rok niepodległości, in: Studia z Dziejów Rosji i Europy Środkowo-Wschodniej 56 (2021), Nr. 1, S. 147-174.

Buchowski, Krzysztof Panowie i żmogusy. Stosunki polsko-litewskie w międzywojennych karykaturach, Białystok 2004.

Buchowski, Krzysztof Polacy w niepodległym państwie litewskim 1918-1940, Białystok 1999.

Bylaitė-Lapinskienė, Andželika Lietuvių etiketas ir bendravimo kultūra XX amžiuje, Klaipėda 2012.

Černiauskas, Norbertas Nedarbas Lietuvoje 1918–1940. Phil. Diss., Vilnius 2014. (MSchr.)

Cholševnikov V. N. Neman. Opisanie gidrografičeskoe i navigacionno-statističeskoe, sostavlennoe po issledovaniju opisnoj partii 1893-1897 g.g. i svidenijam upravlenij vodjanych putej soobščenija, Kostrama 1902.

Coopersmith, Jonathan The electrification of Russia, 1880-1926, Ithaca, London 1992.

Dan, I. Lazdej, in: Lite, Sp. 1597-1599.

Daniliauskas, Antanas Lietuvos miesto gyventujų materialinė kultūra XX a. (Etnografinė apybraiža), Vilnius 1978.

Dieckmann, Christoph Deutsche Besatzungspolitik in Litauen 1941-1944, Bd. 1-2, Göttingen 2011.

Drėmaitė, Marija Das fortschrittliche Litauen. Industrie und Architektur, in: Fortsetzung folgt. Im Zuge der Moderne. Ein Jahrhundert Litauen (1918-2018), hg. von Giedrė Jankevičiūtė und Nerijus Šepetys, Vilnius 2017, S. 98-107.

Eidintas, Alfonsas / Lopata, Raimundas (Hg.) Lietuvos Taryba ir nepriklausomos valstybės atkūrimas 1914-1920 metų, Vilnius 2017.

Frey, Bruno S. Wirtschaftswissenschaftliche Glücksforschung, Wiesbaden 2017.

Gailienė, Danutė Ką jie mums padarė. Lietuvos gyvenimas traumų psichologijos žvilgsniu, Vilnius 2008.

Gailienė, Danutė Why are suicides so widespread in Catholic Lithuania?, in: Religions 9 (2018), Nr. 3, (http://www.mdpi.com/2077-1444/9/3/71, Zugriff am 9.7.2018).

GIMBUTAS, JURGIS / DANYS, JUOZAS V. Steponas Kolupaila, Čikaga 1974.

GLUŠKOV, VIKTOR Grigor'evič Voprosy teorii i metody gidrologičeskich issledovanij, hg. von M. I. L'vovič', Moskva 1961.

GRIFFANTE, ANDREA Children, poverty and nationalism in Lithuania, 1900-1940, Cham 2019.

GRIFFANTE, ANDREA „Irgendetwas in mir ist verhärtet oder abgestorben. Ich bin nicht mehr die, die ich war." Gabrielė Petkevičaitė und ihr Kriegstagebuch, in: Nordost-Archiv N.F. 23 (2014), S. 192-208.

GRIGORAVIČIŪTĖ, AKVILĖ Jidiš literatūra tarpukario Lietuvoje (1918-1940). Savasties paieškos, in: Colloquia (2013), Nr. 29, S. 38-62.

GUESLIN, JULIEN La France et les petits États baltes. Réalités baltes, perceptions françaises et ordre européen (1920-1932), Thèse de doctorat, Paris 2004 (MSchr.), (http://tel.archives-ouvertes.fr.tel-00126331, Zugriff am 19.3.2018).

HASLINGER, PETER / PETRONIS, VYTAUTAS Erster Weltkrieg, Systemkonsolidierung und kollektive Gewalt in Ostmitteleuropa. Litauen und der „Eiserne Wolf", in: Gewaltgemeinschaften. Von der Spätantike bis ins 20. Jahrhundert, hg. von Winfried Speitkamp, Göttingen 2013, S. 343-369.

HERMANN, EDUARD Lietuviškai vokiškų pasikalbėjimų knygelė. Litauisch-Deutsches Gesprächsbüchlein, Kaunas 1931.

JOKUBAUSKAS, VYTAUTAS Lietuvos šauliai tarpukariu: Lietuviai, katalikai, *visuomenės elitas*, in: Paramilitarism in the Eastern Baltics, 1918-1940. Case studies and comparisons, hg. von Vasiljus Safronovas, Klaipėda 2014, S. 75-102. = Acta Historica Universitatis Klaipedensis; 28.

JUREVIČIŪTĖ, AUŠRA Karo invalidų organizacijos Lietuvoje 1923–1940 m., in: Kauno istorijos metraštis 8 (2007), S. 7-54.

KAMINSKAS, RAIMUNDAS Prof. A. Voldemaro likimo keliais, Vilnius 2012.

KARNUPS, VIESTURS Pauls Kārļa Ulmaņa autoritārā režima valdišanas laiks (1934-1940), in: Latvijas tautsaimniecības vēsture, hg. von Gatis Krūmiņš, Rīga 2017, S. 134-162.

KATELBACH, TADEUSZ Za litewskim murem, Warszawa 1938.

KAUBRYS, SAULIUS Lietuvos mokykla 1918-1939 m. Galios gimtis, Vilnius 2000.

KERBELYTĖ, BRONISLAVA (Hg.) Litauische Volksmärchen, Berlin 1978.

KIAUPIENĖ, JŪRATĖ (Hg.) Lietuvos istorija. Bd. 10, Teil 1-2, Vilnius 2013-2015.

KLIMAS, P[ETRAS] u.a. Pirmasis nepriklausomos Lietuvos dešimtmetis 1918-1928, Bd. 1, 2. Aufl. London 1955.

KOHRS, MICHAEL H. Die Litauische Nationale Union – Porträt einer (Staats-) Partei. Die Litauische Nationale Union (LTS) und ihre Bedeutung für das autoritäre Regime der Zwischenkriegszeit in Litauen 1924 bis 1940, Frankfurt am Main u.a. 2012.

Kolupaila, Steponas Die hydrometrischen Arbeiten in Litauen, Kaunas 1927.

Kolupaila, Steponas Kalėdinės mintys apie šviesą. Kuo mes laimingesni už kitus? Kur priežastys skirtumų tarp kaimo ir miesto? Kodėl nesiskubinima su elektrifikacija?, in: XX amžius 23.12.1939, Nr. 295 (1047), S. 5.

Kolupaila, Steponas Latvija ruošiasi elektrifikacijai. 107 lietuviai technikai Kegume, in: XX amžius 13.10.1937, Nr. 233 (391), S. 4.

Komplektov, V. G. (Hg.) Polpredy soobščajut... Sbornik dokumentov ob otnošenijach SSR s Latviej, Litvoj i Ėstoniej avgust 1939 g. – avgust 1940 g., Moskva 1990.

Krikščiūnas, J. Nedarbo klausimu Lietuvoje, in: Tautos ūkis (1933), Nr. 2, S. 39-41.

Kulikauskas, Gediminas Lietuvio kodas. Įpročiai ir būdas senovės lietuvio prieš 100 metų, Vilnius 2018.

Kuodys, Modestas Pacifizmo refleksija tarpukario Lietuvoje (XX a. 3–4 deš.), in: Karo archivas 33 (2018), S. 281-329.

Kužulis, Valdas Genese, Heranbildung und Eigenart des Staatskirchenrechts in Litauen (Theol. Diss. München 2016), Berlin 2017. = Aus Religion und Recht; 21.

L. B. E. Anišok (Anušišok), in: Lite, Sp. 1622-1624.

Latvenergo. Enerģētikas muzejs. o.O. o.J. Ķeguma hidroelektrostacija no idejas līdz mūsdienām (https://energetikasmantojums.lv/keguma-hes-no-idejas-lidz-musdienam, Zugriff am 8.2.2022).

Laurinavičius, Česlovas / Milewski, Jan Jerzy (Hg.) Suvalkų sutartis. Faktai ir interpretacijos. Umowa suwalska. Fakty i interpretacje, Vilnius 2012.

Laurinavičius, Česlovas Lietuvos-Sovietų Rusijos Taikos sutartis (1920 m. liepos 12 d. sutarties problema), Vilnius 1992.

Leonavičius, Juozas / Maksimavičius, Juozas Valstiečių streikas Suvalkijoje ir Dzūkijoje 1935 metais, Vilnius 1958.

Lesčius, Vytautas Lietuvos kariuomenė nepriklausomybės kovose 1918-1920, Vilnius 2004.

Lewandowska, Stanisława Losy Wilnian. Zapis rzeczywistości okupacyjnej. Ludzie, fakty, wydarzenia 1939-1945, 3. Aufl. Warszawa 2004.

Liekis, Šarūnas "A state within a state?" Jewish autonomy in Lithuania 1918-1925, Vilnius 2003.

Łossowski, Piotr Ultimatum polskie do Litwy 17 marca 1938 roku. Studium z dziejów dyplomacji, Warszawa 2010.

Mačiulis, Dangiras Dvarų kultūrinio palikimo likimas Nepriklausomoje Lietuvoje, in: Kultūros paminklai (2002), Nr. 9, S. 33-62.

Mačiulis, Dangiras Valstybės kultūros politika Lietuvoje 1927-1940 metais, Vilnius 2005.

Maier, Helmut „Weiße Kohle" versus Schwarze Kohle. Naturschutz und Ressourcenschonung als Deckmantel nationalsozialistischer Energiepolitik, in: WerkstattGeschichte (1992), Nr. 3, S. 33-38.

Marten, Reiner Die Bedeutung der Etymologie im Denken Martin Heideggers, in: Discours etymologiques. Actes du colloque international organisé à l'occasion du centenaire de la naissance de Walther von Wartburg, Bâle, Freiburg i. Br., Mulhouse, 16-18 mai 1988, hg. von Jean-Pierre Chambon, Tübingen 1991, S. 227-237.

Matz, Israel Mejn geburtštat kalvarie, in: Lite, Sp. 1499-1512.

Mažeika, Vaidotas Danijos santykiai su Lietuva 1918-1940 m., Vilnius 2002.

Mendelsohn, Ezra The Jews of East Central Europe between the World Wars, 3. Aufl. Bloomington 1993.

Mergel, Thomas Geht es weiter voran? Die Modernisierungstheorie auf dem Weg zu einer Theorie der Moderne, in: Geschichte zwischen Kultur und Gesellschaft. Beiträge zur Theoriedebatte. hg. von dems. und Thomas Welskopp, München 1997, S. 203-232.

Mertelsmann, Olaf [Rez.] Christoph Dieckmann. Deutsche Besatzungspolitik in Litauen 1941-1944, Bd. 1-2, Göttingen 2011, in: Forschungen zur baltischen Geschichte 8 (2013), S. 323-326.

Meškauskas, Pr. u.a. (Hg.) Antono Smetonos Didžiosios Mintys, Bd. 1-2, Kaunas 1935-1937 (Neudruck Kaunas 2014).

Meškauskas, Kazimieras u.a. Lietuvos pramonė ikisocialistiniu laikotarpiu, Vilnius 1976.

Mikalauskas, Arvydas Valstybės tarnautojai ir valstybės tarnyba Pirmojoje Lietuvos Respublikoje (1918-1940) m. Phil. Diss., Kaunas 2007 (MSchr.).

Mishell, William W. Kaddish for Kovno. Life and death in a Lithuanian ghetto, Chicago 1988.

Motieka, Egidijus (Hg.) Mykolas Römeris, Vilnius 1996. = Lietuvių Atgimimo istorijos studijos; 13.

Mukdoni, A. A jor in der litvišer meluche. (A bintl zichrojnes fun a durchrejzndikn), in: Lite, Sp. 1071-1098.

Müller, Marcel / Schwarz, Momme Ein übernationales Laboratorium. Juden und Deutsche in der Minderheitendiplomatie der Zwischenkriegszeit, in: osmikon 14.10.2020, (https://www.osmikon.de/themendossiers/sha

red-histories/ein-uebernationales-laboratorium-juden-und-deutsche-in-der-minderheitendiplomatie-der-zwischenkriegszeit, Zugriff am 24.1.2022).

Niendorf, Mathias Geschichte Litauens. Regionen, Reiche, Republiken 1009-2009, Wiesbaden 2022.

Nordlund, Sven Temporary partners or permanent connections? Scandinavian responses to the Baltic-state-markets, 1918-1940, in: Emancipation and interdependence. The Baltic states as new entities in the international economy, 1918-1940, hg. von Anders Johansson u.a., Stockholm 1994, S. 213-260. = Studia Baltica Stockholmiensia; 13.

Norkus, Zenonas Du nepriklausomybės dvidešimtmečiai Lietuvoje. Kapitalizmas, klasės ir demokratija Pirmojoje ir Antrojoje Lietuvos Respublikoje lyginamosios istorinės sociologijos požiūriu, Vilnius 2014.

Norkus, Zenonas Kas turtėjo greičiausiai? Baltijos šalių ūkio augimo 1913–1938 metais palyginimas, in: Politologija (2015), Nr. 3 (79), S. 3-54.

Paleckis, Justas Dviejuose pasauliuose. Atsiminimai, Vilnius 1983.

Paleckis, Justas In zwei Welten. Autobiographie, Berlin 1976.

Paszkiewicz, Bohdan Pod znakiem „Omegi“, hg. von Adam Gałkowski und Piotr Łossowski, Warszawa 2003.

Pauliukonas, Vl. Kur Lietuvos ateitis? Lietuvos vandenų galybė, Kaunas 1923.

Penkaitis, Norbert Agrarentwicklung in Litauen 1918-1992, Berlin 1994. = Gießener Abhandlungen zur Agrar- und Wirtschaftsforschung des europäischen Ostens; 197.

Petronis, Vytautas Guarding the honor of the nation and the prosperity of the state. National Defense of Lithuania ‘Iron Wolf’ (1928-1930), in: Journal of Baltic Studies 48 (2017), Nr. 1, S. 1-25.

Polkaitė-Petkevičienė, Giedrė / Černiauskas, Norbertas Urbanizacija, in: Dalia Bukelevičiūtė u.a. Socialiniai pokyčiai Lietuvos valstybėje 1918-1940 metais, Vilnius 2016, S. 143-193.

Prusin, Alexander V. The lands between. Conflict in the East European borderlands, 1870-1992, Oxford, New York 2010.

Rauch, Georg von Geschichte der baltischen Staaten, Stuttgart u.a. 1970.

Ril, N. Plungian, in: Lite, Sp. 1592-1595.

Römer, Michał Dzienniki, Bd. 6, Warszawa 2018.

Rudis, Gediminas Augustinas Voldemaras – nemokėjęs pralaimėti politikas, in: Lietuvos Respublikos ministrai pirmininkai 1918-1940, hg. von Ričardas Čepas und Vytautas Spečiūnas, Vilnius 1997, S. 11-69.

Safronovas, Vasilijus u.a. Didysis karas visuomenėje ir kultūroje Lietuva ir Rytų Prūsija, Klaipėda 2018.

Schlögel, Karl Jenseits des Großen Oktober. Das Laboratorium der Moderne. Petersburg 1909-1921, Berlin 1988.

Schmidt, Paul Statist auf diplomatischer Bühne 1923-45. Erlebnisse des Chefdolmetschers im Auswärtigen Amt mit den Staatsmännern Europas, 2. Aufl. Bonn 1950.

Senn, Alfred Erich Lithuania in my life, Kaunas 2012.

Sierpowski, Stanisław Piłsudski w Genewie. Dyplomatyczne spory o Wilno w roku 1927. Poznań 1990. = Prace Instytutu Zachodniego; 53.

Smilgevičius, Jonas Nemuno hidroelektros stotis, Kaunas 1930.

Snyder, Timothy Bloodlands. Europa zwischen Hitler und Stalin, 4. Aufl. München 2012.

Snyder, Timothy Bloodlands. Europe between Hitler and Stalin, London 2011.

Staliūnas, Darius Der Kult des Unbekannten Soldaten in Litauen, in: Nordost-Archiv N.F. 17 (2008), S. 248-266.

Štanzel, Arnošt Wasserträume und Wasserräume im Staatssozialismus. Ein umwelthistorischer Vergleich anhand der tschechoslowakischen und rumänischen Wasserwirtschaft 1948-1989, Göttingen 2017. = Schnittstellen. Studien zum östlichen und südöstlichen Europa; 8.

Stranga, Aivars The destiny of the Baltic Entente, 1934-1940, Riga 1994.

Sudarski, Mendl u.a. (Hg.) Lite, Bd. 1, New York 1951.

Surgailis, Gintautas Rusijos kariuomenės išvedimas, 1990-1993, Vilnius 2005.

Surgailis, Gintautas The 1919-1920 Lithuanian War of Liberation, in: The wars of Lithuania. A systematic quantitative analysis of Lithuanian's wars in the nineteenth and twentieth centuries, hg. von Gediminas Vitkus, Vilnius 2014, S. 149-221.

Tarulis, Albertas Die Juden im Wirtschaftsleben Litauens, in: Osteuropa 13 (1938), S. 383-392.

Tauber, Joachim Das Memelgebiet (1919-1945) in der deutschen und litauischen Historiographie nach 1945, in: Nordost-Archiv N.F. 10 (2001), S. 11-44.

Truska, Liudas Lietuviai ir žydai nuo XIX a. pabaigos iki 1941 m. birželio. Antisemitizmo Lietuvoje raida, Vilnius 2005.

Vaitekūnas, Stasys Lietuvos gyventojai. Per du tūkstantmečius, Vilnius 2006.

Vaskela, Gediminas Lietuva 1939-1940 metais. Kursas į valstybės reguliuojamą ekonomiką, Vilnius 2002.

Vaskela, Gediminas Tautiniai aspektai Lietuvos ūkio politikoje 1919-1940 metais, Vilnius 2014.

Volbikaitė, Goda Maža pakraščio šalies sostinė. Kaunas tarpukario jidiš literatūroje, in: Sostinė kaip tapatumo simbolis. Vilnius ir Kaunas tarpukario kultūroje, hg. von Alma Lapinskienė und Viktorija Šeina, Vilnius 2014, S. 185-214.

Voldemaras, Augustinas Raštai, Bd. 2, hg. von Morkus Šimkus, Chicago 1983.

Wirsing, Giselher Zwischeneuropa und die deutsche Zukunft, Jena 1932.

Žalys, Vytautas Lietuvos diplomatijos istorija (1925-1940), Bd. 1-2, Vilnius 2007-2012.

Žalys, Vytautas Ringen um Identität. Warum Litauen zwischen 1923 und 1939 im Memelgebiet keinen Erfolg hatte. Kova dėl identiteto. Kodėl Lietuvai nesisekė Klaipėdoje tarp 1923-1939 m., Lüneburg 1993.

Žepkaitė, Regina Die fehlende Hauptstadt: Litauens Politik im Zeichen der Wilnafrage, in: Nordost-Archiv N.F. 2 (1993), S. 299-316.

Zivion (Dr. B. Hoffmann) Mejne cvej bazuchn in der litvišer meluche, in: Lite, Sp. 1293-1310.

Žulys, Audrius A. Polska w polityce zagranicznej Litwy w latach 1938-1939. Studium z historii dyplomacji, Gdańsk 2015.

Werner Benecke

Zwischen Konsolidierung und entglittener Reform: Die nordöstlichen Grenzgebiete Polens in den 1920er Jahren

Die Kresy Wschodnie der Zweiten Polnischen Republik, also die nach dem Frieden von Riga[1] entstandenen östlichen Wojewodschaften Wilno, Nowogródek, Polesie und Wołyń, sind gewiss im engeren Sinne kein Gegenstand der baltischen Geschichte. Gleichwohl stand aber auch Polen vor der komplizierten Aufgabe, seinen Weg aus dem Krieg zu finden und in dieser national, konfessionell und sozial so sehr heterogenen Zone eine akzeptable und akzeptierte neue Staatlichkeit zu etablieren. Diese Aufgabe wurde durch die Hinterlassenschaften des Ersten Weltkrieges und der ihm folgenden polnisch-ukrainischen und polnisch-sowjetischen Kriege massiv erschwert: Die Kresy Wschodnie waren seit 1915 zum Schauplatz gewaltiger Evakuierungs- und Fluchtwellen geworden, in dieser Region hatte der Stellungskrieg zwischen dem Russischen Reich und den Mittelmächten ebenso wie der Bewegungs- und Verheerungskrieg des Sommers 1920 seine tiefen Spuren hinterlassen, und letztlich strömten seit dem Friedensschluss zwischen Sowjetrussland und Polen im März 1921 riesige Zahlen von Rückwanderern in diesen Teil Europas. Viele durchquerten das östliche Polen nur im Transit. Viele blieben und fanden sich in einem Land wieder, das sie kaum wiedererkannten.[2]

Die Wahrnehmung dieser Grenzregion war in der Polnischen Republik auch aus anderem Grunde problembehaftet: Nach 123 Jahren der Nichtexistenz Polens verfolgten die Regierenden und weite Teile der öffentlichen Meinung jene Phänomene mit extrem geschärfter Aufmerksamkeit, die – tatsächlich oder vermeintlich – die wiedergewonnene nationale Souveränität und Integrität infrage stellten. Die Region grenzte an die UdSSR und an Litauen, mithin an Staaten, die unmissverständlich klar machten, dass sie die faktische Grenzziehung einstweilen zu akzeptieren hatten, sie aber keineswegs als *ultima ratio* ihrer Politik betrachteten. In einer solchen Atmosphäre konnte bisweilen die

---

1 Zum Frieden von Riga siehe den Beitrag von Benjamin Conrad in diesem Sammelband.

2 Benecke, Ostgebiete, S. 27-40.

völlig gerechtfertigte, sachlich begründete Kritik der Bevölkerung etwa an Fragen der Bodenreform oder der Schulpolitik schnell in den Verdacht geraten, die polnische Staatlichkeit als solche zur Disposition zu stellen. Jegliche polnische Politik agierte und reagierte in einem sehr komplexen, extrem empfindlichen Resonanzraum, für den sich übrigens außer den unmittelbaren Anrainern auch das Deutsche Reich massiv interessierte.

Mein Beitrag ist darauf angelegt, an drei Beispielen aufzuzeigen, wie der Staat und die betroffene Bevölkerung mit zentralen Themen umgingen, um letztlich jene Deeskalation zuwege zu bringen, die sich als Wege aus dem Krieg beschreiben ließe. Diese drei Beispiele sind zum einen der staatliche Sicherheitsapparat, zum anderen die dringend notwendige Bodenreform, letztlich der Umgang mit dem Erbe der orthodoxen Kirche in den östlichen Grenzregionen Polens. An diesen drei Punkten mochte sich exemplarisch ausgeprägt haben, was es bedeutete, Bürger der Polnischen Republik nach verheerenden Kriegen an einer umstrittenen Grenze zu sein. Um es vorweg zu nehmen: Die Bilanz fiel ebenso differenziert aus wie es die Herangehensweise der Staatsmacht war. Es ist weder die Geschichte einer gelungenen Integration, noch jene einer unablässigen Konfrontation.

1. Das Beispiel des Sicherheitsapparates

Die Beamtenschaft der Zweiten Polnischen Republik wurde nur einmal, nämlich im Jahre 1923, systematisch gezählt, die Ergebnisse zwei Jahre später veröffentlicht.[3] Die landesweite Zählung kombinierte quantitative Angaben mit den Ergebnissen einer strukturellen Befragung der Staatsdiener aller Sparten: Der interessierte Leser erfuhr Informationen zur Altersstruktur, zur schulischen Bildung, zur Erfahrung im Amt, zur Besoldung, zur Mobilität und zu den Karrieren jener Beamter, die das Gemeinwesen auf allen Ebenen hauptberuflich verwalteten. Die Kombination der einzelnen Parameter erlaubt es dem Betrachter noch heute, eine Morphologie des polnischen Beamtenapparates der frühen zwanziger Jahre zu erkennen und diese regional zu spezifizieren. Im Hinblick auf die im Osten Polens stationierten Kräfte der Polizei ergibt sich ein bemerkenswertes Bild:

Die Kresy Wschodnie wiesen unter allen Regionen Polens die geringste Verwaltungsdichte auf, allerdings war das hier eingesetzte Verwaltungspersonal in quantitativer Hinsicht zweifach auffällig: Zum einen war die Dichte an Lehrern

3 Funkcjonariusze, 1925.

in den öffentlichen Schulen in Polen nirgends so gering wie hier. Der Aufbau des öffentlichen Schulwesens hatte im östlichen Grenzland erst begonnen und traf auf große Schwierigkeiten. 1923 waren die Kresy in dieser Hinsicht ein Gebiet, das noch lange nicht zum Landesdurchschnitt aufgeschlossen hatte. Zum anderen aber waren im Landesvergleich (mit Ausnahme der hochindustrialisierten Verdichtungsregion Oberschlesien) nirgendwo mehr Polizisten stationiert als im östlichen Grenzland. Und nur in den Kresy überstieg die Zahl der Beamten im Sicherheitsdienst jene der in der Volksbildung. Zu diesem sehr markanten quantitativen Profil kamen auffällige qualitative Besonderheiten hinzu: Weit überdurchschnittlich waren hier junge, im Polizeidienst eher unerfahrene Männer tätig, die zu sehr großen Anteilen zuvor im Militär sozialisiert worden waren. Darüber hinaus wiesen sie hinsichtlich ihres nationalen und konfessionellen Bekenntnisses die polnisch-katholischen Attribute der Staatsnation auf. Vieles spricht dafür, dass diese große und teure Ordnungsmacht sich also nur in geringem Maße aus dem Lande selbst rekrutierte. Ihre Besoldung war insgesamt niedriger als im Landesdurchschnitt, dafür besetzten sie zu mehr als 99% feste Planstellen. Der Staat plante mit ihnen also dauerhaft.[4]

Im Zusammenhang mit einer konsequent angewandten allgemeinen Wehrpflicht und mit dem bald erfolgenden massierten Aufbau eines von der Polizei getrennten Grenzschutzes lässt sich m. E. dieser Apparat zum einen als Polens Antwort auf die Freikorpsproblematik beschreiben, mithin als eine Form, die im Lande vorhandene potenzielle physische Gewalt der skizzierten Personengruppe unter staatliche Kontrolle zu bringen und zugleich die Grenzen ebenso wie die verarmte und zum großen Teil entwurzelte Zivilbevölkerung zu pazifizieren.

Diese Funktion wird einem parallel auftretenden Phänomen, das die Zeitgenossen als Militarisierung der Kresy beklagten, nicht zuzuschreiben sein, nämlich der vermeintlich planmäßigen Ansiedlung von Militärkolonisten im Osten Polens.[5] Es war ein hoch umstrittenes, emotionalisiertes Thema, das von seinen Befürwortern zu einer nationalen Heldentat stilisiert wurde, von seinen Gegnern als das vermeintlich „wahre Gesicht“ aggressiver Polonisierungstendenzen apostrophiert wurde.[6] Es war beides nicht. Tatsächlich erwies sich die Idee der Ansiedlung verdienter Veteranen des polnisch-sowjetischen Krieges von 1920 und deren Familien in den Kresy Wschodnie als eines der folgenschwersten

---

4 Benecke, Ostgebiete, S. 139-151.
5 Bocian, Osadnictwo, S. 271; Marquardt, Wehr- und Militärsiedlung, S. 48.
6 Kon, Zapadnaja Belorussija, passim.

Eigentore polnischer Innenpolitik nach 1921, bei dem die symbolische Wirkung in diametralem Gegensatz zur messbaren Veränderung stand.

Es geht um die Dimension von etwas mehr als 9000 Männern, die zwischen 1921 und 1923 in einigen Regionen an der Ostgrenze zu privilegierten Bedingungen angesiedelt wurden. Ihre Zahl war bei weitem zu klein, um einen substanziellen ökonomischen Impuls auszulösen, sie war aber groß genug, um den handfesten Unmut und Protest der ortsansässigen oder nach Flucht und Evakuierung nun zurückkehrenden Bevölkerung auszulösen. Vom Staat so schlecht ausgerüstet, dass die Zahl der siedlungswilligen ehemaligen Soldaten von anfänglich knapp 100.000 Antragstellern auf letztlich 9080 tatsächlich angesiedelte Kolonisten kontinuierlich sank, zogen diese Siedler vor allem dorthin, wo sich mit vertretbarem Aufwand ein relativ schnell erreichbares, eher erträgliches denn lukratives Auskommen erzielen ließ. Dieses war nur im Süden der Kresy, in der Wojewodschaft Wołyń, möglich.[7] Wołyń aber zählte unter den ostpolnischen Bedingungen zu den ohnedies stark besiedelten Regionen, in denen Kolonisation – verstanden als Urbarmachung und Erschließung – am wenigsten nötig, die Konkurrenz um fruchtbares Land indes überdurchschnittlich stark war. Durchaus zu Recht hat die umstrittene Militärkolonisation ihren Platz in der Reihe jener Ereignisse, die zur Erklärung der massiven Gewaltausbrüche des Jahres 1943 in dieser Region heranzuziehen sind.

Was die Staatsmacht also einerseits an potenzieller Gewalt im ersten Beispiel kanalisierte und einhegte, das beförderte sie im zweiten langfristig und folgenschwer. In dieser Hinsicht war der Weg aus dem Krieg eine zwiespältige Erfahrung.

2. Das Beispiel der Bodenreform

Bodenreformen bargen in allen ost- und ostmitteleuropäischen Staaten nach dem Ersten Weltkrieg eine enorme soziale, wirtschaftliche und nationale Sprengkraft: Wie anders als in einer als „gerecht" zu apostrophierenden Bodenreform hätte sich die Neuformung der Agrargesellschaften in den jungen, der nationalen Idee verpflichteten Staaten, ausdrücken sollen? Der Anspruch, das bisweilen jahrzehnte-, wenn nicht gar jahrhundertelange Wirken von Teilungs- und Besatzungsmächten oder als fremd angesehener Oberschichten zu revidieren, Besitzverhältnisse zugunsten der bisher Benachteiligten zu fixieren und dem allgemeinen Wohlstand die Bahn zu brechen, zählt zu den unbestrittenen

7 Brzozowski, Akcja osadnictwa wojskowego, S. 28f.

Grundforderungen jeder Modernisierung als Teil eines besseren Weges aus dem Krieg. Wer immer sich dieser Aufgabe stellte, hatte die Balance zwischen dem ökonomisch Sinnvollen einerseits und der Akzeptanz einer bäuerlichen Bevölkerung andererseits zu finden, deren bisweilen diffusen und hohen Erwartungen nicht enttäuscht werden durften. Er hatte auch in Betracht zu ziehen, welche Maßstäbe das zeitgenössische Sowjetrussland in Bezug auf Enteignung und Umverteilung landwirtschaftlicher Flächen gesetzt hatte, war das durchaus positive Bild eines besseren und gerechteren Lebens in der UdSSR der zwanziger Jahre doch nicht allein auf die Minderheitenpolitik der *korenizacija* fixiert: Vielen Ukrainern und Weißrussen in den Kresy galt die Sowjetunion auch aufgrund ihrer vermeintlich freiheitlicheren Bodenpolitik als ein Vorbild, dem gegenüber die Zustände in Polen ungerecht und nachteilig erscheinen mochten.[8]

Der Vorwurf, die Bodenreform der Zweiten Polnischen Republik sei ein Programm zur nationalen (polnischen) Besitzstandswahrung, im ökonomischen Kern aber eine bis 1939 letztlich nicht gelöste Aufgabe gewesen, trifft in weiten Teilen durchaus zu. Es trifft auch zu, dass sie ein im Kern durchdachtes und wirtschaftlich überzeugendes Grundkonzept verfolgte. Ebenso ist richtig, dass sie über erhebliche Strecken zu einem – oberflächlichen – ökonomischen Erfolg, zu Entspannung und Deeskalation beitrug, die die Situation in den Kresy in den 1920er Jahren entschärfte. Dass sie sich in der Weltwirtschaftskrise auf katastrophale Weise in ihr Gegenteil verkehrte, stand auf demselben Blatt.

Vor der Analyse der Bodenreform sind kurz die spezifischen Rahmenbedingungen anzusprechen. Vorauszusetzen ist erstens, dass weite Teile insbesondere der nordöstlichen Kresy Wschodnie von extremen landwirtschaftlichen Größenunterschieden gekennzeichnet waren: Waren in den vier östlichen Wojewodschaften allein 207 Betriebe zu verzeichnen, deren Betriebsgröße je 3000 ha überstieg, so ballten sich über 95% aller Betriebe in der Größenkategorie von unter 20 ha. Einen landwirtschaftlichen Mittelstand gab es hier kaum ansatzweise.[9]

Hinzuzufügen ist zweitens aber auch, dass die traditionelle Einstufung nach Betriebsgrößen in den östlichen Regionen Polens nur bedingt aussagekräftig ist. Großer Landbesitz bedeutete bei weitem nicht Reichtum, Kleinbetriebe waren aber auch kein sicheres Zeichen für bittere Armut. Stärker als in anderen Regionen Polens arbeiteten die Bauern – neben ihrer Tätigkeit im Ackerbau – in der

---

8 Benecke, Ostgebiete, S. 40-62.

9 Landau, Gospodarka Polski Międzywojennej, S. 144-147; Tomaszewski, Z dziejów Polesia, S. 37f.

Wald-, Weide- und Wasserwirtschaft. Vielfach nutzten sie hierbei Servitute, also tradierte Nutzungsrechte an fremdem Eigentum, um ihr Einkommen aufzubessern. Der Holzeinschlag in eigentumsrechtlich fremden Wäldern, das Fischen in ehemals gutsherrlichen Gewässern, das Weiden des bäuerlichen Viehs auf den Weiden anderer Besitzer kennzeichneten das Wirtschaften noch stark.[10]

Drittens gilt es zu beachten, dass das Land, das sich im Besitz der Bauern befand, bisweilen sehr stark zersplittert war. Um die schmalen Streifen an nutzbarem Land zu erreichen, hatten im Osten Polens die Bauern ihr Arbeitsgerät und ihre Zugtiere über weite Strecken, bisweilen per Boot, zu transportieren, gleiche Beschwernisse galten für die Ernte.[11] Mit einem Wort: Der Begriff „Bodenreform" hatte sich in den Kresy gänzlich anderen Rahmenbedingungen zu stellen als etwa in Großpolen, in der Region Warschau oder im ehemaligen österreichischen Teilungsgebiet. Ein schieres Umverteilen von Grund und Boden als Kern einer Bodenreform kam nicht infrage.

Konturen eines längerfristigen Programms nahm die polnische Bodenpolitik in den Kresy erst um 1922/23, nach Ende der bewaffneten Konflikte, nach der vollzogenen Grenzziehung und nach der ökonomischen Stabilisierung der frühen Nachkriegszeit an. Grundsätzlich orientierte sich dieses Programm an den Grundzügen der russischen Agrarreform der Jahre zwischen 1906 und 1914, deren wirtschaftsliberale Logik auf den seinerzeit höchst umstrittenen Ministerpräsidenten Petr A. Stolypin zurückging.

Jeglicher Eigentumsveränderung hatte eine Strukturreform vorauszugehen, die klare Eigentumsverhältnisse schaffen und den schon vorhandenen kleinen Besitz durch die Kraftanstrengung und auf das Risiko der zum Wandel entschlossenen Bauern arrondieren sollte. Dann erst galt eine Eigentumsreform als sinnvoll, die in aller Regel auf den Erwerb, nicht auf die kostenlose Übernahme zuvor enteigneten Besitzes gründete. Was der Großgrundbesitz freiwillig oder durch staatliche Maßnahmen erzwungen auf dem künftigen Bodenmarkt anbot, sollte von den Bauern regulär gekauft und ihren schon ansatzweise rationalisierten Betrieben zugeschlagen werden, damit auf diese Weise mittelgroße, leistungsfähigere Strukturen entstünden.

Dementsprechend bestand die Bodenreform der Zweiten Polnischen Republik aus

- dem Gesetz über die Abschaffung der Servituten vom Januar 1922;[12]

10 Benecke, Ostgebiete, S. 97-104.

11 Boyd, The Marshes of Pinsk, S. 376-395; Ormicki, Życie gospodarcze, passim.

12 DzURP 1922, poz. 65.

- dem Gesetz über die Zusammenlegung landwirtschaftlicher Nutzflächen zur Überwindung der Landzersplitterung vom Juli 1923;[13]
- dem Gesetz zur Parzellierung des Großgrundbesitzes vom Dezember 1925.[14]

Der Begriff des Eigentums sollte in dieser Reform die zentrale Rolle spielen, wenngleich die ökonomische Tradition viele Bauern noch immer vielfach in der Kategorie von Nutzungsrechten denken ließ. Nutzungsrechte betrafen vor allem den einzigen natürlichen Reichtum der Kresy, den Wald. Genau hier gewann die Reform ihre große Dynamik.

Die Erholung der Weltkonjunktur um 1923 spiegelte sich in Ostmitteleuropa in einer steigenden Nachfrage nach Holz wieder. Den Landbesitzern im östlichen Polen war es keineswegs entgangen, dass exportfähiges Holz eine höchst einträgliche Handelsware wurde, die in großen Mengen in den Kresy vorhanden war.[15] Zwar wuchs Polen in den Jahren des ökonomischen Aufschwungs zwischen 1923 und 1929 zu einem der größten Holzexporteure Europas heran, doch es galt zu beachten, dass nur Wald zu schlagen und zu verkaufen war, der frei von den Nutzungsrechten der Bauern war. Dieses Interesse stand generell im Einklang mit dem ersten Reformgesetz vom Januar 1922, ebenso fügte es sich logisch in die Vorgaben des zweiten Reformgesetzes über die Landzusammenlegung ein. Die starke Nachfrage nach Holz und die grundsätzlich gewollte Abschaffung der Nutzungsrechte führte in den 1920er Jahren zu einem bemerkenswert einfachen, auf den ersten Blick für beide Seiten vorteilhaften Geschäft und zu einer florierenden Bodenreform:

Stand den Bauern, die auf ihre Nutzungsrechte an fremdem Eigentum verzichteten, eine materielle Entschädigung, z. B. in Form von Grund und Boden zu, so bot der am Holz interessierte Großgrundbesitz den Bauern gern und großzügig Grund und Boden an, um so schnell wie möglich an die exklusiven und unbeschränkten Besitzrechte des Waldes zu gelangen. Sein Interesse an einer schnellen Verfügbarkeit der exportfähigen Ressource war so groß, dass es sich lohnen konnte, weit mehr als das Mindestmaß an Kompensation in Form von Grund und Boden anzubieten, wenn die Bauern nur schnell und rigoros ihre vorbehaltlichen Rechte aufgaben. War das Nutzungsrecht erst abgelöst, stand einer großflächigen Rodung und dem lukrativen Verkauf der Ressource nichts mehr im Wege.[16]

13 DzURP 1924, poz. 266.

14 DzURP 1926, poz. 1.

15 Barański, Kwestja drzewna w Polsce, S. 45.

16 Tochtermann, Lasy i gospodarka drzewna, S. 35.

Mochten erste besorgte Stimmen begründeterweise vor einer Devastierung der ostpolnischen Wälder warnen,[17] mochten die tauschwilligen Bauern bald nach dem Geschäft die Einsicht erlangen, für ihr generationslanges Nutzungsrecht nun oftmals mit großen aber wenig nutzbaren Flächen abgefunden worden zu sein, so verschaffte doch die zwischen 1923 und 1929 anhaltende Konjunktur vor der Zäsur der Weltwirtschaftskrise der Bodenreform einen gewaltigen Impuls. Der Bodenmarkt umfasste ein großes Angebot an freiwillig abgegebenen Flächen, vermittelte somit der staatlichen Wirtschaftspolitik und den Kleinbauern in Ostpolen eine Phase von Zuversicht und Stabilität, der Gesellschaft eine Zeit der Deeskalation. Die beeindruckende Zahl von über 155.000 ha Grund und Boden ging im Zeitraum bis 1931 in die Hände ehemaliger Nutzer von Servituten über.[18] Gleichzeitig verzeichnete die zeitgenössische Statistik, dass dem massiv zurückgehenden Waldbestand fast überall in den Kresy ein Zuwachs nur an Gras- und Weideflächen, nicht aber an Ackerland gegenüberstand.[19]

Mit dieser bald offensichtlich werdenden Fehlentwicklung ist die Geschichte der Bodenreform in den Kresy der Zweiten Republik bei weitem nicht auserzählt. Tatsächlich aber verlor der Prozess mit dem Einbruch der zweifelhaften Holzkonjunktur sein entscheidendes impulsgebendes Element. Dennoch sollen noch kurz die anderen Elemente der Reform nachgezeichnet werden:

Ein solch wichtiger Faktor wie die Landzusammenlegung beruhte nach dem Gesetz vom Juli 1923 auf dem freiwilligen Entschluss und dem ökonomischen Risiko der beteiligten Bauern, die den aufwändigen Prozess privat zu bezahlen hatten. Allein die geometrische Aufnahme bisher unvermessenen Landes barg ein erhebliches Konfliktpotenzial, erwartete doch ein jeder Bauer für sein gutes Geld eine vorteilhafte Berechnung, die mehr sein sollte als lediglich mathematisch korrekt. Die Landvermesser indes sahen sich ausschließlich genau hierzu verpflichtet, und das für die bäuerlichen Auftraggeber vielfach komplett undurchsichtig-abstrakte Geschäft der Geodäten enttäuschte die wartenden Bauern oft. Neben finanziellen waren es nicht zuletzt mentale Hürden, denen sie sich in einem solchen Prozess zum ersten Mal in ihrem Leben unterzogen. Stießen die Bauern auf städtisch gebildete Fachleute, die sich zudem der polnischen Staatssprache bedienten, waren bald Gerüchten und Spekulationen Tür und Tor geöffnet.[20] Als sich aber die Prozesse in die Länge zogen und die Aussicht auf

17 Na marginesie, S. 185-188; Broda, Dzieje lasów, leśnictwa i drzewnictwa, S. 329.

18 Roczniki Statystyczne 1924-1938.

19 Roczniki Statystyczne 1923-1931.

20 Tarasiewicz, Scalenie w powiecie brasławskim, S. 225-242; Krzysztofik, Jasienówka, S. 90.

schnelle Verbesserung der materiellen Situation angesichts des Konjunktureinbruches verfinsterte, wagten immer weniger Berechtigte, die Landzusammensetzung anzustoßen. Auch dieses – an sich gut durchdachte Element einer echten Strukturreform – erfüllte sich nicht im erwarteten Maße.

Die Aufteilung des Großgrundbesitzes als Schlussstein der Reform verlor zusehends an Bedeutung. Die tatsächlich stattgehabte Parzellierung von Großgrundbesitz kam – gänzlich anders etwa als im ehemaligen preußischen Teilungsgebiet – weitgehend ohne staatliche Zwangsmaßnahmen aus. In den Jahren guter Konjunktur war ohnedies mehr Land auf dem Markt, als die Reformwilligen aufzunehmen in der Lage gewesen wären. Letztlich fehlte der als Abschluss der Reform gedachten Parzellierung der Unterbau einer modernisierten bäuerlichen Besitzstruktur. Griff der Staat tatsächlich zum allemal vorhandenen Mittel einer amtsseitig angeordneten Parzellierung von Grundbesitz, so orientierte er sich hierbei nicht an nationalen Kategorien. Solche Eingriffe verschonten den zumeist polnischen Großgrundbesitz keineswegs, sie markierten aber keinen wirklichen Substanzverlust. Es kam im Ergebnis weder zu einer nachhaltigen strukturellen Modernisierung, noch zu einem Ausgleich der disparaten Eigentumsverhältnisse.[21]

Insgesamt lässt sich die Geschichte der Bodenreform in den Kresy Wschodnie kaum anders als eine Geschichte des endlichen Scheiterns erzählen. Es existieren verlässliche Angaben dazu, dass die ostpolnische Landwirtschaft am Ende der 1930er Jahre eher weniger effektiv produzierte als zu Beginn des Projektes. Das Scheitern aber war auf die skizzierten ökonomischen Probleme zurückzuführen. Ganz gewiss war diese Bodenreform – weder in der Zeit ihrer Erfolge, noch in der Phase der Misserfolge – nicht der Logik eines national konnotierten Besitzstandskonfliktes geschuldet.

3. Das Beispiel der Konfessionspolitik gegenüber der orthodoxen Kirche

Es entspricht einer durchaus berechtigten Tradition, die Geschichte der Zweiten Polnischen Republik als die Geschichte des Umgangs mit nationalen und konfessionellen Minderheiten zu erzählen. Nach der 1921 abgeschlossenen Grenzziehung ließ sich davon ausgehen, dass ein Anteil von deutlich über 30% der Bevölkerung des neuen Staates sich einer anderen als der polnischen Nation zuordnete. Nationale Zugehörigkeit galt hierbei in manchen Regionen des

21 Benecke, Ostgebiete, S. 117-122.

Landes als durchaus weniger wichtig als das religiöse und konfessionelle Bekenntnis. Die orthodoxen Christen machten mit 2,9 Millionen Gläubigen etwa 10% der Gesamtbevölkerung aus. Mit Ausnahme der UdSSR lebte in keinem Staat Europas eine derart große indigene Bevölkerungsgruppe russisch-orthodoxer Konfession. Nach den Unierten und den Juden waren die Orthodoxen somit die drittgrößte konfessionelle Minderheit Polens, ihr geographischer Schwerpunkt lag in den Kresy Wschodnie.[22] Ohne Zweifel war das Verhältnis zwischen der hier präsenten russisch-orthodoxen Kirche einerseits und der Polnischen Republik andererseits gespannt und voller Brisanz. Das konnte nach den Jahren der Teilungsherrschaft, in denen sich das Russische Imperium zur Sicherung seiner Dominanz auch rigider kirchenpolitischer Schritte bedient hatte, kaum anders sein. Nicht zu vergessen ist in dieser Hinsicht, dass die Territorien der östlichen Wojewodschaften nicht zum 1815 etablierten Königreich Polen gehört hatten, wo es – der plakativen und viel beschriebenen Russifizierungsmaßnahmen des langen 19. Jahrhunderts zum Trotz – zwischen 1815 und 1915 doch so etwas wie eine noch nicht ganz eliminierte Sonderstellung Polens im Zarenreich gegeben hatte. Die Kresy waren gewissermaßen Polens viertes Teilungsgebiet, da hier die Sonderrechte des Kongresskönigreiches nie gegolten hatten. Das betraf auch die Position der Orthodoxie.

Für das Zählungsjahr 1924 ergab sich der folgende orthodoxe Bevölkerungsanteil:

- Wojewodschaft Wilno: 13%
- Wojewodschaft Nowogródek: 34,6%
- Wojewodschaft Polesie: 85,4%
- Wojewodschaft Wołyń: 75,2%

Bildeten die Orthodoxen landesweit die drittgrößte konfessionelle Minderheit, waren sie also in weiten Teilen der Kresy in der massiven Mehrheit.[23]

Zu den beeindruckenden Zahlen gesellte sich das sichtbare kulturelle Erbe der aus polnischer Sicht endlich überwundenen russischen Herrschaft: Die orthodoxe Kirche war ihrer Tradition gemäß fest auf den Synod, seit 1917 auf das wiederhergestellte Patriarchat von Moskau fixiert. Gerade die tiefen Umbrüche der Revolutionen von 1917 ließ den in den Kresy verbliebenen oder dorthin zurückgekehrten Klerus und seine Gläubigen ihren Halt in der Treue zur Mutterkirche suchen, die in Russland unter den existenzbedrohenden Druck der

22 Papierzyńska-Turek, Między tradycją a rzeczywistością, S. 310.
23 Papierzyńska-Turek, Między tradycją a rzeczywistością, S. 310.

Kommunisten geraten war. Keine andere als die russische Sprache galt als *lingua franca* in den Bereichen von Kultur und Bildung, und es galt – nun mehr denn je – die Nähe zum polnisch konnotierten Katholizismus zu scheuen. Wenngleich die Verfassung der Polnischen Republik die Religionsfreiheit garantierte, ließen sich alle Elemente eines zu erwartenden Kulturkampfes finden. Dass dieser zum großen Teil ausblieb, ist eine der wenigen, wenn nicht die einzige, kontinuierlich befolgte politische Leitlinie der polnischen Minderheitenpolitik zwischen 1921 und 1939 gewesen.

Ohne Zweifel versuchte die römisch-katholische Kirche nach 1921 verloren gegangenen materiellen Besitzstand für sich wiederzuerlangen. Rückgabeforderungen bezogen sich vor allem auf ehemals unierte und römisch-katholische Kirchen, und besonders im letztgenannten Fall unterstützte der Staat die Forderungen der *una sancta* massiv, wenn auch nicht vorbehaltlos.[24] Bereits in dieser Frage zeichnete sich jene Linie ab, die die staatliche Politik gegenüber der orthodoxen Kirche bis 1939 kennzeichnen sollte: Der Druck auf die Orthodoxie sollte spürbar hoch, nicht aber existenzgefährdend gehalten werden. Der Staat hatte ein Interesse an einer relativ schwachen, abhängigen und steuerbaren orthodoxen Kirche, nicht aber an ihrer Vernichtung. Er brauchte sie in den problematischen Ostwojewodschaften zur Aufrechterhaltung der öffentlichen Ordnung, und er konnte darauf bauen, dass ihm die Orthodoxie gerade angesichts der gnadenlosen Antikirchenpolitik der sowjetischen Staatsmacht ein gutes Stück des Weges entgegenkam. Der Kompromiss sollte funktionieren.

Ein zentrales Interesse hatte die Polnische Republik daran, die Unterstellung der orthodoxen Gemeinden auf ihrem Territorium unter das Moskauer Zentrum aufzuheben und Klerus wie Gläubigen klarzumachen, dass künftig für sie die Uhren nach Warschauer, nicht Moskauer Zeit zu gehen hatten. Mit viel diplomatischem Geschick und unter Nutzung der nach 1918 neu entstandenen Situation der orthodoxen Gemeinden in ganz Ostmitteleuropa gelang es der polnischen Außenpolitik, den Segen des ökumenischen Patriarchen von Konstantinopel, Meletios IV., zur Begründung einer Autokephalie der auf polnischem Boden existierenden Orthodoxie zu erwirken. Am 17. September 1925 verkündeten Vertreter des Patriarchen in der orthodoxen Warschauer Marienkathedrale den entscheidenden Tomos über die Etablierung der neuen Kirchenstruktur. Mochte die von Moskau losgelöste autokephale Kirche auch nicht generell akzeptiert

---

24 Papierzyńska-Turek, Między tradycją a rzeczywistością, S. 343.

worden sein, so war sie doch von einer unbestritten berufenen und ernst zu nehmenden Instanz proklamiert worden.[25]

In dieser neuen Ordnung hatte sich der Staat maßgebliche Eingriffsrechte vorbehalten. Diese betrafen nicht nur, wie oben bereits gezeigt, Entscheidungsbefugnisse über den materiellen Besitz der autokephalen orthodoxen Kirche in Polen, der Staat nutzte noch andere Hebel, um seine Vorstellungen einer loyalen Orthodoxie durchzusetzen. Hierzu gehörte die Frage der staatsbürgerlichen Rechte der Priester, die vielfach im Zuge des russischen Rückzuges ab 1915 das Land verlassen hatten und nun in Bürgerkriegs- und Nachkriegszeiten zurückgekehrt waren. Oftmals war ihre Staatsangehörigkeit nicht geklärt, und die Behörden verstanden sich meisterhaft darauf, die Entscheidung hierüber zu verkomplizieren und in die Länge zu ziehen. Zeugnisse der Loyalität vermochten natürlich, einzelne positive Entscheidungen zu begünstigen und zu beschleunigen.[26]

Auf der anderen Seite garantierte der Staat der neuen Kirche ein von ihm selbst definiertes Mindestmaß an Besitz, Kompetenzen und Sicherheit. Das betraf auch den Gebrauch der russischen Sprache in den Diensten der orthodoxen Kirche, den die Republik nicht maßgeblich behinderte, wenngleich sie sonst alles dafür tat, dieses offensichtliche Relikt der Teilungszeit aus dem öffentlichen Leben verschwinden zu lassen. Es ist bezeichnend, dass die rechtlich verbindliche Fixierung der Position der Orthodoxen Kirche in der Polnischen Republik erst durch zwei Dekrete aus dem Jahre 1938, das „Äußere Statut"[27] und das „Innere Statut"[28], erfolgte.

Großen Wert legte der Staat darauf, die autokephale Orthodoxie in den nördlichen Kresy Wschodnie nicht unter den Einfluss der mächtigen und auch in weltlich-politischen Belangen gut organisierten Unierten Kirche in den südöstlichen, einst zum Habsburgerreich gehörenden Wojewodschaften gelangen zu lassen. Der Staat, nicht eine verwandte, dem Staat kritisch gegenüberstehende Glaubensgemeinschaft, sollte der zentrale Bezugspunkt der Autokephalie sein. Ihr ließ der Staat nach eigenem Dafürhalten das Nötigste zum Leben, weil er an ihrem Sterben kein Interesse hatte. Es gibt schlechterdings keine Phase in der Geschichte der Zweiten Republik, in der es zu ernst zu nehmenden Spannungen zwischen den ungleichen Partnern gekommen wäre.

---

25 Benecke, Ostgebiete, S. 203f.

26 AAN, MWRiOP, 1247, 14; Iz pečati.

27 DzURP 1938, poz. 597.

28 DzURP 1938, poz. 679.

Diese These lässt sich auch dann aufrechterhalten, wenn man die Augen nicht vor dem am stärksten plakativen und schmachvollsten Kapitel der polnischen Minderheitenpolitik der Zwischenkriegsjahre verschließt: vor den Kirchenzerstörungen von 1938 in der Region Chełm.

Der Tod Marschall Piłsudskis im Mai 1935 markiert die größte Zäsur der polnischen Innenpolitik vor 1939. Der sofort einsetzende staatlich geförderte Kult um Józef Piłsudski war ein hohles Trugbild: Nie wurde der Name des verdienten Staatsgründers lauter gepriesen als nach 1935, nie aber wurden die politischen Konzepte seiner eingeschworenen Gegner schamloser in die Tat umgesetzt als jetzt. Das schlug sich auch in der Politik gegenüber den Orthodoxen nieder. In den Jahren nach seinem Tod formierte sich der Gedanke einer „Wiedergewinnung der Seelen", mithin also einer Wiedererweckung vermeintlich oder tatsächlich verschütteter polnischer und katholischer Traditionen unter einer nur oberflächlich zur Orthodoxie übergetretenen Bevölkerung.[29] Der Fokus dieser Idee war vor allem auf die Region um die Stadt Chełm in der Wojewodschaft Lublin gerichtet, die in der Tat ein sehr spezifisches Erbe trug und trägt: Im März 1875 war die unierte Diözese Chełm als letzte auf ehemals polnischem Boden gewaltsam in den russischen Staatskirchenapparat hineingezwungen worden. Zum Teil unter Einsatz großer militärischer und polizeilicher Gewaltmittel waren die unierten Gläubigen gezwungen worden, „echte" Orthodoxe zu werden und den unierten Traditionen zu entsagen. Die Gläubigen widersetzten sich der Zwangskonversion und leisteten einen zivilen Widerstand, der die große Aufmerksamkeit internationaler zeitgenössischer Beobachter erweckte und bis heute ein Topos der polnischen Literatur und Geschichtsschreibung ist. Die ganze Oberflächlichkeit dieses Unterfangens zeigte sich im Jahre 1905, als die Verkündung des Toleranzediktes die große Mehrheit der zwangsweise zu Orthodoxen Gewordenen wieder zur katholischen Kirche übertreten ließ.[30]

Nach 1921 fand sich immerhin noch ein Anteil von etwa 10% der hier ansässigen Gläubigen in den Gemeinden der orthodoxen Kirche wieder, doch ihr Bekenntnis galt – angesichts der Ereignisse zwischen 1875 und 1905 – als weniger tief im Volk verwurzelt als in den eigentlichen Kresy Wschodnie. Die Anhänger der „Wiedergewinnung der Seelen", unter ihnen einflussreiche Militärs der zweiten und dritten Entscheidungsebene, gedachten, im Sommer 1938 ein Exempel statuieren zu müssen und beseitigten jene orthodoxen Strukturen, die ihrer Mission entgegenstanden: Feuerwehren und Pioniereinheiten der

29 Stawecki, Następcy Komendanta, S. 190f.

30 Kania, Likwidacja cerkwi, S. 50-89.

Armee zerstörten in diesem Sommer des letzten Friedensjahres 91 orthodoxe Kirchen, zehn Kapellen und 26 Bethäuser.[31] Nichts war seinerzeit geeigneter, Polens Namen in der Weltöffentlichkeit auf das Gründlichste zu diskreditieren.[32] Am Ende blieb dieser brutale Auswuchs eine traurige Ausnahme, diese aber dominiert bisweilen bis heute das gängige Bild von Polens Umgang mit seiner orthodoxen Minderheit. Zu Unrecht.

Die skizzierten drei Beispiele markierten wichtige Stationen, die Polens Weg aus dem Krieg ausmachten, bei weitem beschrieben sie nicht den ganzen Weg. Das Gezeigte weist – etwa am Beispiel des schnellen Aufbaus der Beamtenschaft – rationale und m. E. nachvollziehbare Sicherheitsinteressen auf, die dem kurzsichtigen, halbherzigen und gefährlichen Experiment der Militärkolonisation durchaus abzusprechen sind. Es umfasst das konsequente Fortführen nicht eben populärer, aber ökonomisch durchdachter Reformansätze im Bereich der Landfrage, die nach kurzlebigem Erfolg ihre brandgefährliche Eigendynamik entfalteten. Dieser wurde der Staat nicht mehr Herr. Und es verweist auf die einzige konsequente Leitlinie der Minderheitenpolitik vor 1939, die sich die Schwäche der einstmals dominanten Kraft der russisch-orthodoxen Kirche zunutze machte, sie klug nach den Maßstäben von Aufwand und Nutzen führte und von ihrer Deeskalation profitierte.

Literaturverzeichnis

AAN = Archiwum Akt Nowych, Warszawa.

Arner Boyd, Louise The Marshes of Pinsk, in: The Geographical Review, XXVI (1936), S. 376-395.

Barański, Władysław Kwestja drzewna w Polsce, Warschau 1928.

Benecke, Werner Die Ostgebiete der Zweiten Polnischen Republik. Staatsmacht und öffentliche Ordnung in einer Minderheitenregion 1918-1939 (Beiträge zur Geschichte Osteuropas 29), Köln 1999.

Bocian, Franciszek Osadnictwo wojskowe, in: Rocznik Ziem Wschodnich 1 (1935), S. 271-276.

Broda, Józef (Hg.) Dzieje lasów, leśnictwa i drzewnictwa w Polsce, Warszawa 1965.

Brzozowski, Czesław Akcja osadnictwa wojskowego na Kresach Wschodnich (Praca dyplomowa SGH), Warszawa 1938.

31 Stawecki, Następcy Komendanta, S. 193f.

32 Soborny, The Truth About Poland, S. 1f.

DzURP = Dziennik Ustaw Rzeczypospolitej Polskiej.

Funkcjonariusze państwowej służby cywilnej. Wyniki spisu ze stycznia 1923 r., Warszawa 1925. = Statystyka Polski; VI.

Iz pečati, in: Voskresnoe Čtenie 1 (1924), Nr. 30.

Kania, Janusz Likwidacja cerkwi na Lubelszczyżnie w okresie miedzywojennym, in: Chrześcijanin w świecie XIV (1982), Nr. 108, S. 50-89.

Kon, Feliks Zapadnaja Belorussija. Kolonija panskoj Pol'ši, Moskva 1928.

Krzysztofik, Wincenty Jasienówka wieś powiatu sokólskiego. Monografja ze szczególnym uwzględnieniem zmian wywołanych komasacją gruntów, Poznań 1934.

Landau, Zbigniew/Tomaszewski, Jerzy Gospodarka Polski Międzywojennej w czterech tomach (tom I).W dobie inflacji 1918-1923, Warszawa 1967.

LP = Las Polski. Organ Związku Zawodowego Leśnikow w Rzeczypospolitej Polskiej.

Marquardt, Werner Wehr- und Militärsiedlung in den polnischen Ostmarken, in: Reichsplanung 2 (1936), S. 46-50.

MWRiOP = Ministerstwo Wyznań Religijnych i Oświecenia Publicznego.

Na marginesie rozporządzenia o zniesieniu służebności, in: LP 1927, S. 185-188.

Ormicki, Wiktor Życie gospodarcze Kresów Wschodnich, Kraków 1929.

Papierzyńska-Turek, Mirosława Między tradycją a rzeczywistością. Państwo i kościoł prawosławny w Polsce w latach 1918-1939, Warszawa 1989.

Rocznik Statystyczny Rzeczypospolitej Polskiej, Warszawa 1920-1939.

Stawecki, Piotr Następcy Komendanta. Wojsko a polityka wewnętrzna Drugiej Rzeczypospolitej w latach 1935-1939, Warszawa 1969.

Soborny, V./Bukata, Walter The Truth About Poland. A Nation That Perverts The Principles of National Self-Determination to Further Her Imperialistic Designs Upon Other Nations, New York 1938.

Tarasiewicz, Olgierd Scalenie w powieie brasławskim, in: Rocznik Nauk Rolniczych i Leśnych 38 (1937), S. 225-342.

Tochtermann, Jan Jerzy Lasy i gospodarka drzewna Ziem Północno-Wschodnich, Warszawa 1938.

Tomaszewski, Jerzy Z dziejów Polesia 1921-1939. Zarys stosunków społeczno-ekonomicznych, Warszawa 1963.

Christian Müller

Friedenschance oder taktisches Manöver? Der Vorschlag einer Friedenskonferenz für Russland auf Prinkipo 1918/1919

Am 8. Januar 1918 formulierte der amerikanische Präsident Woodrow Wilson sein berühmtes 14-Punkte-Programm vor dem amerikanischen Kongress in Washington, D.C. Ein Jahr später prägte dieses die Pariser Friedenskonferenz; zwei Jahre später erhielt Wilson den Friedensnobelpreis für seinen vierzehnten Punkt, der zur Gründung des Völkerbundes führte.[1] Doch Wilsons sechster Punkt, die Beilegung aller Fragen, die Russland betrafen, konnte in Paris nicht ansatzweise umgesetzt werden. Stattdessen schwebte Russland im Winter 1918/1919 wie ein Gespenst über Paris und der Welt. Zwar war der ehemalige Verbündete nach zwei Revolutionen und einem Friedensschluss mit den Mittelmächten aus dem Krieg und der Entente vorzeitig ausgeschieden; doch in Russland herrschte ein Bürgerkrieg zwischen den Bolschewiki, der Weißen Armee und neu gegründeten Nachfolgestaaten, wobei deutsche und alliierte Soldaten das Chaos noch verschärften. So klagte – und rechtfertigte sich später – Lloyd George: „Russia was a jungle in which no one could say what was within a few yards of him".[2]

Die russische Frage schien unlösbar – bis der Vorschlag einer Friedenskonferenz auf der Insel Prinkipo (türkisch: Büyükada, griechisch: Prinkipos) im Marmarameer aufkam. Nach den Plänen der Alliierten sollten dort sämtliche Parteien des Russischen Bürgerkriegs zusammenkommen und unter alliierter Vermittlung ihre Konflikte beilegen. Aber die Prinkipo-Konferenz kam nie zustande. Stattdessen wurde der Vorschlag nach wenigen Wochen verworfen – nach heftigen Diskussionen und erheblichen diplomatischen Verwicklungen. Frieden in Russland und auch die Anerkennung neu gegründeter Staaten, z. B. im Baltikum, rückten somit in weite Ferne.

Dieser Beitrag geht anhand von ausgewählten diplomatischen Dokumenten der Alliierten der Frage nach, warum und an wem die Idee der Prinkipo-Konferenz gescheitert ist. Die *British Documents on Foreign Affairs* und die

---

1 Cooper, Woodrow Wilson, S. 575f.

2 Lloyd George, The Truth about the Peace Treaties, S. 326f.

Papers Relating to the Foreign Relations of the United States sind daher wichtige Quellen dieser Arbeit.[3] Weitere wichtige Quellendokumente sind die Memoiren von Winston Churchill sowie die Protokolle des britischen Kriegskabinetts, in denen ebenfalls auf die Prinkipo-Konferenz eingegangen wird.[4]

Eine Publikation des sowjetischen Diplomaten Boris E. Štejn über das angebliche Versagen alliierter Russlandpolitik auf der Pariser Friedenskonferenz hat in den 1950er-Jahren auch westliche Historiker auf die Prinkipo-Konferenz aufmerksam gemacht.[5] Es ist daher auch kein Zufall, dass ein Großteil von Autoren, wie John M. Thompson, Richard K. Debo, Arno J. Mayer und Richard H. Ullman, ihre Ergebnisse bereits vor Jahrzehnten publiziert haben.[6] Eine aktuelle Forschungsdiskussion über die Prinkipo-Konferenz ist daher kaum vorhanden, auch weil das Thema seit dem Zerfall der Sowjetunion in den Hintergrund gerückt ist.

1. „Audiatur et altera pars" – Das Friedensangebot der Bolschewiki an die Alliierten

Als die *George Washington* mit Woodrow Wilson an Bord die französische Hafenstadt Brest erreichte, empfing ihn eine begeisterte Menschenmenge mit Sprechchören wie „Vive l'Amérique! Vive Wilson!"[7] Der Bürgermeister von Brest begrüßte Wilson sogar als „Apostel der Freiheit" und auch an anderen Orten wie London und Rom „wurde ihm jeweils ein ähnlicher Empfang zuteil."[8] Der Optimismus und die Hoffnung auf eine bessere Zukunft, die Wilson personifizierte, war in jenen Tagen in Westeuropa allgegenwärtig.

Die Nachricht von Wilsons Ankunft in Europa sorgte selbst bei den antiliberalen Bolschewiki für vorsichtigen Optimismus, endlich mit den Alliierten in direkte Verhandlungen zu treten. Dabei spielten die Bolschewiki ein doppeltes

---

3 BDFA, Teil II, Reihe I (The Paris Peace Conference of 1919), Band 1 (Preparations for the Conference and Early Meetings); FRUS 1919 (Russia).

4 CAB 23/42, British Imperial War Cabinet Minutes (13.08.1918-31.12.1918); CAB 23/9, British Imperial War Cabinet Minutes (08.01.1919-31.03.1919); CHURCHILL, The World Crisis.

5 ŠTEJN, Die „Russische Frage" auf der Pariser Friedenskonferenz 1919-1920.

6 THOMPSON, Russia, Bolshevism, and the Versailles Peace; DEBO, Survival and Consolidation; MAYER, Politics and Diplomacy of Peacemaking; ULLMAN, Britain and the Russian Civil War.

7 MACMILLAN, Paris 1919, S. 15.

8 MANELA, Die Morgenröte einer neuen Ära, S. 28.

Spiel: Einerseits agierten sie aus ideologischen Gründen gegen die als Imperialisten gebrandmarkten Westmächte – was wiederum „einen kaum überwindbaren Graben zwischen den beiden Lagern schuf."[9] Andererseits planten die Bolschewiki, mit den Alliierten – ähnlich wie zuvor mit den Mittelmächten in Brest-Litovsk – durch Verhandlungen einen Frieden Zeit zu gewinnen, um auswärtige Bedrohungen beenden und innere Probleme lösen zu können.[10] Dieser Frieden hätte seinen Preis, aber wie Brest-Litovsk zeigt, waren die Bolschewiki zu erheblichen Zugeständnissen bereit,[11] die für sie angesichts der bevorstehenden kommunistischen Weltrevolution aber nur vorübergehender Natur wären. Die alliierten Militärinterventionen in Murmansk, Vladivostok und Archangel'sk führten im August 1918 jedoch dazu, dass alliierte Bürger im Machtbereich der Bolschewiki festgesetzt wurden.[12] Zusätzlich landeten im November 1918 französische, griechische und polnische Truppen in der Schwarzmeerstadt Odessa.[13] Die informellen Gesprächskanäle zu den Alliierten waren durch diese militärischen Unternehmungen erheblich belastet; es gab aber noch neutrale Staaten, über welche die Bolschewiki weiterhin den Kontakt suchten. So versuchte im Oktober der Volkskommissar für Auswärtige Angelegenheiten, Georgij Vasil'evič Čičerin, mit den Alliierten über Norwegen und Schweden in Kontakt zu treten.[14] Beide Länder fungierten seit August 1918 *de facto* als Schutzmächte für alliierte Interessen in Russland und beherbergten alliierte Sondergesandte sowie ein dichtes Netz alliierter Nachrichtendienste.[15] Nachdem aber seine Bemühungen erneut ergebnislos geblieben waren, schickte der zunehmend ungeduldige Čičerin Anfang Dezember 1918 eine diplomatische Mission unter der Führung seines Stellvertreters Maksim Maksimovič Litvinov

9 Buzinkai, The Bolsheviks, the League of Nations and the Paris Peace Conference, S. 257.

10 Thompson, Russia, S. 88.

11 Siehe Sharp, The Versailles Settlement, S. 157. Hier werden die unmittelbaren Auswirkungen des Friedensschlusses von Brest-Litovsk auf die Bolschewiki verdeutlicht: Russland verlor u.a. Gebiete von Finnland bis in den Kaukasus, 26 Prozent seiner Bevölkerung, 28 Prozent seiner Industriekapazitäten, 75 Prozent seiner Kohle- und Eisenreserven und 37 Prozent seiner Getreidekapazitäten,

12 Debo, The Manuilskii Mission, S. 215f. Richard K. Debo berichtet hier auch von französisch-russischen Geheimverhandlungen, die allerdings sehr schleppend verliefen.

13 Conze, Die große Illusion, S. 305.

14 Debo, Survival and Consolidation, S. 23.

15 Debo, Survival and Consolidation, S. 25f.; Debo, The Manuilskii Mission, S. 217.

nach Stockholm.[16] Allerdings konnte auch Litvinov anfangs nicht direkt mit den Alliierten sprechen und verlegte daher seine Bemühungen darauf, Kontakte zur alliierten Presse zu knüpfen.[17]

Dies änderte sich mit Wilsons Ankunft in Europa. Litvinov ging nun in die Offensive: Zunächst schickte er am 23. Dezember einen Brief an die amerikanischen, britischen, französischen und italienischen Gesandten in Stockholm.[18] Litvinov nannte sich nun „Bevollmächtigter der Russisch-Föderativen Republik der Sowjets" und wollte verhandeln:

> „The Sixth All Russian Congress of Soviets of November last reflecting the sincere desire of the Russian toiling masses to live in undisturbed peace and friendship with all the people of the world addressed to the governments of the Allied powers a formal offer of peace. […] I am told to inform you that I have been authorized by the Soviet Government to enter into preliminary peace negotiations with representative[s] of the Allied countries should their Governments reciprocate the desire of the Russian Republic of a peaceful settlement of all the outstanding questions which may give rise to a continuation of hostilities between the countries concerned."[19]

Doch Litvinov beließ es dieses Mal nicht nur bei einem Schreiben an die eher zögerlichen Gesandten in Stockholm. Stattdessen schrieb Litvinov an Heiligabend 1918 einen persönlichen Brief an Woodrow Wilson, in dem er Friedensverhandlungen zwischen den Alliierten und den Bolschewiki auf Augenhöhe forderte und an Wilsons Liberalismus, Pazifismus und Gerechtigkeitssinn appellierte.[20] Litvinovs Wunsch nach Verhandlungen ohne Vorurteile gipfelt in dem lateinischen Satz *„audiatur et altera pars"* – auch die andere Seite möge gehört werden.[21] Der Zeitpunkt für den Brief war gut gewählt, da ein Treffen zwischen Woodrow Wilson und den britischen Kabinettsmitgliedern für den 26. Dezember in London geplant war[22] – und gerade in Großbritannien hatten Litvinovs Bemühungen Eindruck hinterlassen.

Denn die stetigen Bemühungen der Bolschewiki, mit den Alliierten in Verhandlungen zu treten, waren Lloyd George und dem britischen Kriegskabinett nicht verborgen geblieben. In der Kabinettssitzung vom 23. Dezember 1918

---

16 Mayer, Politics and Diplomacy of Peacemaking, S. 422.

17 Thompson, Russia, S. 89. Der Autor erwähnt z. B. ein Interview mit der *Daily News* aus London.

18 Mayer, Politics and Diplomacy of Peacemaking, S. 422.

19 FRUS 1919 (Russia), S. 1.

20 Debo, Survival and Consolidation, S. 26.

21 Thompson, Russia, S. 90f.

22 Anderson, Die baltische Frage, S. 338.

sorgte Litvinovs Friedensvorschlag daher für Diskussionen – und für die Bildung von politischen Fronten, die ihre gegensätzliche Russlandpolitik auf der Pariser Friedenskonferenz wenige Wochen später weiter austragen sollten. Zwar war seit November 1918 ein britisches Marinegeschwader in der Ostsee aktiv, um die baltischen Staaten in ihrem Unabhängigkeitskrieg gegen russische Verbände („russische Westarmee") und deutsche Freikorps zu unterstützen.[23] Aber einer Gruppe um Winston Churchill ging dieser Schritt nicht weit genug; sie forderte eine großflächige Intervention in Russland, während sich der britische Außenminister Lord Balfour für Verhandlungen mit den Bolschewiki aussprach – allerdings auf informeller Ebene, um die Weißen Armeen, die Großbritannien im Bürgerkrieg unterstützte, nicht zu entmutigen.[24] Lloyd George, der wie Wilson von Litvinovs Friedensangebot überaus angetan war,[25] ging sogar noch einen Schritt weiter und signalisierte Verhandlungsbereitschaft auf Augenhöhe, auch wegen der großen finanziellen, militärischen und politischen Risiken einer großflächigen Intervention in Russland.[26] Diese Linie setzte sich schließlich durch und wurde in der Sitzung des Kriegskabinetts vom 30. Dezember 1918 bekräftigt. Diese Sitzung markiert den Beginn der Idee einer Konferenz auf der Insel Prinkipo, da hier erstmals die Idee einer Zusammenkunft aller Bürgerkriegsparteien und Nachfolgestaaten geäußert wurde.[27] Die Details blieben noch offen, aber diese Idee des kanadischen Premierministers Sir Robert Borden konkretisierte den Vorschlag nach Verhandlungen auf Augenhöhe.[28] Lloyd George, dessen Linie sich durchgesetzt hatte, war mit den Beratungen zufrieden und am 31. Dezember rückte das Kabinett von einer militärischen Intervention in Russland ab – oder wie es das australische Kabinettsmitglied Sir Joseph Cook ausdrückte: „[Our general policy should be that as] walling off a fire in a mine."[29] Auch wenn man den Weißen materielle und politische Unterstützung gegen die Bolschewiki nicht versagte, war man nun an einer nachhaltigen Beilegung des Bürgerkriegs interessiert. Man wollte also, um bei Cooks Metapher zu bleiben, verhindern, dass das Feuer, die kommunistische Revolution im „russischen Bergwerk" weiter loderte und die Oberfläche, also die gesamte Welt, erreichte.

---

23 Bradley, L'intervention alliée dans les états Baltes, S. 75f. Die britische Marineintervention in der Ostsee wurde auch im Jahr 1919 aufrechterhalten.

24 Debo, Survival and Consolidation, S. 26f.

25 Kennan, Russia and the Versailles Conference, S. 16.

26 CAB 23/42, Sitzung vom 23. Dezember 1918 um 11 Uhr, S. 8.

27 Debo, Survival and Consolidation, S. 27; Thompson, Russia, S. 93f.

28 CAB 23/42, Sitzung vom 30. Dezember 1918 um 15.30 Uhr, S. 8.

29 CAB 23/42, Sitzung vom 31. Dezember 1918 um 11 Uhr, S. 5.

2. Der Weg zur Prinkipo-Konferenz

Die amerikanische Regierung arbeitete in den folgenden Tagen und Wochen eng mit der britischen Regierung in der Russland-Frage zusammen. So vereinbarte am 1. Januar 1919 die amerikanische Delegation in Paris, den amerikanischen Diplomaten W. H. Buckler nach Skandinavien zu schicken, um Litvinov persönlich zu treffen.[30] Nur einen Tag später schickte die britische Regierung an sämtliche alliierte und assoziierte Staaten Telegramme, in denen sie vorschlug, dass die Alliierten gemeinsam zu einer Waffenruhe in Russland aufrufen sollten.[31] Sollte diese zustande kommen, könne man auf einer Friedenskonferenz, z. B. in Paris, zusammenkommen. Einige wollten jedoch nicht warten: So drängte Colville Barclay, der britische Chargé d'Affaires in Washington, D.C., alle russischen Bürgerkriegsparteien sofort einzuladen, um zu verhindern, dass u.a. die baltischen Staaten, die besonders bedroht waren, noch vor Beginn der Konferenz zerfielen („some immediate action of this kind would appear to be necessary without awaiting the meeting of the Powers at Paris").[32] Doch britische und amerikanische Diplomaten wollten damit bis zum Beginn der Pariser Friedenskonferenz warten und hielten Barclays Nachricht zurück, um die eigenen Verbündeten nicht zu überrumpeln.[33] Denn diese hatten bereits Kritik an dem Vorpreschen in der Russland-Frage geübt. Über Wilsons Pressesprecher Joseph Patrick Tumulty waren die ursprünglich diskret behandelten anglo-amerikanischen Friedenspläne an die Presse durchgesickert.[34] So kritisierte der ehemalige zarische Außenminister Sergej Sazonov die Idee einer Russland-Konferenz unter Einbeziehung der Bolschewiki scharf; der französische Außenminister Stephen Pichon machte unmissverständlich deutlich:

> „Si les Alliés avaient la faiblesse et l'imprudence d'agir ainsi, ils démentiraient en premier lieu les principes de justice et de droit qui font leur force et leur honneur, et donneraient à la propagande bolchevique dans le monde une puissance et une extension dont ils risqueraient d'être les premières victimes. Le gouvernement français, quant à lui, ne pactisera pas avec le crime."[35]

---

30 Mayer, Politics and Diplomacy of Peacemaking, S. 424.
31 Thompson, Russia, S. 94f.
32 FRUS 1919 (Russia), S. 2.
33 FRUS 1919 (Russia), S. 6f.
34 Neilson, That elusive entity British policy in Russia, S. 80.
35 Dokument 421, DDF Armistices et Paix (1918-1920), Band 1 (1918/19), S. 607f.

Frankreich würde die „anglo-amerikanische Friedensoffensive" also nicht unterstützen. Als dann auch noch *L'Humanité*, das Sprachrohr der französischen Sozialisten, diese negative Reaktion der französischen Regierung fast wortwörtlich veröffentlichte, war die erhoffte Einigkeit der Alliierten dahin, die Buckler Litvinov in Stockholm suggerieren sollte.[36] Nun musste die Pariser Friedenskonferenz diese Differenzen aus dem Weg räumen.

Erste Debatten auf der Pariser Friedenskonferenz

Jeder schaute also jetzt nach Paris, wo Großbritannien, Italien, Frankreich und die USA ihre eigene Friedenskonferenz vorbereiteten. Die russische Frage bereitete dabei erhebliche Probleme: „It seemed unthinkable that the conference should leave the future of such a vast area of Europe unresolved, yet the alternative presupposed an acknowledged and authorised power with which to deal."[37] So hatten sich die Alliierten auch noch nicht entschieden, ob Russland einen Platz auf der Konferenz erhalten sollte. Mit Polen war lediglich ein Nachfolgestaat des Zarenreiches offiziell zugelassen – teils, weil die Alliierten bereits Polen vor der Konferenz als unabhängigen Staat anerkannt hatten; teils, weil polnische Politiker und Intellektuelle wie Dmowski und Paderewski sehr effektive Lobbyarbeit betrieben hatten.[38] Weitere Nachfolgestaaten wie Finnland, Estland oder Lettland blieben außen vor. Lord Balfour hatte im Dezember überlegt, sie nicht doch einzuladen, war aber an Lloyd George gescheitert, der entgegnete, „das sei unmöglich, sofern nicht auch Sowjetrussland eingeladen werde."[39] Die baltischen Staaten erschienen daraufhin als inoffizielle Beobachter.

Dieses Schicksal sollten sämtliche russische Bürgerkriegsparteien teilen; denn am 12. Januar beschlossen die Alliierten „that Russia should not be represented at the Conference."[40] Stattdessen würde man einzelne Gruppen in persönlichen Gesprächen anhören. Das zielte insbesondere auf die antibolschewistischen Kräfte in Paris und die von Frankreich protegierte Lobbygruppe „Russian Political Conference" (RPC).[41] Die von den weißen Generälen Kolčak und Denikin anerkannte RPC unter der Führung von Fürst L'vov umfasste auch Nikolaj

36 Debo, Survival and Consolidation, S. 28.

37 Sharp, The Versailles Settlement, S. 157.

38 MacMillan, Paris 1919, S. 211-214.

39 Anderson, Die baltische Frage, S. 340.

40 FRUS 1919 (Russia), S. 6.

41 Hovi, Cordon Sanitaire or Barriere de l'Est, S. 169. Die RPC firmierte auch unter dem französischen Namen *Conférence Politique Russe*.

Čajkovskij, Boris Savinkov und Sergej Sazonov, der sein Ziel, mit der RPC einen Sitz in Paris zu ergattern, verpasst hatte.[42]

Zuvor hatten diese Gegner der Bolschewiki bereits ihre eigenen Konferenzversuche unternommen, jedoch ohne Erfolg: Sie waren im November und Dezember 1918, von der Weltöffentlichkeit kaum beachtet, zunächst in Jassy und später in Odessa zusammengetroffen, um eine gemeinsame Position in der Russlandfrage zu erreichen[43]. Allerdings offenbarte diese Konferenz gleich mehrere Schwächen der antibolschewistischen Kräfte in Russland: Ihr Beharren auf eine Unteilbarkeit des einst zarischen Staatsgebietes stieß bei alliierten Beobachtern auf wenig Resonanz, ihre eigenen Rahmenbedingungen für eine westliche Intervention berücksichtigten nur unzureichend die politischen Realitäten auf beiden Seiten des Atlantiks und ihre mangelnde Einigkeit in fast allen politischen Fragen führten zu „dem Dilettantismus der Zufallsvereinigung von Jassy".[44] Der erhoffte Befreiungsschlag entwickelte sich zum diplomatischen Fiasko.

Die Alliierten verfolgten im Januar 1919 weitergreifende Pläne für alle Akteure auf dem Gebiet des ehemaligen Zarenreiches. Auf Drängen der britischen und amerikanischen Delegation verhandelten sie nun über eine separate Friedenskonferenz für Russland, die quasi als Ersatzveranstaltung für die in Paris nicht zugelassenen russischen Bürgerkriegsparteien geplant wurde. Zunächst versuchte Lloyd George Missverständnisse der früheren anglo-amerikanischen Friedensinitiative aus dem Weg zu räumen. Er zeigte drei mögliche Wege des Umgangs mit Russland auf: die Zerstörung des Bolschewismus, die Isolierung der Bolschewiki durch einen sog. *cordon sanitaire* und eine Friedenskonferenz mit allen Vertretern russischer Bürgerkriegsparteien.[45] Die letzte Option sei, so Lloyd George, falsch verstanden worden: Man habe den Bolschewiki keinen Sitz auf der Pariser Friedenskonferenz offeriert, sondern wolle lediglich alle Parteien an einen Verhandlungstisch bringen. Wilson unterstützte Lloyd George mit einem weit ausgreifenden Vortrag über den sozialen Wandel, der den Bolschewiki entgegenkäme – womit er aber den französischen Premier Georges Clemenceau kaum überzeugen konnte.[46] Die französische Delegation um

42 Alston, The Suggested Basis for a Russian Federal Republic, S. 26; siehe auch Conze, Die große Illusion, S. 307.

43 Katzer, Die weiße Bewegung in Russland, S. 366; siehe auch Leonhard, Der überforderte Frieden, S. 505.

44 Katzer, Die weiße Bewegung in Russland, S. 366f.

45 FRUS 1919 (Russia), S. 11.

46 Thompson, Russia, S. 101.

Clemenceau und seinem Außenminister Stephen Pichon sowie die italienische Delegation mit dem Ministerpräsidenten Vittorio Orlando und dem Außenminister Sidney Sonnino blieben skeptisch; sie sprachen sich für eine umfangreiche militärische Intervention aus und wurden dabei vom französischen Marschall Ferdinand Foch unterstützt.[47] Immerhin befand sich die französische Regierung nicht zuletzt durch ihr Eingreifen in Odessa „in its most ambitious attempt to reconstruct its former influence in Russia".[48] Daher verlangten diese Befürworter einer militärischen Lösung, mit Joseph Noulens und Harald de Scavenius die Meinung von zwei Russland-Experten zu hören und somit die Entscheidung über eine friedliche Lösung zu vertagen.[49]

Die Vorladung von Noulens und de Scavenius entpuppte sich für die Franzosen und Italiener, die insgeheim gehofft hatten, durch diesen Schachzug die Amerikaner und Briten auf ihre Seite zu ziehen, als kompletter Fehlschlag. Da Noulens und de Scavenius die negative Haltung der weißen Generäle gegenüber den Bolschewiki fast deckungsgleich übernahmen und sich kategorisch für eine Intervention aussprachen, hatte ihr Vortrag am 20. Januar 1919 keine Wirkung auf Lloyd George und Woodrow Wilson.[50] Die Franzosen und Italiener wurden noch weiter in die Defensive gedrängt, weil W. H. Buckler, den die amerikanische Regierung Anfang Januar zu Litvinov nach Stockholm geschickt hatte, in der Zwischenzeit den Alliierten Ergebnisse seiner dortigen Verhandlungen präsentieren konnte – und genau diese Ergebnisse bestärkten diejenigen Politiker auf der Pariser Friedenskonferenz, die sich für einen Frieden mit den Bolschewiki, welche sich nun Sowjets nannten, einsetzten.[51] Buckler schrieb an seine Vorgesetzten in Paris:

> „Litvinoff [sic!] stated that the Soviet Government are anxious for a permanent peace, and fully endorse the telegram which he sent to President Wilson the 24th December. They detest the military preparations and costly campaigns which are now forced upon Russia after four years of exhausting war, and wish to ascertain whether the United States and the Allies have a desire for peace."[52]

---

47 Conze, Die große Illusion, S. 307.

48 Stevenson, The First World War and International Politics, S. 240.

49 FRUS 1919 (Russia), S. 13f. Noulens war der ehemalige französische Botschafter in Russland, de Scavenius ein dänischer Diplomat. Beide waren erst kürzlich aus Russland zurückgekommen.

50 Debo, Survival and Consolidation, S. 31; Mayer, Politics and Diplomacy of Peacemaking, S. 427. Für den Vortrag vom 20. Januar 1919, siehe BDFA, Teil II, Reihe I, Band 1, S. 354-359.

51 MacMillan, Paris 1919, S. 76.

52 BDFA, Teil II, Reihe I, Band 1, Dokument 58, S. 359.

Litvinov hatte also mit Buckler endlich einen Gesprächspartner gefunden, der sein Friedensangebot den Alliierten überbrachte. Durch die offensichtliche Verhandlungsbereitschaft der Bolschewiki, die nun auf eine Antwort aus Paris warteten, waren die Alliierten zu schnellem und diplomatischem – nicht militärischem – Handeln gezwungen.

Der Durchbruch am 21. Januar 1919 – Endlich Frieden für Russland?

Die Sitzung des Supreme War Council am 21. Januar 1919 brachte den Vorschlag einer Friedenskonferenz für Russland auf den Weg. Woodrow Wilson plädierte nun dafür, Lloyd Georges Vorschlag, den das britische Kriegskabinett am 30./31. Dezember abgesegnet hatte, zu modifizieren: Die Bürgerkriegspartien – auch die Bolschewiki – sollten gehört werden, aber nicht in Paris, sondern an einem anderen Ort.[53] Georges Clemenceau war immer noch nicht von einer solchen Konferenz überzeugt, referierte über die bolschewistische Agitation und Aggression in ganz Europa und befürchtete, eine Konferenz würde die Bolschewiki auf dieselbe politische Stufe heben wie die Alliierten.[54] Clemenceaus größtes Problem war, dass er keine realisierbare Alternative aufzeigen konnte. Da die Alliierten ihm entgegenkamen und die Konferenz nicht mehr nach Paris, sondern ins östliche Mittelmeer legten, ließ sich Clemenceau umstimmen, weil er dadurch auch seine Idee eines *cordon sanitaire*, der Frankreich vor den Bolschewiki schützen sollte, indirekt verwirklicht sah.[55] Außerdem taktierte Clemenceau: Er erkannte, dass ein großzügiges Entgegenkommen seinerseits zu einem späteren Zeitpunkt der Konferenz von den Briten und Amerikanern zurückgezahlt werden könnte.[56] Clemenceau stimmte dem Vorschlag einer Russland-Konferenz zu „as it was essential that there should not be even the appearance of disagreement amongst them [the Allies].“[57]

Nach Clemenceaus Einlenken blieb lediglich die italienische Delegation als erklärter Gegner der Konferenz übrig. Lloyd George reagierte gereizt auf Sonninos Vorschlag, alle russischen Parteien außer den Bolschewiki einzuladen. Eine

---

53 Neilson, That Elusive Entity British Policy in Russia, S. 82f.; Walworth, Wilson and His Peacemakers, S. 128f.

54 BDFA, Teil II, Reihe I, Band 1, Dokument 59, S. 362-365. bzw. FRUS 1919 (Russia), S. 19-25, bes. S. 23.

55 Mayer, Politics and Diplomacy of Peacemaking, S. 428.

56 Thompson, Russia, S. 107.

57 BDFA, Teil II, Reihe I, Band 1, S. 363.

Intervention in Russland schlossen die Alliierten schnell aus, weil sie aus Furcht vor Meutereien keine großen Truppenverbände stellen wollten.[58] Damit war auch der italienische Widerstand gebrochen. Die in dieser Frage sehr zurückhaltenden Japaner unter Baron Makino sprachen sich ebenfalls für die Konferenz aus. Thompson vermutet, dass die japanische Delegation hoffte, eine Friedenskonferenz würde zum Abzug alliierter – und v. a. amerikanischer – Interventionstruppen in Sibirien führen, „thus giving the Japanese a free hand in that area."[59] Nachdem die Alliierten in Paris der Russland-Konferenz nun zugestimmt hatten, mussten sie in einem nächsten Schritt noch einen geeigneten Konferenzort finden.

Eine Friedenskonferenz auf einem Hundefriedhof?

Die Wahl eines Konferenzortes gestaltete sich schwieriger als gedacht: Clemenceau hatte nämlich der britischen Delegation vorab unmissverständlich erklärt, dass seine Regierung ihn zum Rücktritt zwingen würde, falls eine Konferenz mit den Bolschewiki in Paris stattfinden würde.[60] Wilson schlug Saloniki oder Lemnos als Konferenzorte vor, die einfach zu erreichen, aber weit genug von Paris entfernt wären.[61] Außerdem würden die Teilnehmer nicht über ein Drittland reisen – was gerade für die revolutionären Bolschewiki einen großen Vorteil darstellte.[62] Warum aber am Ende die Wahl auf Prinkipo fiel, ist bis heute noch nicht geklärt. Wie Mayer schreibt, hätten sich einige alliierte Delegierte gegen Lemnos ausgesprochen, weil „Bolsheviks should not be invited to a vacation island full of fine hotels and endowed with a splendid view of the coastline of Europe and Asia."[63] Dies ist aber ein schwaches Argument, da Prinkipo nach Wilson wegen seiner Hotelkapazitäten ausgewählt wurde.[64] Es ist möglich, dass Lemnos und vor allem Saloniki aus Rücksicht auf die griechischen Verbündeten fallengelassen wurden, die die Bolschewiki nicht in ihrer zweitgrößten Stadt sehen wollten.

---

58 BDFA, Teil II, Reihe I, Band 1, S. 364. De Scavenius rechnete mit 150.000 alliierten Soldaten für eine erfolgreiche Intervention.

59 Thompson, Russia, S. 108.

60 Mayer, Politics and Diplomacy of Peacemaking, S. 428.

61 FRUS 1919 (Russia), S. 25.

62 Kennan, Russia and the Versailles Conference, S. 19.

63 Mayer, Politics and Diplomacy of Peacemaking, S. 431.

64 Wilson, Remarks to Members of the Democratic National Committee, The Papers of Woodrow Wilson, S. 319.

Der geplante Konferenzort Prinkipo ist die größte der sog. Prinzeninseln, die im Marmarameer in Reichweite zu Istanbul liegen, das im Jahr 1919 offiziell noch Konstantinopel hieß. Die Insel lag damit auf dem Staatsgebiet des von den Alliierten besiegten Osmanischen Reiches und war durch seine Lage leicht für die russischen Konferenzteilnehmer zu erreichen. Prinkipos Problem war der Ruf der Inselgruppe: So kursierte in Paris das Gerücht, dass das Osmanische Reich vor dem Ersten Weltkrieg unzählige streunende Hunde auf den Prinzeninseln ausgesetzt hätte, die wegen Nahrungsknappheit qualvoll verendet seien.[65] Prinkipo war im byzantinischen Reich auch Verbannungsort gewesen; es gab Berichte, wonach die Insel Gefangene beherbergte, denen man zuvor die Augen ausgestochen hatte.[66] Wie auch immer, für Kritiker der Prinkipo-Konferenz war dies eine Steilvorlage, um den Vorschlag später ins Lächerliche zu ziehen.[67]

Doch dies ahnte Wilson zu diesem Zeitpunkt noch nicht und formulierte deshalb eine Proklamation an alle russischen Bürgerkriegsparteien, die auf der Sitzung vom 22. Januar in Paris abgesegnet wurde:[68] Die Alliierten äußerten ihren Wunsch nach einer friedlichen Lösung des Russischen Bürgerkriegs, erkannten die Revolution in Russland an und unterstrichen, dass sie nicht in Paris über Frieden in Europa und der Welt verhandeln könnten, wenn in Russland immer noch Krieg tobte.[69] Sie erachteten es daher als ihre Pflicht, „to serve Russia in this matter as generously, as unselfishly, as thoughtfully, as ungrudgingly as they would serve every other friend and ally […].“ Der zweite Teil der Proklamation enthielt die Einladung zur Konferenz:

> „They [the Allies and the Associated Powers] invite every organised group which is now exercising, or attempting to exercise, political authority or military control anywhere in Siberia, or within the boundaries of European Russia as they stood before the war just concluded (except in Finland and Poland[70]), to send representatives […] to the Prince's Islands, Sea of Marmora, where they will be met by Representatives of the Associated Powers, provided, in the meantime, there is a truce of arms amongst the parties invited,

---

65 MacMillan, Paris 1919, S. 74.

66 Mayer, Politics and Diplomacy of Peacemaking, S. 431.

67 Churchill widmet dem Hundefriedhof auf Prinkipo in seinen Memoiren einen ganzen Absatz und behauptet, er habe ihn 1909 mit eigenen Augen gesehen. Siehe Churchill, The World Crisis, S. 170.

68 Anderson, Die baltische Frage, S. 341f.

69 BDFA, Teil II, Reihe I, Band 1, S. 370f. Die folgenden Zitate sind diesem Dokument entnommen.

70 Polen war bereits von den Alliierten anerkannt worden (s. o.).

and that all armed forces […] shall be meanwhile withdrawn, and aggressive military action cease.“

Die Friedenskonferenz für Russland sollte also am 15. Februar beginnen und auf Prinkipo stattfinden – womit Wilson sein Versprechen an Clemenceau eingehalten hatte, die Konferenz nicht in Paris abhalten zu lassen. Die Einladung wurde am 22./23. Januar über Funk und Presse verschickt und am 27. Januar ausdrücklich auf kleinere Nachfolgestaaten des ehemaligen Zarenreiches, z. B. Estland, Georgien, Russisch-Armenien und Dagestan ausgeweitet.[71]

3. Die Kritik an der Prinkipo-Konferenz – „the most fatuous decision of modern times“[72]?

Die Einladungen waren versandt, doch als Antwort kam ein wütender Aufschrei von verschiedenen Seiten, der sich im Laufe der nächsten Wochen von Paris bis nach Sibirien im Osten und bis in die USA im Westen ausbreiten sollte. Erste Kritik an der Prinkipo-Konferenz war bereits geäußert worden, aber nun sollte die Konferenz tatsächlich stattfinden – und dies führte zu deutlichen Protesten.

Die Reaktion der Weißen

Den Anfang machte die RPC unter Sergej Sazonov, der den Alliierten unmissverständlich klar machte, dass man die Teilnahme an der Prinkipo-Konferenz boykottieren würde, ohne jedoch offiziell abzusagen.[73] Dies kam nicht überraschend, da Sazonov bereits die anglo-amerikanische Friedensoffensive abgelehnt hatte.[74] Das Ziel der RPC, ein starkes zentralistisches Russland zu schaffen, schien durch die Prinkipo-Konferenz, an der viele regionale Parteien teilnehmen sollten, bedroht. Sazonov redete sich während eines Interviews mit der französischen Zeitung *Matin* in Rage: „Never, and under no circumstances, will I go to Prinkipo. How dare they even propose it? […] On one side are the murderers, on the other their victims.”[75] Fürst L'vov wies dementsprechend als Vertreter der antikommunistischen Kräfte den Konferenzplan umgehend zurück; eine

71 FRUS 1919 (Russia), S. 30f.

72 Zit. nach NEILSON, That elusive entity British policy in Russia, S. 83. Das Zitat stammt von Lord Hardinge, seinerseits Staatssekretär im britischen Außenministerium – und entschiedener Gegner der Konferenz.

73 THOMPSON, Russia, S. 119.

74 NEILSON, That elusive entity British policy in Russia, S. 80.

75 Zit. nach MAYER, Politics and Diplomacy of Peacemaking, S. 432.

förmliche Absage folgte am 16. Februar.[76] Vor der russischen Botschaft in Paris protestierten russische Emigranten, während im fernen Archangel'sk Bilder, die Präsident Wilson zeigten, aus dem Straßenbild entfernt wurden.[77]

In Russland selbst waren die Regierungen der Weißen von der Idee ebenfalls überrumpelt. In Archangel'sk übernahm Evgenij Karlovič Miller Sazonovs Sichtweise und warnte die Alliierten in seiner Protestnote vor leeren Versprechungen der Bolschewiki.[78] In Omsk war General Kolčak von der Nachricht derart alarmiert, dass er ein Gerücht in Umlauf bringen ließ, wonach die Prinkipo-Konferenz ein kluges diplomatisches Manöver der Alliierten sei, um die Bolschewiki vor der ganzen Welt zunächst zu diskreditieren und danach die Weißen auf ganzer Linie zu unterstützen.[79] Die Omsker Regierung teilte zudem mit, dass die Moral der Truppen spürbar nachgelassen habe.[80] Selbst alliierte Gesandte in Russland waren empört: So reichte der amerikanische Gesandte in Archangel'sk, DeWitt Clinton Poole[81], seine Entlassung ein, weil er von der Russlandpolitik seiner Regierung enttäuscht war.[82] Der Vorschlag habe die russischen Verbündeten in Archangel'sk vor den Kopf gestoßen. Interessant ist, dass selbst Lloyd George, der gemeinsam mit Wilson die Planungen für die Prinkipo-Konferenz vorangetrieben hatte, rückblickend Verständnis für seine größten Konferenzgegner zeigte. In seinem Memoiren schreibt er, unter Zuhilfenahme eines eigenwilligen historischen Vergleichs: „If, at the time of the French Revolution, the Royalist Governments of Europe had proposed to the French Revolutionaries a meeting in Geneva at which not only Britain, Russia, Prussia and Austria, but the Emigrés, the Vendeans and the Royalists of the Midi should also be represented, the proposal would have met with the same disdainful refusal as that which was accorded to our Prinkipo invitation."[83]

---

76 Katzer, Die weiße Bewegung in Russland, S. 370.

77 MacMillan, Paris 1919, S. 76.

78 Katzer, Die weiße Bewegung in Russland, S. 371; siehe auch Neilson, That elusive entity British policy in Russia, S. 83f.

79 Thompson, Russia, S. 120.

80 Thompson, Russia, S. 8.

81 Der amerikanische Gesandte DeWitt Clinton Poole (1885-1942) ist nicht zu verwechseln mit Frederick Cuthbert Poole (1869-1936), der die britischen Expeditionsstreitkräfte in Archangel'sk kommandierte.

82 FRUS 1919 (Russia), S. 42f. Pooles Entlassungsgesuch wurde abgelehnt.

83 Lloyd George, The Truth about the Peace Treaties, S. 366

Die Reaktion der Bolschewiki

Die Reaktionen der Bolschewiki in Moskau auf die geplante Prinkipo-Konferenz fielen gemischt aus: Trockij zögerte, Zinov'ev mahnte in Petrograd zur Vorsicht und einige Parteimitglieder vermuteten eine Falle der Alliierten[84]. Für Lenin wiederum kam der Konferenzvorschlag zu einem günstigen Zeitpunkt, sah er doch die Möglichkeit, sich durch ein zweites Brest-Litovsk Zeit für die unvermeidliche Konfrontation der Systeme zu erkaufen – notfalls auf Kosten wirtschaftlicher oder territorialer Zugeständnisse.[85] Diejenigen, die in Prinkipo eben jene Parallele zu Brest-Litovsk sehen wollten, verbreiteten also vorsichtigen Optimismus, wie z. B. die Parteizeitung *Pravda*, die in einem sarkastisch gefärbten Artikel Prinkipo nicht ablehnte, sondern als Mittel zum größeren Ziel, der Weltrevolution, sah.[86] Čičerin schien diese Meinung zu teilen – und war enttäuscht, dass die Konferenz auf einer Insel stattfand, was keine große Bühne für die Bolschewiki bedeutete.[87] Außerdem zeigte er sich verärgert, dass die Einladungen nicht offiziell verschickt worden waren, sondern an die Presse herausgegeben wurden.[88] Er erbat daher am 28. Januar von Wilson eine offizielle Einladung – was dieser jedoch ablehnte, da eine offizielle Einladung an die Bolschewiki einer Anerkennung der Regierung in Moskau gleichkäme.[89]

Trotz dieser Zurückweisung nahm die Regierung der Bolschewiki die Einladung der Alliierten am 4. Februar als eine der ersten potenziellen Teilnehmer der Prinkipo-Konferenz an.[90] Čičerins Antwort an die Alliierten unterteilte die Verhandlungspunkte der Bolschewiki für die Prinkipo-Konferenz in vier Punkte: finanzielle, materielle, territoriale und politische Streitfragen.[91] Zunächst sei die Sowjetregierung bereit, über das Ausmaß ihrer finanziellen Verpflichtungen, die sich z. B. aus den russischen Kriegsschulden ergäben, zu verhandeln.

84 Debo, Survival and Consolidation, S. 38.

85 Stevenson, The First World War and International Politics, S. 240.

86 Thompson, Russia, S. 113.

87 Ullman, Britain and the Russian Civil War, S. 111.

88 Debo, Survival and Consolidation, S. 38.

89 Walworth, Wilson and His Peacemakers, S. 130.

90 Anderson, Die baltische Frage, S. 342. Nach Walworth (Walworth, Wilson and His Peacemakers, S. 130.) wurde die Antwort der Bolschewiki drei Tage später von der französischen Zeitung *Le Matin* veröffentlicht.

91 Extracts from Chicherin's reply to the Allied Govenments' invitation to a conference on Princes Island, Soviet Documents on Foreign Policy, Band 1 (1917-1924), S. 137-139. Die folgenden Informationen zu Čičerins Antwort sind diesem Dokument entnommen.

Man könne sich vorstellen, einen Teil der Schulden durch die Lieferung von Rohstoffen und die Übertragung von Holz-, Schürf- und anderen Konzessionen an die Alliierten abzubauen. In Grenzfragen wolle man mit Ausnahme Polens und Finnlands keine weiteren Zugeständnisse machen. Jede weitere Gebietsabtretung werde als feindliche Annexion betrachtet. Die sowjetische Regierung werde aber ein Abkommen mit den Alliierten in Betracht ziehen, welches die Bolschewiki verpflichte, sich nicht in die Angelegenheiten anderer Staaten einzumischen. Allerdings könne man dies nur auf diplomatischem Wege garantieren, da man die Freiheit der revolutionären Presse nicht einschränken könne.

Die Reaktionen auf Čičerins Antwort fielen gemischt aus: Für die Alliierten hatte Čičerin mit seinen weitreichenden Zugeständnissen impliziert, dass sie eine ähnliche Politik wie die Deutschen in Brest-Litovsk verfolgten – was den Alliierten nicht gefallen konnte.[92] Wilson, der die Alliierten als Vermittler und nicht als Bittsteller sah, war erbost: „We are not after their money or their concessions or their territory. That is not the point. We are their friends who want to help them and must tell them so."[93] Die innenpolitischen Gegner der Bolschewiki, die Menschewiki und die rechten Sozialrevolutionäre, stellten sich jedoch hinter die Antwort der Sowjetregierung, da nach ihrer Ansicht eine alliierte Intervention den Bolschewiki nur Gründe für innenpolitische Repressionen liefern würde.[94] Diese Befürchtung war nicht unbegründet, denn fast zeitgleich zu der alliierten Einladung zur Prinkipo-Konferenz hatten die Bolschewiki zu der Bildung einer kommunistischen Internationale aufgerufen.[95] In dem Dokument, das die Geburtsstunde der Komintern markierte, verlangten die Bolschewiki „maximum contact between the different parts of the revolutionary proletariat and a close alliance between those countries in which the socialist revolution has already triumphed." Dies sollte erzielt werden durch „mass action by the proletariat right up to open armed conflict with the political power of capital." Dieser Aufruf wirkte für viele Kritiker der Prinkipo-Konferenz aus dem Westen wie eine Bestätigung ihrer Sorgen vor einer kommunistischen Weltrevolution.

---

92 Mayer, Politics and Diplomacy of Peacemaking, S. 438.

93 Wilson, Remarks to Members of the Democratic National Committee, S. 320.

94 Thompson, Russia, S. 116.

95 Extract from the Appeal for the Formation of the Communist International, Soviet Documents on Foreign Policy, S. 136. Die folgenden Zitate sind dem sechsten und siebten Punkt des Aufrufes entnommen.

Die Reaktion der Alliierten – Pressekampagnen und Red Scare

Diese Weltrevolution rückte für einige Amerikaner Anfang 1919 gefährlich nahe. Am 2. Februar fand eine große Kundgebung in Washington, D.C. statt, die den Abzug amerikanischer Truppen aus Sibirien forderte; nur einen Tag später wurde ein Generalstreik in Seattle ausgerufen.[96] Der Senat reagierte sofort und richtete einen Ausschuss ein, um die bolschewistische Propaganda und Unterwanderung in den USA zu untersuchen. Die sog. „Red Scare“ hatte in den USA einen neuen Höhepunkt erreicht. Die Prinkipo-Konferenz wurde von der amerikanischen Presse daher mit Unverständnis registriert. So schrieb die *New York Times* Anfang Februar:

> “It is incredible that the associated powers in council should have perpetrated such a poor joke at such a tragic moment, and on such a subject of gravity. No wonder that even the Bolsheviks are suspicious. For them the news is too good to be true. For those who still hope for the triumph of reason and justice it seems too unrelievedly to be possible.”[97]

Der Kommentar, der außerdem die nahende Niederlage der Bolschewiki ankündigte, steht beispielhaft für die negative amerikanische Berichterstattung über die Prinkipo-Konferenz sowie für die desaströse Nachrichtenlage über Russland, welche zu Fehleinschätzungen der Lage führte. Wilson erhielt selbst von Vertrauten Gegenwind: Joseph Tumulty zeigte sich besorgt über die negative Presse in Washington, Außenminister Lansing schrieb die Konferenz bereits ab und sein Stellvertreter Frank Polk bezweifelte, ob die Bolschewiki sie überhaupt ernst nahmen.[98] Lansing sah Prinkipo gar als Notlösung an, weil man einfach irgendetwas tun wollte.[99]

In Großbritannien waren die öffentlichen und politischen Reaktionen ähnlich, wenn nicht sogar negativer: Konservative Hinterbänkler probten den Aufstand, weil sie nicht mit den Bolschewiki verhandeln wollten.[100] Auch sie verwiesen dabei indirekt auf die Komintern und die Gefahr einer Weltrevolution. Nach einem kurzen Beifallssturm für Lloyd George in der linksliberalen Presse zerpflückten die einflussreichen konservativen Zeitungen *Morning Post*, *Daily Mail* und *Times* den Konferenzvorschlag; Henry Wickham Steed kritisierte

96 Mayer, Politics and Diplomacy of Peacemaking, S. 447.
97 Williams, „It Gives Breating Space to Bolsheviki.
98 Walworth, Wilson and His Peacemakers, S. 128.
99 Kennan, Russia and the Versailles Conference, S. 20.
100 Debo, Survival and Consolidation, S. 40.

die Prinkipo-Konferenz als kontraproduktiven Schnellschuss und Verrat an Sazonovs RPC.[101] Mit Winston Churchill hatten die britischen Prinkipo-Gegner außerdem ein Kabinettsmitglied gefunden, das sich auf ihre Seite stellte – und bereits im Dezember Bedenken gegen die Konferenz geäußert hatte. Churchill, der als Kriegsminister seine engen Kontakte zu Denikin, Kolčak und der Regierung in Archangel'sk betonte, sprach sich für eine Intervention aufseiten der Weißen aus.[102]

Churchills Pläne registrierte Frankreich mit Wohlwollen. Die Nachricht einer Konferenz mit allen russischen Bürgerkriegsparteien hatte die konservative Presse, welche traditionell enge Kontakte zu der RPC um Sazonov unterhielt, regelrecht aufgewühlt.[103] August Gauvain (*Journal des Débats*), Alfred Capus (*Figaro*), Jean Herbette (*Temps*) und Pertinax (*L'Écho de Paris*; *Temps*) zogen eine breite Front gegen die Prinkipo-Konferenz zusammen.[104] So berichtete z. B. der Schweizer Botschafter Dunant von Paris nach Bern: „L'opinion du grand public est nettement mécontente de cette solution. La grande majorité de la presse également."[105]

Zwischen Schadensbegrenzung und Scheitern

Während in Paris und andernorts die Kritik an der Prinkipo-Konferenz immer lauter wurde, bemühten sich Wilson und Lloyd George, ihren Vorschlag zu retten. Die Alliierten, die als Vermittler nach Prinkipo reisen wollten, bestimmten ihre Delegationen – und die Auswahl der Gesandten spiegelte die Haltung der Alliierten zu der Prinkipo-Konferenz wieder. Die Franzosen nominierten mit General Rampont einen Militär und mit Alexandre-Robert Conty ihren Ministre plénipotentiaire in Dänemark, während die Italiener Pietro Tommasi Della Torretta entsenden wollten, der 1917/1918 Ministre plénipotentiaire in St. Petersburg gewesen war.[106] Alle drei Gesandten galten alleine schon auf Grund ihrer Position als skeptisch gegenüber den Bolschewiki. Lloyd George hatte Schwierigkeiten, jemanden zu finden, der überhaupt bereit war, nach Prinkipo zu gehen und beauftragte schließlich einen sichtlich erfreuten Sir Robert Borden, dessen Idee zu der Konferenz geführt hatte[107]. Diese Entscheidung spaltete das

101 Mayer, Politics and Diplomacy of Peacemaking, S. 443.
102 Churchill, The World Crisis, S. 170f.
103 Ullman, Britain and the Russian Civil War, S. 110.
104 Mayer, Politics and Diplomacy of Peacemaking, S. 440.
105 Dokument 167, DDS, Band 7 (1918-1920), 1. Buch, S. 331.
106 Mayer, Politics and Diplomacy of Peacemaking, S. 434.
107 MacMillan, Paris 1919, S. 76.

kanadische Kabinett. Bordens Stellvertreter in Ottawa, William Thomas White, meldete nach Paris, man sei uneinig darüber, ob es wirklich besser für Kanada wäre, wenn Borden als Delegationsleiter nach Prinkipo reise anstatt als Delegationsmitglied bei der wichtigeren Pariser Friedenskonferenz zu bleiben.[108] Borden, der angesichts der vielen Vorabdiskussionen durchaus mit einem Scheitern des Konferenzvorschlags rechnen konnte, beruhigte bereits am 25. Januar: „It is however very doubtful whether the Conference will take place."[109] Diese Einschätzung zeigt, dass selbst die Befürworter der Prinkipo-Konferenz nicht so recht von ihrem eigenen Vorschlag überzeugt waren.

In den USA führte bereits die Suche nach geeigneten Delegierten für die Prinkipo-Konferenz zu weiteren Debatten: Woodrow Wilson legte sich auf William Allen White, einen progressiven Journalisten, und George D. Herron, einen Geistlichen und christlich-sozialen Aktivisten, fest.[110] Doch diese Entscheidung blieb nicht ohne Kritik; Colonel House hatte gegenüber beiden Delegierten erhebliche Bedenken.[111] Und die amerikanische Presse verglich Herrons soziales Programm mit den Bolschewiki und brandmarkte ihn zudem als Ehebrecher.[112] Die *New York Times* zitierte den republikanischen Politiker und Präsidenten der Columbia University, Nicholas Murray Butler, der diese Gelegenheit nutzte, seinen ehemaligen Kollegen und Konkurrenten Woodrow Wilson[113] persönlich zu kritisieren: „We have become accustomed during these last six years to the President's fondness for surrounding himself with intellectual and political midgets, but we have hitherto been spared anything so shocking as this [Harron's] appointment."[114]

Zu diesem Zeitpunkt war immer noch unklar, ob die Delegierten überhaupt aufbrechen würden. Zwar hatten die Bolschewiki bereits zugesagt und die lettische Regierung die Einladung unter Vorbehalten am 12. Februar ebenfalls angenommen.[115] Auch von der litauischen und estnischen Delegation wurde

---

108 Document 41, DCER (Band 2), S. 38 ; Document 43, DCER (Band 2), S. 39.

109 Document 45, DCER (Band 2), S. 40.

110 Thompson, Russia, S. 110.

111 Floto, Colonel House in Paris, S. 109.

112 Walworth, Wilson and His Peacemakers, S. 131, Fußnote 32.

113 Wilson hatte vor seiner politischen Karriere acht Jahre lang die Princeton University geleitet.

114 O.V., „Dr. Butler Assails Wilson's Policies", S. 12.

115 FRUS 1919 (Russia), S. 50. Die lettische Regierung macht hier aber auch deutlich, dass sie am liebsten wie Polen und Finnland von der Konferenz ausgenommen wäre und in Paris verhandeln würde.

vorsichtig Zustimmung signalisiert, wobei ähnlich wie in der lettischen Antwort die Anerkennung der staatlichen Unabhängigkeit als Vorbedingung formuliert wurde.[116] Aber fast zeitgleich lehnten andere Staaten ihre Teilnahme auf Prinkipo unvermittelt ab: Die georgische Delegation unter Gvarjaladze wollte direkt in Paris verhandeln und die Unabhängigkeit Georgiens bestätigt wissen.[117] Die Ukrainische Republik unter Sydorenko wollte auch nicht auf Prinkipo erscheinen und der rumänische Premier Brătianu hatte die Teilnahme Bessarabiens an der Konferenz abgelehnt, weil sich diese Region freiwillig Rumänien angeschlossen habe.[118] Die Konkursmasse des Zarenreiches, die vereinten Regierungen von Sibirien, Archangel'sk und Südrussland, vertreten durch die RPC mit Sazonov, lehnten am 12. Februar offiziell ihre Teilnahme an der Prinkipo-Konferenz ab.[119] Durch diese Absage rückte die Prinkipo-Konferenz in weite Ferne – und Churchill, der dies in London registrierte, sah seine Chance gekommen. Lloyd George war nach London zurückgekehrt, um innenpolitische Probleme zu lösen.[120] Wilsons vorübergehende Abreise aus Paris stand kurz bevor, weil der Präsident den 66. Kongress der USA eröffnen wollte.[121] Die Befürworter der Prinkipo-Politik waren geschwächt.

4. Churchills Intervention und die geheime Sitzung – *Das Ende von Prinkipo*

Der sowjetische Diplomat Boris E. Štejn beschuldigte Churchill später als „Hauptschuldigen am Scheitern der [Prinkipo-] Konferenz und ärgsten Feind des Sowjetvolkes."[122] Zwar stellt sich Štejns Werk über die „Russische Frage" in Paris ganz in den Dienst der sowjetischen Geschichtsschreibung der 1950er-Jahre und ist daher in einer Rezension des amerikanischen Historikers John

116 Alston, The Suggested Basis for a Russian Federal Republic, S. 27; Anderson, Die baltische Frage, S. 342; Leonhard, Der überforderte Frieden. S. 506.

117 FRUS 1919 (Russia), S. 47.

118 Mayer, Politics and Diplomacy of Peacemaking, S. 434. Für Brătianu siehe BDFA, Teil 2, Reihe 1, Band 2, S. 18f.

119 Thompson, Russia, S. 125; Stevenson, The First World War and International Politics, S. 240.

120 Ullman, Britain and the Russian Civil War, S. 117.

121 Mayer, Politics and Diplomacy of Peacemaking, S. 447.

122 Štejn, Die „russische Frage", S. 89.

M. Thompson regelrecht verrissen worden (vgl. „the breadth and depth of the book's coverage is limited").[123] Doch die Frage nach der Rolle Churchills bleibt.

Churchill erreichte Paris am 14. Februar und nahm sofort an der Sitzung des Supreme War Council teil, dem er mitteilte, das britische Kabinett habe ihn angesichts der bevorstehenden Abreise Wilsons gebeten, sofort nach Paris zu kommen: „Mr. Lloyd George had expressed a wish to know whether the Allied policy which had led to the suggestion of the meeting at Prinkipo was to be pursued or, if not, what policy was to be substituted for it."[124] Das ist zweifelhaft, da die Sitzungsprotokolle des Imperial War Cabinets nahelegen, dass das Kabinett zwar vor Wilsons Abreise handeln wollte, sich aber unentschlossen vertagte.[125] Churchills Memoiren legen zudem nahe, dass er nicht auf Wunsch des Kabinetts gekommen war, sondern Lloyd George mit seinen Plänen für die weißen Regierungen so lange bedrängt hatte, bis dieser nachgab und Churchill nach Paris schickte.[126] Dort ließ sich aber Wilson nicht auf die von Churchill gewünschte Intervention ein. Im Gegenteil: „The Allied and Associated Powers ought to withdraw their troops from all parts of Russian territory."[127] Wilson erklärte Churchill auch, warum man die Prinkipo-Konferenz einberufen hatte:

> „The policy tending to a meeting at Prinkipo had been instituted in order to find out what the people in Russia were thinking and purposing to do. As far as he [Wilson] was concerned, he would be quite content that informal American representatives should meet representatives of the Bolsheviks. […] What we were seeking was not a rapprochement with the Bolsheviks, but clear information. The reports received from Russia from various official and unofficial sources were so conflicting that it was impossible to form a coherent picture of the country. Some light on the situation might be obtained by meeting the Russian representatives."

Nach Wilson war die Prinkipo-Konferenz also ein taktisches Manöver, um sich ein genaueres Bild von der Lage in Russland zu verschaffen. Churchills Einwand, ohne militärische Hilfe würden die Weißen untergehen, ließ Wilson, der so kurz vor seiner Abreise selbst keine Entscheidung treffen wollte, kalt. Er teilte lediglich mit, sich während seiner Abwesenheit niemandem in den Weg zu stellen.

---

123 Thompson, Rezension zu Štejns „Russkij vopros" na parižskoj mirnoj konferencii (1919-1920), S. 19.

124 FRUS 1919 (Russia), S. 56.

125 CAB 23/9, Sitzung vom 23.12.1918 um 11 Uhr, S. 6; CAB 23/9, Sitzung vom 13.02.1919 um 12 Uhr, S. 2.

126 Churchill, The Word Crisis, S. 170f.

127 FRUS 1919 (Russia), S. 56.

Dies war aber ein taktischer Fehler, der Churchill freie Hand ließ. Denn der britische Kriegsminister nutzte das darauffolgende Abendessen mit General Wilson und Lloyd Georges Privatsekretär Kerr, um zwei Resolutionen zu formulieren.[128]

Am nächsten Tag stand Russland erneut auf der Tagesordnung in Paris – und Churchill präsentierte seine Resolutionen:[129] Einerseits wollte er von den Bolschewiki eine sofortige Waffenruhe fordern. Erst nach deren Einhaltung könnten sie den Vorschlag der Prinkipo-Konferenz annehmen. Andererseits – und für den Fall, dass die Bolschewiki das Ultimatum zur Waffenruhe verstreichen ließen – wollte Churchill einen interalliierten Kriegsrat bilden, der einen Interventionsplan für Russland ausarbeiten sollte. Am nächsten Tag hatte er mit dem französischen General Alby einen Verbündeten gewonnen, der zu Sitzungsbeginn ein düsteres Bild der russischen Bürgerkriegsfront zeichnete; Alby sah an allen Fronten die Bolschewiki auf dem Vormarsch.[130] Trotz dieser guten Vorlage konnte Churchill noch keinen Beschluss herbeiführen; Lord Balfour und House wollten sich ohne ihre Vorgesetzten nicht sofort auf diese neue Russlandpolitik festlegen und befürchteten, dass die Bolschewiki Churchills Vorschläge propagandistisch nutzen würden.[131] Dennoch wollten sie, nachdem die Prinkipo-Konferenz in weite Ferne gerückt war, nicht tatenlos zusehen, was in Russland passierte, und ein Signal aussenden.[132] Sonnino und Clemenceau nutzten dies, um die Prinkipo-Konferenz endgültig zu begraben. Während Sonnino der Meinung war „the Allies would have to get out of the Prinkipo business", betonte Clemenceau „that French opinion had throughout been unanimously opposed to the Prinkipo policy, and the protests had not been limited to France." Churchills Vorschläge kamen für Clemenceau also zur rechten Zeit, auch wenn sich die Alliierten noch nicht sicher waren, wie man das Ultimatum an die Bolschewiki genau stellen sollte. Es wurde daher vereinbart, die Diskussion auf die Sitzung am folgenden Tag zu vertagen.

Doch auch auf der Sitzung vom 17. Februar wurden Churchills Vorschläge nicht abgesegnet. Stattdessen mussten die Debatten so hitzig verlaufen sein, dass nicht einmal ein Protokoll herausgegeben wurde.[133] So existiert für Russland nur

---

128 Ullman, Britain and the Russian Civil War, S. 121.

129 BDFA, Teil II, Reihe A, Band 1, S. 58f.

130 Ullman, Britain and the Russian Civil War, S. 122.

131 Mayer, Politics and Diplomacy of Peacemaking, S. 452-454.

132 BDFA, Teil II, Reihe I, Band 2, S. 180-185. Die folgenden Zitate sind diesem Protokoll entnommen.

133 Mayer, Politics and Diplomacy of Peacemaking, S. 458f.

eine knappe Mitteilung: „A discussion on the policy to be pursued in Russia ensued, and after an exchange of views, it was decided to postpone the resumption of the discussion until later in the week."[134] Die Debatten wurden geheim gehalten. Allerdings mussten Lansing und House dem abgereisten Wilson Bericht erstatten und fassten so den Meinungsaustausch zusammen: Nach Lansing habe Churchill weiter auf eine große Intervention in Russland und Verteidigungskonzepte für diverse Staaten in Osteuropa gedrängt.[135] Die amerikanische Delegation sei aber gegen eine sofortige Intervention gewesen und habe damit erreicht, dass die Alliierten vor einer Abstimmung zunächst ihre militärischen Berater konsultieren würden; daher sei das Thema vertagt worden. House ergänzte, Lloyd George hätte ihm unmittelbar vor Sitzungsbeginn über seinen Privatsekretär mitgeteilt, dass Churchills Vorschläge zu weit gingen und nicht den Anweisungen entsprächen, die Lloyd George Churchill vor dessen Abreise mitgegeben hatte.[136] Das machte die amerikanische Delegation skeptisch. House sollte später berichten, dass Clemenceau daraufhin erbost die USA aus dieser Angelegenheit ausschließen wollte.[137] Doch er wurde von Balfour ausgebremst, der keinen Konflikt mit Lloyd George in London riskieren wollte. Churchill reiste schließlich enttäuscht aus Paris ab, wobei er die Abwesenheit Wilsons und Lloyd Georges als Grund für den schleppenden Entscheidungsprozess ausmachte.[138]

Neben der Prinkipo-Konferenz war auch Churchills Vorschlag einer Intervention gescheitert. Die Franzosen wendeten sich nach dem Scheitern beider Optionen ihrer Idee eines *cordon sanitaire* zu.[139] In Großbritannien debattierte das Kriegskabinett weiter über die Intervention und in den USA überlegte man, Litvinovs Friedensangebot vom Dezember 1918 quasi zu imitieren und inoffiziell mit den Bolschewiki zu verhandeln. Daraus entwickelte sich später die sog. Bullitt-Mission, die ebenfalls ohne diplomatischen Durchbruch scheiterte.[140] Alles war fast so wie im Dezember 1918. Oder doch nicht?

---

134 BDFA, Teil II, Reihe I, Band 2, S. 189.

135 Telegramm von Lansing an Wilson am 17. Februar 1919, The Papers of Woodrow Wilson, S. 202f.

136 Telegramm von House an Wilson am 17. Februar 1919, The Papers of Woodrow Wilson, S. 203f.

137 Mayer, Politics and Diplomacy of Peacemaking, S. 458f.

138 Churchill, The World Crisis, S. 175.

139 Hovi, Cordon sanitaire or barrière de l'Est, S. 170f.

140 FRUS 1919 (Russia), S. 74. Siehe für eine konzise Zusammenfassung dieses diplomatischen Lösungsversuchs Stevenson, The First World War and International Politics, S. 241f.

5. Die vielen Totengräber der Prinkipo-Konferenz – Ein Scheitern mit Ansage

Die Absage der antikommunistischen Regierungen in Russland ließ die Prinkipo-Konferenz schließlich scheitern. Doch es wäre verfehlt, diese antikommunistischen Kräfte als einzige Totengräber der Konferenz darzustellen. Stattdessen war Prinkipo ein Scheitern mit Ansage: Nach zwei Jahren Bürgerkrieg waren die politischen und ideologischen Gräben in Russland derart tief, dass sie auch keine Verhandlung auf einer Insel im Marmarameer überbrücken konnte. Denn selbst die vordergründig verhandlungsbereiten Bolschewiki hofften, auf Prinkipo ihre Verhandlungsstrategie von Brest-Litovsk wiederholen zu können, womit sie zeigten, dass sie eher an einer Ausbreitung ihrer Revolution als an einem nachhaltigen Frieden für ihr Land interessiert waren. Nur einige wenige neu gegründete Staaten, wie die baltischen Staaten, begriffen die Prinkipo-Konferenz als wirkliche Chance für Frieden in Freiheit. Sie wollten als unabhängige Staaten anerkannt werden und hatten ihre Teilnahme an der Konferenz deshalb nach langem Zögern zugesagt; an ihnen scheiterte die Konferenz nicht.

Stattdessen sind die Alliierten viel mehr an sich selbst gescheitert: Sie waren untereinander zu zerstritten, um den nötigen Druck auf die einzelnen russischen Bürgerkriegsfraktionen auszuüben, die Konferenz wahrzunehmen. Die heftige französische Kritik dämpfte die britisch-amerikanischen Friedensbemühungen noch zum Jahreswechsel 1918/1919 – und machte den Optimismus, den Wilson und Lloyd George nach Litvinovs Friedensangebot ausgestrahlt hatten, wieder zunichte. Für die Franzosen und Italiener stellte die Prinkipo-Konferenz nur ein taktisches Manöver dar, von dem sie hofften, dass es nie zustande kommen würde. Für die Briten und Amerikaner um Lloyd George und Wilson stellte Prinkipo dagegen auch eine Friedenschance für Russland dar. Aber gerade für Wilson war die gescheiterte Prinkipo-Konferenz nur die erste von vielen Enttäuschungen, die er auf der Pariser Friedenskonferenz erlebte. Die Lagerbildung zwischen Großbritannien und den USA einerseits und Frankreich und Italien andererseits setzte sich bei der Pariser Friedenskonferenz fort.

Doch Prinkipo scheiterte nicht nur in Paris, sondern auch an der alliierten Heimatfront, wo Politik und Presse den Konferenzvorschlag gleichermaßen vehement ablehnten. Kritik an der Prinkipo-Konferenz war von Anfang an vorhanden; dass die Franzosen und Italiener dem britisch-amerikanischen Konferenzvorschlag überhaupt zustimmten, war die eigentliche Leistung von Lloyd George und Woodrow Wilson. Dass die Alliierten aber keinen klaren Plan B für den Fall entwickelten, dass die Prinkipo-Konferenz scheiterte, ja dass sie nicht einmal ein klar formuliertes Ultimatum zur Waffenruhe an die russischen

Bürgerkriegsparteien richteten, war ein schwerer diplomatischer Fehler, den die Alliierten in der Folge nicht mehr korrigieren wollten oder konnten. Stattdessen fuhren sie weiter einen diplomatischen Zickzackkurs, der durch Churchills Kurzintervention nicht nur offengelegt, sondern auch weiterverfolgt wurde. Ein Politikwechsel der Alliierten fand also nach dem Scheitern von Prinkipo nicht statt. Die Prinkipo-Konferenz hätte eine zweite Pariser Friedenskonferenz werden können. Stattdessen war Prinkipo der Anfang einer unglücklichen und manchmal unverständlichen Russlandpolitik auf der Pariser Friedenskonferenz, die mit Idealismus und großen Zielen begonnen hatte, aber viele offene Fragen in Russland nicht lösen konnte.

Literaturverzeichnis

Alston, Charlotte "The Suggested Basis for a Russian Federal Republic". Britain, Anti-Bolshevik Russia and the Border States at the Paris Peace Conference, 1919, in: History 91 (2006), Nr. 301, S. 24-44.

Anderson, Edgar Die baltische Frage und die internationale Politik der Alliierten und assoziierten Mächte 1918-1921, in: Von den baltischen Provinzen zu den baltischen Staaten. Beiträge zur Entstehungsgeschichte der Republiken Estland und Lettland 1918-1920, hg. von Jürgen von Hehn u. a., Marburg 1977, S. 327-377.

Bradley, John F. N. L'intervention alliée dans les états Baltes, in: Études Slaves et Est- Européennes 12 (1967), Heft 2-3, S. 71-83.

Buzinkai, Donald I. The Bolsheviks, the League of Nations and the Paris Peace Conference,

1919, in: Soviet Studies 19 (1967), Nr. 2, S. 257-263.

BDFA = British Documents on Foreign Affairs, Teil 2, Reihe 1 (The Paris Peace Conference of 1919), Band 1 (Preparations for the Conference and Early Meetings) und Band 2 (The Paris Peace Conference of 1919, Supreme Council Minutes, January-March 1919). Frederick (MD) 1989.

CAB 23/9 = British Imperial War Cabinet Minutes 23/9 (08.01.1919-31.03.1919), URL: http://filestore.nationalarchives.gov.uk/pdfs/large/cab-23-9.pdf" http://filestore.nationalarchives.gov.uk/pdfs/large/cab-23-9.pdf, 25.02.2017.

CAB 23/42 = British Imperial War Cabinet Minutes 23/42 (13.08.1918-31.12.1918), URL: http://filestore.nationalarchives.gov.uk/pdfs/large/cab-23-42.pdf, 25.02.2017.

Churchill, Winston The World Crisis, Band 5 (The Aftermath), London 1929.

Conze, Eckart Die große Illusion. Versailles 1919 und die Neuordnung der Welt, München 2018.

COOPER, JOHN MILTON Woodrow Wilson. A Biography, New York 2009.

DCER = Documents on Canadian External Relations, Band 2. The Paris Peace Conference 1919, Ottawa 1969.

DDF = Documents Diplomatiques Français. Armistices et Paix (1918-1920), Band 1 (1918/19), Bruxelles 2014.

DDS = Documents Diplomatiques Suisses, Band 7 (1918-1920), 1. Buch, Bern 1979.

DEBO, RICHARD K. Survival and Consolidation. The Foreign Policy of Soviet Russia 1918-1921, Montreal u. a. 1992.

DEBO, RICHARD K. The Manuilskii Mission. An Early Soviet Effort to Negotiate with France, August 1918-April 1919, in: The International History Review 8 (1986), Nr. 2, S. 214-235.

DEGRAS, JANE Soviet Documents on Foreign Policy, Band 1 (1917-1924), London 1951.

FLOTO, INGA Colonel House in Paris. A Study of American Policy at the Paris Peace Conference, 1919, Aarhus 1979.

FRUS = Papers Relating to the Foreign Relations of the United States 1919 (Russia). New York 1969.

HOVI, KARLERVO Cordon Sanitaire or Barriere de l'Est? The Emergence of the New French Eastern European Alliance Policy 1917-1919, Turku 1975.

KENNAN, GEORGE Russia and the Versailles Conference, in: The American Scholar 30 (1960/61), Nr. 1, S. 13-42.

KATZER, NIKOLAUS Die weiße Bewegung in Russland. Herrschaftsbildung, praktische Politik und politische Programmatik im Bürgerkrieg, Köln 1999.

LEONHARD, JÖRN Der überforderte Frieden. Versailles und die Welt 1918-1923, München 2018.

LLOYD GEORGE, DAVID The Truth about the Peace Treaties (Band 1), London 1938.

MACMILLAN, MARGARET Paris 1919. Six Months That Changed the World, New York 2003.

MANELA, EREZ Die Morgenröte einer neuen Ära. Der „Wilsonische Augenblick" und die Transformation der kolonialen Ordnung der Welt, 1917-1920, in: Globalgeschichte. Theorien, Ansätze, Themen, hg von SEBASTIAN CONRAD u. a., Frankfurt/New York 2007, S. 282-312.

MAYER, ARNO J. Politics and Diplomacy of Peacemaking. Containment and Counterrevolution at Versailles, 1918-1919, London 1967.

NEILSON, KEITH 'That elusive entity British policy in Russia': the Impact of Russia on British Policy at the Paris Peace Conference, in: The Paris Peace

Conference, 1919. Peace without Victory?, hg. von MICHAEL DOCKRILL u. a., New York 2001, S. 67-102.

SHARP, ALAN The Versailles Settlement. Peacemaking in Paris, London ³2018.

ŠTEJN, BORIS E. Die „Russische Frage" auf der Pariser Friedenskonferenz 1919-1920, Leipzig 1953.

STEVENSON, DAVID The First World War and International Politics, Oxford 1988.

THOMPSON, JOHN M. Rezension zu Štejn, Boris E. „Russkij vopros" na parižskoj mirnoj konferencii (1919-1920), in: The American Slavic and East European Review 9 (1950), Nr. 3, S. 218f.

THOMPSON, JOHN M. Russia, Bolshevism, and the Versailles Peace, Princeton 1966.

ULLMAN, RICHARD H. Britain and the Russian Civil War (Anglo-Soviet Relations, 1917-1921), Princeton 1968.

WALWORTH, ARTHUR Wilson and His Peacemakers, New York 1986.

WILLIAMS, HAROLD „It Gives Breating Space to Bolsheviki, Says Former Correspondent in Russia", in: NYT, 13.02.1919, S. 14, URL: www.nytimes.com/1919/02/13/archives/the-prinkipo-conference-it-gives-new-breating-space-to-bolsheviki.html?searchResultPosition=1, 23.07.2019.

WILSON, WOODROW The Papers of Woodrow Wilson, Band 55, Princeton 1986.

O. V. „Dr. Butler Assails Wilson's Policies", in: NYT, 12.02.1919, S. 12, URL: https://www.nytimes.com/1919/02/12/archives/dr-butler-assails-wilsons-policies-says-american-people-are-tired.html?searchResultPosition=1, 23.07.2019.

Benjamin Conrad

Eine Paris-Rigaer Friedensordnung? Zur historischen Verortung der Friedenskonferenz von Riga 1920-1921 nach dem Ersten Weltkrieg

Kaum zwei Jahre jung spielte die Republik Lettland zu Beginn der 1920er Jahre eine Rolle, deren Bedeutung weit über die Geschichte des Landes, ja des Baltikums hinausreichte: 1920 und 1921 war die Stadt Riga neutraler Gastgeber der nach ihr benannten Rigaer Friedenskonferenz. Diese Konferenz beendete den Polnisch-Sowjetischen Krieg, der seit April 1920 gewährt hatte.

Damals hatte sich der seit eineinhalb Jahren amtierende Staatschef Józef Piłsudski dagegen entschieden, einen möglichen Friedensvertrag mit den Sowjets abzuschließen – ganz anders als dies beispielsweise Estland nach dem Sieg der Bolschewiki im Russischen Bürgerkrieg 1919 getan hatte. Stattdessen sollte in einem Feldzug gemeinsam mit der Regierung und den Truppen der Ukrainischen Volksrepublik (UNR) unter Ataman Symon Petljura die im Gange begriffene Inkorporation der Ukraine in den sowjetischen Machtbereich abgewendet werden.[1]

Die Offensive begann am 25. April 1920. Nach Anfangserfolgen – so konnte am 7. Mai 1920 Kiew besetzt werden – blieb der polnische Angriff stecken. Die Gegenoffensive der Roten Armee führte diese im Norden Polens bis nach Soldau, das noch wenige Monate zuvor zum Deutschen Reich gehört hatte, in der Mitte bis 25 Kilometer vor Warschau und im Süden Polens bis vor Lemberg. Zwischen Warschau und Lemberg konnte im August 1920 das polnische Militär unter Piłsudski eine neuerliche Wende erreichen, die später als *Cud nad Wisłą* (Wunder an der Weichsel) in die Geschichtsbücher einging – obwohl dies ein Begriff war, der von Piłsudskis Gegnern ersonnen worden war. Im Anschluss kam es zu einem erneuten polnischen Vormarsch, beide Seiten waren jedoch ausgelaugt und begannen parallel mit Verhandlungen.[2]

---

1 Palij, Ukrainian-Polish Defensive Alliance, S. 62-91.

2 Zum Kriegsverlauf aus der reichhaltigen Literatur: Palij, Ukrainian-Polish Defensive Alliance, S. 99-160.

Auf der Rigaer Konferenz wurde zwischen Delegierten Polens und der Sowjets von September 1920 an zunächst um einen Waffenstillstand und dann um einen Frieden für die beiden größten Staaten im Osteuropa der Zwischenkriegszeit verhandelt. Schon am 12. Oktober 1920 konnte ein Waffenstillstands- und Vorfriedensvertrag abgeschlossen werden,[3] die Unterzeichnung des endgültigen Friedensvertrags zog sich dann allerdings bis zum 18. März 1921.[4]

Im Vordergrund der Rigaer Friedenskonferenz standen Regelungen der Grenzziehung. Diese wurden hauptsächlich mit dem Waffenstillstands- und Vorfriedensvertrag vom Oktober 1920 ausgehandelt. Die endgültige Fassung enthielt nur geringfügige Änderungen zu Gunsten Polens in Gebieten nordwestlich und südwestlich von Minsk.[5] Um die Frage der Grenzen Polens soll es in nachfolgendem Aufsatz jedoch nicht gehen. Dieser Text beschäftigt sich vielmehr mit der historischen Einordnung der Friedenskonferenz.

Der Frieden wurde zeitgleich mit zwei anderen Ereignissen geschlossen, die für die Zwischenkriegszeit Polens Weichen stellten: Tags zuvor, am 17. März 1921, hatte der Verfassungsgebende Sejm das Kernelement seiner Arbeit vollendet und die Märzverfassung der Zweiten Republik Polens verabschiedet. Zwei Tage nach der Vertragsunterzeichnung in Riga fand am 20. März 1921 der für das deutsch-polnische Verhältnis prägende Volksentscheid über die Zugehörigkeit Oberschlesiens statt, der den letzten Abschnitt bei der Formierung der Westgrenze Polens besiegelte. Somit fiel der Vertragsschluss von Riga in eine Zeit, in der sich das Ende für verschiedene Prozesse abzeichnete, die die Jahre nach dem Ersten Weltkrieg und die verschiedenen Folgekriege in Osteuropa prägten – gemeint sind insbesondere der Russische Bürgerkrieg, die Unabhängigkeitskriege der verschiedenen, vormals auf zarisch-russischem Gebiet gelegenen, Staaten und schließlich der Polnisch-Sowjetische Krieg.

Nahezu allen baltischen Außenpolitikern war nach diesen Ereignissen an einer stabilen Ordnung gelegen. Gerade aus diesem Bedürfnis nach Sicherheit hatte Lettlands Außenminister Zigfrīds Anna Meierovics den Regierungen

---

3 Russische Fassung des Vertrags: Dokumenty vnešnej politiki SSSR, Bd. 3, S. 245-258. Polnische Fassung: Dokumenty i materiały do historii stosunków polsko-radzieckich, Bd. 3, S. 465-475; Palij, Ukrainian-Polish Defensive Alliance, S. 155-160; Conrad, Umkämpfte Grenzen, umkämpfte Bevölkerung, S. 239-245.

4 Russische Fassung des Vertrags: Dokumenty vnešnej politiki SSSR, Bd. 3, S. 618-658. Polnische Fassung: Dokumenty i materiały do historii stosunków polsko-radzieckich, Bd. 3, S. 572-609; Conrad, Umkämpfte Grenzen, umkämpfte Bevölkerung, S. 245-248.

5 Dąbski, Pokój ryski, S. 142-144, S. 170-171; Conrad, Umkämpfte Grenzen, umkämpfte Bevölkerung, S. 246.

Polens und Sowjetrusslands Riga als Austragungsort einer solchen Friedenskonferenz zugesagt und sie am 21. September 1920 auch persönlich eröffnet.[6]

Tagungsort war das bekannte Schwarzhäupterhaus im Zentrum der Altstadt Rigas. 1941 von der deutschen Wehrmacht zerstört, wurde in den 1990er Jahren ein originalgetreuer Wiederaufbau des Schwarzhäupterhauses errichtet. Bevor 2011 der Präsidentensitz Lettlands vom baufälligen Deutschordensschloss hierherwechselte, erinnerten Ausstellungsobjekte im damaligen Museum des Schwarzhäupterhauses an die Rigaer Friedenskonferenz. Dort vermittelte ein groß dimensioniertes Gruppenfoto der Konferenzteilnehmer einen Eindruck der Größe bei insgesamt etwa 150 Teilnehmern. Ebenfalls fand sich eine von der polnischen Botschaft in den 1990er Jahren an die Republik Lettland geschenkte Kopie des Friedensvertrags, die in einer Vitrine zu sehen war. Sowohl die polnische Titelseite links mit der Aufschrift *Traktat pokoju między Polską a Rosją i Ukrainą* (Friedensvertrag zwischen Polen und Russland sowie der Ukraine) als auch die Seite der Signatare und der Siegelkopien rechts waren aufgeschlagen. Zu diesen beiden Objekten kam noch eine zweisprachig lettisch-polnische Tafel, finanziert von der Warschauer Firma *BISS International*, hinzu. Diese war im Treppenhaus des Schwarzhäupterhauses angeschlagen und enthielt folgenden Text:

> „Melngalvju Namā 1921 g. 18 marta starp Polijas Republiku, Padomju Krieviju un Ukrainu tika noslēgts miera traktāts pazīstams arī kā Rīgas Miera Līgums izbeidzot karu un noliegot Polijas austrumu robežas. Polijas Republikas Vēstniecība. (Polnisch) Tu w domu czarnogłowych 18 marca 1921 roku zawarto między Rzecząpospolitą Polską a Radziecką Rosją i Ukrainą traktat pokoju znany jako Traktat Ryski kończący wojnę oraz ustalający wschodnie granice Polski. Ambasada RP w Rydze.“[7]

(Hier im Schwarzhäupterhaus wurde am 18. März 1921 zwischen der Republik Polen und Sowjetrussland und der Ukraine ein Friedensvertrag geschlossen, der als Frieden von Riga bekannt ist. Dieser beendete den Krieg und die Festlegung der Ostgrenze Polens. Die Botschaft der Republik Polen).

Die Beteiligung der „Ukraine“ bedarf einer Präzisierung: Zum Zeitpunkt des Friedensvertrags gab es verschiedene Akteure, die für sich reklamierten, Repräsentanten der Ukraine zu sein. Der Bekannteste war der bereits genannte Symon Petljura, dessen Regierung der UNR in Kontinuität zum 1917 gegründeten Ukrainischen Zentralen Rat stand. Diese Regierung konnte am ehesten den Rückhalt

---

6 AAN, Bestand 322 Ministerstwo spraw zagranicznych, Sign. 6737, S. 46; Dąbski, Pokój ryski, S. 77f.; Wandycz, Soviet-Polish Relations, S. 259.

7 Die Tafel wurde durch den Verfasser dieses Aufsatzes am 2. August 2008 abfotografiert.

der Mehrheit der ukrainischen Bevölkerung behaupten. Nach dem Scheitern der polnischen Offensive befand sich Petljura mit seiner Regierung jedoch im Exil in Polen. Die andere ukrainische Staatlichkeit war die Ukrainische Sozialistische Sowjetrepublik, die Ende 1917 von einer Gruppe meist russischsprachiger Ukrainer ausgerufen worden war. Ihre Machtbasis innerhalb der ukrainischen Bevölkerung war wesentlich schwächer, mit Hilfe der im Russischen Bürgerkrieg erfolgreichen Roten Armee hatte sich der Rat der Volkskommissare der Ukrainischen SSR als moskau-höriges Regime 1918-1920 jedoch Stück um Stück in der Ukraine durchsetzen können.[8]

Im Vorfeld der Friedenskonferenz sagte die polnische Regierung die Akzeptanz einer sowjetukrainischen Delegation zu. Delegierte der UNR waren hingegen offiziell nicht zugelassen, auch wenn es eine UNR-Gruppe vor Ort gab, die freilich Zaungast blieb.[9] Damit hatte die polnische Regierung bereits zu Beginn der Verhandlungen ihr ursprüngliches Kriegsziel, nämlich die Inkorporation der Ukraine in das Sowjetsystem zu verhindern, preisgegeben. Piłsudski war in seinen Zielen vom April 1920 gescheitert.

Die formal selbstständige ukrainische Delegation war kaum mehr als eine sowjetische Marionettenveranstaltung. Ihre Hilflosigkeit wurde ganz am Ende der Konferenz deutlich, als es darum ging, neben der russischen und polnischen auch eine ukrainische Fassung des Waffenstillstands- und Vorfriedensvertrags vom Oktober 1920 als auch des definitiven Friedensvertrags vom März 1921 anzufertigen. Die „ukrainischen“ Delegierten waren hierzu nicht in der Lage, da sie das Ukrainische nicht ausreichend beherrschten und es den Sowjets offenkundig von Oktober 1920, als das Problem erstmalig aufgetreten war, bis März 1921 nicht möglich war, geeignetes Personal nach Riga zu entsenden. Aus der polnischen Delegation behob Leon Wasilewski, der der Delegation angehörende, sehr gut Ukrainisch sprechende polnische Gesandte in Estland, diese für die Sowjets peinliche wie entlarvende Situation. Wasilewski, der 1918 erster Außenminister Polens gewesen war, galt als enger Vertrauter Piłsudskis. Durch eine Übersetzung beider Verträge ermöglichte Wasilewski den Sowjets den Schein einer selbstständigen und souveränen ukrainischen Beteiligung zu wahren.[10]

---

8 Vgl. aus der zahlreichen Literatur u. a. MAGOCSI, A History of Ukraine, S. 481-511.

9 WANDYCZ, Soviet-Polish Relations, S. 259, 269.

10 KUMANIECKI, Tajny raport, S. 163; POBÓG-MALINOWSKI, Najnowsza historia polityczna Polski, S. 552; PIETRZAK, Leon Wasilewski, S. 351f.; CONRAD, Umkämpfte Grenzen, umkämpfte Bevölkerung, S. 249.

Warum die polnische Botschaft auf der bereits genannten Tafel im Schwarzhäupterhaus die damaligen Machtverhältnisse nicht durch Hinzufügung der Worte *Padomju* vor Lettisch *Ukrainu* bzw. *Radziecką* vor Polnisch *Ukrainą* – die in der deutschen Übersetzung aus dem Wort *Ukraine* das Wort *Sowjetukraine* gemacht hätten – kenntlich machte, muss auf sich gestellt bleiben. Im Folgenden bleibt die Ukraine außer Betracht und es wird lediglich aufgrund der tatsächlichen Machtverhältnisse von zwei Vertragsparteien, der polnischen und der sowjetrussischen, die Rede sein.

Sowohl die im Schwarzhäupterhaus ausgestellte Vertragskopie als auch die angeschlagene Tafel zeigen bereits klar, für welche der beiden Vertragsparteien dieser Frieden eine besondere Bedeutung hatte und bis heute hat. Ein Blick in die Forschungsliteratur bestätigt, dass der Frieden vor allem von polnischer Seite erforscht worden ist. Bereits in der Volksrepublik Polen gab es einen Spezialisten, der sich schwerpunktmäßig mit diesem Frieden, seiner Genese wie auch seiner Auswirkungen beschäftige. Solch eine Herausbildung eines zentralen Spezialisten für eine historische Einzelfragestellung war typisch für die Volksrepublik Polen.

Im Falle der Rigaer Friedenskonferenz war dieser Spezialist Jerzy Kumaniecki (1938-1991), der am Institut für Geschichte der Polnischen Akademie der Wissenschaften in Warschau tätig war. Neben Aufsätzen[11] veröffentlichte Kumaniecki zwei Monografien zum Thema, nämlich 1971 *Po traktacie ryskim. Stosunki polsko-radzieckie 1921-1923* (Nach dem Rigaer Vertrag. Die polnisch-sowjetischen Beziehungen 1921-1923) und 1985 *Pokój polsko-radziecki 1921. Geneza, rokowania, traktat, komisje mieszane* (Der polnisch-sowjetische Friede 1921. Genese, Verhandlungen, Vertrag, gemischte Kommissionen).[12]

Kumaniecki gehörte dabei der zweiten Generation von in der Volksrepublik Polen publizierenden Historikern an. Diese veröffentlichten in den 1970er und 1980er Jahren Werke, die nur noch selten die Methodologie des Historischen Materialismus und die üblichen sozialistischen Propagandadarstellungen nutzten, was beispielsweise zeitgleich in der DDR oder der UdSSR noch vielfach unmöglich gewesen war. Sozialistische Gehirnakrobatik dahingehend, den polnischen Lesern die sowjetische Position in den Vertragsverhandlungen als die berechtigtere darzustellen, weil die polnische Delegation überwiegend aus

11 Aus dessen Œuvre zum Thema: Kumaniecki, Polska a powstanie Związku Socjalistycznych Republik Rad; Kumaniecki, Uznanie wschodniej granicy Polski; Kumaniecki, Z genezy traktatu ryskiego; Kumaniecki, Dwa oblicza dyplomacji radzieckiej.

12 Kumaniecki, Po traktacie ryskim; Kumaniecki, Pokój polsko-radziecki 1921.

„bourgeoisen" Politikern bestanden hatte, kommt bei Kumaniecki 1971 nur in zurückhaltendem Umfang, 1985 sogar kaum noch vor.

Dennoch würdigte er selbstverständlich die sowjetische Position ausführlich – eine Tatsache, die nach dem Zusammenbruch des Ostblocks 1989 in polnischen Publikationen nicht mehr zwingend nötig war. Spätere Werke, wie die von Jacek Arkadiusz Goclon aus den Jahren 2000-2006, nehmen bereits mit der Titelwahl die zu erzählende Heils- und Heldengeschichte vorweg; hier finden sich zum Beispiel: *1920: Ojczyzna w niebezpieczeństwie* (1920: Das Vaterland in Gefahr) und *Wojna z bolszewicką Rosją o niepodległość Polski 1919-1920* (Der Krieg mit dem bolschewistischen Russland um die Unabhängigkeit Polens 1919-1920) sowie *W obronie Europy. Wojna z bolszewicką Rosją w 1920 roku* (In Verteidigung Europas. Der Krieg mit dem bolschewistischen Russland im Jahr 1920).[13] Solche Titel gehen anders als bei Kumaniecki wiederum fast zwangsläufig mit einer bedingten Einseitigkeit einher.

1991, im Jahre seines Todes und unmittelbar nach dem Ende der Volksrepublik, publizierte Kumaniecki noch eine von ihm selbst gehaltene Rede über Pëtr Vojkov, den späteren sowjetischen Botschafter in Warschau. Vojkov war Mitglied einer der fünf durch den Friedensvertrag von Riga eingesetzten polnisch-sowjetischen gemischten Kommissionen. Dieser setzte sich mit Erfolg für eine Taktik der Verhinderung der Rückgabe polnischen Kulturguts ein, das im Ersten Weltkrieg vom Zarenreich gen Osten abtransportiert worden war. Im November 1923 berichtete Vojkov in einem geheimen Bericht, der in 45 Exemplaren in der Druckerei des damaligen sowjetischen Staatssicherheitsdiensts GPU gedruckt worden war, an die Sowjetführung. Kumaniecki konnte diesen Bericht in den 1960er Jahren bei eigenen Recherchen in Moskau einsehen. Die Übersetzung des in der polnischen Übersetzung 107 Seiten starken Vojkov-Berichts fertigte Aleksander Achmatowicz an.[14]

In der postkommunistischen Zeit erschienen zu Jubiläen des Rigaer Friedens eine ganze Reihe von Publikationen polnischer Provenienz. Zum 75. Jubiläum erschien der umfangreiche und von den Zwängen sozialistischer Forschung vollständig befreite Band *Traktat ryski 1921 roku po 75 lat* (Der Rigaer Vertrag von 1921 nach 75 Jahren), herausgegeben von Mieczysław Wojciechowski.[15]

---

13 Goclon, 1920. Ojczyzna w niebezpieczeństwie; Goclon, Wojna z bolszewicką Rosją; Goclon, W obronie Europy. Sehr ähnlich: Zamoyski, Warszawa 1920. Ebenso neuere Werke wie Chwalba, Przegrane zwycięstwo, Śledziński, Wojna polsko-bolszewicka.

14 Kumaniecki, Tajny raport, S. 9f.

15 Wojciechowski, Traktat ryski.

In diesem Werk publizierte auch der eben genannte Aleksander Achmatowicz einen Artikel, der einen weitgehenden Deutungsanspruch formulierte, auf den noch ausführlich zu sprechen gekommen wird.[16]

2006 erschien ein Neudruck des Vertragstextes unter dem Titel *Traktat Pokoju między Polską a Rosją i Ukrainą. Ryga 18 marca 1921* (Der Friedensvertrag zwischen Polen und Russland und der Ukraine. Riga, 18. März 1921) zum 85. Jubiläum des Vertrags. Dieser von Bronisław Komorowski eingeleitete und herausgegebene Neudruck trägt als Cover auf der Titelseite das wiederaufgebaute Schwarzhäupterhaus. Komorowski, ein studierter Historiker, amtierte zu diesem Zeitpunkt für die Partei *Platforma Obywatelska* (Bürgerplattform) als Vizemarschall des Sejm. 2010-2015 sollte er das Staatspräsidentenamt Polens bekleiden. Der Neudruck unterstreicht die hohe Symbolik und die weit über das Fachinteresse von Historikern hinausgehende öffentliche Interesse an dem Vertrag in Polen.[17]

Im Umfeld des 90. Jahrestags des Friedensvertrags entstanden einige Publikationen des polnisch-kanadischen Historikers Jerzy Borzęcki, der in der Tradition der nordamerikanischen exilpolnischen Forschung steht. 23 Jahre nach Jerzy Kumanieckis Werk erschien seine Monografie *Soviet-Polish peace of 1921 and the creation of interwar Europe*; ein Werk, das bereits im Titel einen weitergehenden Deutungsanspruch erhebt. 2012 gab das Polnische Institut für internationale Beziehungen eine polnische Übersetzung dieses Buches unter dem Titel *Pokój ryski 1921 roku i kształtowanie się międzywojennej Europy Wschodniej* (Der Friede von Riga von 1921 und die Ausgestaltung Osteuropas in der Zwischenkriegszeit) heraus.[18]

Der vormalige Direktor des Polnischen Instituts für internationale Beziehungen (2007-2010), Sławomir Dębski, der 2011-2016 als Direktor des Warschauer Zentrums für den polnisch-russischen Dialog und Verständigung amtierte, gab schließlich 2013 einen weiteren umfangreichen Sammelband mit dem Titel *Zapomniany pokój. Traktat ryski. Interpretacje i kontrowersje 90 lat później* (Der vergessene Friede. Der Friede von Riga. Interpretationen und Kontroversen 90 Jahre danach) heraus, an dem auch Borzęcki mitgewirkt hatte.[19]

---

16 Achmatowicz, Traktat ryski.

17 Komorowski, Traktat Pokoju. Dass es sich bei dem Herausgeber der Quellenedition in der Tat um den späteren Staatspräsidenten handelt, bestätigte Maciej Ptaszyński, Universität Warschau, ein früherer Mitarbeiter Komorowskis, dem Autor dieses Aufsatzes.

18 Borzęcki, Soviet-Polish peace; Borzęcki, Pokój ryski 1921 roku. Weiterer einschlägiger Titel des Autors: Borzęcki, Niełatwy kompromis.

19 Dębski, Zapomniany pokój; Borzęcki, Pokój ryski w historii Europy.

Neben dem großen Interesse der polnischen Forschung leisten die restriktiven Archivzugänge in Russland ebenfalls ihren Beitrag zu einseitigen Studien über die Konferenz.[20] Dennoch hätte eine stärkere Erforschung der Friedenskonferenz aus russischer Perspektive das Ungleichgewicht vermindert, sicher aber nicht beseitigt. Es überrascht daher nicht, dass es polnische Historiker waren, die den Vorschlag einer Erweiterung des bislang im Deutschen allgemein als *Pariser Friedensordnung* bezeichneten internationalen Systems nach dem Ersten Weltkrieg gemacht haben, worum es im Folgenden gehen soll.

Erstmalig sprach 1998 Achmatowicz in seinem Beitrag zum Sammelband zum 75. Jahrestag von der *ład wersalsko-ryski*, also der Versailles-Rigaer Ordnung.[21] Dies griff 2008 und 2012 Jerzy Borzęcki im Schluss seiner Monografie zum Friedensvertrag unter expliziter Berufung auf Achmatowicz auf, grenzte den Begriff aber vorsichtiger zu einem *Versailles-Riga system in East-Central Europe*[22] bzw. in der polnischen Ausgabe zu einer *ład wersalsko-ryski w Europie Środkowo-Wschodniej* ein.[23] Sławomir Dębski proklamierte in seiner Einführung zum 2013 erschienen Band zum 90. Jubiläum des Friedens hingegen wie Achmatowicz erneut ein *system wersalsko-ryski*, also ein Versailles-Rigaer System, dies mit dem Verweis auf die Möglichkeit der Etablierung von Staatlichkeit für die kleineren und mittelgroßen osteuropäischen Nationalitäten.[24]

Dębski war auch Mitglied der 2002 ins Leben gerufenen, 27-köpfigen polnisch-russischen Studiengruppe für schwierige Fragen der gemeinsamen Beziehungsgeschichte.[25] Diese Gruppe, die ihre Namen in beiden Sprachen verschiedentlich wechselte, entfaltete 2008-2013 den Höhepunkt ihrer Tätigkeit.[26] Aus Anlass des 90. Jahrestags des Friedens von Riga fand auch eine Sitzung der

20 Der Autor dieses Aufsatzes hat 2009 versucht, in das Archiv der auswärtigen Politik der Russländischen Föderation (*Archiv Vnešnej Politiki Rossijskoj Federacii*) eingelassen zu werden. Dieses stellt kein Staatsarchiv im eigentlichen Sinne dar, sondern ein Behördenarchiv. Als Beschäftigte eines Behördenarchivs dürfen seine Bediensteten wählerisch bei der Genehmigung von Zugängen sein und erfanden damals gegenüber vielen ausländischen Promovierenden kreative Ausreden, warum ein Archivzugang nicht möglich wäre.

21 Achmatowicz, Traktat ryski, S. 366.

22 Borzęcki, Soviet-Polish peace, S. 281.

23 Borzęcki, Pokój ryski 1921 roku i, S. 391f.

24 Dębski, Zapomniany pokój, S. 31.

25 Rotfeld/Torkunow, Białe plamy, czarne plamy, S. 891f.

26 Rotfeld/Torkunov, White Spots – Black Spots, S. 656-658.

Gruppe im Juni 2011 im wiederaufgebauten Rigaer Schwarzhäupterhaus statt.[27] 2010 wurden voluminöse Berichtsbände in polnischer und russischer Sprache publizierte, wobei für die polnische Fassung offenbar signifikant höhere Mittel zur Verfügung gestanden haben.[28] 2015 erschien noch eine verkürzte englische Fassung, dies ein Jahr nachdem der Angriff Russlands auf die Ukraine den Zusammenbruch der Gruppe herbeigeführt hatte.[29] Im Anschluss trat der polnische Ko-Vorsitzende Adam Rotfeld Ende 2015 zurück.[30] Eine Wiederbelebung 2017 in anderer Zusammensetzung entfaltete keine nennenswerten Aktivitäten mehr.[31] Russlands Angriff auf die Ukraine 2022 verunmöglichte schließlich auf unbestimmte Zeit derartige Studiengruppen.

In den Publikationen der Studiengruppe agierte die polnische Seite begrifflich zurückhaltender. Der polnische Beitrag zum Beginn der polnisch-sowjetischen Beziehungen von Daria und Tomasz Nałęcz betont die Bedeutung des Friedens von Riga nicht nur für Polen und Sowjetrussland, sondern auch für die Stabilisierung Osteuropas insgesamt, vermied jedoch eine begriffliche Definition der Friedensordnung.[32] Dębski hingegen nannte sie in seinem Aufsatz abweichend zu seinen bereits genannten Publikationen schon im Titel *system wersalski* (poln.) sowie *Versailles System* (engl.).[33] In der russischen Fassung hat der Aufsatz zwar einen anderen Titel, der Begriff *Versal'skaja sistema* wird aber im Text genannt.[34] Das russische Pendant zum Aufsatz von Daria und Tomasz Nałęcz, verfasst von Gennadij Matveev, betrachtete – ganz den sowjetischen Traditionen folgend – den Frieden von Riga lediglich aus Perspektive der Erfolglosigkeit der Politik Piłsudskis und der Instabilität Polens aufgrund der großen nationalen Minderheiten. Die politische Ordnung nach dem Ersten Weltkrieg benannte Matveev identisch zu Dębski *ład wersalski*, *Versal'skaja sistema* und *Versailles*

---

27 Latvijas Reitingi, Konference Polija, Krievija, Eiropa; ROTFELD/TORKUNOV, White Spots – Black Spots, S. 648f.

28 ROTFELD/TORKUNOW, Białe plamy, czarne plamy; TORKUNOV/ROTFELD, Belye pjatna – černye pjatna.

29 ROTFELD/TORKUNOV, White Spots – Black Spots,

30 E-Mail des 2021 verstorbenen Prof. Włodzimierz BORODZIEJ, Universität Warschau, an den Verfasser vom 15. April 2018.

31 Ministerstwo Spraw Zagranicznych, Wznowienie.

32 NAŁĘCZ/NAŁĘCZ, Stosunki polsko-sowieckie, S. 40; LIPIN'SKAJA-NALENČ/NALENČ, Načalo, S. 67; NAŁĘCZ/NAŁĘCZ, Polish-Soviet Relations, S. 27.

33 DĘBSKI, Przyczyny II wojny światowej, S. 141; DĘBSKI, Crisis of the Versailles System, S. 105.

34 DEMBSKIJ, Proischoždenie vtoroj mirovoj vojny, S. 166.

System,[35] wobei die geringfügig abweichende begriffliche Wiedergabe im Polnischen sicher nicht auf Matveev selbst zurückgeht.

Die genannten Neuinterpretationen polnischer Historiker stießen also innerhalb der Studiengruppe nicht auf Resonanz, ja, wurden vielleicht aus diplomatischer Zurückhaltung gar nicht genannt. Auch anderswo waren diese Neuinterpretationen nicht anschlussfähig. Im letzten Abschnitt dieses Aufsatzes soll die bisherige internationale Nicht-Resonanz durchbrochen und eine über die bisherige Interpretation hinausgehende mögliche Bedeutung für Ostmitteleuropa oder sogar für ganz Europa im Folgenden etwas genauer untersucht werden.

Als Hauptgrund für die vorgeschlagene Terminologie wird von den polnischen Historikern die rund zwanzigjährige Unterbrechung der sowjetischen Expansion in den ostmitteleuropäischen und südosteuropäischen Raum angeführt, die durch den Frieden erreicht worden wäre. Achmatowicz formulierte 1998 die inhaltlich weitestgehende Deutung der Signifikanz des Vertrages, die in – womöglich von ihm nicht zu vertretenen – englischen Übersetzung besonders weitläufig ausfällt:

> Historic weight of the Treaty of Riga lies in the fact that countries like Poland, Lithuania, Latvia, Estonia and Finland as well as former states of Habsburgian Monarchy (Austria, Hungary, Czech Republic and Slovak Republic) and the republics of former Yugoslavia can be found on a political map of Europe.[36]

Im polnischen Original des Beitrags von Achmatowicz entfällt die Einbeziehung der gegenwärtigen Nachfolgestaaten der Tschechoslowakei und Jugoslawiens. Finnland, Estland, Lettland, Litauen, Polen sowie die Tschechoslowakei und der SHS-Staat als Nachfolgestaaten Österreich-Ungarns werden allerdings auch im polnischen Original explizit genannt.[37] Wäre der Friede von Riga also 1921 nicht geschlossen worden, wären demnach die 1917/1918 ausgerufenen genannten Staaten nicht auf der politischen Landkarte Europas zurückgekehrt – eine Behauptung, die schon aus chronologischer Sicht nicht unproblematisch ist.

Achmatowicz, Borzęcki und Dębski haben mit ihrer Bedeutungsdiskussion nicht vollständig unrecht: Die in Paris 1919-1920 vereinbarte Friedensordnung umschloss zwar ganz weitgehend Ostmittel- und Südosteuropa, nicht aber die Gebiete des alten Zarenreiches. Verantwortlich dafür war der Sieg der Sowjets

---

35 Matwiejew, Stosunki polsko-sowieckie, S. 55, 91; Matveev, Načalo, S. 24, 41; Matveyev, Polish-Soviet Relations, S. 39, 56.

36 Achmatowicz, Traktat ryski, S. 370.

37 Achmatowicz, Traktat ryski, S. 368.

im Russischen Bürgerkrieg. Diesen Erfolg hatten die Westalliierten nicht auf ihrer Rechnung, als sie 1918 und 1919 die Weiße Bewegung Russlands genauso wie diverse nationale Separationsbewegungen direkt oder zumindest indirekt unterstützten. Und in der Tat hätte die Haltbarkeit der Friedensverträge Sowjetrusslands von Dorpat mit Estland und später mit Finnland sowie von Moskau mit Litauen und von Riga mit Lettland möglicherweise ohne den polnisch-sowjetrussischen Frieden anders ausgesehen.[38] Die in den Friedensverträgen von Dorpat, Moskau und Riga 1920 von den Sowjets versprochene Anerkennung der Unabhängigkeit der drei baltischen Staaten *na večnye vremena*[39] (für alle Zeiten) und Finnlands[40] wäre vielleicht noch kürzer ausgefallen, hätte sich Polen im Polnisch-Sowjetischen Krieg nicht behaupten können.[41] Der erfolglose Putschversuch der Kommunisten in Estland 1924 war nämlich schon zeitgenössisch ein stichhaltiger Beweis für die weiter bestehenden territorialen Aspirationen der UdSSR abseits der Verträge, mit denen es die Regierung in Moskau schon 1924 nicht so genau nahm – von 1939/40 ganz abgesehen.

Sollte aber deshalb begrifflich die *Pariser* einer *Versailles-Rigaer Friedensordnung* weichen? Diese Begrifflichkeit erscheint die polnische Rolle am Ausgang des Ersten Weltkriegs etwas zu hoch zu hängen. In Versailles wurden mit dem Frieden mit Deutschland die außenpolitischen Rahmenbedingungen der Wiedergründung Polens festgelegt, ebenso der Völkerbund gegründet und der Minderheitenschutzvertrag der Alliierten mit der Republik Polen geschlossen. Für andere Teile Osteuropas, insbesondere für Südosteuropa, spielen jedoch auch die Verträge von St. Germain und Neuilly-sur-Seine, insbesondere aber derjenige von Trianon zentrale Rollen. Wollte man also einen neuen Globalbegriff schaffen, der auch über das polnische Beispiel hinaus Gültigkeit entfalten sollte, so sollte nicht von einer Versailles-Rigaer Ordnung, sondern wenn überhaupt von einer Paris-Rigaer Ordnung gesprochen werden – um somit allen Pariser Vorortverträgen gerecht zu werden.

---

38 Russische Fassungen des Vertrags von Dorpat mit Estland vom 2. Februar 1920: Dokumenty vnešnej politiki SSSR, Bd. 2, S. 339-354, von Moskau mit Litauen vom 12. Juli 1920: Dokumenty vnešnej politiki SSSR, Bd. 3, S. 28-42, von Riga mit Lettland vom 11. August 1920: Dokumenty vnešnej politiki SSSR, Bd. 3, S. 101-116, von Dorpat mit Finnland vom 14. Oktober 1920: Dokumenty vnešnej politiki SSSR, Bd. 3, S. 265-282.

39 Vgl. Dokumenty vnešnej politiki SSSR, Bd. 2, 340, Bd. 3, S. 29, 102.

40 Der Vertrag mit Finnland enthält die Floskel „für alle Zeiten“ nicht, vgl. Dokumenty vnešnej politiki SSSR, Bd. 3, S. 265f.

41 Dieselbe Ansicht vertritt in diesem Band Karsten Brüggemann.

Ein solcher Begriff der Paris-Rigaer Friedensordnung könnte zu einem Paradigmenwechsel in der Betrachtung der Zwischenkriegszeit führen. Dass er sich durchsetzen wird, ist allerdings nicht zu erwarten – zu viele Punkte sprechen dagegen. Im Folgenden werden zwei Themenkomplexe besprochen, die der Etablierung dieses Begriffs im Wege stehen und die von den genannten polnischen Autoren in ihrem Streben nach Erhöhung des Rigaer Friedens zu wenig gewürdigt worden sind.

Im ersten dieser zwei Themenkomplexe soll es um die Frage gehen, ob der in Riga zwischen Polen und den Sowjets vereinbarte Friede eine neue Friedensperiode für Europa oder wenigstens Ostmitteleuropa begründete. Einerseits könnte eine solche Sichtweise befürwortet werden, da der Polnisch-Sowjetische Krieg die letzte Auseinandersetzung in den Nachwehen des Ersten Weltkriegs in Europa war, in dem mit Millionenheeren gekämpft worden war. Im Kern erreichte der Friedensvertrag allerdings den Friedenszustand nur für die beiden beteiligten Mächte. Denn das neben Polen auch Finnland, Estland, Lettland und Litauen nicht mehr einem irgendwie gearteten Russland angehören sollten, war anders als Achmatowicz behauptete, kaum ein Ergebnis des Rigaer Friedensvertrags von 1921, sondern bereits im vorangegangenen Jahr 1920 vertraglich vereinbart worden. Es unterschlägt auch das westalliierte Engagement für die Etablierung der Unabhängigkeit dieser Staaten ab Ende 1919, von dem gleich noch die Rede sein wird. Schon gar nicht spielte der Rigaer Friede für die von Achmatowicz angesprochene Tschechoslowakei oder für das spätere Jugoslawien eine Rolle.

Für die Gründung und Stabilisierung Finnlands, Estlands, Lettlands, Litauens und Polens hatten sich die Alliierten aus unterschiedlichen Beweggründen und auch mit gänzlich unterschiedlicher Intensität beginnend mit Polen seit 1917, also seit dem Ersten Weltkrieg, allmählich immer stärker engagiert. Diese Frage war auch Bestandteil der Pariser Konferenzberatungen von 1919. Im Juni 1919 ging Admiral Aleksandr Kolčak, der Anführer der Weißen Bewegung, auf eine Forderung der Alliierten ein und erkannte die Unabhängigkeit Finnlands und Polens definitiv für ein künftiges nicht-kommunistisches Russland an. Er schloss zudem eine Unabhängigkeit für Estland, Lettland und Litauen nicht kategorisch aus, wobei allerdings fast alle Akteure der Weißen einer Unabhängigkeit der baltischen Staaten ablehnend gegenüber standen.[42] Die 1919 bereits vorhandene Unabhängigkeit der genannten Staaten, wenn auch teilweise embryonenhaft und instabil, wäre also womöglich auch bei einem anderen Ausgang

42 Documents on British Foreign Policy, Serie I, Bd. III, S. 331f., 362-364; Katzer, Weiße Bewegung, S. 372f.

des Russischen Bürgerkriegs bestehen geblieben. Dies bleibt allerdings Spekulation. Genauso wäre denkbar, dass die Weißen ihre zahlreichen Zugeständnisse im Falle eines Erfolgs wieder kassiert hätten. Generäle wie der Kommandant der Weißen Bewegung im Süden Russlands und in der Ukraine, Anton Denikin, lehnten eine Unabhängigkeit der baltischen Staaten stets ab. Er drohte zudem der polnischen Regierung unter Piłsudski für den Falle eines Sieges der Weißen mit Repressalien.[43]

Darüber hinaus stellte der Rigaer Friede von 1921 eben nur einen, wenn auch den wichtigsten Friedensvertrag der Sowjetmacht mit einem ehemaligen Teilgebiet des untergegangenen Zarenreichs dar. Wie genannt hatte der Vertrag Sowjetrusslands mit Estland von Dorpat im Februar 1920 den ersten dieser Verträge dargestellt, der die Isolation Sowjetrusslands in der internationalen Staatenwelt durchbrochen hatte. Der Dorpater Frieden stellte ein Muster für die nachfolgenden Frieden von Moskau mit Litauen vom Juli, von Riga mit Lettland vom August und erneut von Dorpat mit Finnland vom Oktober 1920 dar. Ebenso ist in dieser Kette zu nennen, dass die sowjetische Regierung im Mai 1920 den Frieden von Moskau mit Georgien geschlossen hatte,[44] den sie allerdings schon nicht einmal ein Jahr später bereits wieder brach, um Georgien zu annektieren.

Von diesem Standpunkt aus schloss demnach der Friede von Riga zwischen Polen und Sowjetrussland 1921 eher die bereits eingetretene Entwicklung des allmählichen Ausklingens sowohl des Ersten Weltkriegs, insbesondere aber des Russischen Bürgerkriegs und der Unabhängigkeitskriege in Osteuropa auf dem vormals zarisch-russländischen Territorium ab. Bei der wechselseitigen Anerkennung der Sowjetherrschaft in Moskau im Tausch gegen die Bestätigung der bereits eingetretenen Unabhängigkeit vormals russischer Nationalitäten nahm Polen chronologisch somit lediglich Platz 6 hinter Estland, Georgien, Litauen, Lettland und Finnland ein. Dies wäre anders gewesen, hätte das von den Sowjets ab Dezember 1919 betriebene Werben um einen Friedensschluss mit Polen Früchte getragen, was aber beide Seiten endgültig im April 1920 durch kleinliche Streitereien um einen geeigneten Konferenzort verhindert hatten.[45] Gerade aber

43 Dokumenty i materiały do historii stosunków polsko-radzieckich, Bd. 2, S. 411; Cisek, Sąsiedzi wobec wojny 1920 roku, S. 43; Katzer, Weiße Bewegung, S. 375-377; Palij, Ukrainian-Polish Defensive Alliance, S. 85f.

44 Batsell, Soviet Rule in Russia, S. 247-254.

45 Dokumenty vnešnej politiki SSSR, Bd. 2, S. 427f., 480-482; Dokumenty i materiały do historii stosunków polsko-radzieckich, Bd. 2, S. 693, S. 718-719, S. 743-744; Conrad, Umkämpfte Grenzen, umkämpfte Bevölkerung, S. 221-225.

weil er damit den Prozess des Herauswachsens aus dem Krieg nicht einleitete, sondern abschloss, begründete der Rigaer Frieden eher keine Ordnung.

Der zweite Themenkomplex ist aus Perspektive von 1921 in die Zukunft gerichtet und kreist um die Frage, ob der Friede von Riga einen überregionalen Beitrag zur Begründung eines Systems der Friedenswahrung über die reine Beendigung des Krieges und die Schaffung des Friedenszustands hinaus leistete. Auch dies ist kaum zu bejahen. Die zumindest bis Anfang der 1930er Jahre auch für Osteuropa außerhalb der UdSSR relevante internationale Organisation war mit dem Völkerbund wiederum in Paris gegründet worden. Dem Völkerbund gehörte Polen als Gründungsmitglied an. Finnland, Estland, Lettland und Litauen wurden nach einigem Zögern 1920 und 1921 aufgenommen. Auch Georgien wäre als Mitglied willkommen gewesen, hätte nicht die Invasion der Sowjets 1921 die Möglichkeit des Beitritts zerschlagen.

Die Sowjetunion trat hingegen dem Völkerbund erst 1934 bei, als er nach dem Austritt des Deutschen Reiches im internationalen Mächtefeld bereits stark an Bedeutung eingebüßt hatte. In Richtung einer Integration der Sowjets in die internationale Staatengemeinschaft gingen von Riga 1920 und 1921 demnach aus naheliegenden Gründen keinerlei Impulse aus. Weder war Polen Hauptsiegermacht des Ersten Weltkriegs und hätte damit einen solchen Prozess grundsätzlich anstoßen können, noch lag eine solche Politik auch nur im Entferntesten überhaupt im Interesse der polnischen Regierung. Vielmehr waren sowohl Polens Staatschef Józef Piłsudski als auch die sich abwechselnden Ministerpräsidenten entschiedene Gegner des Sowjetstaates. Sie betrachteten den Frieden von Riga vorrangig aus Perspektive der Staatsräson. Die genannten Politiker waren, wie die Regierungen der Westalliierten, Anhänger des Gedankens des *cordon sanitaire*, also der Eindämmung der kommunistischen Staatlichkeit auf die ostslawischen Gebiete Osteuropas.

In besagter Vorstellung des *cordon sanitaire* nahm Polen sowohl als größter Staat Ostmitteleuropas einen bedeutenden Platz ein. Andererseits nahm Polen auch einen großen Platz beim Scheitern dieser Konzeption ein. Seine unflexible und oft kleinkarierte Außenpolitik, die manchmal auf ein einziges, sich auf der vermeintlich falschen Seite der Grenze befindendes Dorf zielte,[46]

46 Gemeint ist hier die Ortschaft Jaworzyna in den Karpaten, die auf Slowakisch (Tatranska) Javorina und auf Deutsch Uhrngarten heißt. Diese Ortschaft war mehrmals 1918-1920 kurzzeitig militärisch in polnischem Besitz. Bei den polnisch-tschechoslowakischen Grenzverhandlungen, die während des Polnisch-Sowjetischen Kriegs stattfanden, war die polnische Delegation auf Nachschub und Waffenlieferungen durch die Tschechoslowakei angewiesen und stimmte deshalb einer den tschechoslowakischen Wünschen

verunmöglichte sowohl den Brückenschlag gen Norden Richtung Litauen und den anderen Ostseestaaten als auch gen Süden Richtung Tschechoslowakei und den Rest der Kleine Entente.

Die größeren Staaten Europas bereinigten ihr offizielles diplomatisches Nicht-Verhältnis zur entstehenden Sowjetunion, dies sei noch nachgeschoben, ohnehin ohne jedweden Bezug zum Frieden von Riga, so Großbritannien zeitgleich bereits 1920/21, das Deutsche Reich im Rahmen des Rapallo-Vertrages 1922 und schließlich nach längerem Zögern Frankreich 1924.

Zuletzt muss die Frage auch vom Ende her gestellt werden: Bei aller Kritik an der Politik des Appeasements gegenüber dem nationalsozialistischen Deutschland blieben sich die ideologisch sehr fern stehenden Regierungen Großbritanniens, Frankreichs und Italiens 1938 treu in ihrer Linie, die von ihnen in Paris geschaffene Friedensordnung zunächst mit friedlichen Mitteln erhalten zu wollen, auch wenn dies erhebliche Konzessionen an das expansionistische Deutsche Reich beinhaltete. 1939 entschlossen sich dann mit der britischen und französischen zwei der drei genannten Regierungen, sich auch mit Gewalt der Expansionspolitik Deutschlands entgegen zu stellen. Beide Politiken, sowohl die des Appeasements als auch die des militärischen Widerstands scheiterten, lassen aber eine gemeinsame Grundhaltung erkennen.

Wie agierten die Regierungen Polens und der Sowjetunion 1938 und 1939? Zunächst befand sich Polen im Fahrwasser der nationalsozialistischen deutschen Außenpolitik, was sich 1938 vor allem wiederum gegen die Tschechoslowakei und Litauen niederschlug. Die Sowjets versuchten zeitgleich vergeblich, an der vermeintlich im Entstehen begriffenen neuen europäischen Sicherheitsarchitektur überhaupt beteiligt zu werden. Im Frühjahr 1939 kam es dann zum Allianzwechsel Polens, als es selbst ins Visier der Expansionspolitik des Dritten

---

entgegenkommenden Grenzlinie am 31. Juli 1920 zu, vgl. Documents on British Foreign Policy, Serie I, Bd. X., S. 715; Conrad, Umkämpfte Grenzen, umkämpfte Bevölkerung, S. 187f. Fortan lag Javorina 1,5 km östlich der Grenze der Tschechoslowakei zu Polen auf tschechoslowakischem Hoheitsgebiet. Nach Kriegsende 1921 verlangte die polnische Regierung eine Grenzkorrektur, was am Ende ein Verfahren vor dem Völkerbund nach sich zog. Die polnische Regierung behauptete, sich 1920 in einer Notlage befunden zu haben und von der Tschechoslowakei daher übervorteilt worden zu sein. Das Verfahren endete 1924 aus polnischer Sicht erfolglos, beschädigte jedoch das ohnehin fragile polnisch-tschechoslowakische Verhältnis weiter, vgl. AAN, Bestand 503 Ambasada Rzeczypospolitej Polskiej w Londynie, Sign. 325, S. 230. Publications de la Cour permanente, Serie B, Nr. 8, S. 57; Conrad, Umkämpfte Grenzen, umkämpfte Bevölkerung, S. 189f., 284, 287, 297.

Reiches geraten war. Im August 1939 schloss sich die sowjetische Regierung dann der NS-Expansionspolitik an und brach mit ihrem Angriff auf Polen den Frieden von Riga am 17. September 1939. Ein gemeinsames Vorgehen Polens und der Sowjetunion zur Friedenswahrung im Sinne eines „Geistes von Riga“ ist nirgends zu erkennen. Wie bereits genannt kannte der Friedensvertrag nämlich keine über die üblichen Bestimmungen hinausgehenden Instrumente der Friedenswahrung.

Auch wenn polnische Forscher die Bedeutung des Rigaer Friedens verständlicherweise nicht in Vergessenheit geraten lassen wollen, so schießt das Ziel einer Anhebung auf Augenhöhe mit den Pariser Vorortverträgen selbst für Ostmitteleuropa über das Ziel hinaus. Die langfristige Bedeutung des Friedens von Riga liegt darin, der bedeutendste und abschließende unter denjenigen der Sowjetmacht mit den früheren nationalen Minderheiten des Zarenreichs zu sein und somit die eingetretenen Entwicklungen hinsichtlich der Unabhängigkeiten Polens, Finnlands, Estlands, Lettlands und Litauens abgeschlossen zu haben. In dieser Kette der Letzte zu sein, schmälert die historische Signifikanz des Friedens von Riga keineswegs. Der bereits genannte frühere Präsident Polens, Bronisław Komorowski, hatte 2006 ein anderes, nüchterneres Urteil über den Rigaer Vertrag gefällt und dabei folgende Worte gewählt: *Traktat rozwiązywał jedynie część polsko-rosyjskich sprzeczności związanych z odrodzeniem państwa polskiego. Oddalał aktualne zagrożenie Polski, ale nie tworzył warunków trwałego bezpieczeństwa.*[47] (Der Vertrag löste nur einen Teil der polnisch-russischen Widersprüche im Zusammenhang mit der Wiedergeburt des polnischen Staates. Er beseitigte die aktuelle Bedrohung Polens, aber er schuf keine Grundlagen dauerhafter Sicherheit.)

Angesicht all der genannten Einordnungsprobleme scheint von der behaupteten Signifikanz des Rigaer Friedens selbst Sławomir Dębski nicht vollständig überzeugt zu sein, der 2016 auf seinen früheren Posten als Direktor des Instituts für internationale Angelegenheiten Polens zurückkehrte. Den von ihm zum 90. Jubiläum herausgegebene Sammelband betitelte er nämlich, wie bereits genannt, mit den Worten *Zapomniany pokój*, zu Deutsch „Der vergessene Friede“ – was den Leser ohne Antwort auf die Frage zurücklässt, wie es denn hatte passieren können, dass der Friede von Riga in Vergessenheit geraten konnte, wenn er doch so wichtig gewesen war.

---

47 Komorowski, Traktat Pokoju, S. 6.

Literaturverzeichnis

ACHMATOWICZ, ALEKSANDER Traktat ryski w kontekście polsko-rosyjskiego konfliktu i jego znaczenie dziejów, in: Traktat ryski 1921 roku po 75 latach, hg. von MIECZYSŁAW WOJCIECHOWSKI, Toruń 1998, S. 361-370.

BATSELL, WALTER RUSSELL Soviet Rule in Russia, New York 1929.

BORZĘCKI, JERZY Niełatwy kompromis. Granica ryska w świetle rokowań w Mińsku i Rydze. Teil 1, in: Arcana 58/59 (2004), S. 73-92, Teil 2, in: Arcana 61/62 (2005), S. 213-249.

BORZĘCKI, JERZY Soviet-Polish peace of 1921 and the creation of interwar Europe, New Haven 2008.

BORZĘCKI, JERZY Pokój ryski 1921 roku i kształtowanie się międzywojennej Europy Wschodniej, Warszawa 2012.

BORZĘCKI, JERZY Pokój ryski w historii Europy, in: Zapomniany pokój. Traktat ryski. Interpretacje i kontrowersje 90 lat później, hg. v. Sławomir Dębski, Warszawa 2013, S. 77-96.

CHWALBA, Andrzej Przegrane zwycięstwo. Wojna polsko-bolszewicka 1918-1920. Wołowiec 2020.

CISEK, JANUSZ Sąsiedzi wobec wojny 1920 roku. Wybór dokumentów, Londyn 1990.

CONRAD, BENJAMIN Umkämpfte Grenzen, umkämpfte Bevölkerung. Die Entstehung der Staatsgrenzen der Zweiten Polnischen Republik 1918-1923, Stuttgart 2014.

DĄBSKI, JAN Pokój ryski. Wspomnienia, pertraktacje, tajny układy z Joffem, listy, Warszawa 1931.

DĘBSKI, SŁAWOMIR Poland, the Soviet Union, and the Crisis of the Versailles System, in: White Spots – Black Spots. Difficult Matters in Polish-Russian Relations, 1918-2008, hg. von ADAM DANIEL ROTFELD/ANATOLY V. TORKUNOV, Pittsburgh 2015, S. 105-124.

DĘBSKI, SŁAWOMIR (Hg.) Zapomniany pokój. Traktat ryski. Interpretacje i kontrowersje 90 lat później, Warszawa 2013.

DĘBSKI, SŁAWOMIR Kilka uwag o systemie wersalsko-ryskim i znaczeniu traktatu ryskiego w historii Europy, in: Zapomniany pokój. Traktat ryski. Interpretacje i kontrowersje 90 lat później, hg. von SŁAWOMIR DĘBSKI, Warszawa 2013, S. 13-31.

DĘBSKI, SŁAWOMIR Przyczyny II wojny światowej. Polska, Związek Sowiecki i kryzys system wersalskiego, in: Białe plamy – czarne plamy. Sprawy trudne w polsko-rosyjskich stosunkach 1918-2008, hg. von ADAM D. ROTFELD/ANATOLIJ W. TORKUNOW, Warszawa 2010, S. 141-176.

Dembskij, S. Proischoždenie vtoroj mirovoj vojny, in: Belye pjatna – černye pjatna. Složnye voprosy v rossijsko-pol'skich otnošenijach, hg. von Anatolij V. Torkunov/ Adam D. Rotfel'd, Moskva 2010, S. 165-201.

Documents on British Foreign Policy, Serie I, Bd. III. London 1949. Bd. X, London 1960.

Dokumenty i materiały do historii stosunków polsko-radzieckich, Bd. 2: listopad 1918-kwiecień 1920, Warszawa 1961, Bd. 3: kwiecień 1920–marzec 1921, Warszawa 1964.

Dokumenty vnešnej politiki SSSR, Bd. 2: 1 janvarja 1919 g.–30 ijunja 1920 g, Moskva 1958. Bd. 3: 1 ijulja 1920 g.–18 marta 1921 g, Moskva 1959.

Goclon, Jacek Arkadiusz W obronie Europy. Wojna z bolszewicką Rosją w 1920 roku, Toruń 2006.

Goclon, Jacek Arkadiusz Wojna z bolszewicką Rosją o niepodległość Polski 1919-1920, Wrocław 2003.

Goclon, Jacek Arkadiusz 1920. Ojczyzna w niebezpieczeństwie, Wrocław 2000.

Katzer, Nikolaus Die weiße Bewegung in Russland. Herrschaftsbildung, praktische Politik und politische Programmatik im Bürgerkrieg, Köln u. a. 1999.

Komorowski, Bronisław (Hg.) Traktat Pokoju między Polską a Rosją i Ukrainą. Ryga 18 marca 1921, Warszawa 2006.

Komorowski, Bronisław Wstęp, in: Traktat Pokoju między Polską a Rosją i Ukrainą. Ryga 18 marca 1921, hg. v. Bronisław Komorowski, Warszawa 2006, S. 5-24.

Kumaniecki, Jerzy Polska a powstanie Związku Socjalistycznych Republik Rad, in: Z dziejów stosunków polsko-radzieckich. Studia i materiały V (1969), S. 141-148.

Kumaniecki, Jerzy Uznanie wschodniej granicy Polski przez Radę Ambasadorów, in: Kwartalnik Historyczny LXXVI (1969), S. 73-92.

Kumaniecki, Jerzy Po traktacie ryskim. Stosunki polsko-radzieckie 1921-1923, Warszawa 1971.

Kumaniecki, Jerzy Z genezy traktatu ryskiego, in: Z dziejów stosunków polsko-radzieckich i rozwoju wspólnoty państw socjalistycznych XXIV (1982), S. 157-170.

Kumaniecki, Jerzy Pokój polsko-radziecki 1921. Geneza, rokowania, traktat, komisje mieszane, Warszawa 1985.

Kumaniecki, Jerzy Dwa oblicza dyplomacji radzieckiej. Rokowania w Mińsku i w Rydze, in: Wojna polsko-sowiecka 1920 roku. Przebieg walki i tło międzynarodowe, hg. von Andrzej Koryn, Warszawa 1991, S. 159-171.

KUMANIECKI, JERZY Tajny raport Wojkowa czyli Radziecka taktyka zwrotu polskiego mienia gospodarczego i kulturalnego po pokoju ryskim; Piotr Wojkow, 1921-1923 – dwa lata prac delegacji rosyjsko-ukraińskiej, rosyjsko-ukraińsko-polskich Komisji Mieszanych Reewakuacyjnej i Specjalnej nad wykonaniem Ryskiego Traktatu Pokojowego. Sprawozdanie, tł. dokumentu z ros. Aleksander Achmatowicz, Warszawa 1991.

Latvijas Reitingi Konference Polija, Krievija, Eiropa. No kara līdz mieram, 28.05.2011, URL: www.reitingi.lv/lv/news/5/54392.html (01.04.2023).

LIPIN'SKAJA-NALENČ, DARIA/NALENČ, TOMAŠ Načalo, in: Belye pjatna – černye pjatna. Složnye voprosy v rossijsko-pol'skich otnošenijach, hg. von ANATOLIJ V. TORKUNOV/ ADAM D. ROTFEL'D, Moskva 2010, S. 51-73.

MAGOCSI, PAUL ROBERT A History of Ukraine, Seattle 1996.

MATVEEV, G. F. Načalo, in: Belye pjatna – černye pjatna. Složnye voprosy v rossijsko-pol'skich otnošenijach, hg. von ANATOLIJ V. TORKUNOV/ ADAM D. ROTFEL'D, Moskva 2010, S. 15-50.

MATVEYEV, GENNADY F. Polish-Soviet Relations, in: White Spots – Black Spots. Difficult Matters in Polish-Russian Relations, 1918-2008, hg. von ANATOLY V. TORKUNOV/ ADAM D. ROTFELD, Pittsburgh 2015, S. 30-58.

MATWIEJEW, GIENNADIJ F. Stosunki polsko-sowieckie w latach 1917-1921, in: Białe plamy – czarne plamy. Sprawy trudne w polsko-rosyjskich stosunkach 1918-2008, hg. von ANATOLIJ W. TORKUNOW/ ADAM D. ROTFELD, Warszawa 2010, S. 45-81.

Ministerstwo Spraw Zagranicznych Wznowienie działalności Polsko-Rosyjskiej Grupy ds. Trudnych, 09.03.2017 (komunikat), URL: https://pap-mediaroom.pl/polityka-i-spoleczenstwo/msz-wznowienie-dzialalnosci-polsko-rosyjsk iej-grupy-ds-trudnych-komunikat (01.04.2023).

NAŁĘCZ, DARIA/NAŁĘCZ, TOMASZ Polish-Soviet Relations, 1917-1921, in: White Spots – Black Spots. Difficult Matters in Polish-Russian Relations, 1918-2008, hg. von ANATOLY V. TORKUNOV/ ADAM D. ROTFELD, Pittsburgh 2015, S. 17-29.

NAŁĘCZ, DARIA/NAŁĘCZ, TOMASZ Stosunki polsko-sowieckie w latach 1917-1921, in: Białe plamy – czarne plamy. Sprawy trudne w polsko-rosyjskich stosunkach 1918-2008, hg. von ANATOLIJ W. TORKUNOW/ ADAM D. ROTFELD, Warszawa 2010, S. 25-44.

PALIJ, MICHAEL The Ukrainian-Polish Defensive Alliance, 1919-1921. An Aspect of the Ukrainian Revolution, Toronto 1995.

PIETRZAK, BEATA Leon Wasilewski na konferencji w Rydze, in: Traktat ryski 1921 roku po 75 latach, hg. v. MIECZYSŁAW WOJCIECHOWSKI, Toruń 1998, S. 347-353.

Pobóg-Malinowski, Władysław Najnowsza historia polityczna Polski, Bd. 2: 1914-1939, 2. Aufl. Londyn 1967.

Publications de la Cour permanente de la Justice internationale. Serie B, Nr. 8: Recueil des avis consultatifs. Affaire de Jaworzina [sic] (frontière polono-tchécoslovaque), Leyde 1923.

Rotfeld, Adam D./Torkunow, Anatolij W. (Hgs.) Białe plamy – czarne plamy. Sprawy trudne w polsko-rosyjskich stosunkach 1918-2008, Warszawa 2010.

Rotfeld, Adam D./Torkunov, Anatoly W. (Hgs.) White Spots – Black Spots. Difficult Matters in Polish-Russian Relations 1918-2008, Pittsburgh 2015.

Rotfel'd, Adam D./Torkunov, Anatolij V. (Hgs.) Belye pjatna – černye pjatna. Složnye voprosy v rossijsko-pol'skich otnošenijach, Moskva 2010.

Śledziński, Kacper Wojna polsko-bolszewicka. Konflikt, który zmienił bieg historii. Kraków 2020.

Wandycz, Piotr S. Soviet-Polish Relations, 1917-1921, Cambridge (Massachusetts) 1969.

Wojciechowski, Mieczysław (Hg.) Traktat ryski 1921 roku po 75 lat, Toruń 1998.

Zamoyski, Adam Warszawa 1920. Nieudany podbój Europy. Klęska Lenina. Kraków 2009.

Timo Nahler

Im Blick der USA? Krieg, Kommunismus und die lettische Gesellschaft aus Sicht der amerikanischen Gesandtschaft in Riga. 1920/22-34

Aus Perspektive der USA wurde 1918 mit dem Ende des Ersten Weltkriegs und dem Sturz der Monarchie in Deutschland das bolschewistische Regime in Russland zum Hauptfeind der westlichen Demokratie. Dieses hatte ein Jahr zuvor in der Oktoberrevolution die Macht ergriffen, eine Demokratisierung des einstigen Zarenreiches gewaltsam verhindert und ehedem eine globale Ausweitung der Revolution propagiert. In den USA hatten die innerrussischen Entwicklungen in weiten Teilen der Bevölkerung sowie unter konservativen Politikern zu einer regelrechten Panik vor einem Ausgreifen des Bolschewismus und einer mit ihm assoziierten Zerstörung der westlichen, freiheitlich-demokratischen Lebensweise geführt. Dieser „Red Scare“ sollte sich in der Zwischenkriegszeit ganz wesentlich auf die amerikanische Außenpolitik gegenüber Sowjetrussland (ab Ende 1922 Sowjetunion) sowie gegenüber Europa auswirken.[1] Nach Abschluss der Pariser Friedensverhandlungen kehrte die amerikanische Außenpolitik alsbald zu ihrer traditionellen Abschirmung bezüglich europäischer Angelegenheiten zurück, welche sie 1917 mit dem Kriegseintritt unter der Prämisse „die Welt für die Demokratie sicher zu machen“[2] durchbrochen hatten. Einer Ratifikation des Versailler Vertrags hatte der Kongress im November 1919 eine Absage erteilt, dem von ihrem Präsidenten Woodrow Wilson initiierten Völkerbund traten die USA selbst nicht bei und standen der europäischen Nachkriegsordnung somit nicht als Garantiemacht zur Verfügung. Von sicherheitspolitischen Verpflichtungen entbunden, beschränkte sich die amerikanische Überseepolitik fortan v. a. auf wirtschaftliche Aspekte.[3]

Gleichwohl bestand vor dem Hintergrund des ideologischen Gegensatzes zum Sowjetregime, welchem die Vereinigten Staaten bis 1933 die Anerkennung und somit jegliche offiziellen diplomatischen Beziehungen verweigerten,[4] ein

1 Little, Antibolshevism, S. 377-379.
2 Schwabe, Weltmacht, S. 59.
3 Schwabe, Weltmacht, S. 76f.
4 Breuer, Russische Sektion, S. 33; Schwabe, Weltmacht, S. 69, 98.

großes amerikanisches Interesse an einer Eindämmung des Bolschewismus. Von den zwischen 1918 und 1920 aus der „Konkursmasse"[5] des Russischen Imperiums hervorgegangen baltischen Staaten Lettland, Estland und Litauen erhoffte man sich in diesem Zusammenhang eine Barrierefunktion. Die innere Stabilität der an der Grenze zum sowjetischen Russland in Form parlamentarischer Demokratien gegründeten Nationalstaaten wurde zweifellos als Grundvoraussetzung einer widerstandsfähigen nordosteuropäischen Friedensordnung gesehen. Einen wesentlichen Gradmesser für Demokratie- und Staatsfähigkeit der baltischen Völker bildete aus Sicht der USA deren Umgang mit Versuchen sowjetischer Einflussnahme von außen sowie mit kommunistischer Subversion im Inneren. Anhand der Berichte, mit denen die amerikanische Gesandtschaft in Riga in der Zwischenkriegszeit ihr Außenministerium in Washington über die inneren Verhältnisse und Entwicklungen Lettlands unterrichtete, lässt sich dies exemplarisch nachvollziehen.[6] Im Folgenden soll auf Grundlage dieser, von der Historiografie zu Lettland bisher weitgehend unberücksichtigten Quellen zum einen vergegenwärtigt werden, welches Bild sich den amerikanischen Vertretern in Riga von der lettischen kommunistischen Bewegung, ihrer Vorgehensweise sowie ihrem Gefahrenpotenzial bot. Zum anderen soll nachvollzogen werden, wie amerikanischerseits die Abwehr- und Sicherheitsmaßnahmen des lettischen Staatsapparts gegenüber kommunistischen Aktivitäten beurteilt wurden.[7]

Ziel ist es dabei nicht, die Entwicklung der Bewegung in den 1920er und 1930er Jahren vollständig zu rekonstruieren. Aufgrund z. T. erheblicher quantitativer und qualitativer Schwankungen in der amerikanischen Berichterstattung, deren Ursachen sich kaum mit Gewissheit benennen lassen, wäre dies unmöglich. Auch eine analytische Abdeckung des gesamten Zeitraums der lettischen Unabhängigkeit bis 1940 ist auf Grundlage der vorliegenden Berichte nicht machbar, da diese bereits ab 1933 nur noch sporadisch kommunistische Aktivitäten behandelten. Der Staatsstreich Ulmanis' im Mai 1934 ist daher aus pragmatischen Gründen als Endpunkt des Untersuchungszeitraums gewählt.

---

5 Altrichter/Bernecker, Geschichte Europas, S. 105.

6 Records of the Department of State Relating to Internal Affairs of Latvia 1910-1944.

7 Bei der vorliegenden Arbeit handelt es sich um eine gekürzte Fassung der Masterarbeit, die der Verfasser im Dezember 2016 unter dem Titel *Im Blick der USA? Kommunismus im Lettland der Zwischenkriegszeit. Von der Oktoberrevolution bis zum Staatsstreich Ulmanis' (1917/20-34)* am Fachbereich 07 – Geschichts- und Kulturwissenschaften der Johannes Gutenberg-Universität Mainz bei Prof. Dr. Jan Kusber vorgelegt hat.

Eine eingehende geschichtswissenschaftliche Auseinandersetzung mit der kommunistischen Bewegung im Lettland der Zwischenkriegszeit steht bislang noch aus. Eine Arbeit von Ādolfs Šilde aus dem Jahr 1967 über die Sowjetisierung Lettlands ab 1940 vermag auf die Genese der Bewegung in den 1920er und 1930er Jahren zumindest einige Schlaglichter zu werfen.[8] Ebenso tut dies der knappe Artikel, den Edgar Anderson über die Lettische Kommunistische Partei (LKP) für das 1973 von Witold S. Sworakowski herausgegebene Lexikon *World Communism*[9] amerikanischen Europa- und Russlandpolitik sowie der amerikanisch-lettischen Beziehungen in der Zwischenkriegszeit, die es im folgenden Abschnitt zu erläutern gilt, sind v. a. das Standartwerk Klaus Schwabes zur Außenpolitik der USA[10] sowie die 1995 erschienene Untersuchung zur Russischen Sektion der Rigaer US-Gesandtschaft von Claudia Breuer[11] wichtig.

1. Die USA und die Republik Lettland 1918/22-34

1918 hoffte man auf Seiten der USA noch, dass sich das russische Volk alsbald aus eigenem Willen und eigener Kraft von dem Regime befreien würde, welches im Vorjahr ohne demokratische Legitimation an die Macht gelangt war. Auf dieser Wunschvorstellung fußte das Ideal eines starken, ungeteilten demokratischen Russlands, welches der amerikanische Präsident Woodrow Wilson im Januar 1918 im Rahmen seines 14-Punkte-Programms als integralen Bestandteil und Gleichgewichtsfaktor der zu schaffenden Friedensordnung definiert hatte.[12]

Eine etwaige territoriale Beeinträchtigung des Russischen Reichs stellte vor diesem Hintergrund einen Störfaktor dar. Die Unabhängigkeitserklärungen der baltischen Staaten – Litauens und Estlands im Februar sowie jene Lettlands im November 1918 – wurden daher von den USA nicht anerkannt. Bestärkt wurde die amerikanische Haltung durch die Annahme, dass die kleinen, militärisch wie wirtschaftlich schwachen Staaten losgelöst von Russland nicht überlebensfähig seien. Zudem wurden die baltischen Völker, von deren Mentalität und Kultur bei den amerikanischen Offiziellen offenbar nur geringe Kenntnisse vorhanden waren, stereotyp als „engstirnig", „ungebildet" und „undemokratisch" eingestuft. Im Gegensatz zu den Deutschbalten, die als zuverlässig antikommunistisch

8 Šilde, Sowjetisierung.
9 Anderson, Latvia.
10 Schwabe, Weltmacht.
11 Breuer, Russische Sektion.
12 Schwabe, Weltmacht, S. 62f.

galten, erschienen sie den Amerikanern als leichte Opfer für kommunistische Propaganda.[13]

Bezüglich Lettlands wurde dieses Misstrauen sicher durch die Tatsache genährt, dass große Teile der lettischen Bevölkerung die im Dezember 1918 einrückende Rote Armee sowie im Januar 1919 die anschließende Bildung einer Lettischen Sowjetrepublik (LSSR) zunächst begrüßten und somit der am 18. November 1918 durch den Lettischen Volksrat proklamierten demokratischen Republik Lettland eine vermeintliche Absage erteilten. Die vom Grunderwerb ausgeschlossene lettische Landbevölkerung, die rund 60% der rund 1,6 Millionen Landeseinwohner ausmachte und auf eine radikale Neuverteilung des bis dato v. a. in deutschbaltischem Besitz konzentrierten Bodens hoffte, neigte den kommunistischen Verheißungen eher zu als der ursprünglich bürgerlichen Idee eines unabhängigen demokratischen Lettlands.[14] Angesichts der unter Pēteris Stučka errichteten kommunistischen Terrorherrschaft wichen diese Sympathien rasch. Der eingeführte Kriegskommunismus ließ die ohnehin angespannte Versorgungslage binnen kürzester Zeit dramatische Züge annehmen, die große Masse verhafteter „Konterrevolutionäre" machte die Einrichtung von Konzentrationslagern erforderlich und die Zahl der Exekutierten dürfte zwischen 3500 und 5000 Personen gelegen haben.[15] Nichtsdestotrotz: Aufgrund der Einschätzung, dass die baltischen Staaten und ihre Titularvölker kein ernsthaftes Hindernis für die Ausbreitung des Bolschewismus nach Westen darstellten, riet Warwick Greene, der Leiter einer alliierten Beobachtungsmission im Baltikum, noch im Sommer 1919, als die Rote Armee bereits durch deutschbaltische, estnische sowie lettische Verbände bis nach Lettgallen zurückgedrängt worden war, von einer Anerkennung der baltischen Staaten ab; diese sei „wenig angemessen", so Greene.[16]

Anders als in Nordrussland oder Sibirien, wo sich ab September 1918 amerikanische Truppen an alliierten Militärmissionen beteiligten,[17] schlossen die USA eine eigene gegen die Bolschewiki gerichtete militärische Intervention im Baltikum kategorisch aus. Wie zuvor in Mitteleuropa, beschränkten sie sich dort auf eine *Food as a Weapon*-Strategie, um die durch Krieg und Bürgerkrieg

---

13 Tarulis, American-Baltic Relations, S. 211f; Nies, Lettland, S. 209.

14 Bleiere, Geschichte Lettlands, S. 195; Hehn, Baltischer Freiheitskrieg, S. 2, 5.

15 Bleiere, Geschichte Lettlands, S. 127; Rauch, Bolschewistische Staatsgründungen, S. 61f.; Stranga, Communist Dictatorship, S. 168f.

16 Hehn, Baltischer Freiheitskrieg, S. 22f.; Nies, Lettland, S. 210.

17 Schild, Ideology and Realpolitik, S. 70-90; Rhodes, Anglo-American Winter War.

ausgezehrte Bevölkerung gegenüber der kommunistischen Propaganda zu immunisieren. Zwischen April und August 1919 lieferte die halbstaatliche *American Relief Administration* Nahrungsmittel ins Baltikum. Darüber hinaus unterstützten die USA die baltischen Regierungen beim Aufbau nationaler Streitkräfte, indem sie ihnen durch die Gewährung von Krediten die Möglichkeit boten, ausrangiertes Kriegsmaterial der US-Armee zu kaufen.[18]

Spätestens mit der amerikanischen Ablehnung des Versailler Vertrags im November 1919 war klar, dass sich nach einer etwaigen amerikanischen Anerkennung der baltischen Staaten die diplomatischen Beziehungen zwischen den USA und Lettland, das im Januar 1920 durch die Vertreibung der Roten Armee aus Lettgallen und dessen Anschluss an die beiden anderen ethnisch lettischen Gebiete Kurland und Südlivland seine territoriale Konsolidierung abgeschlossen hatte,[19] auf ein Mindestmaß beschränken würden: Lettland hatte im Falle einer äußeren Aggression – z. B. von sowjetischer oder deutscher Seite – von den Amerikanern keinen militärischen Beistand zu erwarten und aus Sicht der USA waren sowohl der kleine Absatzmarkt, als auch die wenigen Ressourcen und Produkte Lettlands wirtschaftlich unattraktiv.[20] Auch die Funktion Lettlands als Transitland für den amerikanisch-sowjetischen Handel, der trotz des ideologischen Gegensatzes schon zu Beginn der 1920er Jahre einen beträchtlichen Umfang annahm, sollte lediglich von kurzer Dauer sein. Die amerikanische Hoffnung auf einen zollfreien Handel *via* lettisch-sowjetische Grenze erfüllte sich nicht dauerhaft.[21]

Die amerikanische Skepsis ob der Unabhängigkeit der baltischen Staaten hatte auch über die erfolgreiche Beendigung der Befreiungskämpfe hinaus Bestand. Gleichwohl ließen die Entscheidung des russischen Bürgerkriegs zugunsten der Bolschewiki im Jahre 1920 sowie die allmähliche innerliche Stabilisierung Sowjetrusslands nach Einführung der Neuen Ökonomischen Politik (NEP) im März 1921[22] die Hoffnung auf einen kurzfristigen Zusammenbruch des bolschewistischen Regimes schwinden. Ohne Aussicht auf eine kurzfristige

---

18 Anderson, Baltische Frage, S. 343f., 362; Schwabe, Weltmacht, S. 76f.

19 Hehn, Baltischer Freiheitskrieg, S. 41f.

20 Breuer, Russische Sektion, S. 49f., Anm. 13; Nies, Lettland, S. 208f.; Schwabe, Weltmacht, S. 77.

21 Breuer, Russische Sektion, S. 29; Nies, Lettland, S. 213; White, Gateway to Russia, S. 42, 51-54.

22 Die NEP löste den Kriegskommunismus ab und ließ sowohl privates Wirtschaften als auch ausländische Investitionen in begrenztem Maße zu: Altrichter, Neue Ökonomische Politik, S. 216-218.

Demokratisierung Russlands erfolgte die Anerkennung Lettlands *de jure* durch die Administration Präsident Warren G. Hardings im Juli 1922 – wie es hieß „unter Vorbehalt“ und mit der Absicht, durch diese Geste das lettische Volk in seiner Moral gegenüber dem Bolschewismus zu stärken.[23]

Die marginale Bedeutung der diplomatischen Beziehungen zwischen den USA und Lettland sowie zwischen den USA und den baltischen Staaten im Allgemeinen manifestierte sich u. a. darin, dass das US-Außenministerium nach der Anerkennung der baltischen Staaten in der lettischen Hauptstadt nicht etwa eine Botschaft, sondern lediglich eine Gesandtschaft einrichtete.[24] Zudem entsandte das State Department zu seiner Vertretung bei den drei baltischen Staaten mit dem Juristen Frederick W. B. Coleman einen diplomatischen Laien nach Riga, dessen Qualifikation für das Amt des Gesandten wohl in erster Linie in persönlichen Kontakten zur republikanischen Regierungspartei bestand. Seine Tätigkeit in Riga von 1922 bis 1931 beschränkte sich daher weitgehend auf repräsentative Aspekte.[25]

Trotz der knappen diplomatischen und wirtschaftlichen Zusammenarbeit zwischen den Vereinigten Staaten und Lettland, bildete die Gesandtschaft in Riga eine der personell stärksten amerikanischen Auslandsvertretungen in der Zwischenkriegszeit.[26] Im Zuge von Oktoberrevolution und Bürgerkrieg hatte das amerikanische Außenministerium seine Diplomaten aus Russland abgezogen.[27] Vor dem Hintergrund der bedingungslosen amerikanischen Nicht-Anerkennungspolitik gegenüber den Sowjets, stellte sich den USA die lettische Hauptstadt in ihrer traditionellen Funktion als logistischer und informationeller Knotenpunkt als unentbehrlicher Beobachtungsposten für die inneren Verhältnisse Russlands dar. Auf Empfehlung Warwick Greenes hatte das State Department bereits 1919 in Riga eine Beobachtungs-Kommission – die *Commission to the Baltic Provinces* (bis Mai 1920 *Commission to the Baltic Provinces of Russia*) – eingerichtet,[28] die binnen kurzer Zeit „zu einem kleinen Informationszentrum über Russland” ausgebaut wurde.[29] Die sogenannte „Russische Sektion“ der Rigaer US-Gesandtschaft konnte Mitte 1922 somit an solide Vorarbeiten

23 Tarulis, American-Baltic Relations, S. 306; Bleiere, Geschichte Lettlands, S. 138f.; Nies, Lettland, S. 208, 210f.

24 Breuer, Russische Sektion, S. 44f.

25 Breuer, Russische Sektion, S. 66-68.

26 Breuer, Russische Sektion, S. 49.

27 Breuer, Russische Sektion, S. 37.

28 Breuer, Russische Sektion, S. 14, 40f.; Nies, Lettland, S. 208-210.

29 Breuer, Russische Sektion, S. 44; Tarulis, American-Baltic Relations, S. 214, 218.

anknüpfen. Durch die Sammlung sämtlicher verfügbarer Informationen über die Sowjetunion lieferte diese Sektion die „notwendige Wissensgrundlage", auf der das Außenministerium in Washington „seine Empfehlungen zur amerikanischen Rußlandpolitik" aufbauen konnte.[30]

Formal war die Russische Sektion dem Gesandten unterstellt, wurde jedoch durch einen eigenen Leiter geführt – zwischen 1922 und 1931 David B. Macgowan – und behauptete eine weitgehende Eigenständigkeit gegenüber der Baltischen Sektion, welche für die Auslandsvertretung *vis-à-vis* der baltischen Staaten zuständig war. Dass dem Auftrag der Russischen Sektion eine tatsächliche Vorrangstellung zukam, zeigte sich u. a. darin, dass fast alle der ständig in der Gesandtschaft tätigen Mitarbeiter – Ende der 1920er Jahre im Schnitt etwa 24 Personen – in der Russischen Sektion beschäftigt waren. Die Baltische Sektion bestand hingegen lediglich aus dem Gesandten und einem Sekretär. Die Behandlung baltischer Angelegenheiten geschah sozusagen nebenher.[31]

2. Die Berichterstattung über kommunistische Aktivitäten in Lettland

Spielte Lettland für die USA weder als politischer noch als wirtschaftlicher Akteur eine nennenswerte Rolle, so war der amerikanische Blick auf den in unmittelbarer Nachbarschaft zum sowjetischen Russland gelegenen jungen Nationalstaat ganz wesentlich von der Frage bestimmt, ob der lettische Staatsapparat sowie die lettische Gesellschaft dazu in der Lage waren, kommunistischer Subversion von innen wie von außen standzuhalten und einen demokratischen Stabilitätsfaktor zwischen Ost und West zu bilden. Dem entsprechend nahmen kommunistische Aktivitäten in der Berichterstattung der Rigaer US-Gesandtschaft über Lettland einen vergleichsweise großen Rahmen ein.

Die maßgebliche Quelle zu kommunistischen Aktivitäten in Lettland stellte der Politische Administration des lettischen Innenministeriums dar, zu der bereits 1920 der Kontakt geknüpft worden war. Bei der „*Political Police*" – so die übliche Bezeichnung in den amerikanischen Dispatches – handelte es sich um den lettischen Inlandsgeheimdienst (Lettisch: *politiskā pārvalde*), der zur Abwehr staatsgefährdender Aktivitäten eine große Zahl von Agenten und Spitzeln unterhielt.[32] Voldemārs Ozoliņš, Leiter der Politischen Polizei von 1924 bis

30 Breuer, Russische Sektion, S. 15.

31 Breuer, Russische Sektion, S. 49, 63, 69f.

32 Bleiere, Geschichte Lettlands, S. 159; Breuer, Russische Sektion, S. 108; Šilde, Sowjetisierung, S. 11; Tarulis, American-Baltic Relations, S. 215; nach eigenen Angaben

zum Staatsstreich Ulmanis' im Jahr 1934,[33] war in Bezug auf innenpolitische Entwicklungen Lettlands ein wichtiger Ansprechpartner für die amerikanischen Vertreter in Riga. Der Gesandte Coleman schätzte den lettischen Geheimdienstchef als einen „Beamten von großer Energie und Effizienz".[34] Nicht selten wurden dessen Berichte lediglich ins Englische übersetzt und ohne größere Anmerkungen nach Washington übermittelt. Auch die von der Gesandtschaft selbst verfassten Rapporte bezogen sich meist ausdrücklich auf Angaben Ozoliņš'. Anzeichen einer kritischen Rezeption seiner Auskünfte durch die übermittelnden Amerikaner sucht man in den vorliegenden Quellen vergebens und nur in seltenen Fällen wurde eine Deutung oder Einordnung seiner Meldungen versucht.[35] Für die Pflege des Kontakts zu Ozoliņš war auf Seiten der US-Gesandtschaft zwischen 1922 und 1929 Hugh S. Martin als nachrichtendienstlicher Mitarbeiter zuständig, der in den vorliegenden Dispatches diverse Male als Autor beigefügter Berichte und Memoranden in Erscheinung tritt.[36]

Das Bild, das sich die amerikanischen Vertreter in Riga auf Grundlage der ihnen zur Verfügung stehenden Informationen von den organisatorischen Grundzügen der kommunistischen Bewegung Lettlands machen konnten, hatte sich allem Anschein nach bis Mitte der 1920er Jahre weitgehend etabliert: Getragen wurde sie durch die bereits während des Unabhängigkeitskrieges verbotene Lettische Kommunistische Partei – die LKP,[37] welche unmittelbar nach dem Sturz der LSSR 1919/20 mit dem Aufbau von Untergrundstrukturen begonnen

---

unterhielt die Politische Polizei sogar in Moskau Agenten: *Memorandum concerning secret intelligence work with regard to the Soviet Union* […], In: Nr. 7937, Coleman, 10.8.31, 860p.202 61/7, S. 2 [die Zitation der Gesandtschaftsberichte geschieht Arbeit wie folgt: ggf. Titel der Anlage in kursiver Schreibweise, Nummer der Sendung, Name des unterzeichnenden Absenders, Sendungsdatum, Ablagesignatur, ggf. Seitenzahl].

33 Bērziņš, Latvijas Vēsture II, S. 943; Bleiere, Geschichte Lettlands, S. 167.

34 Nr. 3558, Coleman, 30.1.1926, 860p.00B/35, S. 3.

35 Laut Natalie Grant war zwischen 1922 und 1928 auch die Berichterstattung der Russischen Sektion dadurch gekennzeichnet, dass „facts and events took precedence over analysis": Grant, Russian Section, S. 111.

36 Die Stelle des nachrichtendienstlichen Mitarbeiters war vor Martin durch Sergius M. Riis (1920-22) und Michael C. Perts (1922) besetzt worden, die in den vorliegenden Unterlagen jedoch nicht namentlich genannt werden. Nach Martins Versetzung 1929 wurde die Stelle nicht mehr neubesetzt und deren Aufgaben dem Ressort des Wirtschaftsberichterstatters übertragen: Breuer, Russische Sektion, S. 108-111.

37 Die LKP war im März 1919 – also zur Zeit der LSSR – aus der Lettischen Sozialdemokratischen Arbeiterpartei (LSDSP) hervorgegangen: Skultans, Lettland, S. 372; Anderson, Latvia, S. 297f.

hatte.[38] Die Parteiführung der LKP, ihr Zentralkomitee (ZK der LKP), hatte sich indessen nach Moskau abgesetzt, von wo aus sie fortan die Arbeit der lettischen Kommunisten anleitete – und das angeblich mit demselben Personal, welches auch zuvor dem Sowjetregime in Lettland vorgestanden hatte. Als prominentestes Mitglied des ZK der LKP galt den Amerikanern der ehemalige Präsident der LSSR, Pēteris Stučka.[39] Zwar fanden in den amerikanischen Berichten auch Namen weiterer ‚altgedienter' lettischer Kommunisten als mutmaßliche Angehörige der LKP-Spitze Erwähnung,[40] auf deren Funktionen wurde jedoch nicht näher eingegangen. Etwaige personelle Wechsel lassen sich nicht nachvollziehen. Die Parteiführung in Moskau taucht in den amerikanischen Berichten als nebulöses, ungreifbares Korpus auf, von dem man annahm, dass es voll und ganz im Dienste der Kommunistischen Internationale stehe.[41] Von einer Zugehörigkeit der LKP zur Komintern waren die Amerikaner spätestens Ende 1922 ausgegangen,[42] bevor die Resolutionen des im Februar 1923 abgehaltenen VII. Parteikongresses der LKP diesbezüglich Klarheit schufen. Diese lagen der US-Gesandtschaft im Mai 1923 vor und sprachen von einer „vollständigen

38 Martin, *A History of Bolshevik Activities in Latvia. Methods of Organization*, in: Nr. 132, Coleman, 11.12.22, 860p.00B/14, S. 1f.; Nr. 2727, Coleman, 19.3.25, 860p.00B/32, S. 1f.

39 Nr. 189, Gade, 13.5.20, 860p.00/7; *Translation of communication*, in: Nr. 2183, Coleman, 14.8.24, 860p.00B/25, S. 1; Ozoliņš, *The Relations between the Communist International and the Latvian Communist Party*, in: Nr. 6567, Sussdorff, 19.11.29, 860p.00B/63; Nr. 204, Skinner, 31.3.32, 860p.00B/85, S. 4; laut Ādolfs Šilde bestand das Moskauer Auslandsbüro des ZK der LKP aus fünf Personen und war Ende Januar 1920 eingerichtet worden: Šilde, Sowjetisierung, S. 9; Stučka verstarb 1932 in Moskau: Bleiere, Geschichte Lettlands, S. 158.

40 So etwa Jānis Lencmanis, Dāvids Beika, Jānis Krumiņš-Pilāts und Jānis Bērziņš: Nr. 189, Gade, 13.5.20, 860p.00/7; *Translation of communication*, in: Nr. 2183, Coleman, 14.8.24, 860p.00B/25, S. 1; Jānis Lencmanis, ehemals Vizepräsident und Volkskommissar der LSSR für innere Angelegenheiten: Bērziņš, Latvijas Vēsture II, S. 935; Skultans, Lettland, S. 372; Dāvids Beika, ehemals Volkskommissar der LSSR für Wirtschaft: Bērziņš, Latvijas Vēsture II, S. 904; Jānis Krumiņš-Pilāts, Sekretär des ZK LKP in Moskau: Bērziņš, Latvijas Vēsture II, S. 931; Jānis Bērziņš-Ziemelis, ehemals Volkskommissar der LSSR für Bildung: Bērziņš, Latvijas Vēsture II, S. 905.

41 Die Komintern war auf Initiative Lenins in Moskau als Organisation zur weltweiten Verbreitung der sozialistischen Revolution gegründet worden: Müller, Komintern, S. 149f.; Sworakowski, Communist International, S. 78-92.

42 Martin, *A History of Bolshevik Activities in Latvia. Methods of Organization* in: Nr. 132. Coleman, 11.12.22, 860p.00B/14; die LKP war der Komintern bereits im März 1919 beigetreten: Anderson, Latvia, S. 297f.

Unterordnung" der Partei unter die Komintern.[43] Das Auslandsbüro des ZK der LKP in Moskau bildete die sogenannte „Lettische Sektion der Komintern" und wurde daher in den amerikanischen Berichten meist als „Latvian Section" bezeichnet.[44] Für die Umsetzung der Komintern-Weisungen sowie für die Kommunikation zwischen Parteiführung in Moskau und ihren Organisationen in Lettland war ein weiteres mutmaßliches Mitglied des ZK der LKP namens Krastiņš[45] verantwortlich. Unter seiner Direktive wurden zahlreiche Agitatoren und Propagandisten von Moskau nach Lettland entsandt, um dort die Durchführung der kommunistischen Untergrundaktivitäten entlang der in Moskau bestimmten Richtlinien sicherzustellen.[46]

Die kommunistische Untergrundstruktur war landesweit in acht Regionen unterteilt, welche jeweils durch Regionalkomitees (RKs) geleitet wurden. Das Rigaer Komitee nahm gegenüber den übrigen RKs, deren Standorte anhand der amerikanischen Berichte nicht zu bestimmen sind, eine übergeordnete Position ein und wurde aufgrund seiner Führungsrolle von den Amerikanern häufig als „*Central Committee*" bezeichnet.[47] Es war für die Umsetzung der Vorgaben der Lettischen Sektion innerhalb seines regionalen Zuständigkeitsbereichs verantwortlich und fungierte gleichzeitig als Transmissionsriemen zwischen der Moskauer Führung und den einzelnen RKs. Die Regionen waren jeweils in mehrere Distrikte unterteilt, innerhalb derer die Basiseinheiten – kleine, lokal operierende Zellen von drei bis zehn Personen – durch eine Distrikt-Organisation koordiniert wurden.[48] Ergänzt wurde dieses System durch eine überregional angelegte

---

43 *Resolutions of the recent 7th Congress of Lettish Communist Party*, in: Nr. 851, Coleman, 25.5.23, 860p.00B/18; der VII. Parteikongress der LKP fand im Februar 1923 in Moskau statt, bei der Zählweise wurde von den vorangegangenen Kongressen der LSDSP ausgegangen: ANDERSON, Latvia, S. 299.

44 Vgl. ŠILDE, Sowjetisierung, S. 9.

45 Kārlis Krastiņš, Angehöriger des ZK LKP: BĒRZIŅŠ, Latvijas Vēsture II, S. 930; STRANGA, Economic Relations, S. 161.

46 *Translation of communication*, in: Nr. 2333, Coleman, 14.8.24, 860p.00B/25, S. 1; Nr. 2921, Coleman, 8.6.25, 860p.00B/33; Nr. 3558, Coleman, 30.01.26, 860p.00B/35, S. 2; OZOLIŅŠ, *The Relations between the Communist International and the Latvian Communist Party*, in: Nr. 6567, Sussdorff, 19.11.29, 860p.00B/63.

47 Vgl. *Confidential Memorandum for the Minister*, in: Nr. 5996, Coleman, 22.3.29, 860p.00Party, Communist/1.

48 Vgl. Lenins Vorstellungen vom hierarchischen Führungsprinzip des „demokratischen Zentralismus", welches die Komintern 1920 für ihre nationalen Sektionen verbindlich machte: WEBER, Lenin in Selbstzeugnissen, S. 50; *Die „21 Bedingungen" für die*

Organisationseinheit. Dem sogenannten „Legalen Zentrum“, welches sich aus einem Repräsentanten des ZK der LKP sowie je einem Vertreter der acht RKs zusammensetzte, oblag die Anleitung und Koordination kommunistischer Zellen innerhalb legaler Organisationen, wie Gewerk- und Genossenschaften, karitativen Einrichtungen, Sportvereinen oder auch in der lokalen Administration.[49] Der Lettische Kommunistische Jugendverband (Lettischer Komsomol),[50] der in den amerikanischen Berichten des Jahres 1924 erstmalig als aktiver Akteur auftritt, war in organisatorischer wie programmatischer Hinsicht der Führung der LKP unterstellt.[51]

Bereits Ende 1921 ging man auf amerikanischer Seite davon aus, dass die lettischen Kommunisten und ihre Organisationen durch die offiziellen, in der lettischen Hauptstadt stationierten sowjetischen Institutionen unterstützt würden.[52] Der diplomatische Postweg aus Moskau sowie die durch die sowjetische Vertretung in Riga genutzten Gebäude waren durch exterritoriale Privilegien vor dem Zugriff der lettischen Behörden geschützt.[53] Spätestens Mitte der 1920er Jahre nahm man an, dass die „*Soviet Mission*“ – so der in den Berichten verwendete Sammelbegriff, unter dem Sowjetgesandtschaft und -konsulat sowie die sowjetische Außenhandelsvertretung zusammengefasst wurden – innerhalb ihrer Einrichtungen verdeckt operierende Funktionäre der Komintern unterhielt. Diese versorgten die örtliche Bewegung mit Propagandamaterial und Finanzmitteln

---

Aufnahme in die Komintern (1920), in: Weber, Kommunistische Internationale, S. 55-62, hier S. 60.

49 *Translation of communication*, in: Nr. 2333, Coleman, 14.8.24, 860p.00B/25, S. 1f.; vgl. Anderson, Latvia, S. 299.

50 Beim *Lettischen Kommunistischen Jugendverband*, handelte es sich um ein lettisches Äquivalent zum *Gesamtsowjetischen Leninschen Kommunistischen Jugendverband* (*Komsomol*), eine Hilfsorganisation der Kommunistischen Partei, durch die Jugendliche im Alter von 14 bis 28 Jahren auf den Dienst in der Partei vorbereitet werden sollten: Anderson, Latvia, S. 299; Long, Communist Youth Organizations, S. 228-235; Ziemelis/Kadiķe, Komsomol of Latvia, S. 270f.

51 Nr. 2727, Coleman, 19.3.25, 860p.00B/32; *Resolutions of the recent 7th Congress of Lettish Communist Party*, in: Nr. 851, Coleman, 25.5.23, 860p.00B/18.

52 Telegramm Konsul Hurleys, 16.4.21, 860p.00/16; Konsul Hurley, 14.7.21, 860p.504/-; Nr. 1506, Young, 20.12.21, 860p.00B/4; Nr. 1531, Young, 22.12.21, 860p.00B/3.

53 Nr. 2921, Coleman, 8.6.25, 860p.00B/33; vgl. Stranga, Economic Relations, S. 171; Martin, *A History of Bolshevik Activities in Latvia. Methods of Organization*, in: Nr. 132, Coleman, 11.12.22, 860p.00B/14, S. 12; Nr. 3558, Coleman, 30.1.26, 860p.00B/35, S. 4.

und hielten deren Verbindung zu den Weisungsgebern in Moskau aufrecht.[54] Eine enge Verbindung der Sowjetmission zur LKP manifestierte sich scheinbar auch in der großen Anzahl lettischer Staatsbürger, die in sowjetischen Institutionen beschäftigt waren und daher unter kommunistischem Einfluss standen. Insbesondere die von der sowjetischen Handelssektion betriebenen Lagerräume boten zahlreiche Arbeitsplätze. Nach Angaben der Politischen Polizei machten lettische Staatsangehörige Anfang 1926 rund 75% des Gesamtpersonals der Sowjet-Vertretung aus. Für diese Angestellten war eine Unterordnung unter die Beschlüsse der Kommunistischen Partei wohl ebenso obligatorisch wie die Mitgliedschaft in einer der kommunistisch geführten Gewerkschaften.[55]

In ihrer nationalen Zusammensetzung war die kommunistische Bewegung in Lettland klar lettisch-dominiert. Lediglich die Komsomolorganisationen in Riga und Lettgallen zeichneten sich durch einen überdurchschnittlichen Anteil jüdischer Mitglieder aus (50% in Riga, bzw. 75% in Lettgallen), während es in den übrigen Organisationen wohl nur wenige Juden gab. Auch die Anzahl ethnisch russischer Kommunisten in Lettland wurde mit denselben regionalen Ausnahmen als „insignifikant“ eingeschätzt.[56]

3. Kommunistische Konsolidierungsversuche 1919/22-26

Wie Claudia Breuer in ihrer Arbeit über die Russische Sektion der Rigaer US-Gesandtschaft festgehalten hat, ließ „die Berichterstattung der [...] amerikanischen Kommission in Riga“ vor 1922 „die Züge einer wirklich systematischen Beobachtung noch in vielem vermissen“.[57] In den Kommissionsberichten über kommunistische Aktivitäten innerhalb Lettlands findet sich dieses Urteil bestätigt. Bis Jahresende 1921 war von der Kommission tatsächlich nur über die

---

54 *Communist Agitation and Soviet Russian Ambassies*, in: Nr. 985, Coleman, 25.6.23, 860p.00B/19; Nr. 3558, Coleman, 30.1.26, 860p.00B/35, S. 3f.

55 Nr. 3558, Coleman, 30.1.26, 860p.00B/35, S. 4; siehe auch Nr. 2727, Coleman, 19.3.25, 860p.00B/32, S. 10; vgl. Angaben zum lettischen Anteil an der Belegschaft der sowjetischen Handelsvertretung in Riga. Ende 1922 waren in der Sowjetmission insgesamt 291 Personen beschäftigt, Ende 1924 rund 200 alleine in der Handelsvertretung: Stranga, Economic Relations, S. 170.

56 Ozoliņš, *Brief Report Concerning the Communist Movement in Latvia, up to March 20, 1926*, in: Nr. 3701, Coleman, 9.4.26, 860p.00B/36, S. 2; Hinweise zu den absoluten Mitgliederzahlen der kommunistischen Organisationen in Lettland finden sich in Abschnitt 3. *Kommunistische Konsolidierungsversuche 1919/22-26.*

57 Breuer, Russische Sektion, S. 130.

Aushebung einer Organisation kommunistischer „Terroristen“ durch die lettische Polizei im Juni 1921 berichtet worden. Neun lettische Kommunisten wurden damals zum Tode verurteilt, weitere nach Russland abgeschoben. Diese Angelegenheit hatte nicht nur Niederschlag in der sowjetischen Presse gefunden, sondern auch zu Friktionen zwischen dem lettischen Außenministerium und der sowjetischen Vertretung in Riga geführt. Trotz der Drohung des sowjetischen Gesandten, im Falle einer Vollstreckung der Todesurteile abzureisen, waren die Exekutionen durchgeführt worden. Commissioner Evan E. Young sah darin seinerzeit einen Beleg für das Bestreben und das Vermögen der lettischen Autoritäten, sowohl die kommunistische Bedrohung von innen, als auch die bolschewistischen Versuche der Einflussnahme von außen – hier der Versuch, unter Androhung diplomatischer Konsequenzen eine Schutzfunktion für lettische Staatsbürger zu übernehmen und somit lettisches Recht auszuhebeln – einzudämmen bzw. abzuwehren. Ausdrücklich lobte Young das „entschlossene“ lettische Vorgehen, welches vorerst zum Bruch der kommunistischen Organisation in Lettland geführt habe.[58] Als Befürworter einer amerikanischen Anerkennung Lettlands war Young darum bemüht, den lettischen Staat und dessen Regierung als stabil und unbeugsam gegenüber dem Kommunismus darzustellen.[59]

Bis zum Ausbau der Kommission zur Gesandtschaft ab Juli 1922 waren die übrigen Berichte mit Bezug auf die kommunistische Bewegung in Lettland spärlich und lieferten lediglich bruchstückhafte Informationen. Gut denkbar, dass es eben dieser Umstand war, der Hugh S. Martin im Dezember 1922 dazu veranlasste, auf Grundlage lettischer Geheimdienstinformationen eine ausführliche Darstellung der Entwicklung zu verfassen, welche die kommunistische Bewegung seit dem Fall des Sowjetregimes 1919/20 in Lettland genommen hatte.[60]

Laut den Schilderungen Martins hätten die in Lettland verbliebenen Kommunisten 1919 damit gerechnet, dass ihr Machtverlust lediglich vorübergehend sei und dass die Revolution mit einer baldigen Wiederkehr der Roten Armee zurückgebracht werden würde.[61] Die „werktätigen Massen“ Lettlands hätten

---

58 Der sowjetische Gesandte hatte seine Drohung letztendlich nicht wahrgemacht; Telegramm Youngs, 11.6.21, 860p.00/18; Nr. 1008, Young, 18.6.21, 860p.00/21; *In Latvia – The Soviet Russian Note (Pravda Nr. 131, 17.6.21)*, in: Nr. 1013, Young, 27.6.21, 860p.00/22.

59 Vgl. Anderson, Baltische Frage, S. 375; Breuer, Russische Sektion, S. 43.

60 Martin: *A History of Bolshevik Activities in Latvia. Methods of Organization*, in: Nr. 132, Coleman, 11.12.22, 860p.00B/14.

61 Bis 1920 wurde sowohl von Seiten der Komintern als auch von Seiten der sowjetischen Führung prophezeit, dass der Ausbruch der „Weltrevolution“ unmittelbar bevorstehe.

jedoch vor dem Hintergrund des während „bolschewistischen Regimes" erlebten „Terrors" 1919 keine Neigung mehr gezeigt, die kommunistische Bewegung zu unterstützen.[62] Unter dem Eindruck der sich herausstellenden militärischen Schwäche der (russischen) „Bolschewiken" und deren Unfähigkeit, den Kampf gegen Lettland fortzusetzen, seien die Massen in ihrem „Geist" gestärkt worden und hätten der kommunistischen Agitation immer weniger Beachtung geschenkt. Die zunehmend „antibolschewistische" Haltung der lettischen Arbeiter habe die Kommunisten dazu gezwungen, ihre offene Propaganda einzustellen und eine neue Taktik zu wählen: Indem sie sich als parteiunabhängige Verteidigerin der sozialen und wirtschaftlichen Interessen der lettischen Arbeiter ausgegeben hätte, sei es der „kleinen Gruppe gut getarnter und gut organisierter Kommunisten" binnen kurzer Zeit gelungen, machtvolle Positionen innerhalb von Gewerk- und Genossenschaften[63] zu besetzen und den Einfluss zu minimieren, den die lettischen Sozialdemokraten[64] bis dahin auf die Massen ausgeübt hätten. Da sie zu dieser Zeit aus großen finanziellen Ressourcen habe schöpfen können – „Millionen von Rubel" seien „regelmäßig" aus Moskau eingetroffen[65] –, habe die kommunistische Bewegung ihre Mitglieder und Funktionäre mit großzügigen Gehältern bezahlen können, weshalb sie einen regen personellen Zulauf genossen habe.

Das Jahr 1921 habe für die Kommunisten dann jedoch eine negative Trendwende bedeutet. Nicht nur hätten die Sozialdemokraten im Verbund mit dem lettischen Geheimdienst einen „energischen Gegenangriff" gestartet. Auch habe die Komintern ihre Aufwendungen wegen angeblicher Engpässe beträchtlich gekürzt und die LKP so vor erhebliche finanzielle Schwierigkeiten gestellt. Zahlreiche Mitglieder seien daraufhin aus der Partei ausgetreten; Aktivität und Agitation der LKP hätten deutlich nachgelassen.[66] Der Versuch der Lettischen

---

Der Rückzug der Roten Armee 1919 wurde von den lettischen Kommunisten vor diesem Hintergrund wohl als temporär interpretiert: vgl. Weber, Kommunistische Internationale, S. 19.

62 Vgl. Bleiere, Geschichte Lettlands, S. 127.

63 Über eine mutmaßliche kommunistische Kontrolle der Rigaer Genossenschaften war Ende 1921 durch die Kommission knapp berichtet worden: Nr. 1506, Young, 20.12.21, 860p.00B/4.

64 Lettische Sozialdemokratische Arbeiterpartei (LSDSP): Skultans, Lettland, S. 375f.

65 Die Finanzierung der nationalen Kommunistischen Parteien bewältigte die Komintern wohl v. a. aus den Reichtümern der Zarenfamilie: Agnew/McDermott, Comintern, S. 21f.

66 Martin, *A History of Bolshevik Activities in Latvia. Methods of Organization*, in: Nr. 132, Coleman, 11.12.22, 860p.00B/14, S. 1-6.

Sektion, ab Jahresende dieser Entwicklung durch die Übermittlung gefälschter Lettischer Rubel entgegenzuwirken,[67] habe die Krise der Partei zusätzlich verschärft: Das vermehrte Auftauchen gefälschter Banknoten hatte die lettischen Behörden offenbar recht schnell auf die Spur von Kommunisten geführt, sodass bis Mitte 1922 zahlreiche Angehörige der LKP verhaftet werden konnten. Das Rigaer Komitee, als ‚verlängerter Arm' der Lettischen Sektion, sei daraufhin von den übrigen kommunistischen Organisationen beschuldigt worden, durch die Verteilung von Falschgeld die Sicherheit der lettischen Kommunisten aufs Spiel gesetzt zu haben.[68] Anfang August habe die lettische Politische Polizei schließlich zugeschlagen und ein Treffen verantwortlicher Parteifunktionäre ausgehoben. Nicht nur „alle Geheimunterlagen" seien dabei sichergestellt, sondern auch „praktisch alle" (lokalen) Führer der LKP verhaftet worden. Seit diesem Rückschlag, der die Stärke der Partei „vollständig gebrochen" habe, hätten die lettischen Kommunisten lediglich schwache Versuche unternommen, die „zerstreuten kommunistischen Kräfte" zu reorganisieren. Während die inhaftierten Führer kurz davor stünden, nach Russland deportiert zu werden, herrsche unter den Kommunisten gegenseitiges Misstrauen, da ihre Bewegung von „Spitzeln und Provokateuren" durchsetzt sei.[69]

Nachdem es den lettischen Kommunisten mittels „opportunistischer Methoden"[70] und trotz einer ablehnenden Haltung der Bevölkerung offenbar gelungen war, zwischen 1919 und 1921 beträchtlichen politischen Einfluss zu entfalten, waren sie bis Ende 1922 doch letztlich an finanziellen Problemen sowie am entschlossenen Vorgehen der lettischen Behörden gescheitert. Das Fazit, mit welchem Martin seinen Bericht Ende 1922 schloss, prognostizierte der nunmehr

---

67 Laut Berichten Commissioner Youngs aus dem Jahr 1922 sei bereits im August 1921 durch die Sowjetmission in Riga damit begonnen worden, die LKP mit in Sowjetrussland gedrucktem lettischem Falschgeld auszustatten: Nr. 2005, Young, 4.5.22, 860p.00B/8; Nr. 2523, Young, 18.8.22, 860p.5158/1; dass die Komintern womöglich Falschgeld nach Lettland einschleuste, um das lettische Wirtschafts- und Finanzwesen zu destabilisieren um somit günstigere Voraussetzungen für ökonomisch bedingte Arbeiterunruhen zu schaffen, wurde 1922 von amerikanischer Seite offenbar nicht in Erwägung gezogen: vgl. STRANGA, Economic Relations, S. 159, 164.

68 MARTIN, *A History of Bolshevik Activities in Latvia. Methods of Organization*, in: Nr. 132, Coleman, 11.12.22, 860p.00B/14, S. 7f.

69 MARTIN, *A History of Bolshevik Activities in Latvia. Methods of Organization*, in: Nr. 132, Coleman, 11.12.22, 860p.00B/14, S. 8f.

70 MARTIN, *A History of Bolshevik Activities in Latvia. Methods of Organization*, in: Nr. 132, Coleman, 11.12.22, 860p.00B/14, S. 3.

vermeintlich führungslosen kommunistischen Bewegung Lettlands keine Aussicht auf eine kurzfristige Erholung:

> „[W]hile the Bolsheviks have not abandoned the idea of eventually forcing an overthrow of the Latvian Government, they have no hope of accomplishing their aim in the near future. It will take a very long time and very much money to regain even the strength and organization which they formerly had, and from the present outlook [...] the Third International is not disposed to grant any considerable financial assistance to the Latvian Communists."[71]

Nach diesem mutmaßlichen Niedergang waren die lettischen Kommunisten aber allem Anschein nach sehr wohl gewillt, ihre Kräfte zu konsolidieren. Der VII. Parteikongress der LKP im Frühjahr 1923, von dem die amerikanische Gesandtschaft in Riga durch die Moskauer *Pravda* erfuhr, hatte ganz im Zeichen einer Reorganisation gestanden. Wie es in dem betreffenden Artikel heißt, habe die LKP die schwere Krise der „Kommunistischen Weltpartei" im Jahr 1921[72] im Untergrund bewältigen müssen, in den sie durch die Demokratie gedrängt worden sei. Der Kongress sei notwendig gewesen, um die „Taktik zu klären" sowie die „Standpunkte auszumachen", auf welche sich die Kommunisten in Lettland zurückgezogen hätten und es seien „Maßnahmen" für den Kampf gegen die Regierung ausgearbeitet worden.[73]

In den Augen der amerikanischen Gesandtschaft handelte es sich bei den „Maßnahmen", mit welchen die Kommunisten in Lettland gedachten, die „Republik zu stürzen, den Kommunismus einzuführen und Lettland der Sowjetischen Föderation anzugliedern" um eine konsequente Übernahme der durch die Komintern ausgegebenen Weisungen. Jedoch kam David B. Macgowan im August 1924 nicht umhin festzustellen, dass die lettischen Kommunisten „ungewöhnlich systematisch", „intelligent und beharrlich" vorgingen und gezielt die „unzweifelhaft schwachen Punkte der lettischen sozialen und politischen Struktur" attackierten. Dabei bezog er sich auf eine „sorgfältige Analyse" des LKP-Programms

---

71 Martin, *A History of Bolshevik Activities in Latvia. Methods of Organization*, in: Nr. 132, Coleman, 11.12.22, 860p.00B/14, S. 13.

72 Das sowjetische Scheitern im Krieg gegen Polen und mehrere fehlgeschlagene militante, von der Komintern initiierte Aktionen – u. a. Generalstreiks in Rumänien, der Tschechoslowakei und Jugoslawien sowie nicht zuletzt die „Märzaktion" in Deutschland – hatten die kommunistische Hoffnung auf einen kurzfristigen Ausbruch der Weltrevolution enttäuscht: Agnew/McDermott, Comintern, S. 28.

73 *Communists and Social-Democrats in Latvia (Extracts* [...] *from Moscow Pravda, No. 81, April 14, 1923)*, in: Nr. 825, Coleman, 23.5.23, 860p.00B/17.

vom Frühjahr 1923, welche der deutschbaltische Saeima-Abgeordnete Paul Schiemann[74] kurz zuvor in der *Rigaschen Rundschau* vorgenommen hatte.[75] Die wesentliche Waffe der Kommunisten bestehe demnach nicht mehr im Terror,[76] sondern in einer „friedlichen Durchdringung der Bevölkerung mit den Ideen der [Kommunistischen] Internationale". Es gelte ihr, überall dort „den Hebel anzusetzen, wo Unzufriedenheit mit den bestehenden Verhältnissen, oder unerfüllte Wünsche" zum Ausdruck kämen.[77] Dabei beschränkten sich die lettischen Kommunisten nicht darauf, ökonomische, soziale und politische Forderungen der Arbeiter – etwa Fragen der Arbeitszeit, des Mindestlohns, der staatlichen Fürsorge oder politischer Freiheiten[78] – für Agitationszwecke zu instrumentalisieren. Auch versuche die LKP, die Agrar- sowie die nationale Minderheitenfrage für die kommunistische Sache nutzbar zu machen – eben jene sensiblen Aspekte, deren Behandlung durch die bürgerliche Regierung während und unmittelbar nach dem Unabhängigkeitskrieg über Durchsetzung und Stabilität der Republik entschieden hatte.[79] War es ab 1919 gelungen, die landlosen Bauern, die

74 Paul Schiemann, deutschbaltischer Politiker und Publizist: Bērziņš, Latvijas Vēsture II, S. 956.

75 Die deutschbaltische *Rigasche Rundschau* galt den Amerikanern als „ultrakonservative" Tageszeitung. Das Programm der LKP war nach Angaben Macgowans zuvor durch den *Latvijas Kareivis* (Lettischer Soldat), die offizielle Zeitung der lettischen Armee, an die Öffentlichkeit gelangt. Zum *Latvijas Kareivis* sowie zur *Rigaschen Rundschau* siehe: *List of the Principal Newspapers in Latvia*, in: Nr. 330, Coleman, 22.1.23, 860p.911/1.

76 Der kommunistische Terror des LSSR-Regimes (1919) war von der deutschbaltischen Minderheit als Trauma erlebt worden: Kusber, Zwischen den Imperien, S. 41.

77 Schiemann, *Communist Tactics in Latvia (Summary from Rigasche Rundschau, No. 191, August 25, 1924)*, in: American Foreign Service Report No. 177, Macgowan, 28.8.24, 860p.00B/26; vgl. *Resolutions of the Recent 7th Congress of Lettish Communist Party*, in: Nr. 825, Coleman, 23.5.23, 860p.00B/17.

78 Dem Recht auf wirtschaftliche und politische Streiks waren in Lettland ebenso Grenzen gesetzt wie der Versammlungsfreiheit. Die lettische Verfassung sah keine umfangreichen persönlichen Grundrechte vor: Bleiere, Geschichte Lettlands, S. 151; Loit, Trade Union Movement, S. 344.

79 Um die bei Kriegsende in Lettland herrschenden ethnokulturellen und sozioökonomischen Gegensätze auszugleichen und die Republik auf eine stabile gesellschaftliche Basis zu stellen, war im September 1920 eine radikale Landreform begonnen worden, die den Großgrundbesitz weitgehend liquidierte und den Anteil landloser Bauern bis 1938 von 61,2% auf 18% senkte: Bleiere, Geschichte Lettlands, S. 195-199; Hehn, Demokratie, S. 7f.; Pistohlkors, Agrarische Umwälzungen. Die Loyalität der Angehörigen nationaler Minderheiten (ca. 27,2% der lettischen Gesamtbevölkerung) sollte durch eine Kultur- und Schulautonomie gewonnen werden: Bleiere, Geschichte

zuvor großenteils den Verheißungen der Kommunisten gefolgt waren, durch das Versprechen auf Landbesitz für die bürgerliche Idee eines demokratischen Nationalstaats zu gewinnen, so erschienen den Kommunisten noch 1923 die 1920 begonnenen staatlichen Landreformen als neuralgischer Punkt des herrschenden Systems. Die Verbitterung all jener, die sich bislang bei der Landvergabe benachteiligt fühlten, sollte daher agitatorisch forciert und die bürgerliche Regierung als Sympathisantin der Großgrundbesitzer bloßgestellt werden.[80] Ebenso meinten die Kommunisten durch das Anfachen nationaler Gefühle und Bestrebungen der nationalen Minderheiten Lettlands einen destabilisierenden Effekt für den Staat erzeugen zu können. Insbesondere in der Integration Lettgallens, für das die LKP eine „weitreichende Autonomie" forderte, sahen sie einen Ansatzpunkt dafür, etwaige Empfindungen der dortigen, national sehr heterogenen Bevölkerung ob einer sprachlichen und kulturellen Diskriminierung zu schüren. Der lettische Staat sollte als nationalistisches Regime und als Unterdrücker nationaler Selbstbestimmung dargestellt werden.[81]

Die amerikanischen Gesandtschaftsberichte zeugen davon, dass sich die kommunistische Bewegung 1923 darum bemühte, sich auf die ökonomischen, sozialen und nationalen Spezifika des lettischen Staats und seiner Gesellschaft einzustellen. Auch gelang es ihr wohl, ihre Lähmung zu überwinden, in welcher sie sich Ende 1922 angeblich befunden hatte. Spätestens bis Mitte 1923 war eine „spürbare Zunahme kommunistischer Aktivitäten" festzustellen.[82] Im August des Folgejahres setzte Ozoliņš die Amerikaner darüber in Kenntnis, dass

---

Lettlands, S. 153f.; ZESTOVSKA, Autoritäres Regime, S. 7. Vgl. hierzu auch den Beitrag von SVETLANA BOGOJAVLENSKA in diesem Band.

80 Die Nachfrage nach Land war so groß, dass lediglich Parzellen mit einer durchschnittlichen Fläche von 17 ha vergeben wurden. Die gesetzliche Obergrenze lag bei 22 ha. Obwohl die Saeima im April 1924 eine entschädigungslose Enteignung der Großgrundbesitzer beschloss, wurden insbesondere lettischen Alteigentümern – den „grauen Baronen" – i. d. R. 100 ha belassen: BLEIERE, Geschichte Lettlands, S. 196f.; PISTOHLKORS, Agrarische Umwälzungen, S. 185.

81 SCHIEMANN, *Communist Tactics in Latvia (Summary from Rigasche Rundschau, No. 191, August 25, 1924)*, in: American Foreign Service Report No. 177, Macgowan, 28.8.24, 860p.00B/26; vgl. *Resolutions of the Recent 7th Congress of Lettish Communist Party*, in: Nr. 825, Coleman, 23.5.23, 860p.00B/17; v. a. die große russische und weißrussische Minderheit Lettgallens stand einer Zugehörigkeit zum lettischen Nationalstaat ablehnend gegenüber. In Jürgen von Hehns Worten standen „Wirtschaft- und Kulturleben" in Lettgallen „auf einem wesentlich tieferen Niveau" als in den „Schwesterprovinzen": HEHN, Demokratie, S. 6f.

82 Nr. 985, Coleman, 25.6.23, 860p.00B/19.

die Tätigkeit der Kommunisten „auf keinen Fall“ nachgelassen habe und dass es ihren Agitatoren „von Zeit zu Zeit“ gelänge, Streiks zu organisieren. Der lettische Geheimdienstchef fügte jedoch hinzu, dass es keine Anzeichen für ein Anwachsen der kommunistischen Bewegung gebe. Die „große Mehrheit“ des lettischen Volkes „bleibe entschieden antibolschewistisch“ eingestellt.[83] Auf eine in Lettland herrschende, „allgemeine“ ablehnende Haltung gegenüber dem Kommunismus hatte Coleman das State Department bereits im Mai 1923 hingewiesen.[84]

Trotz einer gewissen Konstanz, welche kommunistische Aktivitäten bis Mitte 1924 aus amerikanischer Perspektive offenbar gewannen, war von ihnen bis dato keine Gefahr für die innere Sicherheit Lettlands ausgegangen. Auch nach dem gescheiterten kommunistischen Aufstand in Estland im Dezember 1924[85] blieben die amerikanischen Sorgen bezüglich einer ähnlichen Entwicklung in Lettland gering. Zwar war auch hier eine deutliche Steigerung kommunistischer Aktivitäten gegen Jahresende wahrgenommen worden,[86] in einem Bericht, den Coleman im März 1925 nach Washington sandte, heißt es jedoch, dass in der Gesamtschau des Jahres 1924 nicht behauptet werden könne, dass die Kommunisten aktiver als in den Vorjahren gewesen seien. Die Bewegung wurde als personell schwach und kaum waffentauglich eingeschätzt: Die rund 600 Parteimitglieder würden durch nicht mehr als 350 Angehörige des Kommunistischen Jugendverbandes ergänzt. In beiden Organisationen sei die Hälfte der Mitglieder weiblich, was sie aus Sicht des Berichtenden anscheinend für einen bewaffneten Kampf disqualifizierte: Würden die Kommunisten dazu aufgefordert, „die Waffen aufzunehmen“, seien unter ihnen nicht mehr als 200 Erwachsene dazu in der Lage.[87]

Den Hauptgrund dafür, dass es die kommunistische Bewegung bis Anfang 1925 nicht vermocht hatte, sich zu einer ernsthaften Bedrohung zu entwickeln, wurde von Seiten der amerikanischen Gesandtschaft in einem „effektiven und intelligenten“ Vorgehen der lettischen Autoritäten im Allgemeinen[88] sowie der Politischen Polizei im Speziellen gesehen:

---

83 Nr. 2183, Coleman, 9.6.24, 860p.00B/24.

84 Nr. 791, Coleman, 12.5.23, 860p.00/34.

85 Der „Revaler Kommunistenputsch“ vom 1. Dezember 1924 war wohl unter Anleitung der Komintern von etwa 500 estnischen Kommunisten unternommen, jedoch binnen Tagesfrist durch die estnischen Autoritäten niedergeschlagen worden: Rauch, Geschichte der baltischen Staaten, S. 101.

86 Telegramm Nr. 177, White, 13.11.24, 860p.00B/28.

87 Nr. 2727, Coleman, 19.3.25, 860p.00B/32, S. 1-3.

88 Nr. 2851, Coleman, 13.5.25, 860p.00/68.

„Notwithstanding [their] continued propaganda activities, [...] it may be said that since 1920 the Communists in Latvia have never constituted a real danger to the State, as a very efficient and active political police department has been prepared at all times to frustrate any attempts at open action, or extensive organization for open action."[89]

Auf Grundlage eines Gesetzes der Russischen Provisorischen Regierung,[90] welches durch die lettische Regierung einst übernommen worden war, hätten die Autoritäten die Möglichkeit, „unerwünschte Elemente" des Staatsgebietes zu verweisen. Allein 1922 waren nach Angaben der Politischen Polizei 356 Personen wegen kommunistischer Aktivitäten des Landes verwiesen worden.[91]

In den vorliegenden amerikanischen Berichten des Jahres 1926 taucht erstmals der Begriff der „Bolschewisierung" auf.[92] Nach ihrem V. Weltkongress im Juni und Juli 1924, hatte die Komintern eine Ausformung ihrer nationalen Sektionen zu Massenparteien und eine intensivierte ideologische und methodologische Ausbildung der Mitglieder angeordnet.[93] Vor diesem Hintergrund waren die lettischen Kommunisten wohl spätestens ab 1925 angehalten, sich um eine deutliche Steigerung ihrer Mitgliederzahlen, den Aufbau von Frontorganisationen[94] sowie die Schaffung von Zellen zur theoretischen Unterweisung ihrer Jugendlichen zu bemühen.[95]

---

89 Nr. 2727, Coleman, 19.3.25, 860p.00B/32, S. 8.

90 Mit Gesetz vom 2. August 1917 hatte die Russische Provisorische Regierung Kriegs- und Innenminister dazu ermächtigt, nach gegenseitiger Absprache Personen, welche eine Gefahr für die äußere und innere Sicherheit des Staates darstellten, zu inhaftieren und des Landes zu verweisen: Dokument Nr. 1219, S. 1440f.

91 Nr. 2727, Coleman, 19.3.25, 860p.00B/32, S. 8.

92 Nr. 3558, Coleman, 30.1.26, 860p.00B/35, S. 7.

93 Vgl. SINOWJEW, *Die Bolschewisierung der kommunistischen Parteien (1925)*, in: WEBER, Kommunistische Internationale, S. 118-123; AGNEW/MCDERMOTT, Comintern, S. 45f.: Ziel war es, alle KPs nach dem Vorbild der KPR (B) auszurichten und deren Direktive zu unterwerfen. Nach Lenins Tod (21.1.24) und mit dem folgenden Machtaufstieg Stalins sollten die nationalen Komintern-Sektionen von Tendenzen gesäubert werden, die von den Grundsätzen des Leninismus abwichen.

94 In Lettland, wo die kommunistische Bewegung verboten war, war es Aufgabe der kommunistischen Frontorganisationen, unter dem Deckmantel gemeinnütziger Vereine oder anderer gesetzeskonformer Körperschaften Propaganda unter den Massen zu verbreiten und diese für kommunistische Ziele zu gewinnen: vgl. SWORAKOWSKI, International Communist Front Organizations, S. 210.

95 Vorgesehen war u. a. eine Unterrichtung in den Regeln und Taktiken konspirativer Arbeit, in Parteidisziplin, in der Arbeit innerhalb von Arbeiterorganisationen sowie in den Theorien des Leninismus: Nr. 3558, Coleman, 30.1.26, 860p.00B/35, S. 7f.; vgl. AGNEW/MCDERMOTT, Comintern, S. 46.

Das Bild, das Ozoliņš der amerikanischen Gesandtschaft im April 1926 in Form eines ausführlichen Berichts vom Zustand der kommunistischen Bewegung zeichnete, ließ jedoch in dieser Hinsicht keine baldigen Fortschritte erwarten. Selbstbewusst führte der Geheimdienstchef aus, dass die stete Aktivität seiner Behörde die Tätigkeit der Kommunistischen Partei vollständig „paralysiert" habe. Aus Angst davor, verhaftet zu werden, verweilten die Angehörigen der kommunistischen Organisationen in Passivität und die ohnehin „insignifikanten" Mitgliederzahlen seien „erheblich" gesunken.[96] Im Juni des Vorjahres war es Ozoliņš' Behörde gelungen, das Rigaer Hauptquartier der LKP auszuheben. Nicht nur diverse kommunistische Funktionäre seien dabei verhaftet, sondern auch die Archive sowie Geldvorräte der Partei sichergestellt worden.[97] In den folgenden sechs Monaten hätten bei Razzien insgesamt rund 170 Kommunisten – *„practically all of the most active workers"* sowie viele aus Moskau entsandte „Agitatoren und Organisatoren" – festgenommen und vor Gericht gestellt werden können. Zudem seien große Mengen „aufrührerischer Literatur" sowie diverse Gerätschaften zum Druck von Propagandamaterial beschlagnahmt worden. Ein weiterer ‚Coup' der Politischen Polizei war die Dekodierung von Chiffren gewesen, mit welchen die Lettische Sektion in Moskau ihre Schreiben an das Rigaer Komitee ehedem verschlüsselt hatte.[98]

Diese Erfolge des lettischen Geheimdienstes machten es den Kommunisten anscheinend völlig unmöglich, die von der Komintern vorgegebenen personellen Zuwächse zu erzielen und die Strukturen für eine den Moskauer Weisungen entsprechende Massenbewegung aufzubauen: Die Bildung eines lettischen Zweiges der Internationalen Roten Hilfe[99] war offenbar ebenso an personellen Engpässen gescheitert, wie der Erhalt der im Frühjahr 1925 in Riga eingerichteten „theoretischen Keimzellen" zur Ausbildung der kommunistischen Jugend. Diese waren bereits zum Jahresende wieder aufgelöst worden.[100] Lediglich die

---

96 Ozoliņš, *Brief Report Concerning the Communist Movement in Latvia, up to March 20, 1926*. In: Nr. 3701, Coleman, 9.4.26, 860p.00B/36, S. 1.

97 Nr. 2921, Coleman, 8.6.25, 860p.00B/33.

98 Nr. 3558, Coleman, 30.1.26, 860p.00B/35.

99 Die Internationale Rote Hilfe war 1922 in Moskau gegründet worden, um als kommunistisches Äquivalent zum Internationalen Roten Kreuz, für die materielle und moralische Unterstützung von in „kapitalistischen" Gefängnissen inhaftierten Kommunisten und deren Familien zu sorgen. Dabei unterstand sie der Direktive der Komintern: Sworakowski, International Organization, S. 216.

100 Ozoliņš: *Brief Report Concerning the Communist Movement in Latvia, up to March 20, 1926*, in: Nr. 3701, Coleman, 9.4.26, 860p.00B/36, S. 13, 17.

Gründung des Sportvereins „Energie“ in Riga, der mit rund 150 Mitgliedern eine lettische Abteilung der Roten Sportinternationale bildete,[101] stellte einen gewissen, gleichwohl überschaubaren kommunistischen Teilerfolg dar.[102]

Eine weitere Ursache für die Mitte der 1920er Jahre als prekär erachtete Lage der kommunistischen Bewegung in Lettland waren neben dem effizienten Vorgehen der Politischen Polizei interne Unstimmigkeiten und Konflikte. Obwohl die LKP und der ihr zugehörige Jugendverband eng zusammenarbeiten sollten,[103] vertraten die beiden Organisationen anscheinend vollkommen divergierende Vorstellungen von revolutionärer Untergrundarbeit innerhalb eines subversive Tendenzen rigoros unterdrückenden Staates. Wie Ozoliņš 1926 erklärte, herrsche zwischen Partei und Komsomol eine stete Feindseligkeit. Diese erwachse daraus, dass die jugendlichen Kommunisten die Mitglieder sowie die Führung der LKP der Passivität beschuldigten, während sie selbst von Seiten der Partei eines allzu forschen, provokanten und zu wenig auf Diskretion bedachten Vorgehens bezichtigt würden. In diesem Zusammenhang merkte Ozoliņš an, dass rund 50% der Verhaftungen aus einer Vernachlässigung „konspirativer Methoden“ durch Angehörige des Kommunistischen Jugendverbands resultierten. Indem diese versuchten, so viele Neu-Mitglieder wie möglich in ihre Reihen zu ziehen, sprächen sie häufig offen mit Außenstehenden über ihre Aktivitäten und kämen dabei oft unbemerkt in Kontakt mit verdeckten Ermittlern. Nicht selten führe dies zur Aufdeckung von Untergrundstrukturen. Im Gegensatz dazu seien die „altbewährten“ LKP-Mitglieder äußerst vorsichtig und ließen lediglich in seltenen Fällen und nur nach gründlicher Prüfung Beitritte zu ihrer Partei zu.[104]

---

101 Die Rote Sportinternationale war 1921 gegründet worden und agierte in enger Kooperation mit der Jugendinternationale. Ziel war es, Jugendliche im Bereich des Sports ideologisch zu durchdringen und somit Generationen wehrfähiger Kommunisten zu formieren: Sworakowski, Red Sport International, S. 377f.

102 Nr. 3558, Coleman, 30.1.26, 860p.00B/35, S. 7; Ozoliņš: *Brief Report Concerning the Communist Movement in Latvia, up to March 20, 1926*, in: Nr. 3701, Coleman, 9.4.26, 860p.00B/36, S. 2f.

103 *Resolutions of the recent 7th Congress of Lettish Communist Party*, in: Nr. 851, Coleman, 25.5.23, 860p.00B/18.

104 Ozoliņš: *Brief Report concerning the Communist Movement in Latvia, up to March 20, 1926*, in: Nr. 3701, Coleman, 9.4.26, 860p.00B/36, S. 7f; als Massenorganisation bemühte sich der Komsomol sehr viel enthusiastischer um personelle Zuwächse als die LKP. Unter deren „altbewährten“ Parteimitgliedern befanden sich womöglich noch viele Anhänger der Lenin'schen Idee kommunistischer Elitenparteien, die einen massiven personellen Zuwachs ablehnten. Nach Lenins Vorstellungen sollte die KP

Unter dem Eindruck der vorliegenden Informationen gab man sich 1926 auf Seiten der amerikanischen Gesandtschaft in Riga bezüglich des kommunistischen Gefahrenpotenzials in Lettland gelassen und meldete mit Überzeugung nach Washington,

> „that, on the whole, all recent attempts at active revolutionary work on the part of the Communists in Latvia have led to a series of liquidations and failures. In view of the apathy of the Communist Party and the vigilance of the political police authorities, it is believed that any serious activity on the part of the Communists in Latvia, certainly for some time to come, is entirely out of question."[105]

4. Gewerkschaften als „kommunistische Festungen"?

Aus amerikanischer Perspektive stellte die kommunistische Bewegung in Lettland bis Mitte der 1920er Jahre also keine ernsthafte Bedrohung für den lettischen Staat dar. Worüber man sich jedoch nicht sicher sein konnte, war die Zahl mit dem Kommunismus sympathisierender Arbeiter innerhalb der lettischen Gewerkschaften. Da in den meist kleinen Betrieben nur in wenigen Fällen genügend Parteimitglieder beschäftigt waren, die sich zu einer Betriebszelle hätten zusammenfinden können, boten den Kommunisten in Lettland die Gewerkschaften das am besten geeignete Betätigungsfeld.[106] Insbesondere bei der Initiierung von Streiks und Demonstrationen spielten kommunistische Gewerkschaften in den 1920er Jahren eine gewisse Rolle.[107]

In einem Memorandum des lettischen Geheimdienstes, das Commissioner Young im März 1922 an das State Department übermittelte, heißt es:

> „The trade unions are regarded by the Communists as their very stronghold. In the trade unions the Communists have the opportunity to get into close contact with the labor masses to establish legitimate relations with them, and to imbue them with hatred and

---

als kommunistische Avantgarde die Revolution anleiten und die Massen zum Kommunismus erziehen: vgl. WEBER, Lenin in Selbstzeugnissen, S. 50.

105 Nr. 3558, Coleman, 30.1.26, 860p.00B/35, S. 8f.

106 Vgl. *Organisationsbericht des EKKI über den Stand der Parteien (1926)*, in: WEBER, Kommunistische Internationale, S. 144: im Durchschnitt waren pro Betrieb etwa 20 Arbeiter beschäftigt; vgl. zur Größe lettischer Betriebe und Fabriken auch: BLEIERE, Geschichte Lettlands, S. 200.

107 Siehe z. B. *Translation of Communication*, in: Nr. 2333, Coleman, 14.8.24, 860p.00B/25, S. 3; Nr. 2727, Coleman, 19.3.25, 860p.00B/32, S. 9f; Nr. [nicht lesbar], Coleman, 15.3.26, 860p.00/88.

> hostility towards the existing order of things. Therefore, the Communist Party are using their best endeavors to get the management of the trade unions into their hands.“[108]

Zu diesem Zweck sei es für jedes LKP-Mitglied seit 1920 obligatorisch, einer Gewerkschaft anzugehören, dort gemeinsam mit anderen Kommunisten konspirative „Fraktionen“ von drei bis zwölf Personen zu bilden und zu versuchen, die Führung der jeweiligen Arbeiterorganisation zu erobern. Wie Martin in seinem Bericht aus dem Dezember 1922 schilderte, war es den lettischen Kommunisten bis zu ihrer Krise des Jahres 1921 offenbar in vielen Fällen gelungen, die Führer von bis dato sozialdemokratisch dominierten Gewerkschaften durch eigene Leute zu ersetzen. Dabei hatten sie das Zentralbüro der Gewerkschaften in Riga, einen überregionalen Gewerkschaftsdachverband, unter ihre Kontrolle bringen können.[109] Dieses unterlag von da an den Weisungen des „Legalen Zentrums“ der LKP und bildete ein kommunistisches Gegenstück zum Lettischen Zentralbüro,[110] unter dem die sozialdemokratischen Gewerkschaften zusammengeschlossen waren und dessen Ziele von amerikanischer Seite im sozioökonomischen, nicht aber im weltanschaulichen Bereich gesehen wurden. Ende 1921 gingen die Amerikaner davon aus, dass von den 60.000 bis 65.000 lettischen Arbeitern lediglich etwas mehr als 3000 dem Rigaer Zentralbüro angehörten.[111] Zudem, so musste auf Grundlage der vagen, nicht näher bezifferten Informationen des lettischen Geheimdienstes vermutet werden, existierten in zahlreichen Organisationen des Lettischen Zentralbüros kommunistische Fraktionen, über deren tatsächliche Stärke und Einflussmöglichkeiten Unklarheit herrschte.[112]

Spätestens ab Mitte 1924 wurden durch die Kommunisten Versuche unternommen, die Spaltung des Gewerkschaftswesens zu überwinden, um somit den sozialdemokratischen Einfluss auf die lettischen Arbeiter zurückzudrängen.

---

108 *The Work of Communists in Trade Unions*, in: Nr. 1869, Young, 24.3.22, 860p.00B/7.

109 Martin, *A History of Bolshevik Activities in Latvia. Methods of Organization*, in: Nr. 132, Coleman, 11.12.22, 860p.00B/14, S. 2f; vgl. *The Work of Communists in Trade Unions*, in: Nr. 1869, Young, 24.3.22, 860p.00B/7.

110 Das Lettische Zentralbüro der Gewerkschaften war 1920 als Dachverband aller sozialdemokratischen lettischen Gewerkschaften gegründet worden und im Folgejahr dem Internationalen Gewerkschaftsbund (IGB) beigetreten. 1921 war es zu einer Spaltung gekommen, bei der sich jene Organisationen mit kommunistischer Mehrheit vom Lettischen Zentralbüro lösten und sich unter dem Zentralbüro der Gewerkschaften in Riga zusammenschlossen: Loit, Trade Union Movement, S. 342.

111 Vgl. *Labor and Industrial Conditions in Latvia*, in: Nr. -[*sic.*], Hurley, 24.5.22, 860p.504/1, S. 64f.

112 *The Work of Communists in Trade Unions*, in: Nr. 1869, Young, 24.3.22, 860p.00B/7.

Bereits die Resolutionen des VII. LKP-Kongresses hatten 1923 von einer „Einnahme der Gewerkschaften“[113] gesprochen und dies mit dem Slogan einer „vereinten Gewerkschaftsbewegung“[114] verbunden.

Die kommunistischen Bemühungen zur Umsetzung dieses Vorhabens konnten sich bis März 1925 anhand der relativen Entwicklung der Mitgliederzahlen von kommunistisch- und sozialdemokratisch-dominierten Gewerkschaften nachvollziehen lassen: Waren Ende 1924 noch 4500 Arbeiter unter dem Rigaer Zentralbüro organisiert gewesen, so hatte sich deren Zahl innerhalb von nur zwei Monaten auf 3000 reduziert. Im gleichen Zeitraum war die Mitgliederzahl des Lettischen Zentralbüros von rund 10.000 auf etwa 14.000 angewachsen.[115] Zwar wurde diese deutliche Verschiebung von Seiten des lettischen Geheimdienstchefs Ozoliņš auch damit zu erklären versucht, dass die lettischen Arbeiter immer „konservativer“ und weniger „anfällig für radikale Propaganda“ würden. Den Hauptgrund dieser abrupten personellen Entwicklung sah er jedoch in einem Taktikwechsel der kommunistischen Gewerkschaftsarbeit: Es gäbe Beweise dafür, dass die Führer des Rigaer Zentralbüros ihre Mitglieder angewiesen hätten, sich sozialdemokratischen Gewerkschaften anzuschließen, um diese mittels kommunistischer „Keimzellen“ zu unterminieren. Es sei daher unmöglich abzuschätzen, wie viele Mitglieder des Rigaer Zentralbüros aus „seriösen Motiven“ übergewechselt seien.[116]

Zur Veranschaulichung der Intentionen der kommunistischen Unterwanderungs-Taktik übermittelte der Gesandte Coleman Auszüge eines im Januar 1925 von der LKP in Umlauf gesetzten Pamphlets nach Washington. Wie

113 *Resolutions of the Recent 7th Congress of Lettish Communist Party*, in: Nr. 851, Coleman, 25.5.23, 860p.00B/18.

114 Vgl. Schiemann, *Communist Tactics in Latvia (Summary from Rigasche Rundschau, No. 191, August 25, 1924)*, in: American Foreign Service Report No. 177, Macgowan, 28.8.24, 860p.00B/26, S. 1.

115 Zu den Zahlenverhältnissen im Jahr 1924 siehe auch: *Translation of Communication*, in: Nr. 2333, Coleman, 14.8.24, 860p.00B/25, S. 2; Aleksander Loit gibt für das Jahr 1925 ähnliche personellen Größenordnungen an: Während das Lettische Zentralbüro rund 17.000 Angehörige gezählt haben soll, habe das Rigaer Zentralbüro etwa 4000 Mitglieder vereint: Loit, Trade Union Movement, S. 342.

116 Nr. 2727, Coleman, 19.3.25, 860p.00B/32, S. 3f.; beim V. Weltkongress der Komintern war u. a. beschlossen worden, sämtliche kommunistischen Gewerkschaften in die freien Gewerkschaften zu überführen, um somit die „Gewerkschaftseinheit“ wiederherzustellen: vgl. *Die Gewerkschaftsfrage (1924)*, in: Weber, Kommunistische Internationale, S. 112-116; Loit, Trade Union Movement, S. 349.

diesen entnommen werden konnte, waren die Kommunisten zu dem Schluss gelangt, dass unter den „unaufhörlichen Repressionen" von Seiten der „reaktionären Regierung" sowie der Politischen Polizei eine „wahre" Arbeiterbewegung in Lettland unmöglich sei und dass daher „ein neuer Weg" gefunden werden müsse. Dieser bestehe in der Bildung kleiner „Gruppen kommunistischer Sympathisanten" innerhalb aller legalen Arbeiterorganisationen und insbesondere in den „von den verräterischen Sozialdemokraten geführten Gewerkschaften".[117] Die Aufgabe dieser Gruppen bestand nun offenbar nicht mehr länger in einer schnellstmöglichen Eroberung der Gewerkschaftsspitzen. Vielmehr sollten sie „so geheim wie möglich" agieren und bis zum „Sieg des Arbeiters" – bis zu einer proletarischen Revolution – Zellen bilden, welche zu einer Führung von „kommunalen Organen" in der Lage wären. Erst die Errichtung einer „Arbeiter- und Bauernregierung",[118] so heißt es in der kommunistischen Schrift, werde die Situation der lettischen Arbeiterbewegung verbessern.[119] Aus amerikanischer Sicht stellte dieser Taktikwechsel in der kommunistischen Gewerkschaftsarbeit einerseits einen Versuch dar, den Einfluss auf die lettischen Arbeiter zu erhöhen und organisatorische Strukturen für eine revolutionäre Machtübernahme zu schaffen. Andererseits hatten die lettischen Sicherheitsbehörden nach dem estnischen Kommunistenputsch im Dezember 1924 ihre Präventivmaßnahmen gegenüber subversiven Aktivitäten deutlich verschärft.[120] Während sie ihre eigenen legalen Organisationen offenbar zusehends staatlicher Kontrolle ausgesetzt sahen,[121] erhofften sich die Kommunisten von einem Aufgehen ihrer Gewerkschafter in

117 *Organize Groups of Communist Sympathizers (Laukstrādnieku Cīna No. 1, January 1925)*, in: Nr. 2727, Coleman, 19.3.19, 860p.00B/32; vgl. *Resolution on Trade Union Work*, in: Nr. 3558, Coleman, 860p.00B/35.

118 Die Parole der „Arbeiter- bzw. der „Arbeiter- und Bauernregierung" diente der Komintern spätestens ab ihrem IV. Weltkongress (1922) als wesentliche Losung zur Mobilisierung der Arbeiter innerhalb bürgerlicher Länder: *Einheitsfronttaktik und Arbeiterregierung (1922/23)*, in: Weber, Kommunistische Internationale, S. 99-107, hier S. 101f.

119 Ab 1924/25 wurde auf Seiten der Komintern von einer Periode „relativer Stabilität" des westlichen Kapitalismus ausgegangen – von einer Art Transitphase zwischen zwei revolutionären „Schüben", in dem sich der kapitalistische Westen und die durch die NEP sich ebenfalls stabilisierende UdSSR in einem gewissen Gleichgewicht befänden. Auch wenn damit akzeptiert wurde, dass die Weltrevolution zunächst nicht realisierbar sein würde, galt es dennoch organisatorische und strukturelle Vorbereitungen für sie zu treffen: vgl. Agnew/McDermott, Comintern, S. 52.

120 Nr. 2727, Coleman, 19.3.19, 860p.00B/32, S. 5.

121 Vgl. Nr. [nicht lesbar], Coleman, 15.3.26, 860p.00/88.

den sozialdemokratischen Organisationen wohl auch eine bessere Tarnung ihrer Massenarbeit.

Das Prinzip einer „vereinten Gewerkschaftsbewegung“ versuchten die lettischen Kommunisten allerdings nicht allein auf dem Wege konspirativer Unterwanderung zu verwirklichen. Im April 1926 informierte Ozoliņš die amerikanische Gesandtschaft darüber, dass das ZK der LKP entsprechenden Anordnungen der Komintern folgend das Rigaer Zentralbüro dazu angewiesen habe, mit dem Lettischen Zentralbüro „überein zu kommen“ und die beiden Verbände organisatorisch zu „verschmelzen“. Zwar habe es vereinzelt gemeinsame Aktionen (z. B. Demonstrationen) gegeben, bei diesen sei es jedoch zu gewalttätigen Auseinandersetzungen zwischen den Anhängern beider Lager gekommen. Da die sozialdemokratischen Gewerkschaftsführer genau über die „wahren Absichten“ des Rigaer Zentralbüros Bescheid wüssten, lehnten sie eine organisatorische Vereinigung mit dem kommunistischen Verband ab. Gleichzeitig seien sie in ihren Organisationen äußerst wachsam und stets in der Lage, die geringste Tendenz zugunsten der Kommunisten zu unterdrücken. Bislang, so Ozoliņš, hätten sich alle kommunistischen Initiativen unter der Losung einer gegen den Kapitalismus gerichteten „Einheitsfront“[122] als „nutzlos“ erwiesen. Trotz großer Anstrengungen gelänge es den Kommunisten nicht, den Einfluss der Sozialdemokraten auf die Arbeitermassen zu schwächen. Die Situation des Rigaer Zentralbüros, dessen Mitgliederzahl sich stetig verringere, werde indessen immer „jämmerlicher“.[123] Gleichwohl: Das lettische Gewerkschaftswesen, davon konnten die amerikanischen Vertreter in Riga Mitte der 1920er Jahre ausgehen, stellte für die kommunistische Bewegung jenes Betätigungsfeld dar, auf welchem sie mit Abstand den größten Einfluss geltend machen konnte und um den sie sich folglich am meisten bemühte. In der Spaltung der linken Gewerkschaftsorganisationen manifestierte sich ein von Kommunisten und Sozialdemokraten um die lettischen Arbeiter geführter Konkurrenzkampf, in dem der Vorteil aber eindeutig auf Seiten der Sozialdemokraten zu liegen schien.

---

122 Unter „Einheitsfront“ verstand die Komintern eine gemeinsame Aktionsbasis aller sozialistisch gesinnten Arbeiter im Kampf gegen die „kapitalistische Bourgeoisie“. Sie ging davon aus, dass die Erfahrung des gemeinsamen Kampfes die Werktätigen von den kommunistischen Methoden überzeugen würde: *Einheitsfronttaktik und Arbeiterregierung (1922/23)*, in: Weber, Kommunistische Internationale, S. 99-107, hier: S. 100f.; Agnew/ McDermott, Comintern, S. 27.

123 Ozoliņš, *Brief Report Concerning the Communist Movement in Latvia, up to March 20, 1926*, in: Nr. 3701, Coleman, 9.4.26, 860p.00B/36, S. 15-17.

5. Abwege 1927

Das Jahr 1927 bildet in der amerikanischen Berichterstattung über die kommunistische Bewegung Lettlands eine auf den ersten Blick unerklärliche Lücke. Lediglich im Rahmen diverser Monatsberichte über die allgemeinen innenpolitischen Verhältnisse in Lettland finden sich vereinzelte, bruchstückhafte Hinweise auf kommunistische Aktivitäten.[124] Auffällig ist dabei, dass die knappen Kenntnisse offenbar vollständig aus der lokalen Presse gezogen worden waren – Bezüge auf Ozoliņš und die Politische Polizei als etwaige Informanten sucht man in den betreffenden Berichten vergeblich.

1927 war das Jahr der Amtszeit der sozialdemokratisch-dominierten Regierungskoalition Ministerpräsident Marģers Skujenieks' gewesen – der zweiten und längeren der beiden sozialdemokratischen Regierungsbeteiligungen vor 1934.[125] Unter Initiative ihres Außenministers Fēlikss Cielēns[126] hatte diese Administration eine engere sicherheitspolitische und wirtschaftliche Zusammenarbeit mit der Sowjetunion angestrebt, was im Juni zur Unterzeichnung eines Handelsabkommens geführt hatte. Verhandlungen über einen Nichtangriffspakt waren hingegen erfolglos geblieben.[127] Wie der amerikanische Gesandte Coleman im April 1929 in einer Analyse der lettisch-sowjetischen Beziehungen rückblickend darstellte, hatte sich die 1927 vollzogene Annäherung der beiden Staaten merklich in den Aktivitäten der lettischen Kommunisten abgezeichnet. Es sei „offensichtlich" gewesen, dass die „Cielēns-Regierung" seinerzeit versucht habe, einerseits dem „radikalen proletarischen Element" im Inneren durch „diverse Zugeständnisse" zu gefallen, während sie andererseits durch die handelspolitische Annäherung an die UdSSR die Unterstützung der Wirtschaft gesucht habe. Da beide Aspekte im Interesse der Sowjets gelegen hätten, habe die „Diktatur in Moskau" beschlossen, die lettische Regierung so wenig wie möglich zu behindern. Zwar seien die „übliche Propaganda" und die „geheime Agitation" nicht vollständig eingestellt, jedoch mit deutlich reduzierter Intensität

---

124 So z. B. Nr. [nicht lesbar], Coleman, 7.1.27, 860p.00/104; Nr. [nicht lesbar], Coleman, 11.2.27, 860p.00/105; Nr. [nicht lesbar], Coleman, 2.6.27, 860p.00/110; Nr. 4657, Coleman, 13.8.27, 860p.00/114.

125 Das Kabinett Marģers Skujenieks (Partei der sozialdemokratischen Minderheit) amtierte von Dezember 1926 bis Januar 1928: Bērziņš, Latvijas Vēsture I, S. 800; Bleiere, Geschichte Lettlands, S. 158; Conrad, Loyalitäten, S. 175.

126 Zu Fēlikss Cielēns (LSDSP) vgl.: Bērziņš, Latvijas Vēsture I, S. 764.

127 Anderson, USSR Trades with Latvia, S. 303-305.

fortgeführt worden.[128] Demnach wäre es also denkbar, dass sich die LKP 1927 auf Anweisung der Komintern in ihren Tätigkeiten zurückgehalten hatte, um die außenpolitischen Ziele der Sowjet-Führung nicht zu gefährden. Ebenso ließe sich aus den Ausführungen Colemans schließen, dass die lettischen Kommunisten unter sozialdemokratischer Regierung größere Freiheiten genossen hatten, als unter den vorangegangenen bürgerlichen Koalitionen.[129]

Der vermeintlich Moskau-freundliche Kurs der Regierung Skujenieks' wurde von amerikanischer Seite nicht zuletzt vor dem Hintergrund der diplomatischen Spannungen zwischen Großbritannien und der UdSSR sehr kritisch betrachtet. Die britisch-sowjetischen Beziehungen waren gerade erst im Mai durch die konservative britische Regierung abgebrochen worden. Wie sich herausgestellt hatte, hatten die Sowjets die exterritorialen Privilegien ihrer Außenhandelsvertretung in London zu Spionagezwecken missbraucht. Der Abschluss des lettisch-sowjetischen Handelsabkommens erfolgte aus amerikanischer Perspektive somit sicherlich zu einem unglücklichen Zeitpunkt.[130]

Ohnehin befürchtete man, dass die UdSSR das handelspolitische Entgegenkommen der lettischen Regierung für politische und ideologische Zwecke missbrauchen würde, um den sowjetischen Einflussbereich nach Westen zu verschieben. Die amerikanische Annahme, dass die durch das Abkommen vorgesehene Niederlassung sowjetischer Handelsinstitutionen innerhalb Lettlands einer Einrichtung getarnter Stützpunkte für Propaganda- und Spionageaktivitäten gleichkommen würde, war indessen nicht gegenstandslos. So sollte sich etwa im Februar 1929 bei Durchsuchungen durch die Politische Polizei in den Rigaer Lagerhäusern der sowjetischen Handelsflotte (*Sovtorgflot*) zeigen, dass diese Räume von der LKP ehedem als Zentrallager für Propagandamaterial und als Ausgangspunkt für kommunistische Streikaufrufe genutzt worden waren.[131]

---

128 Aufgrund ihrer besonderen außenpolitischen Schwerpunktsetzung wurde die Skujenieks-Regierung von Seiten der amerikanischen Vertreter in Riga auch als „Cielēns-Regierung" bezeichnet: Nr. 6099, Coleman, 24.4.29, 860p.00B/57, S. 3.

129 Von einer mutmaßlichen Nähe der Regierung zu kommunistischen Organisationen hatte Coleman bereits im Juni 1927 im Zusammenhang mit einer Interpellation des Bauernbunds gegen die „sozialistische Regierung" berichtet. Grundlage dieser Interpellation war die Anschuldigung, dass die Regierung die Polizei in ihrem Bemühen um die öffentliche Sicherheit nicht unterstütze: Nr. 4540, Coleman, 6.6.27, 860p.032/9.

130 Vgl. Nr. [nicht lesbar], Coleman, 9.5.27, 860p.00/109; vgl. auch Anderson, USSR Trades with Latvia, S. 303, 310.

131 Nr. 5957, Coleman, 9.3.29, 860p.504/9; vgl. Anderson, USSR Trades with Latvia, S. 305; Stranga, Economic Relations, S. 166.

Dass die lettischen Kommunisten 1927 nicht gänzlich tatenlos geblieben waren, veranschaulichte ein Manuskript des lettischen Geheimdienstchefs Ozoliņš, welches Coleman im Frühjahr 1928 an das State Department übermittelte, um von den Aktivitäten der LKP während des soeben zu Ende gegangenen Vorjahres zu berichten. Demnach hätten die Kommunisten „jede Mühe aufgebracht", ihre Situation zu stärken, neue Mitglieder zu rekrutieren, Propagandisten auszubilden und eine strikte Parteidisziplin unter ihren Angehörigen einzuführen.[132] Dabei hatte die kommunistische Agitation neue Motive erhalten: Neben dem Kampf gegen eine „angeblich wachsende faschistische Bewegung" beherrsche das Szenario einer bevorstehenden „Intervention" der „internationalen Bourgeoisie" gegen die Sowjetunion sowohl die Sitzungen der kommunistischen Gewerkschaften, als auch die kommunistische Presse.[133] Großbritannien gelte den Kommunisten in diesem Szenario als „Initiator, Organisator und Führer der internationalen Reaktion", welche sich dazu bereit mache, „die Waffen aufzunehmen, um die Gegensätze zwischen dem sozialistischen Russland und der kapitalistischen Welt zu lösen".[134] Mit dieser Absicht unterstütze Großbritannien „faschistische Revolten" in den baltischen Staaten, um diese gegen die Sowjetunion in Stellung zu bringen – die „bourgeoise Diktatur" in Polen sowie der „faschistische Putsch" in Litauen wurden dafür als Beweise angeführt.[135]

132 Ozoliņš, *Activities of the Communist Party of Latvia during the Year 1927*, in: Nr. 5964, Coleman, 24.2.28, 860p.00B/46, S. 7.

133 Ozoliņš, *Activities of the Communist Party of Latvia during the Year 1927*, in: Nr. 5964, Coleman, 24.2.28, 860p.00B/46, S. 3f.

134 Spätestens seit dem alliierten Eingreifen in den Russischen Bürgerkrieg unter britischer Initiative galt Großbritannien, das Ursprungsland des Kapitalismus, den Kommunisten als Führer der „internationalen Reaktion": Thesen der LKP zitiert von Ozoliņš in: Ozoliņš, *Activities of the Communist Party of Latvia during the Year 1927*, in: Nr. 5964, Coleman, 24.2.28, 860p.00B/46, S. 8; Breuer, Russische Sektion, S. 134; als Vorzeichen einer bevorstehenden Intervention der kapitalistischen Staaten wurde von sowjetischer Seite auch die Ermordung des sowjetischen Repräsentanten durch einen Weißgardisten in Warschau im Juni sowie die Ausweisung des sowjetischen Botschafters durch die französische Regierung im September 1927 gedeutet: Eichwede, Eintritt Sowjetrusslands in die internationale Politik, S. 207-212; siehe auch Sontag, Soviet War Scare, S. 71.

135 In Polen hatte nach der „Mairevolution" 1926 das sogenannte (konservative) *Sanacja*-Regime Józef Piłsudskis die Herrschaft übernommen: Borodziej, Geschichte Polens, S. 162-164; mit dem Militärputsch vom 17. Dezember 1926 war in Litauen die dortige Regierungskoalition von Volkssozialisten und Sozialdemokraten gestürzt und zunächst durch eine konservative Regierung ersetzt worden, bevor im April 1927

Auch in Lettland, wo die Bildung der linken Skujenieks-Regierung Ende 1926 in bürgerlichen Kreisen zu einer wachsenden Kritik an den innenpolitischen Verhältnissen und dem Parlamentarismus *per se* geführt hatte,[136] sei der Faschismus laut den Kommunisten auf dem Vormarsch: Würde die linke Regierung fallen, so könne die Macht „unter den gegenwärtigen Umständen" nur in die Hände „extremer Reaktionäre" fallen, was den Weg bereiten würde für die Errichtung einer „faschistischen Diktatur". Da sich die Sozialdemokraten weigerten, sich dem „antifaschistischen Kampf" der Kommunisten anzuschließen, begünstigten sie angeblich sowohl den Aufstieg des Faschismus, als auch gleichzeitig die „imperialistischen" Kriegspläne.[137] Vor diesem Hintergrund hatte die LKP ihre Agitation 1927 nicht nur auf die Bekämpfung des Faschismus, sondern auch auf eine verstärkte Solidarisierung der lettischen Arbeiter mit jenen der UdSSR ausgerichtet: Laut Ozoliņš habe die Partei vehement für die Ratifikation des lettisch-sowjetischen Handelsabkommens sowie für den Abschluss eines Nichtangriffspakts geworben. Die kommunistischen Gewerkschaften hätten zudem im Sommer Arbeiterdelegationen mit der Aufgabe in die Sowjetunion entsandt, nach ihrer Rückkehr „in höchstattraktiver Form" von den Lebensbedingungen in Russland zu berichten.[138]

Ab der Jahreswende 1927/28 stand die sowjetische Außenpolitik offiziell unter einem „Primat der Sicherheit" und der Losung einer „friedlichen Koexistenz" mit den kapitalistischen Staaten. Dem lag die Absicht zugrunde, eine etwaige militärische Auseinandersetzung mit dem Westen, wie sie sich 1927 aus sowjetischer Perspektive angedeutet hatte, unbedingt zu vermeiden, um die innenpolitische Entwicklung der UdSSR – den sogenannten „Aufbau des Sozialismus in einem Land" – sicherzustellen. Zu diesem Zweck hatte die Sowjetunion Ende 1927 erstmals ihren Willen demonstriert, sich an den Beratungen des Völkerbunds um internationale Friedenssicherung und allgemeine Abrüstung

---

das litauische Parlament aufgelöst und das autoritäre rechts-nationalistische Regime Antanas Smetonas errichtet wurde: Hellmann, Geschichte Litauens, S. 154-156.

136 Aus Sicht diverser bürgerlicher Politiker hatten sich die „Allmacht des Parlaments" und die häufigen Regierungswechsel als schädlich für die innenpolitische Entwicklung erwiesen, sodass bisweilen sogar eine Nachahmung des autoritären, litauischen Vorbilds in Erwägung gezogen wurde: Hehn, Demokratie, S. 13, 19.

137 Thesen der LKP zitiert von Ozoliņš in: Ozoliņš, *Activities of the Communist Party of Latvia during the Year 1927*, in: Nr. 5964, Coleman, 24.2.28, 860p.00B/46, S. 11-13.

138 Ozoliņš, *Activities of the Communist Party of Latvia during the Year 1927*, in: Nr. 5964, Coleman, 24.2.28, 860p.00B/46, S. 4f.; vgl. Agnew/McDermott, Comintern, S. 94.

zu beteiligen.[139] Aus der Retrospektive konnten die amerikanischen Vertreter in Riga Anfang 1928 nachvollziehen, dass sich das erhöhte sowjetische Sicherheitsbedürfnis 1927 ganz offenbar auch in den Aktivitäten der kommunistischen Bewegung in Lettland widergespiegelt hatte. Als Sektion der Komintern kam der LKP nicht allein eine (welt-) revolutionäre Rolle zu, sondern auch eine unterstützende Funktion für die außen- und sicherheitspolitischen Interessen der UdSSR.[140] Nichtsdestotrotz war es der LKP auch unter einer linken, gegenüber den Kommunisten vermeintlich duldsameren Regierung nicht gelungen, ihre Stellung zu verbessern: Wie Ozoliņš im Frühjahr 1928 konstatierte, verliere die kommunistische Bewegung stetig an Einfluss und ihr Bemühen um die Schaffung einer Einheitsfront sei ein totaler Fehlschlag gewesen.[141]

6. Shorn of Power for Evil 1928-1934

Mit dem Fall der Regierung Skujenieks' Ende 1927 und der anschließenden Bildung einer Regierung des „rechten Zentrums" im Januar 1928, kehrte die Regierungsgewalt ins bürgerlich-konservative Lager zurück.[142] Die lettische Außenpolitik vollzog daraufhin eine Abkehr von der UdSSR und orientierte sich in der Folge wieder stärker am Westen, was eine spürbare „Wiederbelebung" der legalen und illegalen kommunistischen Organisationen innerhalb Lettlands nach sich zog.[143]

Auf die intensivierte Agitation und das verstärkte Auftauchen kommunistischer Propagandaschriften reagierten die lettischen Behörden mit einem verschärften Vorgehen, welches sich am deutlichsten in der Schließung von 19

139 Mit der von Stalin seit 1927 ausgegebenen Parole vom „Aufbau des Sozialismus in einem Land" wurde die Notwendigkeit der Weltrevolution für einen erfolgreichen Aufbau eines sozialistischen Systems in Russland in Frage gestellt: Jacobsen, Primat der Sicherheit, S. 213, 218, 222.

140 Vgl. *Das Programm der Kommunistischen Internationale (1928)*, in: Weber, Kommunistische Internationale, S. 225: Der Komintern kam u. a. die Aufgabe zu, die Sowjetunion „mit allen Mitteln gegen die Angriffe der kapitalistischen Mächte zu verteidigen".

141 Ozoliņš, *Activities of the Communist Party of Latvia during the Year 1927*, in: Nr. 5964, Coleman, 24.2.28, 860p.00B/46, S. 16-18.

142 Die Regierung Skujenieks' war Mitte Dezember 1927 zurückgetreten, bis zur Einsetzung der neuen Regierung Pēteris Juraševskis (Demokratisches Zentrum) im Januar 1928 aber formell im Amt geblieben: vgl. Conrad, Loyalitäten, S. 69, 175; Bērziņš, Latvijas Vēsture II, S. 925.

143 Nr. 6099, Coleman, 24.4.29, 860p.00B/57, S. 4.

mutmaßlich kommunistischen Gewerkschaften manifestierte. Wie Coleman im September 1928 nach Washington meldete, habe sich herausgestellt, dass das Rigaer Zentralbüro, dem die betreffenden Organisationen allesamt angehört hätten, über ein „lokales sowjetisches Bankinstitut" – die Kooperative Transitbank[144] – finanzielle Unterstützung der Roten Gewerkschaftsinternationale (RGI)[145] in Moskau bezogen habe. Infolge der Schließungen im August sei es in Riga zu Demonstrationen und sogar Angriffen auf die Ordnungskräfte gekommen. Erfolglos hätten die Kommunisten den Versuch unternommen, einen Generalstreik zu provozieren. 200 Personen seien festgenommen worden.[146] Hatten die Gewerkschaften bisher das erfolgreichste Feld kommunistischer Arbeit in Lettland dargestellt, so bedeutete deren Stilllegung für die LKP zweifellos einen schweren Schlag.[147]

Umso mehr stellte es für die amerikanische Gesandtschaft ebenso wie für die lettische Öffentlichkeit eine „unerwartete Demonstration kommunistischer Stärke"[148] dar, als es im Oktober desselben Jahres bei den Wahlen zur III. Saeima „zwei getarnten kommunistischen Gruppen" gelang, insgesamt sieben Parlamentsmandate zu gewinnen.[149] Aus einem Memorandum, das Martin Ende November anlässlich dieses Wahlerfolgs verfasste, geht hervor, dass die lettischen Kommunisten Ende 1927 durch die Komintern angewiesen worden waren, bei den bevorstehenden Wahlen „um jeden Preis" kommunistische Abgeordnete in der Saeima zu platzieren. Während die LKP dementsprechend ihre Kandidaten

---

144 Nach Angaben des amerikanischen Konsulats in Riga handelte es sich bei der Kooperativen Transitbank um eine sowjetische Aktiengesellschaft, die 1923 in Riga zur Förderung des sowjetischen Transithandels durch Lettland eingerichtet worden war: Nr. 36, Kliefoth, 23.11.27, 860p.516/35; Nr. 37, Kliefoth, 28.11.27, 860p.516/33.

145 Die Rote Gewerkschaftsinternationale war 1921 auf Initiative der Komintern gegründet worden, um den revolutionären Einfluss innerhalb der europäischen, vornehmlich sozialdemokratisch-dominierten Gewerkschaften zu steigern und somit ein kommunistisches Gegenstück zum sozialistischen IGB zu bilden: Sworakowski, Red International of Labor Unions, S. 375-377; siehe auch Loit, Trade Union Movement, S. 337f.

146 Nr. 5543, Coleman, 10.9.28, 860p.504/7.

147 Vgl. Nr. 6099, Coleman, 24.4.29, 860p.00B/57, S. 3-5; *Review of the Activity and Condition of the Communist Party of Latvia, up to March 15, 1929*, in: Nr. [nicht lesbar], Coleman, 2.5.29, 860p.00B/60, S. 1f.

148 Martin, *Strictly Confidential Memorandum Concerning Communist Activities in Latvia since January 1, 1928*, in: Nr. 5739, Sussdorff, 3.12.28, 860p.00B/49, S. 14.

149 Nr. 5643, Sussdorff, 23.10.28, 860p.00/123, S. 2.

unter dem Decknamen einer Arbeiter- und Bauernpartei[150] aufgestellt habe, habe sie zudem – angeblich aus Gründen der Tarnung – in Gestalt der Unabhängigen Sozialisten eine zweite Partei formiert, deren Mitglieder sich aus linken Gewerkschaften, kommunistischen Organisationen und nicht zuletzt aus dem linken Flügel der LSDSP rekrutiert hätten.[151] Nach „energetischen Bemühungen" im Vorfeld der Wahlen hätten beide Parteien zusammen 8% bzw. 75.000 aller abgegebenen Stimmen auf sich vereinen können.[152] Ein Sitz entfiel dabei auf die Unabhängigen Sozialisten; die Linke Arbeiter- und Bauernpartei erreichte sechs Mandate.[153]

75.000 erreichte Wählerstimmen bedeuteten aus amerikanischer Sicht sicher eine ganz andere Größenordnung als die knapp 1000 Angehörigen von LKP und Komsomol oder die rund 4000 Mitglieder kommunistischer Gewerkschaften. Zumal diese Zahl nur wahlberechtigte Personen mit einem Mindestalter von 21 Lebensjahren repräsentierte und jugendliche Sympathisanten ebenso ausklammerte, wie einen Großteil der Angehörigen des Kommunistischen Jugendverbands.[154] Gleichwohl wurde vermerkt, dass ein Großteil der auf die Kommunisten entfallenen Stimmen von Industriearbeitern abgegeben worden sei, von denen rund die Hälfte aus der lettischen Hauptstadt stamme. Die mutmaßlich kommunistische Wählerschaft beschränkte sich also sowohl weitgehend auf eine spezifische Klientel als auch auf einen lokalen Schwerpunkt. Unter der Landbevölkerung des agrarisch geprägten Lettland schienen die Kommunisten hingegen keinen großen Einfluss zu besitzen. Relativierend führte Martin

---

150 In den amerikanischen Berichten findet sich auch die Bezeichnung der „Linken Gewerkschaftspartei". Offenbar waren beide Bezeichnungen gebräuchlich. In Anlehnung an Jürgen von Hehn und Ādolfs Šilde wird hier die Bezeichnung „Linke Arbeiter- und Bauernpartei" verwendet: Hehn, Demokratie, S. 11; Šilde, Sowjetisierung, S. 11.

151 Bei der Partei der Unabhängigen Sozialisten handelte es sich wohl tatsächlich um eine Splittergruppe des linken Flügels der LSDSP: Anderson, Latvia, S. 298; Hehn, Demokratie, S. 11.

152 Martin berief sich bei diesen Zahlen auf offizielle Angaben des Lettischen Statistikamtes: Martin, *Strictly Confidential Memorandum Concerning Communist Activities in Latvia since January 1, 1928*, in: Nr. 5739, Sussdorff, 3.12.28, 860p.00B/49, S. 1f.; vgl. Šilde, Sowjetisierung Lettlands, S. 10.

153 *Review of the Activity and Condition of the Communist Party of Latvia, up to March 15, 1929*, in: Nr. [nicht lesbar], Coleman, 2.5.29, 860p.00B/60, S. 9; Bilmanis, History of Latvia, S. 342.

154 Vgl. *Review of the Activity and Condition of the Communist Party of Latvia, up to March 15, 1929*, in: Nr. [nicht lesbar], Coleman, 2.5.29, 860p.00B/60, S. 14.

an, dass es nach Ansicht „vieler" besser sei, den Kommunisten zu erlauben offen ihre Stärke zu zeigen und mit ihren Abgeordneten in das Parlament einzuziehen. Bereits in der Vergangenheit seien Kommunisten verdeckt in die Saeima gewählt worden – so etwa in den Reihen der LSDSP[155] –, nun aber wisse man wo sie stehen. Zudem, so Martin, würden die lettischen Polizeibehörden die „Aktivitäten subversiver Elemente" sehr aufmerksam überwachen und nicht davon ausgehen, dass die kommunistische Bewegung in irgendeiner Weise die Staatssicherheit gefährde.[156]

Warum Linke Arbeiter- und Bauernpartei sowie Unabhängige Sozialisten trotz ihres unzweifelhaft linksradikalen Programms – neben einer Wiederherstellung der (revolutionären) Gewerkschaften wurde u. a. ein Anschluss Lettlands an die UdSSR, eine Bewaffnung der Arbeiter sowie die Bildung einer Arbeiter- und Bauernregierung gefordert[157] – zu den Wahlen im Oktober 1928 zugelassen worden waren, lässt sich anhand der amerikanischen Gesandtschaftsberichte lediglich spekulieren. Laut Politischer Administration, seien 1928 im Vorfeld der Wahlen Artikel in der bürgerlichen Presse erschienen, die es als ratsam suggeriert hätten, den Einzug von Kommunisten in die Saeima zu gestatten, um die sozialdemokratische Parlamentsopposition zu schwächen.[158] Dieser Überlegung hätte wieder die Annahme zugrunde gelegen, dass sich in den Reihen des linken LSDSP-Flügels verdeckte Kommunisten befänden, die sich bei entsprechender Gelegenheit einer legalen kommunistischen Partei anschließen würden. Tatsächlich hatte die lettische Sozialdemokratie (inklusive ihrer rechten Minderheit) gegenüber den Parlamentswahlen von 1925 ebenso viele Prozentpunkte verloren, wie die kommunistische Fraktion nunmehr gewonnen hatte. Dies war von amerikanischer Seite bereits kurz nach den Wahlen im Oktober vermerkt

155 Auf Seiten der amerikanischen Gesandtschaft ging man 1928 offenbar davon aus, dass die LSDSP seit dem Verbot der LKP im Jahre 1920 stetig durch kommunistische Zellen unterwandert würde: *Study of Latvian political parties*, in: Nr. [nicht lesbar], Coleman, 21.2.28, 860p.00/117, S. 4.

156 Martin, *Strictly Confidential Memorandum Concerning Communist Activities in Latvia since January 1, 1928*, in: Nr. 5739, Sussdorff, 3.12.28, 860p.00B/49, S. 14f.

157 Nr. 6119, Coleman, 2.5.29, 860p.00/127; *Review of the Activity and Condition of the Communist Party of Latvia, up to March 15, 1929*, in: Nr. [nicht lesbar], Coleman, 2.5.29, 860p.00B/60, S. 9.

158 Nr. 6119, Coleman, 2.5.29, 860p.00/127; *Review of the Activity and Condition of the Communist Party of Latvia, up to March 15, 1929*, in: Nr. [nicht lesbar], Coleman, 2.5.29, 860p.00B/60, S. 4f.

worden.[159] Die Kommunisten hätten, laut Politischer Polizei, nach ihrem Einzug in die Saeima „endgültig" mit der LSDSP „gebrochen", sodass die Möglichkeit einer Zusammenarbeit vollkommen ausgeschlossen sei.[160] Durch die Bildung einer „noch konservativeren" Regierung „als der vorangegangenen"[161] und einer nunmehr gespaltenen linken Opposition scheint das in der bürgerlichen Presse geäußerte Ziel erreicht worden zu sein. In den amerikanischen Berichten erscheint der kommunistische Parlamentseinzug weniger als gut getarnter, konspirativer Coup, sondern mehr als ein von den lettischen Autoritäten antizipiertes und in kontrollierten Bahnen gelenktes Zugeständnis.

Fortan bildete die kommunistische Saeima-Fraktion das neue Zentrum der legalen Aktivitäten der LKP. Wie der lettische Geheimdienst 1929 mitteilte, habe das ZK der LKP ihren Abgeordneten die volle Verantwortung für die Konsolidierung der Bewegung übertragen. Sämtliche Versuche der Fraktion, Arbeiter-, Bauern- und Arbeitslosenkomitees zu initiieren, scheiterten jedoch daran, dass solche Gremien prinzipiell verboten und Personen, die sich um deren Schaffung bemühten, umgehend verhaftet würden. Während die kommunistischen Deputierten – geschützt durch parlamentarische Immunität – mit „ihren provokanten Taktiken" die Arbeiter zu illegalen Aktivitäten „drängten", setzten sie diese der Verfolgung und Verhaftung aus und ernteten somit v. a. deren Misstrauen.[162]

Dass die kommunistische Fraktion überdies ihre Präsenz in der Saeima allein zu demagogischen Zwecken sowie zur Behinderung der parlamentarischen

---

159 Nr. 5643, Sussdorff, 23.10.28, 860p.00B/123, S. 2; die LSDSP und die Partei der sozialdemokratischen (rechten) Minderheit, die sich zur Zeit der lettischen Konstituante von der (linken) Mehrheit der LSDSP abgespalten hatte, hatten 1925 zusammen 35%, 1928 aber nur noch 27% erhalten, während die Linke Arbeiter- und Bauernpartei gemeinsam mit der Partei der Unabhängigen Sozialisten 1928 8% erreichte: Bilmanis, History of Latvia, S. 342; zur Spaltung der lettischen Sozialdemokratie 1921 siehe: Bleiere, Geschichte Lettlands, S. 152.

160 *Review of the Activity and Condition of the Communist Party of Latvia, up to March 15, 1929*, in: Nr. [nicht lesbar], Coleman, 2.5.29, 860p.00B/60, S. 34; seit Ende 1928 vollzog sich in der Komintern die sogenannte „ultralinke Wendung", die v. a. einen verschärften Kampf gegen die Sozialdemokratie und eine Beseitigung „sozialdemokratischer Tendenzen" innerhalb kommunistischer Parteien – so z. B. die Bereitschaft zu konstruktiver parlamentarischer Arbeit – bedeutete: vgl. *Die ultralinke Wendung (1929)*, in: Weber, Kommunistische Internationale, S. 246-248.

161 Nr. 6099, Coleman, 24.4.29, 860p.00B/57, S. 6; Regierung Hugo Celmiņš (Bauernbund): Conrad, Loyalitäten, S. 175; Bērziņš, Latvijas Vēsture II, S. 910.

162 *Review of the Activity and Condition of the Communist Party of Latvia, up to March 15, 1929*, in: Nr. [nicht lesbar], Coleman, 2.5.29, 860p.00B/60, S. 34f.

Abläufe zu nutzten beabsichtigte,[163] konnte von amerikanischer Seite spätestens im Februar 1929 geschlossen werden, als die Fraktion gegen eine Ratifikation des Litvinov-Protokolls stimmte – und das obwohl dieses auf sowjetische Initiative zurückgegangen und dem seit 1927 gesteigerten Sicherheitsbedürfnis der UdSSR Rechnung getragen hatte.[164] Weder in diesem speziellen Fall, noch im Allgemeinen, vermochte es die kommunistische Parlamentsfraktion, in irgendeiner Weise dem Funktionieren der Saeima zu schaden oder eine ernstzunehmende oppositionelle Rolle einzunehmen.[165] Im November 1929 meldete der Gesandte Coleman nach Washington: „Communism is an illegal institution and, while in [...] Parliament there is a small group of Communists which masquerades under another party name, they are without influence and are shorn of power for evil."[166] Weder die verfassungsmäßige Regierungsform noch die öffentliche Ordnung sah er in Lettland gefährdet.

Nach dem kommunistischen Wahlerfolg des Herbsts 1928 war der lettische Geheimdienstchef Ozoliņš sichtlich darum bemüht, den amerikanischen Vertretern zu veranschaulichen, dass sich an der bis dato stets als insignifikant beschriebenen Gefährdungslage im Grunde nichts geändert habe. Zwar wurde eingeräumt, dass kommunistische Aktivitäten seit 1928 zugenommen hätten, dem seien jedoch sogleich verstärkte Maßnahmen entgegengestellt worden. Sei es den Kommunisten Anfang 1928 noch möglich gewesen, eine legale Presse zu publizieren, so würde diese seit Dezember durch die Justiz vollständig konfisziert. Massenversammlungen – selbst solche, die nunmehr durch die kommunistischen Parlamentarier einberufen würden – würden zumeist verboten. Im Jahresverlauf seien insgesamt 24 legale kommunistische Massenorganisationen

---

163 Vgl. *Leitsätze über die kommunistischen Parteien und den Parlamentarismus (1920)*, in: Weber, Kommunistische Internationale, S. 79-82: die Komintern lehnte den Parlamentarismus und einen auf parlamentarischem Wege erreichten Machtgewinn ab. KPs, die durch Wahlen in ein Parlament gelangt waren, sollten dieses als Instrument der „bourgeoisen" Diktatur entlarven und in seiner Funktion stören.

164 Nr. 5902, Coleman, 20.2.29, 860p.00B/51; das nach dem stellvertretenden sowjetischen Volkskommissar für äußere Angelegenheiten Maksim Litvinov benannte Protokoll war eine Zusatzerklärung zum Briand-Kellogg-Pakt des 27. August 1928, in dem die unterzeichnenden Staaten Krieg als Mittel der Politik offiziell verurteilten. Durch das Protokoll trat der Pakt zwischen der Sowjetunion und Estland, Lettland, Polen sowie Rumänien unverzüglich und nicht, wie im Vertragstext des Paktes vorgesehen, erst ein Jahr nach Abschluss in Kraft: Jacobsen, Primat der Sicherheit, S. 219f.

165 Nr. 6099, Coleman, 24.4.29, 860p.00B/57, S. 8.

166 Nr. 6592, Coleman, 21.11.29. 860p.00/131, S. 4.

geschlossen und 299 Kommunisten verhaftet worden. Die neuen Gewerkschaften,[167] welche im Dezember 1928 anstelle der im August aufgelösten Organisationen geschaffen worden seien, stünden seitdem unter strenger behördlicher Aufsicht und verzeichneten kaum Zulauf, da die Arbeiter staatliche Repressionen fürchteten.[168] Diverse kommunistische Ansätze, Demonstrationen und Streiks zu initiieren, seien „komplett fehlgeschlagen".[169]

Das nach den Wahlen verschärfte Vorgehen der Politischen Polizei gegen kommunistische Untergrundaktivitäten wurde insbesondere anhand der Ermittlungserfolge deutlich, welche Ozoliņš' Behörde in den Ersten Monaten des Jahres 1929 hatte vorweisen können: Der bereits erwähnten *Sovtorgflot*-Enttarnung im Februar 1929 war Mitte März eine erneute Aushebung des LKP-„Hauptquartiers" in Riga gefolgt, in deren Zuge sieben mutmaßliche Angehörige des Rigaer Komitees festgenommen worden waren. Diese Schläge des lettischen Geheimdienstes schienen der amerikanischen Gesandtschaft das Scheitern *per se* der kommunistischen Untergrundaktivitäten zu demonstrieren: Die Partei hatte nicht nur für den Moment ihre lokale Führungsriege verloren, auch hatte die Politische Polizei umfangreiche Informationen zu den übrigen in Lettland agierenden Organisationen der Kommunisten sicherstellen können.[170] Im November 1929 setzte Ozoliņš die amerikanische Gesandtschaft davon in Kenntnis, dass die in ihrem Umfang stark reduzierten kommunistischen Aktivitäten nur noch durch „eine oder zwei radikale Gewerkschaften" am Leben gehalten würden. Bei deren rund 700 Angehörigen handele es sich ausschließlich um Arbeitskräfte sowjetischer Handelsunternehmen, die durch ihre Arbeitgeber zur Mitgliedschaft in diesen Organisationen verpflichtet würden. Ohne solche Einflussnahmen der offiziellen und wirtschaftlichen sowjetischen Institutionen innerhalb Lettlands, so der lettische Geheimdienstchef, würde die lokale kommunistische Bewegung alsbald

---

167 Laut *Great Soviet Encyclopedia* habe ein von den Kommunisten organisierter Generalstreik am 22. August 1928 die lettischen Behörden dazu gezwungen, das Verbot der kommunistischen Gewerkschaften aufzuheben: Pūriņš, [Latvian] Trade Unions, S. 271.

168 *Review of the Activity and Condition of the Communist Party of Latvia, up to March 15, 1929*, in: Nr. [nicht lesbar], Coleman, 2.5.29, 860p.00B/60, S. 35f.

169 *Review of the Activity and Condition of the Communist Party of Latvia, up to March 15, 1929*, in: Nr. [nicht lesbar], Coleman, 2.5.29, 860p.00B/60, S. 10.

170 Nr. 5998, Coleman, 22.3.29, 860p.00Party, Communist/1; vgl. Nr. 6099, Coleman, 24.4.29, 860p.00B/57, S. 7f.: um welche Organisationen es sich dabei handelte wird nicht angegeben.

so „insignifikant“ werden, dass die Stärke der Politischen Polizei um die Hälfte reduziert werden könne.[171]

Bis auf wenige Ausnahmen blieben die amerikanischen Berichte über kommunistische Aktivitäten in Lettland in den Jahren 1930 bis 1934 oberflächlich und detailarm. Dies lag zum einen sicherlich an der Abberufung Hugh S. Martins aus Riga im Jahre 1929 sowie an der Entscheidung des State Departments, die Funktion des nachrichtendienstlichen Mitarbeiters nicht neu zu besetzen.[172] Zum anderen machte sich hier wohl ein Trend bemerkbar, den Claudia Breuer in Bezug auf die Berichterstattung der Russischen Sektion über die UdSSR beschrieben hat. Aus Gründen der Verifizierbarkeit war man dort gegen Ende der 1920er Jahre dazu übergegangen, sich auf offizielle, frei zugängliche Informationsquellen zu beschränken. Auf inoffiziellem Wege gewonnene Auskünfte verloren hingegen sukzessive an Bedeutung, da diese oft nicht auf Richtigkeit geprüft werden konnten.[173] Auch für die Berichterstattung über die kommunistische Bewegung Lettlands verloren Geheimdienstinformationen ab 1930 ihre maßgebliche Relevanz. Anhand der diplomatischen Korrespondenz aus Riga lässt sich daher kaum nachvollziehen, wie sich die kommunistische Bewegung in den letzten vier Jahren der lettischen Demokratie entwickelte – in einer Zeit, die sowohl von den sozioökonomischen Auswirkungen der Weltwirtschaftskrise,[174] als auch von einem eng damit einhergehenden politischen und gesellschaftlichen Rechtstrend[175] geprägt wurde und somit eigentlich eine deutliche

---

171 Nr. 6567, Coleman, 10.11.29, 860p.00B/63.

172 Eine der wichtigsten Quellen der Russischen Sektion für die Berichterstattung über die UdSSR hatte der britische Geheimdienst dargestellt. Diese Zusammenarbeit reduzierte sich ab 1927 auf ein Minimum, sodass die Stelle des nachrichtendienstlichen Mitarbeiters erheblich an Bedeutung verlor. Martins Aufgaben wurden dem Ressort des Wirtschaftsberichterstatters der Russischen Sektion, John Lehrs, übertragen: Breuer, Russische Sektion, S. 110.

173 Zum Konzept der „Wissenschaftlichkeit“ und „Objektivität“ siehe Breuer, Russische Sektion, S. 121-126.

174 Infolge fallender Preise für lettische Exportgüter sowie einer verfehlten Bankenpolitik kam es in Lettland ab 1930 zu Steuererhöhungen, Lohnkürzungen und einer wachsenden Arbeitslosenzahl. In den Städten wuchs diese bis 1933 von unter 7000 bis auf fast 18.000 an: Zestovska, Autoritäres Regime, S. 16.

175 In der lettischen Bevölkerung verstärkten sich ab 1930 aufgrund der Auswirkungen der Weltwirtschaftskrise nationalistische, gegen die Minderheiten gerichtete Strömungen und übertrugen sich z. T. auch auf Parteien, die ursprünglich in der Mitte des politischen Spektrums gestanden hatten (z. B. auf das Demokratische Zentrum

Steigerung kommunistischer Aktivitäten erwarten lassen würde.[176] Anhand der Gesandtschaftsberichte aus Riga lässt sich eine solche Intensivierung allenfalls erahnen, so z. B. an der Auflagenhöhe eines kommunistischen Propagandaflugblattes, welches Coleman Mitte 1931 mit der Anmerkung übermittelte, dass dessen große Auflage von angeblich 12.000 Kopien mehr von Interesse sei, als der Inhalt der Schrift selbst. Die darin enthaltene Agitation – die wirtschaftliche Krise wurde als Symptom eines „verfaulenden Kapitalismus" dargestellt, welchen die „Faschisten und Sozialfaschisten"[177] durch die Unterdrückung der Arbeiterklasse sowie durch eine Intervention gegen die UdSSR zu retten beabsichtigten[178] – hielt aus Sicht des Gesandten keine neuen Aspekte bereit. Beinahe wöchentlich stelle die lettische Polizei solche Appelle sicher und verhafte kommunistische Agenten. Die Gerichte seien konstant mit der Verurteilung von Kommunisten beschäftigt, die lettische Presse schenke diesen Verfahren aber nur sehr wenig Aufmerksamkeit, um die Begeisterung für den Kommunismus gering zu halten.[179]

Eine solche Taktik würde zu dem Bild passen, das Coleman vom bürgerlichen Lettland und seinen Autoritäten hatte. Gelegenheit, diesem Bild in einer knappen Stellungnahme Ausdruck zu verleihen, bot ihm der obligatorische Bericht zum Verlauf des Maifeiertages, welcher den amerikanischen Vertretern als regelmäßiger Gradmesser der allgemeinen politischen und gesellschaftlichen Stimmung diente. Von Sozialdemokraten und Kommunisten als „Tag der Arbeit" begangen, wurde der 1. Mai auch durch die lettische Nation gefeiert – als Jahrestag des

---

sowie den Bauernbund): Hehn, Demokratie, S. 11, 15-28; Zestovska, Autoritäres Regime, S. 17-20.

176 Eine solche Annahme wird beispielsweise durch die Angaben Edgar Andersons gestützt, wonach die LKP 1934 mit 1150 Mitgliedern ihren personellen Zwischenkriegs-Höchststand erreichte: Anderson, Latvia, S. 298.

177 Ab Mitte 1929 gehörte die sogenannte „Sozialfaschismus"-These zur offiziellen Linie der Komintern, wonach die Sozialdemokratie lediglich eine besonders gefährliche, getarnte Form des Faschismus sei: Luks, Kommunistische Faschismustheorie, S. 137-139.

178 *Summary of* [...] *a Proclamation* [...] *of the Latvian Communist Party*, in: Nr. 7789, Coleman, 16.6.1931, 860p.00B/74; siehe ebenso: *The Latvian Communist Party (Section of the Communist International)*, in: Nr. 7815, Coleman, 19.6.31, 860p.00B/75; das von der kommunistischen Propaganda entworfene Szenario blieb bis 1933 im Wesentlichen dasselbe, vgl. Flugblätter im Anhang zu: Nr. 1149, Hewes, 10.2.1933, 860p.00B/94.

179 Nr. 7789, Coleman, 16.6.31, 860p.00B/74.

Zusammentretens der Konstituierenden Versammlung im Jahre 1920.[180] Ende April 1931 habe die Politische Polizei, um etwaigen Ausschreitungen vorzubeugen, in Riga diverse Razzien durchgeführt und dabei lokale Kommunisten und deren Propagandamaterial aus dem Verkehr gezogen.[181] Die am Maifeiertag selbst abgehaltene Militärparade, so Coleman, habe zudem ihren Zweck nicht verfehlt, den vielen Zuschauern eindrücklich die Stärke der verfassungsmäßigen Autoritäten zu demonstrieren, patriotische Gefühle zu stimulieren und dazu beizutragen, potenzielle Unruhestifter einzuschüchtern. Alles in allem habe die Ordnung, welche am 1. Mai in Riga geherrscht habe, deutlich den Weitblick, die Wachsamkeit und das „gesunde Urteilsvermögen“ der lettischen Offiziellen sowie die allgemeinen konservativen Tendenzen des lettischen Volkes widergespiegelt.[182] Im Jahr der IV. Saeima-Wahlen waren aus Perspektive des amerikanischen Gesandten die Voraussetzungen für kommunistische Erfolge in Lettland also alles andere als günstig – und das trotz wirtschaftlicher Krise. Dass die lettischen Autoritäten in Hinblick auf die im Oktober anstehenden Parlamentswahlen nichts dem Zufall überlassen wollten, konnte zudem daraus geschlossen werden, dass sie, wie bereits im Vorfeld der Wahlen zur III. Saeima 1928, erneut gegen linke Gewerkschaften vorgingen. Auf Grundlage eines Gerichtsbeschlusses von Ende Juli wurden 14 von ihnen wegen mutmaßlicher Beteiligung an kommunistischen Aktivitäten geschlossen. Was die Leningrader *Pravda* seinerzeit als eine „neue Welle des Terrors“ der „faschistischen“ Ulmanis-Regierung bezeichnete,[183] stellte sich Coleman als Ausdruck „besonderer Wachsamkeit“ der lettischen Autoritäten während einer Zeit „ausgeprägter ökonomischer Depression“ dar.[184]

Der erneute Parlamentseinzug der kommunistischen Arbeiter- und Bauernfraktion nach den Saeima-Wahlen im Oktober 1931 – wieder hatten die erhaltenen Wählerstimmen für 7 Mandate gereicht[185] – wird in den Berichten über

---

180 Bleiere, Geschichte Lettlands, S. 147; den 1. Mai als lettischen Nationalfeiertag zu begehen sollte ganz gezielt den sozialistischen Feiertag kontern: Nr. [nicht lesbar], Sussdorff, 9.5.1927, 860p.00/109.

181 Vgl. Nr. 6963, Sussdorff, 13.5.30, 860p.00B/66.

182 Nr. 7693, Coleman, 3.5.31, 860p.00B/73.

183 *The New Wave of Terror (Leningrad Pravda No. 224, August 15, 1931, p. 2)*, in: Nr. 7994, Coleman, 24.8.31, 860p.00B/80; Koalition Ministerpräsident Kārlis Ulmanis' (Bauernbund), amtierend von März bis Dezember 1931: Conrad, Loyalitäten, S. 175.

184 Nr. 7994, Coleman, 24.8.31, 860p.00B/80.

185 Die Arbeiter- und Bauernfraktion hatte 7,2% der Stimmen erhalten: Šilde, Sowjetisierung, S. 10.

kommunistische Aktivitäten nicht explizit erwähnt, was die geringe Relevanz zeigt, die dieser Fraktion von Seiten der amerikanischen Gesandtschaft beigemessen wurde. Erst mit dem Beginn ihrer sukzessiven Ausschaltung ab März 1932 rückte die Arbeiter- und Bauernfraktion in den Fokus der Berichterstattung. Nachdem die Saeima zunächst die Immunität einzelner kommunistischer Abgeordneter ausgesetzt hatte,[186] wurde die Arbeiter- und Bauernfraktion im November 1933 aufgelöst und ihre Angehörigen verhaftet. Wie Felix Cole – seit 1931 Leiter der Russischen Sektion – dem State Department wenig später schilderte, hätten der lettischen Regierung[187] seit langem ausreichend Beweise vorgelegen, um gegen die „allgemein" als kommunistisch bekannte Arbeiter- und Bauernfraktion vorzugehen. Den letztlichen Auslöser sah Cole jedoch nicht in unlängst intensivierten subversiven Aktivitäten der Fraktion, sondern in dem sich wandelnden politischen Klima Lettlands. Innerhalb politischer Kreise sowie in der Öffentlichkeit zeige die Tendenz klar nach rechts. Die Regierung habe gerade jetzt die Initiative ergriffen, da sie sich sowohl im Parlament als auch in der lettischen Bevölkerung des nötigen Rückhalts sicher gewesen sei. Als weitere Belege des besagten Rechtskurses führte Cole die im Oktober 1933 durch den Bauernbund vorgestellten Vorschläge zur Änderung der Verfassung[188] sowie die Schließung der „sogenannten" Sportorganisation[189] der Sozialdemokraten im September desselben Jahres an.[190]

Nach Auflösung der Arbeiter- und Bauernfraktion spielte die kommunistische Bewegung bis zum Staatsstreich vom 15./16. Mai 1934 in den amerikanischen

---

186 Nr. 204, Skinner, 31.3.32, 860p.00B/85; Nr. 459, Cole, 15.6.32, 860p.00B/87; u. a. Linards Laicens, der die Arbeiter- und Bauernfraktion bis August 1932 geleitet hatte: Nr. 773, Cole, 26.9.32, 860p.00B/93; siehe auch Bērziņš, Latvijas Vēsture II, S. 933.

187 Koalition Ministerpräsident Ādolfs Bļodnieks' (Neubauern- und Kleinlandwirtepartei), amtierend von März 1933 bis März 1934: Conrad, Loyalitäten, S. 175, 182.

188 Die Reformvorschläge sahen eine Stärkung der Stellung des Staatspräsidenten gegenüber eines in Personal und Kompetenzen erheblich einzuschränkenden Parlaments vor. Eine solche Reform hätte die parlamentarische Republik praktisch in eine autoritäre Präsidialdiktatur verwandelt: Hehn, Demokratie, S. 29f.; Bleiere, Geschichte Lettlands, S. 165f.

189 Bei der Sportorganisation *Strādnieku sports un sargs* (Arbeiter-Sport und Verteidigung) hatte es sich um die „Wehrorganisation" der LSDSP gehandelt. Diese war u. a. wegen der „militärischen Ausbildung seiner Mitglieder" durch eine vorläufige Verordnung geschlossen worden: Nr. 1640, Cole, 6.10.33, 860p.00/166; Hehn, Demokratie, S. 27.

190 Nr. 1731, Cole, 29.11.33, 860p.00B/95.

Gesandtschaftsberichten keine Rolle mehr und auch in den Mitteilungen über die Hintergründe des Ulmanis-Coups war von Kommunisten keine Rede. Etwaige linke Umsturzabsichten, die Ulmanis offiziell als Teilgrund für den *coup d'état* nannte, wurden von Seiten der Gesandtschaft allenfalls mit den Sozialdemokraten in Verbindung gebracht und ohnehin als unrealistisch eingeschätzt.[191] Ob und inwieweit zu diesem Zeitpunkt eine eventuelle gemeinsame Aktionsbasis lettischer Kommunisten und Sozialdemokraten bestand, darüber lassen die amerikanischen Gesandtschaftsberichte bis Mai 1934 keine Schlüsse zu. Erst 1935 lagen anscheinend vage Hinweise darauf vor, dass unter den Bedingungen des autoritären Regimes eine gewisse Kooperation von Kommunisten und Sozialisten existiere.[192]

Das autoritäre Regime, das in Lettland nach dem 15. Mai 1934 errichtet wurde, schränkte den ohnehin bereits sehr engen Betätigungsrahmen der kommunistischen Bewegung noch weiter ein. Die gesamte Gesellschaft wurde einer strengen politischen Kontrolle unterworfen. Sämtliche legalen Aktivitäten der Kommunisten waren unmöglich geworden: Parlament und Parteien hatte das Regime ebenso aufgelöst wie die Gewerkschaften; gesellschaftliche Organisationen wurden sukzessive gleichgeschaltet.[193]

Arthur Bliss Lane, der 1936 das Amt des amerikanischen Gesandten in Riga übernahm,[194] kam bereits wenige Wochen nach seiner Ankunft in der lettischen Hauptstadt nicht umhin die „effektive Kontrolle“ zu attestieren, die die Regierung über das Land ausübe. Der lettische Präsident, so informierte Lane das State Department im September, habe ihm in einem persönlichen Gespräch versichert, dass jedweder kommunistischen Propaganda und Aktivität rigoros Einhalt geboten würde. Wörtlich habe Ulmanis zu verstehen gegeben: „*We won't allow any nonsense here.*“[195]

7. 14 Jahre Kommunismus in Lettland aus amerikanischer Perspektive

Die amerikanischen Gesandtschaftsberichte der 1920er Jahre zeugen davon, dass die Kommunisten im unabhängigen Lettland nach anfänglichen Erfolgen

191 Telegramm Nr. 38, Cole, 16.5.34, 860p.00/177; Nr. 297, Cole, 19.5.34, 860p.00/179; Nr. 298, Cole, 19.5.34, 860p.00/180; vgl. Hehn, Demokratie, S. 40f.

192 Nr. 945, Cole, 30.10.35, 860p.00/201.

193 Stranga, Regime von Kārlis Ulmanis, S. 103-112.

194 Breuer, Russische Sektion, S. 74f.

195 Nr. 199, Lane, 4.9.36, 860p.00B/100.

recht schnell an Grenzen stießen, die es ihnen unmöglich machten, sich zu einer ernsthaften Bedrohung für den sich mehr und mehr konsolidierenden Staat zu entwickeln. Zwar stellten kommunistische Propagandaaktivitäten offenbar eine konstante Erscheinung dar, vermochten es jedoch nicht, größere Massen zu mobilisieren. Die von der Komintern ausgegebenen Anweisungen zum personellen und strukturellen Ausbau der Bewegung blieben wohl weitestgehend unerfüllt. Der Aufbau kommunistischer Frontorganisationen verlief schleppend und die Mitgliederzahlen der kommunistischen Organisationen bewegten sich ebenso in einem vermeintlich überschaubaren Rahmen wie deren Potenzial, einen bewaffneten Aufstand durchzuführen oder auch nur für nennenswerte Unruhe zu sorgen.

Hauptgrund für die als aussichtslos eingeschätzte Situation der lettischen Kommunisten, war aus amerikanischer Perspektive ein rigoroses und effizientes Vorgehen der lettischen Politischen Polizei, in dem sich eine kompromisslose Haltung des Staats gegenüber kommunistischer Subversion manifestierte. Diese Behörde war allem Anschein nach gut über die organisatorischen Zusammenhänge der Bewegung informiert und vermochte es, flexibel auf die Aktivitäten der Kommunisten zu reagieren. Indem es ihr immer wieder gelang, mutmaßliche Parteifunktionäre und -aktivisten aus dem Verkehr zu ziehen, schien sie die Bewegung regelrecht zu paralysieren.

Ein weiterer wichtiger, jedoch durch die amerikanischen Vertreter kaum näher erläuterter Grund für die Wirkungslosigkeit der kommunistischen Bewegung in Lettland, war eine als antikommunistisch und zunehmend konservativ wahrgenommene Grundhaltung der Bevölkerungsmehrheit, die sich infolge der schlechten Erfahrungen mit dem lettischen Sowjetregime der Jahre 1919 und 1920 eingestellt hatte. Obwohl die Kommunisten versuchten, mit ihrer Propaganda gezielt an den neuralgischen Punkten des sozialen und nationalen Gefüges des lettischen Staats anzusetzen, trafen sie damit nicht auf den Zuspruch und die Bedürfnisse größerer Bevölkerungsteile. Der kommunistische Einfluss beschränkte sich weitgehend auf die insgesamt schmale lettische Industriearbeiterschaft in den Städten.

Das wesentliche und zugleich erfolgreichste Betätigungsfeld der lettischen Kommunisten stellte die linke Gewerkschaftsbewegung dar, die den Kommunisten eine Möglichkeit dazu bot, innerhalb eines legalen Rahmens mit einer breiteren Masse von Arbeitern in Kontakt zu treten, diese im kommunistischen Sinne zu beeinflussen und bisweilen zu Streiks und Demonstrationen zu animieren. Anhand der Spaltung der linken Gewerkschaftsorganisationen konnte ein Antagonismus zwischen Kommunisten und Sozialdemokraten nachvollzogen werden, der einer gemeinsamen Aktionsbasis beider Lager im Wege stand.

Während die Mitgliederzahlen der kommunistischen Gewerkschaften als unbedenklich erachtet wurden und eine klare Mehrheit der linksorientierten Arbeiter der LSDSP zuzuneigen schien, sorgten lediglich Indizien einer kommunistischen Unterwanderung sozialdemokratischer Arbeiterorganisationen für eine gewisse amerikanische Skepsis.

Wie die amerikanischen Berichte erkennen lassen, stellte der Fall der sozialdemokratisch-dominierten Regierung Skujenieks' an der Jahreswende 1927/28 eine Zäsur für die kommunistische Bewegung in Lettland dar. Nachdem die lettischen Behörden im Sommer 1928 in Reaktion auf merklich intensivierte kommunistische Aktivitäten die kommunistischen Gewerkschaften aufgelöst und die Bewegung somit ihrer vermeintlich wichtigsten Aktionsbasis entledigt hatten, stellte der Parlamentseinzug einer verdeckten kommunistischen Fraktion nach den Saeima-Wahlen im Oktober aus amerikanischer Perspektive zwar eine Überraschung, auf längere Frist jedoch keinen Grund zu ernsthafter Besorgnis dar. Die nach dem sozialdemokratischen Interregnum des Jahres 1927 wiederhergestellte bürgerliche Regierungsgewalt schien gefestigt und die Politische Polizei gewohnt wachsam zu sein.

Auch wenn die knappe und detailarme Form der amerikanischen Gesandtschaftsberichte der Jahre 1930 bis 1934 keine konkreten Schlüsse auf die Entwicklung der kommunistischen Bewegung innerhalb dieses Zeitraums ermöglicht, so lässt sich doch konstatieren, dass sich kommunistische Aktivitäten in Lettland auch unter den Auswirkungen der Weltwirtschaftskrise nicht zu einem wirklichen Unruhefaktor entwickeln konnten. Hinter der sukzessiven Ausschaltung der kommunistischen Saeima-Fraktion bis 1933 wurde von amerikanischer Seite weniger eine Reaktion auf eine unmittelbare Gefährdungslage, als vielmehr das Ergebnis eines allgemeinen politischen Klimawandels gesehen, welcher sich nicht nur gegen die Kommunisten allein, sondern gegen das gesamte linke Spektrum richtete und letztlich im Mai 1934 seinen Höhepunkt im Staatsstreich Kārlis Ulmanis' finden sollte.

Alles in allem gab es aus Sicht der amerikanischen Gesandtschaft in Riga kaum Grund, an der Fähigkeit Lettlands zu zweifeln, mit der kommunistischen Bedrohung im Inneren fertig zu werden. Zu keinem Zeitpunkt zwischen 1922 und 1934 stellten die Kommunisten eine ernsthafte Gefahr für die demokratische Verfassungsordnung des Staats dar. Trotz schwieriger wirtschaftlicher und sozialer Startvoraussetzungen und trotz der problematischen geostrategischen Lage als Nachbar der Sowjetunion schienen der lettische Staat und seine Gesellschaft zumindest die inneren Bedingungen erfüllt zu haben, um einen Beitrag zur Eindämmung des Kommunismus und somit auch zu einer stabilen nordosteuropäischen Friedensordnung zu leisten.

Literaturverzeichnis

AGNEW, JEREMY/MCDERMOTT, KEVIN The Comintern. A History of International Communism from Lenin to Stalin, Basingstoke u. a. 1996.

ALTRICHTER, HELMUT Neue Ökonomische Politik, in: Historisches Lexikon der Sowjetunion 1917/22 bis 1991, hg. von HANS-JOACHIM TORKE, München 1993, S. 216-218.

ANDERSON, EDGAR Die baltische Frage und die internationale Politik der alliierten und assoziierten Mächte 1918-1921, in: Von den baltischen Provinzen zu den baltischen Staaten. Beiträge zur Entstehungsgeschichte der Republiken Estland und Lettland 1918-1920, hg. von JÜRGEN VON HEHN u. a., Marburg 1977, S. 327-377.

ANDERSON, EDGAR Latvia, in: World Communism. A Handbook. 1918-1965, hg. von WITOLD S. SWORAKOWSKI, Stanford 1973, S. 297-299.

ANDERSON, EDGAR The USSR Trades with Latvia: The Treaty of 1927, in: Slavic Review Vol. 21, No. 2 (1962), S. 296-321.

BĒRZIŅŠ, VALDIS 20. Gadsimta Latvijas Vēsture I: Latvija no gadsimta sākuma lids neatkarības pasludināšani 1900-1918, Rīga 2000.

BĒRZIŅŠ, VALDIS 20. Gadsimta Latvijas Vēsture II: Neatkarīgā valsts 1918-1940, Rīga 2003.

BILMANIS, ALFRED A History of Latvia, Princeton 1951.

BLEIERE, DAINA u. a. Geschichte Lettlands. 20. Jahrhundert, Riga 2008.

BORODZIEJ, WŁODZIMIERZ Geschichte Polens im 20. Jahrhundert, München 2010.

BREUER, CLAUDIA Die „Russische Sektion" in Riga. Amerikanische diplomatische Berichterstattung über die Sowjetunion, 1922-1933/40, Stuttgart 1995. = Transatlantische Historische Studien ; 3.

CONRAD BENJAMIN Loyalitäten, Identitäten und Interessen. Deutsche Parlamentarier im Lettland und Polen der Zwischenkriegszeit, Göttingen 2016.

Dokument Nr. 1219: Governmental Authority for Administrative Arrest and Deportation (Sob. Uzak., I, 2, No. 1131.), in: The Russian Provisional Government 1917. Documents. Volume III, hg. von ROBERT PAUL BROWDER/ALEXANDER F. KERENSKY, Stanford 1961, S. 1440f.

EICHWEDE, WOLFGANG Der Eintritt Sowjetrusslands in die internationale Politik, 1921-1927, in: Osteuropa-Handbuch: Sowjetunion. Außenpolitik 1917-1955, hg. von DIETRICH GEYER, Köln/Wien 1972, S. 150-212.

GRANT, NATALIE The Russian Section. A Window on the Soviet Union, in: Diplomatic History 2 (1978), S. 101-115.

HEHN, JÜRGEN VON Der baltische Freiheitskrieg. Umrisse und Probleme. 1918-1920, in: Von den baltischen Provinzen zu den baltischen Staaten. Beiträge zur Entstehungsgeschichte der Republiken Estland und Lettland 1918-1920, hg. von JÜRGEN VON HEHN u. a., Marburg 1977, S. 1-43.

HEHN, JÜRGEN VON Lettland zwischen Demokratie und Diktatur. Zur Geschichte des lettländischen Staatsstreichs vom 15. Mai 1934, München 1957. = Jahrbücher für Geschichte Osteuropas, Beiheft ; 3.

HELLMANN, MANFRED Grundzüge der Geschichte Litauens und des litauischen Volkes, 4. Aufl. Darmstadt 1990.

JACOBSEN, HANS-ADOLF Primat der Sicherheit, 1928-1938, in: Osteuropa-Handbuch. Sowjetunion. Außenpolitik 1917-1955, hg. von DIETRICH GEYER, Köln/Wien 1972, S. 213-269.

KUSBER, JAN Zwischen den Imperien. Baltische Erfahrungen in Weltkrieg und Revolution, in: Der Erste Weltkrieg – Regionale Perspektiven, hg. von BIRGIT ASCHMANN U. A., Stuttgart 2016, S. 30-43. = Historische Mitteilungen; 28.

LITTLE, DOUGLAS Antibolshevism and American Foreign Policy, 1919-1939. The Diplomacy of Self-Delusion, in: American Quarterly, 35 (1983), Nr. 4, S. 376-390.

LOIT, ALEKSANDER Amsterdam or Moscow? The Trade Union Movement in the Baltic Countries caught between the Reformist and the Revolutionary Internationals in the 1920s, in: The Baltic in International Relations between the Two World Wars, hg. von JOHN HIDEN/ALEKSANDER LOIT, Stockholm 1988, S. 335-375. = Acta Universitatis Stockholmiensis. Studia Baltica Stockholmiensia; 3.

LONG, JOHN W. Communist Youth Organizations of the Soviet Union, in: The Modern Encyclopedia of Russian and Soviet History Vol. 7, hg. von JOSEPH L. WIECZYNSKI, Gulf Breeze 1978, S. 228-235.

LUKS, LEONID Entstehung der kommunistischen Faschismustheorie. Die Auseinandersetzung der Komintern mit Faschismus und Nationalsozialismus 1921-1935, Stuttgart 1985. = Studien zur Zeitgeschichte ; 26.

MÜLLER, MICHAEL G. Komintern, in: Historisches Lexikon der Sowjetunion 1917/22 bis 1991, hg. von HANS-JOACHIM TORKE, München 1993, S. 149f.

NIES, SUSANNE Lettland in der internationalen Politik. Aspekte seiner Außenpolitik (1918-95), Münster 1995. = Bonner Beiträge zur Politikwissenschaft ; 6.

PISTOHLKORS, GERT VON Tiefgreifende agrarische Umwälzungen und Umstrukturierungen in den neu gegründeten baltischen Staaten Estland, Lettland und Litauen 1919/1920/1922. Motivationen und Ergebnisse bis 1940, in: Agrarreformen und ethnodemographische Veränderungen. Südosteuropa vom ausgehenden 18. Jahrhundert bis in die Gegenwart, hg. von KRAUSS, KARL-PETER,

Stuttgart 2009, S. 175-205. = Schriftenreihe des Instituts für donauschwäbische Geschichte und Landeskunde; 15.

Pūriņš, V. R. [Latvian] Trade Unions, in: Great Soviet Encyclopedia – A Translation of the Third Edition, Bd. 14, New York 1977, S. 271.

Rauch, Georg von Die bolschewistischen Staatsgründungen im baltischen Raum und die sovetische Politik, in: Von den baltischen Provinzen zu den baltischen Staaten. Beiträge zur Entstehungsgeschichte der Republiken Estland und Lettland 1918-1920, hg. von Jürgen von Hehn u. a., Marburg 1977, S. 44-69.

Rauch, Georg von Geschichte der baltischen Staaten, Stuttgart u. a. 1970.

Records of the Department of State Relating to Internal Affairs of Latvia 1910-1944. Decimal file 860p, Washington D.C. 1981. = National Archives Microfilm Publication.

Rhodes, Benjamin D. The Anglo-American Winter War in Russia, 1918-1919. A Diplomatic and Military Tragicomedy, Westport 1988.

Schild, Georg Between Ideology and *Realpolitik*. Woodrow Wilson and the Russian Revolution, 1917-1921, Westport 1995.

Schwabe, Klaus Weltmacht und Weltordnung. Amerikanische Außenpolitik von 1898 bis zur Gegenwart. Eine Jahrhundertgeschichte, 3. Aufl. Paderborn 2011.

Šilde, Ādolfs Die Sowjetisierung Lettlands, Köln 1967. = Berichte des Bundesinstituts für ostwissenschaftliche und internationale Studien; 1.

Skultans, Vilis Lettland, in: Lexikon der Geschichte der Parteien in Europa, hg. von Frank Wende, S. 369-376.

Sontag, John P. The Soviet War Scare of 1926-27, in: The Russian Review Vol. 34, No. 1 (1975), S. 66-77.

Stranga, Aivars Latvian-Russian Economic Relations and Soviet Foreign Policy, 1920-1932, in: Emancipation and Independence. The Baltic States as New Entities in the International Economy, 1918-1940, hg. von Anders Johansson u. a., Stockholm 1994, S. 157-175. = Acta Universitatis Stockholmiensis. Studia Baltica Stockholmiensia; 13.

Stranga, Aivars Communist Dictatorship in Latvia: December 1918 – January 1920. Ethnic Policy, in: Lithuanian Historical Studies 13 (2008), S. 161-178.

Stranga, Aivars Das Regime von Kārlis Ulmanis in Lettland 1934-1940. Genesis, Entwicklung, Inhalt, in: Autoritäre Regime in Ostmitteleuropa 1919-1944, hg. von Erwin Oberländer, Mainz 1995, S. 103-112.

SWORAKOWSKI, WITOLD S. The Communist International, in: World Communism. A Handbook. 1918-1965, hg. von WITOLD S. SWORAKOWSKI, Stanford 1973, S. 78-92.

SWORAKOWSKI, WITOLD S. The Communist Front Organizations, in: World Communism. A Handbook. 1918-1965, hg. von WITOLD S. SWORAKOWSKI, Stanford 1973, S. 210-212.

SWORAKOWSKI, WITOLD S. The International Organization for Aid to Revolutionaries, in: World Communism. A Handbook. 1918-1965, hg. von WITOLD S. SWORAKOWSKI, Stanford 1973, S. 216.

SWORAKOWSKI, WITOLD S. The Red International of Labor Unions, in: World Communism. A Handbook. 1918-1965, hg. von WITOLD S. SWORAKOWSKI, Stanford 1973, S. 375-377.

SWORAKOWSKI, WITOLD S. The Red Sport International, in: World Communism. A Handbook. 1918-1965, hg. von WITOLD S. SWORAKOWSKI, Stanford 1973, S. 377f.

TARULIS, ALBERT N. American-Baltic Relations 1918-1922. The Struggle Over Recognition, Washington D.C. 1965.

WEBER, HERMANN Die Kommunistische Internationale. Eine Dokumentation, Hannover 1966.

WEBER, HERMANN Lenin in Selbstzeugnissen und Bilddokumenten, Reinbek 1970.

WHITE, CHRISTINE A. The Gateway to Russia. The Baltic States as a Conduit for British and American Trade with Soviet Russia, 1918-1924, in: Emancipation and Independence. The Baltic States as New Entities in the International Economy, 1918-1940, hg. von ANDERS JOHANSSON U. A., Stockholm 1994, S. 41-62. = Acta Universitatis Stockholmiensis. Studia Baltica Stockholmiensia; 13.

ZESTOVSKA, KRISTINE, Das autoritäre Regime in Lettland im Spiegel der Reden Karlis Ulmanis, Mainz 1995.

ZIEMELIS, S.V./KADIĶE, I.V., Lenin Communist Youth League (Komsomol) of Latvia, in: Great Soviet Encyclopedia – A Translation of the Third Edition, Bd. 14, New York 1977, S. 270-271.

Jan Kusber

Auf der Suche nach Sicherheit im Nordosten Europas – bilateral und multilateral (1918-1939)

Ohne den Zusammenbruch des Russischen Imperiums der Zaren und des Deutschen Kaiserreichs hätten Lettland, Estland und Litauen aber auch Polen ihre Unabhängigkeit kaum und vor allem nicht in so kurzer Zeit erreicht.[1] Nachdem sich die Staaten konstituiert, ihre Grenzstreitigkeiten zum Teil gelöst, zum Teil allerdings lediglich eingefroren hatten, begann für die drei baltischen Staaten das, was John Hiden als „*Diplomacy of Survival*" bezeichnet hat.[2] Sie fiel in eine Phase der Neuordnung der Welt, die nicht nur im östlichen Europa ein Vakuum hatte entstehen lassen, das sich als Nachfrage nach neuen Ordnungsmodellen zeigte – politischen, gesellschaftlichen und ökonomischen Modellen, aber auch solchen der internationalen Beziehungen. Der Zusammenbruch und die Suche nach Orientierung in diesem Vakuum erklärt die fast messianischen Hoffnungen, die sich ab 1917/18 auch in Ostmittel- und Nordosteuropa vor allem auf den amerikanischen Präsidenten Woodrow Wilson konzentrierten. Der globale „*Wilsonian Moment*" von 1918/19 illustrierte,[3] wie enttäuschte Erwartungen, etwa auf eine Umsetzung der Vierzehn Punkte, in Desillusion und Gewalt umschlugen.[4]

Polen, dessen Wiederentstehen und Unabhängigkeit Woodrow Wilson einen eigenen Punkt in seinen berühmten Vierzehn Punkten gewidmet hatte, besaß in den USA und den Westalliierten Staaten starke Advokaten. Sie setzten sich im Rahmen der Verhandlungen über die Pariser Vorortverträge für einen arrondierten polnischen Staat ein, während die polnischen Politiker und Politikexperten vor Ort geschickt die polnische Sache verfolgten.[5] Letten, Esten und Litauer hingegen wurden nicht von vornherein gleichberechtigte Partner der Versailler

---

1 Vgl. Kusber, Wegscheide Krieg, S. 233-246.
2 Hiden/ Salmon, The Baltic Nations and Europe, S. 59.
3 Manela, The Wilsonian Moment.
4 Hierzu umfassend mit unterschiedlichen Zugängen: Conze, Die große Illusion; Leonhard, Der überforderte Frieden.
5 Vgl. Conrad, Der Geograph und die Grenzen, S. 89-96.

Ordnung, sondern allerhöchstens als solche im Wartestand angesehen.[6] Die so genannte Zweite Polnische Republik durfte man getrost zu den Siegern zählten, die ihre Grenzen im Westen nach den in Versailles festgelegten, von blutigen Auseinandersetzungen begleiteten Abstimmungen und im Osten im polnisch-sowjetischen Krieg sichern konnten. Deutschland und Sowjetrussland waren Objekte und nicht Subjekte der Pariser Ordnung. Sie bildeten in dieser Konstellation dennoch die Größen, die ökonomisch, geopolitisch, im Falle der Sowjets auch weltanschaulich als potenzielle Bedrohung wahrgenommen wurden. Beide besaßen in den baltischen Staaten jeweils unterschiedlich große und strukturierte Minderheiten.[7]

Gegenüber Sowjetrussland dominierte zudem bekanntermaßen das ideologische Moment. Nicht nur die polnische, auch die französische, amerikanische, vor allem aber auch britische Öffentlichkeit stilisierten etwa das „Wunder an der Weichsel" zu einer Schlacht, von ihrer Bedeutung so groß wie der Sieg Karl Martells gegen die Sarazenen in der Rettung eines christlichen Abendlandes.[8] In den USA wurde diese Konstellation zum Scenario einer ersten *„Red Scare"*.[9]

Die Zukunftsperspektive für den Nordosten Europas war aus Sicht George Clemenceaus die eines Cordon Sanitaire (Dezember 1919), während der britische Außenminister Balfour etwa zeitgleich davon sprach, man brauche einen *„barbed wired fence"*.[10] Und für Deutschland bleibt schon die Bezeichnung der Archivablage des Politischen Archivs des Auswärtigen Amtes sprechend: Die Rede war von den „Randstaaten". Vor diesem Hintergrund ist nicht selten die Schwierigkeit, ja Unmöglichkeit von Frieden und Sicherheit im Nordosten Europas betont worden.[11] Dabei wurde zumeist von der Katastrophe des deutschen Überfalls am 1. September auf Polen und dem Einmarsch der Sowjetunion am 17. September 1939 her gedacht – dem von Deutschland verursachten und

6 Vgl. den Beitrag von Christian Müller in diesem Band sowie: Thomas, Georgi Tschitscherin, S. 125-137.

7 Vgl. den Beitrag von Svetlana Bogojavlenska in diesem Band.

8 Vgl. Davies, The Polish-Soviet War, S. 265.

9 Als Beispiel das Buch des ehemaligen Bürgermeisters von Seattle: Hanson, Americanism versus Bolshevism; Hagedorn, Savage Peace.

10 Documents on British Foreign Policy, Series 1, Vol. II, S. 738-748.

11 Vgl. Beyrau, Schlachtfeld der Diktatoren.

ausgelösten Zweiten Weltkrieg und der sowjetischen Aggression auf der Grundlage der beiden Molotov-Ribbentrop-Pakte vom August und September 1939.[12]

Im Folgenden soll nicht vom Ende her erzählt werden, obwohl das Wissen um die Vergeblichkeit diplomatischer Bemühungen um eine dauerhafte Friedenskonstruktion nicht ausgeblendet werden kann. Vielmehr sollen fragmentarisch Perspektiven auf den Nordosten Europas unter der Frage erörtert werden, ob und welche Chancen des Gelingens es für Sicherheit und Frieden im östlichen Europa existierten.

Litauen, Lettland und Estland wurden in einer Konstellation unabhängig, in der künftigen Staatsnationen vor dem Problem standen, stabile Grenzen, stabile Staatlichkeit und Stabilität in den jeweiligen Gesellschaften zu schaffen, die jeweils durch soziale Unterschiede und durch ethnische Mehrheits- und Minderheitskonstellationen geprägt waren, die immer auch die Möglichkeit außenpolitischer Intervention in sich trugen – zumal dann, wenn das politische System differierte. Dies war bei Sowjetrussland der Fall, für das sich die russischen Minderheiten für eine irredentistische Politik nicht ohne weiteres Nutzen ließen, die der alten Ordnung Russlands vor 1917 nachtrauerten, aber eventuell mit kommunistischen Gruppierungen sympathisierten. Polen und Deutschland hingegen versuchten die jeweiligen Minderheiten für außenpolitische Zwecke zu instrumentalisieren.[13] Für die neu entstandenen Staaten im Nordosten Europas war daher die vertragliche, möglichst auch multilaterale Absicherung von hohem Interesse. Dabei war in der Endphase des Ersten Weltkrieges den Akteuren nicht klar, wie der Wunsch nach nationaler Selbstbestimmung in einer eigenen Staatlichkeit umzusetzen sei, waren sie selbst doch zunächst bestenfalls von Autonomiekonzepten innerhalb der nun untergehenden Imperien ausgegangen. Und es war keineswegs sicher, welche Erfolge der Weg in eine Eigenstaatlichkeit haben würde. Der Weg der kurzlebigen ukrainischen oder belarussischen staatlichen Konstrukte, die in der Sowjetunion aufgehen sollte, die wie das Zarenreich ein Imperium war, stehen für diesen Weg.[14]

Die baltischen Staaten und Finnland waren hier erfolgreicher. Der Völkerbund in Genf war eine Zukunft verheißende Neugründung, der die eigene

---

12 Vgl. Kusber, Ressentiment, Konflikt und Vernichtung, S. 9-22. Ausführlich: Snyder, Bloodlands, insbesondere S. 9-22 und 135-168. Nicht mit einem Schwerpunkt auf den Folgen für die Baltischen Staaten: Weber, Der Pakt.

13 Vgl. Krekeler, Revisionsanspruch und geheime Ostpolitik; Hiden, The Weimar Republic, S. 273-289; Jaworski, Der auslandsdeutsche Gedanke, S. 369-386.

14 Vgl. Michaluk/ Rudling, From the Grand Duchy of Lithuania, S. 3-36.

Existenz flankierend abzusichern versprach. Schon 1920 versuchten Lettland, Litauen und Estland, dem Völkerbund beizutreten, was zunächst abgelehnt wurde.[15] Aber als ein sowjetischer Sieg im Bürgerkrieg immer wahrscheinlicher wurde und nachdem die lettische Außenpolitik unter Außenminister Zigfrīds Anna Meierovics, der dominierenden Figur lettischer Außenpolitik in der ersten Hälfte der 1920er Jahre,[16] massive Lobbyarbeit betrieben hatte, erkannte zunächst der Alliierte höchste Kriegsrat, in dem immerhin Großbritannien, Frankreich, Belgien, Italien und Japan vertreten waren, Lettlands Unabhängigkeit am 26. Januar 1921 an. Dies war der internationale Durchbruch, dem die Anerkennung durch zahlreiche andere Staaten folgte. Lettland wurde schließlich am 22. September 1921 Mitglied des Völkerbundes, die USA erkannten den lettischen Staat im Juli des folgenden Jahres an. Ähnlich verlief die Entwicklung für Estland und Litauen.

Generell lassen sich folgende Charakteristika für die baltischen Staaten festhalten: So tiefgreifend der innere Wandel von der Demokratie zum autoritären Präsidialregimen jeweils für die Innenpolitiken auch war, außenpolitisch waren die Umstürze mit keiner nennenswerten Neuorientierung verbunden. Schon in der Phase der Kämpfe um die Unabhängigkeit hatte sich gezeigt, dass die estnischen und lettischen Erfahrungen und Schlussfolgerungen sich von den litauischen unterschieden. In Tallinn und Riga sah man – wenig überraschend nach dem Vormarsch der Roten Armee 1919 – die Sowjetunion und in geringerem Maße das Deutschen Reich als diejenigen Staaten, von denen am ehesten eine außenpolitische Gefährdung ausgehen konnte; denn das Streben Deutschlands nach einer Revision des Versailler Vertrages konnte in der weit von den Grenzen des zarischen Russlands abgedrängten Sowjetunion in den 1920er Jahren durchaus auf wohlwollendes Verständnis treffen. Stimmen, die einen Dreibund der baltischen Staaten befürworteten, dies schon aus ökonomischen Gründen, sowie die Schaffung eines gemeinsamen Wirtschaftsraumes mit gemeinsamer Währung propagierten, was vor allem Riga zu Gute gekommen wäre – ein Beispiel wäre Alfred von Frauenstein mit seiner Artikelserie „Der Dreibund der drei Baltischen Staaten" – konnten sich nicht durchsetzen.[17]

15 Zum Völkerbund grundlegend: Housden, The League of Nations.

16 Vgl. den Nachruf von Paul Schiemann, Zum Tode von Meierowicz'; Conrad, Loyalität gegenüber einem lettischen Staat, S. 49.

17 Frauenstein, Der Dreibund der Baltischen. Auch in Großbritannien wurde für Anerkennung und Unterstützung aus ökonomischen Gründen geworben: Hinkkanen Lievonen, British Trade and Enterprises, S. 88.

Verheißungsvolle Anfänge, wie die Konferenz von Bulduri 1920, heute ein Teil von Jūrmala, blieben stecken.[18] Die „tanzende Konferenz von Bulduri“, wie Marko Lethi es formulierte, fand im eleganten Hotel Bilderlingshof statt, das eigens mit einer Telegrafenleitung versehen worden war, scheiterte als multilateraler Versuch, bei dem nicht nur Lettland Estland, Litauen, Polen und ukrainische Vertreter anwesend waren und über ihre Beziehungen zu Sowjetrussland redeten, wie auch über Möglichkeiten politscher, ökonomischer und institutioneller Kooperation. Es mangelte nicht an Ideen für eine gemeinsame regionale Zukunft, sondern an der Fähigkeit, diese Ideen in Übereinstimmung zu bringen.[19] So war die Anerkennung der sowjetisch-baltischen Verträge durch jeweils bilaterale Verträge für die neuen Staaten das Wichtigere in der Absicherung einer gemeinsamen Zukunft, die sich in der letztlich doch zügigen Beilegung von Grenzstreitigkeiten zwischen Lettland, Litauen und Estland, teils durch britische Vermittlung, zeigte.

Die jeweiligen Perspektiven auf die Region waren jedoch divergent. Da der deutsche und der sowjetische Revisionismus ihren gemeinsamen Nenner in einer antipolnischen Ausrichtung fanden, lag es nahe, dass Lettland und Estland ausgesprochen gute Beziehungen zu Warschau unterhielten. Dies führte zum Abschluss eines Nichtangriffs- und Konsultationspakts zwischen Polen, Finnland, Estland und Lettland, der am 17. März 1922 in Warschau unterzeichnet wurde.[20] Ganz anders stellte sich die litauische Analyse der Lage dar: Sowohl die Sowjetunion als auch das Deutsche Reich unterstützten – aufgrund ihrer antipolnischen Politik – die litauischen Ansprüche auf Vilnius. Eine Verschärfung der polnisch-litauischen Spannungen entsprach den deutschen und sowjetischen Interessen, so dass in Kaunas mehr oder weniger offen (Sowjetunion) bzw. verdeckt (Deutschland) Litauen zu einem Ausharren in der so genannten Wilnafrage geraten wurde. Zur Schwierigkeit der Situation trug bei, dass der litauische Handstreich auf das Memelgebiet im Januar 1923 zwar mit stillschweigender deutscher Zustimmung geschehen war, aber die deutsch-litauischen Beziehungen doch zunehmend durch den Streit um Memel belastet wurden.[21] Das strategische Dilemma Litauens lag auf der Hand: Während man in Memel Vertreter der Versailler Ordnung war, zählte man bei der Wilnafrage zu den revisionistischen Mächten. Eine außenpolitische Abstimmung der baltischen Staaten

18 Ausführlich: Minutes of the Conference held at Bulduri.

19 Vgl. Lehti, The Dancing Conference, S. 71-94.

20 Vgl. Rauch, Geschichte der baltischen Staaten, S. 108.

21 Vgl. Knudsen, The Foreign Policies of the Baltic States, S. 51.

untereinander konnte unter diesen Umständen nie erreicht werden. Die Konferenzen und Gipfeltreffen in den 1920er Jahren bestätigten immer wieder den grundsätzlichen Antagonismus. Litauen boykottierte alle Gespräche mit polnischer Teilnahme und versuchte beharrlich, Lettland und Estland auf die eigene Seite zu ziehen.[22] Im Kern des Scheiterns aller baltischen Bündnispläne stand der polnisch-litauische Antagonismus, er verhinderte jegliche tiefere politische und militärische Zusammenarbeit im nördlichen Ostmitteleuropa. Damit besaß der Streit um Vilnius eine internationale Dimension, die weit über alle anderen territorialen Streitigkeiten unter den 1918/19 neuentstandenen ostmitteleuropäischen Staaten hinausreichte.[23]

Er war auch für die deutsche Außenpolitik der Weimarer Republik von Bedeutung.[24] Deren Angelpunkt in Osteuropa war insbesondere die Außenpolitik gegenüber Polen, für die die rhetorische Figur von den „blutenden Grenzen" vor allem nach der Abstimmung in Oberschlesien[25] 1921 bis zum deutsch-polnischen Nichtangriffsvertrag von 1934, der nur scheinbar einen *modus vivendi* herzustellen schien, leitend wurde. Für die Staaten Nordosteuropas hatte zunächst kein kohärentes Konzept bestanden. Einerseits waren die Versuche, am Ende des Ersten Weltkrieges und im Verlaufe des Jahres 1918 Monarchien zu errichten, die sich über die schon ausgewählten Dynastien in Abhängigkeit zu Deutschland befinden sollten, im Zuge der Unabhängigkeitserklärungen gescheitert. Andererseits zwangen die fortgesetzte Anwesenheit deutscher Truppen und der sich teilweise aus ihnen formierenden Freikorps die deutsche Außenpolitik immer wieder zu offiziellem oder inoffiziellem Handeln. Ein Objekt waren hier immer auch die deutschen Minderheiten. Während jene in Estland und Lettland lange unabhängig agierten, waren die Memelländer ein Sonderfall.

Insgesamt war die deutsche Diplomatie mit der Niederlage im Ersten Weltkrieg und dem Ende der Freikorps zunächst eine des Rückzugs mit der Anerkennung der baltischen Staaten. Die Fragen des Minderheitenschutzes und der Kriegsentschädigungen standen im Mittelpunkt der Außenpolitik der Weimarer Republik. Rapallo machte Deutschland umgekehrt für die baltischen Staaten, vor allem aber auch für Polen zu einem eher schwierigen Faktor. Die Furcht

---

22 Und zum Folgenden: Jena, Polnische Ostpolitik, S. 100-140.

23 Noch immer wertvoll: Senn, The Great Powers.

24 Kompakte und problemorientierte Überblicke: Elz, Versailles und Weimar, S. 31-38; Elz, Foreign policy, S. 50-77, 286-288.

25 Nitsche, Der Reichstag und die Festlegung, S. 335-361; Jaworski, „Wählt deutsch!", S. 85-97.

vor einer Verständigung mit dem sowjetischen Russland auf Kosten der neuen Staaten war ubiquitär.[26]

Das „Krisenjahr 1923" bedeutete auch für das Verhältnis zwischen der Weimarer Republik und den baltischen Staaten einen Einschnitt: Als französische und belgische Truppen am 10. Januar 1923 das Ruhrgebiet besetzten, marschierten gleichzeitig litauische Soldaten in das dem Völkerbund unterstellte Memelgebiet ein. Dieser Coup brachte die deutsch-litauischen Beziehungen nicht auf einen Nullpunkt: Auch die Proteste der Memelländer konnten das Auswärtige Amt nicht daran hindern, die Wirtschaftsgespräche mit Litauen fortzusetzen, die am 31. Mai 1923 zu einem deutsch-litauischen Wirtschaftsabkommen führten. In diesem Vertrag setzte die deutsche Seite erstmals seit Rapallo das Prinzip des gegenseitigen Verzichts auf Schadenersatz für Kriegs- und Enteignungsverluste durch. Der Abschluss mit Litauen erleichterte wiederum die Unterzeichnung eines Wirtschaftsvertrags mit Estland am 27. Juni 1923. Dieser deutsch-estnische Vertrag vereinbarte die gegenseitige Meistbegünstigung und sicherte freien Transithandel durch Estland zu. Die deutsche Delegation akzeptierte, dass Estland seinen Nachbarstaaten Lettland und Litauen und – bezeichnenderweise erst nach Rapallo – auch Sowjetrussland Vorzugsbedingungen einräumte. Die beiden Abkommen von 1923 waren mithin eine Frucht des Rapallo-Vertrages und ein Erfolg für die Diplomaten des Auswärtigen Amtes. Jedoch unterzeichneten Estland und Lettland schon am 1. November 1923 ein Verteidigungsbündnis, das im Auswärtigen Amt alte Ängste vor einem baltisch-polnischen Block wiedererwachen ließ.[27]

Am 28./29. November 1923 trafen sich in Riga die deutschen Gesandten in den baltischen Staaten mit dem zuständigen Referenten im Auswärtigen Amt, Konsul Thermann, um die Bedeutung des lettisch-estnischen Vertrages zu diskutieren. Alle waren sich einig, dass diese Allianz erst der Beginn eines größeren Blocks von Randstaaten mit dem Ziel einer gemeinsamen Verteidigung gegen Russland war. Als Position des Auswärtigen Amtes wurde zum wiederholten Male festgehalten: Deutschland habe ein starkes Interesse an den „Randstaaten"; Rapallo richte sich gegen Polen, aber nicht gegen die baltischen Staaten.[28] Die sowjetische Führung dagegen schien die bloße Existenz der baltischen Staaten

---

26 Und zum Folgenden: Borowksy, Die deutsche Politik, S. 153-172. Zum Forschungsstand: Fleischhauer, Rathenau in Rapallo, S. 365-415.

27 Lettländisch-estländisches Schutzbündnis. Der Grundstein zum baltischen Staatenbunde gelegt, in: Keruss, Lettland in der Zwischenkriegszeit.

28 Vgl. Creuzberger, Das Deutsch-russische Jahrhundert, S. 356-380.

schon als Bedrohung betrachtet zu haben, konnten diese doch als Einfallstore für eine wirtschaftliche und politische Einflussnahme des kapitalistischen Westens auf Sowjetrussland dienen. Der kommunistische Putschversuch gegen die estnische Regierung am 1. Dezember 1924 scheiterte zwar, auf die ganze Region wirkte er aber als Alarmsignal.[29] Im Januar 1925 trafen sich auf Initiative des finnischen Außenministers die Außenminister Finnlands, Polens, Lettlands und Estlands in Helsinki und unterzeichneten einen Schiedsvertrag.

Die Idee eines baltischen Blocks stand erneut auf der Tagesordnung und beunruhigte die Sowjetunion und Deutschland in höchstem Maße.[30] Wollte die deutsche Politik die baltischen Staaten von einem Pakt mit Polen abhalten, dann musste sie deren Sicherheitsinteressen ernstnehmen. Der deutsche Gesandte in Riga, Adolf Köster, schlug daher im April 1925 vor, Deutschland und Sowjetrussland sollten gemeinsam einen Garantiepakt mit den baltischen Staaten abschließen, um einen polnisch-baltischen Bund zu verhindern. Inspiriert hatte ihn dazu offenbar der lettische Außenminister Zigfrīds Anna Meierovics. Doch dieser Plan fand im Auswärtigen Amt keine Zustimmung – und zwar aus allgemeinpolitischen Überlegungen, die mit Stresemanns Locarno-Politik zusammenhingen. In einer Aufzeichnung vom 24. April 1925 kam Ministerialdirektor Herbert von Dirksen (1928 bis 1933 Botschafter in Moskau) zu dem Schluss, für die Reichsregierung sei weder ein Nichtangriffspakt noch ein Garantievertrag möglich, sondern lediglich ein Schiedsvertrag, denn alles andere würde nur zu verstärktem Druck von Seiten Frankreichs und Polens führen, einen Garantie- oder Nichtangriffspakt auch mit Polen und der Tschechoslowakei abzuschließen. Gerade das aber wollte die deutsche Regierung vermeiden.[31]

Ein Nichtangriffspakt mit indirekter Garantie der Grenzen hätte eine gefährliche Durchbrechung der Grundprinzipien des Locarno-Vertrages dargestellt, welcher die Grenzfragen im Osten grundsätzlich anders behandelte als im Westen. Ein „Ost-Locarno“ sollte es nach dem Willen der Reichsregierung nicht geben. In dieser Situation erwies sich das Instrument des Schiedsvertrages als nützlich. Weil sie territoriale und politische Probleme ausklammerten und nur juristische Streitfragen einer Schlichtungskommission überantworteten, sind die Schiedsverträge in der Debatte über Stresemanns Außenpolitik gelegentlich als lediglich

29 Borowsky, S. 157f.; siehe auch den Beitrag von Karsten Brüggemann in diesem Band.

30 Zum Gesamtkontext ausführlich: Lehti, Baltic League.

31 Vgl. Borowsky, S. 159; Hiden, The Baltic States, S. 158.

taktische Mittel gesehen worden, die nichts weiter bezweckten, als Deutschland die Option für eine spätere Revision der Ostgrenzen offenzuhalten.[32]

Dabei ist vielfach übersehen worden, dass eine Politik der friedlichen Konfliktregelung zu den ernstgemeinten Prinzipien der Weimarer Außenpolitik gehörte. Ein System von Schiedsverträgen sollte die Haager Konvention konkretisieren, die Regelungen des Völkerbundes ergänzen und Einzelkonflikte begrenzen helfen. Der Abschluss von Schiedsverträgen mit den baltischen Staaten bot Gustav Stresemann und seinem Staatssekretär von Schubert eine Möglichkeit, ihren Vorschlag, solche Verträge mit Polen und der Tschechoslowakei abzuschließen, besser zu begründen. Außerdem und vor allem sollten die Verträge dazu dienen, das lästige Problem der Kriegs- und Enteignungsschäden zu lösen. Am 14. März 1925 schloss das Deutsche Reich einen Schiedsvertrag mit Finnland, am 10. August 1925 folgte ein ähnlicher Vertrag mit Estland. Im Zusammenhang mit Locarno wurden am 16. Oktober 1925 die Schiedsverträge mit Polen und der Tschechoslowakei unterzeichnet. Am 29. Januar 1928 schloss Deutschland auch einen Schiedsvertrag mit Litauen. Nur mit Lettland kam ein Schiedsvertrag nicht zustande.[33]

Im Sommer 1925 scheiterte das Projekt eines baltischen Blocks, das zuletzt der estnische Außenminister Pusta betrieben hatte, endgültig. Gleichwohl verfolgte das deutsche Auswärtige Amt weiterhin das Ziel, die Unabhängigkeit der baltischen Staaten durch eine sowjetische Garantieerklärung abzusichern. Wozu Deutschland selbst nicht bereit gewesen war, das sollte nun die Sowjetunion leisten. Der Berliner Vertrag zwischen Deutschland und der Sowjetunion vom 24. April 1926, der den Rapallo-Vertrag als Grundlage der Beziehungen zwischen beiden Staaten bezeichnete und die wechselseitige Neutralität im Konfliktfall festlegte,[34] wirkte in den baltischen Staaten als Anregung, ähnliche Abkommen mit der Sowjetunion zu schließen. In Lettland beschleunigte der Berliner Vertrag die Verhandlungen über einen deutsch-lettischen Handelsvertrag, der im Juni 1926 unterzeichnet wurde und auch ein Entschädigungsabkommen enthielt.[35] Außerdem paraphierte am 9. März 1927 der sozialdemokratische Außenminister Fēlikss Ciēlens einen Nichtangriffsvertrag mit der Sowjetunion.[36] Dieser Vertrag

---

32 Vgl. Höltje, Die Weimarer Republik.

33 Vgl. Niedhart, Die Außenpolitik der Weimarer Republik, S. 32.

34 Vgl. Thomas, Georgi Tschitscherin, S. 217-228.

35 Vgl. Westenberger, Die handelspolitischen und wirtschaftlichen Beziehungen, S. 656-667.

36 Vgl. Duhanovs/ Feldmanis/ Stranga, Latvia and the Year of Fateful Decisions, S. 12.

wurde jedoch nicht mehr unterzeichnet, als die sozialdemokratische Regierung Lettlands Ende 1927 gestürzt wurde. Erst am 5. Februar 1932 wurden unter veränderten Bedingungen ein lettisch-sowjetischer Nichtangriffsvertrag und später eine Schlichtungsvereinbarung unterzeichnet.[37]

Ein weiteres Beispiel für deutsch-sowjetische Zusammenarbeit im Baltikum nach Unterzeichnung des Berliner Vertrages war Litauen. Hier verfolgte das Auswärtige Amt seine Linie weiter, wonach die Memelfrage die Beziehungen zu Litauen, vor allem die wirtschaftlichen, nicht stören durfte. So wurde im Mai 1926 das deutsch-litauische Handelsabkommen ratifiziert, obwohl Litauen seine Zusage, Reichsdeutschen im Memelland die Gleichberechtigung zu gewähren, nicht gehalten hatte.

Im Mai 1926 kam durch einen Staatsstreich Marschall Piłsudski in Polen an die Macht. Er personifizierte gleichsam den Anspruch auf Vilnius, machte einen Interessenausgleich zwischen Polen und Litauen unwahrscheinlicher denn je zuvor und veranlasste die litauische Regierung unter dem Sozialdemokraten Šleževičius, eine politische Annäherung an Deutschland zu suchen. Stresemann und Staatssekretär von Schubert scheuten aber vor einem direkten politischen Abkommen mit Litauen wegen der Memelfrage zurück. Sie ermutigten daher die litauische Regierung zu einem Abkommen mit Moskau, das den Sicherheitsinteressen Litauens dienen sollte. In die nunmehr einsetzenden litauisch-sowjetischen Verhandlungen griff das Auswärtige Amt insofern ein, als Schubert und Stresemann in verschiedenen Unterredungen mit dem sowjetischen Botschafter Krestinskij in Berlin erreichen konnten, dass in dem litauisch-sowjetischen Nichtangriffspakt vom 28. September 1926 das Memelgebiet nicht erwähnt, wohl aber der litauische Anspruch auf Wilna von der Sowjetunion unterstützt wurde. Gegen diese – wie sie es sahen – einseitige Orientierung auf die Sowjetunion wehrten sich die litauischen Nationalisten und das Militär. Am 16./17. Dezember 1926 stürzten sie die Regierung und errichteten eine autoritäre Regierung unter Augustinas Voldemaras, die aber die Zusammenarbeit mit Deutschland fortsetzte. 1928 wurde ein deutsch-litauischer Grenzvertrag und 1929 ein deutsch-litauische Handelsvertrag unterzeichnet. Erst litauische Eingriffe in die Autonomie des Memellandes verschlechterten 1932 die Beziehungen zwischen beiden Staaten und die deutsch-polnische Verständigung des Jahres 1934 nach der Machtergreifung Hitlers wurde als eine Zäsur gesehen – auch in der Sowjetunion.

---

37 Vgl. Kusber, Überleben zwischen den Großmächten, S. 57; Hochmann, The Soviet Union and the Failure, S. 34.

Selbst als es im Jahre 1934 endlich zu einer „Baltischen Entente“ kam, stand die Wilnafrage im Hintergrund. Litauens außenpolitische Situation hatte sich durch die polnisch-deutsche Entspannung nach der Nichtangriffserklärung vom Januar 1934 sowie durch die Verschärfung der Lage im Memelgebiet massiv verschlechtert. Parallel zu Sondierungen in Polen war Kaunas nun bereit, auch eine engere Kooperation mit den baltischen Nachbarn anzustreben. Der Wandel der litauischen Politik führte zu einem ersten Gipfeltreffen in Kaunas im Juli 1934. Der schwierigste Punkt der Verhandlungen war einmal mehr die Wilnafrage. Litauen wollte von den potenziellen Partnern zumindest die Versicherung einer wohlwollenden Neutralität abringen, doch dazu waren Lettland und vor allem das polenfreundliche Estland nicht bereit. Nachdem die Gespräche im August 1934 in Riga fortgesetzt worden waren, kam es schließlich doch noch zu dem Vertrag über „Freundschaft und Zusammenarbeit“, der am 12. September 1934 in Genf beim Völkerbund unterzeichnet wurde. Im Artikel 1 vereinbarten die baltischen Staaten eine Zusammenarbeit in der Außenpolitik und gegenseitige Unterstützung in internationalen Angelegenheiten. Im Artikel 3 wurde indessen zugleich festgehalten, dass Litauens „spezifische Probleme“ nicht unter den Artikel 1 fielen. Mindestens zweimal im Jahr sollten sich die Außenminister zu Gipfelgesprächen treffen, die Auslandsvertretungen eng zusammenarbeiten. Dem Vertrag konnten weitere Staaten beitreten, wenn alle drei (!) baltischen Staaten dem zustimmten.[38] In einem vertraulichen Protokoll erklärten Lettland und Estland, unter „spezifischen Problemen“ sei nur die Wilnafrage zu verstehen. Bereits in den lettisch-estnischen Vorgesprächen zum Treffen in Kaunas herrschte nämlich Einigkeit, dass die nationalsozialistische Aktivität im Memelgebiet auch eine Bedrohung für die eigenen Länder darstelle, weswegen man Litauen unterstützen müsse.[39] Dieses Engagement erleichterte Litauen die Zustimmung zum Vertrag, doch bereits ab 1935 distanzierte man sich in Riga und Tallinn mehr oder weniger von einer Unterstützung Litauens in Memel. Besonders deutlich wurde zwei Jahre später der estnische Gesandte in Kaunas: In einem Gespräch im November 1937 entgegnete er dem litauischen Außenminister Lozoraitis auf dessen Klarstellung, im Falle eines Angriffs auf Memel werde Litauen „bis zum Ende kämpfen“, ungerührt, keine Nation werde auch „nur einen Finger heben“, um Litauen zu helfen.[40] Die Bedeutung der Baltischen Entente wird in der Historiographie daher übereinstimmend als gering bezeichnet. Es habe sich

38 Vgl.: Treaty of Good Understanding and Co-operation, signed at Geneva.

39 Vgl. FELDMANIS/ STRANGA, The Destiny, S. 30f.

40 FELDMANIS/ STRANGA, The Destiny, S. 87.

um ein moribundes Bündnis gehandelt,[41] das sich auf gegenseitige Konsultation beschränkt habe. In der Tat ist die Bezeichnung „Entente" übertrieben und war allenfalls für die Außenwirkung wichtig, denn weder eine wirtschaftliche noch gar eine militärische Zusammenarbeit wurde vereinbart bzw. erreicht. Die regelmäßigen Außenministertreffen sollten sich als Pflichtübungen erweisen.

Die entscheidende Schwäche der Baltischen Entente in den 1930er Jahren lag wie bereits am Ende des Ersten Weltkrieges in den völlig unterschiedlichen Bedrohungsperzeptionen der baltischen Staaten. Während Estland vor allem in der Sowjetunion eine potenziell aggressive Macht sah, unterhielt Kaunas außergewöhnlich gute Beziehungen zu Moskau. *Vice versa* galt Estland als der „polnische Freund" unter den Balten, was dem Grundkonsens der litauischen antipolnischen Politik diametral entgegenstand. Und die Letten fühlten sich sowohl von Moskau als auch Berlin bedroht. Der amtierende lettische Außenminister Vilhelms Munters brachte 1935 die inneren Widersprüche auf den Punkt:[42]

> „Litauen mit zwei ernsthaften Problemen und einer starken Orientierung auf Moskau, die realistisch gesehen kaum gerechtfertigt ist. Estland mit seiner pathologischen Manie über Polen und seinen verkalkten Doktrinen in der Außenpolitik … und einer besonderen Orientierung auf Finnland. Und uns – ein Land, das das Gleichgewicht zwischen allen dreien aufrechtzuerhalten hat und das den Druck von Staaten aushalten muss, die mit der unabhängigen Politik der baltischen Staaten unzufrieden sind, unsere Verbündeten, die Esten, manchmal eingeschlossen."[43]

Immerhin saßen Lettland, Litauen und Estland regelmäßig an einem Tisch. Und im Oktober 1936 feierte die lettische Außenpolitik einen prestigeträchtigen Erfolg: Lettland wurde als nichtständiges Mitglied in den Rat des Völkerbundes gewählt. Im Jahr zuvor war die lettische Botschaft in Washington wiedereröffnet worden, die im Jahre 1927 aus Kostengründen geschlossen worden war.

Jedoch vermochten diese Momente internationaler Geltung nicht darüber hinwegzutäuschen, dass die Sicherheitsoptionen für die baltischen Staaten schwanden. Auf die Erklärung der Außenministerkonferenz der Entente in Riga vom 11. Dezember 1936, es sei zu vermeiden, sich der einen oder anderen Seite zuzuneigen und man werde sich an keiner Art von Blockkonstellation beteiligen,

---

41 Vgl. Eidintas/ Žalys/ Senn, Lithuania in European Politics, S. 154.

42 Munters, Außenminister von 1936-1940, erwies sich in seiner Orientierung zwischen Deutschland und der Sowjetunion als äußerst flexibel: Ahmann, Rusofils, Anglofils vai Germanophils, S. 122-139.

43 Zitiert nach: Feldmanis/ Stranga, The Destiny, S. 85.

reagierte die sowjetische Politik deutlich. Neutralität rege, so der sowjetische Gesandte Karskij in Kaunas, den Appetit des Angreifers an. Nur die Sowjetunion könne die baltischen Staaten schützen.[44] Der Besuch des Generalstabschefs der Roten Armee, Marschall A. I. Egorov, der sich ähnlich äußerte, wurde eher als bedrohlich, denn als beruhigend empfunden.[45]

Die fehlende außenpolitische Kohärenz leistete den Entwicklungen ab März 1938 Vorschub,[46] obwohl eine über die bloße Deklaration hinausgehende Baltische Entente das Kommende auch nicht hätte verhindern können. Bereits im März 1938 hatte Kaunas, durch ein polnisches Ultimatum gezwungen, als dessen Anlass eine (aufgrund des Schmuggels durchaus nicht seltene) Schießerei an der Demarkationslinie, bei der ein polnischer Grenzer ums Leben gekommen war, vorgeschoben wurde, die Aufnahme diplomatischer Beziehungen zwischen Litauen und Polen erzwungen. Damit war die litauische Politik in der Wilnafrage gescheitert, auch wenn Polen die Regierung in Kaunas nicht zu einem offiziellen Verzicht ihrer Ansprüche nötigte. Auch die zweite außenpolitische Besonderheit des größten baltischen Staates fand eine erzwungene Lösung. Am 23. März 1939 stimmte Litauen nach einer ultimativen Drohung des deutschen Außenministers der „Rückkehr“ des Memelgebietes in das Deutsche Reich zu.[47]

Bereits das Abkommen von München vom September 1938 war für die baltischen Staaten komplett desillusionierend, weil es verdeutlichte, dass die baltischen Staaten mit französischem und britischem Schutz nicht würden rechnen können. Das Prinzip jeder kollektiven Sicherheit schien gescheitert zu sein. Unter dem Eindruck, zwischen Hammer und Amboss geraten zu sein, proklamierte die lettische Regierung am 13. Dezember 1938 in einer Geste der Hilflosigkeit seine absolute Neutralität. Dass die Sowjetunion am 28. März 1939 ohne Absprache mit der lettischen Regierung erklärte, sie sei interessiert an der Aufrechterhaltung und Verteidigung der lettischen Unabhängigkeit, wurde als weitere Drohung empfunden.

Während die sowjetische Regierung in ihren Verhandlungen mit Großbritannien und Frankreich, den schwachen Garanten der europäischen Nachkriegsordnung, seit dem Frühsommer 1939 auch eine Garantie der Unabhängigkeit der baltischen Staaten adressierte, blieben die lettische und die estnische Regierung

---

44 Vgl. Beloff, The Foreign Policy of Soviet Russia, S. 79.

45 Vgl. Kusber, Überleben, S. 60.

46 Vgl. Duhanovs/ Feldmanis/ Stranga, Latvia and the Year of Fateful Decisions, S. 46-57.

47 Tauber, Die Memelfrage, S. 115-118.

skeptisch gegenüber den Absichten des Nachbarn im Osten und flüchteten sich jeweils in gegenseitige Nichtangriffspakte mit Deutschland.[48] Der lettisch-deutsche wurde am 7. Juni 1939 in Berlin von den Außenministern Vilhelms Munters und Joachim von Ribbentrop unterzeichnet. Am darauf folgenden Tag betonte Adolf Hitler selbst bei einem Empfang sein Interesse insbesondere an ausgezeichneten Handelsbeziehungen mit den baltischen Staaten.

Auch wenn sich die lettische Regierung über die Qualität solcher Bekundungen keinen großen Illusionen hingab, glaubte man in Riga, eine Atempause zu haben, während der Weg in die Katastrophe am 23. August 1939 in Moskau beschritten wurde. Das nationalsozialistische Deutschland und die stalinistische Sowjetunion einigten sich bekanntermaßen nicht nur auf einen Nichtangriffspakt, sondern in dem Geheimen Zusatzprotokoll über die Ein- und Aufteilung Nordost- und Ostmitteleuropas. Der für die baltischen Staaten entscheidende Passus lautete:

> „Für den Fall einer territorial-politischen Umgestaltung in den zu den baltischen Staaten (Finnland, Estland, Lettland, Litauen) gehörenden Gebieten bildet die nördliche Grenze Litauens zugleich die Grenze der Interessensphäre Deutschlands und der UdSSR. Hierbei wird das Interesse Litauens am Wilnaer Gebiet beiderseits anerkannt."[49]

Damit beanspruchten die Deutschen Territorien Litauens, die sie schon während des Ersten Weltkrieges besetzt gehalten hatten, während den Regierungen der baltischen Staaten nach dem Überfall auf Polen am 1. September 1939 die Sinnlosigkeit der mit Deutschland geschlossen Verträge vor Augen stand.

Die sowjetischen Pläne waren dreistufig und schlossen die Absicht, die baltischen Staaten komplett zu besetzen, ein. Am Beginn stand jeweils, so auch im Falle Lettlands, einen Vertrag über gegenseitige Unterstützung und Hilfe, dem dann die Stationierung von Truppen der Roten Armee folgen sollten, bis dann eine „friedliche sozialistische" Revolution erfolgen sollte. Die Akteure in der lettischen Politik, allen voran Präsident Ulmanis und Außenminister Munters, ahnten natürlich nicht die Details des Szenarios, doch musste ihnen spätestens nach dem Einmarsch sowjetischer Truppen im Osten der Zweiten Polnischen Republik am 17. September 1939 klar sein, dass die Annexion der baltischen Staaten bevorstand.

---

48 Vgl. AHMANN, The German Treaties, S. 337-364.

49 Nichtangriffsvertrag zwischen Deutschland und der Union der Sozialistischen Sowjetrepubliken.

Seit dem 28. September 1939 massierte die Sowjetunion Truppen an der Grenze zu Lettland, nachdem in einem weiteren Vertrag und einem weiteren geheimen Protokoll vom gleichen Tag zwischen der Sowjetunion und Deutschland die Interessensphären erneut abgeglichen worden waren. Danach erhielt Munters eine Einladung zu Gesprächen für den 2. Oktober nach Moskau, deren Inhalt nicht näher spezifiziert wurde. Als sich Munters und Kočiņs, der lettische Gesandte in Moskau, mit den Forderungen Stalins und seines Außenministers Molotov konfrontiert sahen, wurde deutlich, welchen Weg Lettland gehen würde.

Folgt man Munters, so erinnerte ihn Molotov an das Ziel Peters des Großen, Russland einen Zugang an der Ostsee zu verschaffen. Molotov soll gesagt haben: „...Wir müssen grundsätzlich an uns selbst denken. Was 1920 bestimmt wurde, kann nicht immer bestand haben."[50] In gewisser Weise war mit diesen Entwicklungen eine eigenständige Außenpolitik der baltischen Staaten damit an ihr Ende gekommen. Für Lettland, um bei diesem Beispiel zu bleiben, endete sie mit dem am 5. Oktober 1939 geschlossenen Beistandsvertrag.[51] 25.000 Soldaten der Roten Armee sollten auf Stützpunkten in Kurland stationiert werden. Auch wenn Stalin beim abendlichen Bankett das „Ehrenwort eines Bolschewiken"[52] gab, dass sich die Sowjetunion nicht in die inneren Angelegenheiten Lettlands einmischen werde, war dies das Ende. An militärischen Widerstand war angesichts der Kräfteverhältnisse kaum zu denken. Dass der Schritt Stalins in Abstimmung mit dem Deutschen Reich erfolgte, war offensichtlich. Vergeblich hatte sich Munters vor seiner Reise um eine Garantierklärung der Regierung Hitlers bemüht; nach Abschluss des Moskauer Vertrages zwischen Lettland und der UdSSR erfolgte die Aussiedlung der deutschbaltischen Minderheit.

Illustrativ und bezeichnend war, dass sich alle drei baltischen Staaten im Völkerbund, auf den die baltischen Staaten und andere der neuen Staaten in Europa so stark gesetzt hatten und der inzwischen ein Relikt vergangener Zeiten schien, sich bei der Abstimmung über den Ausschluss der Sowjetunion als Aggressor der Stimme enthielten.

Das Ende der Idee der kollektiven Sicherheit, der Niedergang des Völkerbundes, der in den frühen territorialen Streitigkeiten durchaus hatte vermitteln können, sowie der Mangel an Visionen für eine multilaterale Ordnung im nordöstlichen Europa trugen mit Sicherheit dazu bei, dass Hitler und Stalin in der

50 Myllyniemi, Die baltische Krise, S. 65.

51 Pakt o vzaimopomošči meždu SSSR i Latviej.

52 So Beržins, The unpunished crime, S. 50.

Hemmungslosigkeit des Hitlers-Stalin-Paktes Nordosteuropa und ihre Länder in die Katstrophe führten. Festzuhalten bleibt, dass sich an der nördlichen Flanke Ostmitteleuropas kein Sicherheits- und Bündnissystem entwickelte, das sich zwischen Deutschland und der Sowjetunion hätte behaupten können.

Eine baltische Kooperation blieb letztlich – erstens – von den Konjunkturen des litauisch-polnischen Antagonismus abhängig. Als sich Ende 1939 und Anfang 1940 die baltischen Außenminister zum, wie sich zeigen sollte, letzten Mal trafen und bereits die exterritorialen Basen der Roten Armee in den baltischen Ländern stationiert waren, stieß die litauische Aufforderung, das Vilniusgebiet als litauisches Territorium anzuerkennen, auf die strikte Ablehnung Lettlands und Estlands. Dabei begründeten Riga und Tallinn ihre Haltung mit der angesichts der faktischen Situation überraschenden Erklärung, Litauen habe das Vilniusgebiet von der Sowjetunion erhalten, was nicht der litauischen Neutralitätspolitik entspräche und daher illegal sei.[53]

Diese Verwicklungen am Ende der Unabhängigkeit der baltischen Staaten in der Zwischenkriegszeit verdeutlichen – zweitens – in welch hohem Maße die baltischen Staaten, denen es zunächst um eine diplomatische Absicherung der Unabhängigkeit gegangen waren, in ihren Spielräumen von der geopolitischen Großwetterlage und den Interessen der großen Akteure in der Region abhängig waren. Für die Staaten wie Polen und die Tschechoslowakei waren sie vor diesem Hintergrund auch Player nachgeordneten Ranges. Diese Erfahrungen leiteten sicher auch die historiographischen Zugänge nach der Wiedererlangung der Unabhängigkeit 1991,[54] aber auch die konkrete auswärtige Politik. Seit 2004 gewährleisten die Europäische Union und NATO eine multilaterale Einbindung, die in ihrer Bedeutung kaum zu unterschätzen ist und auf den Erfahrungen mit wenig erfolgreichen Sicherheitskonstruktionen der Zwischenkriegszeit beruht.

Literaturverzeichnis

AHMANN, ROLF Rusofils, Anglofils vai Germanophils. Neizprastais Latvijas Arlietu Ministrs Vilhelms Munters Nacionalsocialistu Vertejuma (1936-1939), in: Latvijas Vestures Instituta Zuurnals 8 (1993) Heft 3, S. 122-139.

AHMANN, ROLF The German Treaties with Estonia and Latvia of 7 June 1939. Bargaining Ploy or an Alternative for German Soviet Understanding?, in: Journal of Baltic Studies 20 (1989) Heft 4, S. 337-364.

---

53 Vgl. FELDMANIS/ STRANGA, The Destiny, S. 102.

54 Für das lettische Beispiel: DUHANOVS/ FELDMANIS/ STRANGA, Latvia and the Year of Fateful Decisions.

BELOFF, MAX The Foreign Policy of Soviet Russia, Vol. II (1936-1941), London 1949.

BERŽINS, ALFRED The unpunished crime, New York 1963.

BEYRAU, DIETRICH Schlachtfeld der Diktatoren. Osteuropa im Schatten von Hitler und Stalin, Göttingen 2000.

BOROWKSY, PETER Die deutsche Politik gegenüber den baltischen Staaten 1923 bis 1933. Diplomatie im Spannungsfeld von Wirtschaftsinteressen und Minderheitenschutz (1991), in: Schlaglichter historischer Forschung. Studien zur deutschen Geschichte im 19. und 20. Jahrhundert, hg. aus dem Nachlass von RAINER HERING/ RAINER NICOLAYSEN, Hamburg 2005, S. 153-172.

CONRAD, BENJAMIN Der Geograph und die Grenzen. Eugeniusz Romers Einfluss auf Polens Staatsgebiet, in: Osteuropa 67 (2017) Heft 1-2, S. 89-96.

CONRAD, BENJAMIN Loyalität gegenüber einem lettischen Staat? Deutschbaltische Politiker und die Gründung Lettlands 1918-1920, in: Tradition und Neuanfang. Forschungen zur Geschichte Lettlands an der Wende vom 20. zum 21. Jahrhundert. Kleine Festschrift für Erwin Oberländer, hg. von SVETLANA BOGOJAVLENSKA/ JAN KUSBER, Berlin 2014, S. 33-53.

CONZE, ECKART Die große Illusion. Versailles 1919 und die Neuordnung der Welt, München 2018.

CREUZBERGER, STEFAN Das Deutsch-russische Jahrhundert. Geschichte einer besonderen Beziehung, 2. Aufl. München 2022.

DAVIES, NORMAN The Polish-Soviet War, London 1972.

Documents on British Foreign Policy, Series 1, Vol. II, S. 738-748.

DUHANOVS, MAKSIMS/ FELDMANIS, INESIS/ STRANGA, AIVARS Latvia and the Year of Fateful Decisions – 1939, Riga 1994.

EIDINTAS, ALFONSAS/ ŽALYS, VYTAUTAS/ SENN, ALFRED ERICH Lithuania in European Politics. The Years of First Republic, 1918-1940, London 1987.

ELZ, WOLFGANG Foreign policy, in: Weimar Germany (Short Oxford History of Germany), hg. von ANTHONY MCELLIGOTT, Oxford 2009, S. 50-77, 286-288.

ELZ, WOLFGANG Versailles und Weimar, in: APuZ 50-51 (2008), S. 31-38.

FELDMANIS, INESIS/ STRANGA, AIVARS The Destiny of the Baltic Entente 1934-1940, Riga 1994.

FLEISCHHAUER, EVA INGEBORG Rathenau in Rapallo. Eine Notwendige Korrektur des Forschungsstandes, in: Vierteljahrshefte für Zeitgeschichte 54 (2006), Nr. 3, S. 365-415.

FRAUENSTEIN, ALFRED VON Der Dreibund der Baltischen Staaten Lettland, Estland und Litauen. Sonderabzug aus der Rigaer Zeitung, [Riga 1920].

HAGEDORN, ANN Savage Peace. Hope and Fear in America, 1919, New York 2007.

HANSON, OLE Americanism versus Bolshevism, New York 1920.

HIDEN, JOHN The Baltic States and Weimar Ostpolitik, Cambridge 1987.

HIDEN, JOHN The Weimar Republic and the problem of the Auslandsdeutsche, in: Journal of Contemporary History 12 (1977) Heft 2, S. 273-289.

HIDEN, JOHN/ SALMON, PATRICK The Baltic Nations and Europe. Estonia, Latvia and Lithuania in the Twentieth Century, London 2014.

HINKKANEN LIEVONEN, MERJA-LIISA British Trade and Enterprises in the Baltic States 1919-1925, Helsinki 1984.

HOCHMANN, JIRI The Soviet Union and the Failure of Collective Security, 1934-1938, Ithaca 1984.

HÖLTJE, CHRISTIAN Die Weimarer Republik und das Ostlocarno-Problem 1919-1934 (Marburger Ostforschungen 8), Würzburg 1958.

HOUSDEN, MARTYN The league of nations and the organization of peace, Harlow 2012.

JAWORSKI, RUDOLF „Wählt deutsch!" – „Głosuj za Polską!" Postkartenpropaganda in Oberschlesien, in: Jahrbuch Polen: Oberschlesien 2021, S. 85-97.

JAWORSKI, RUDOLF Der auslandsdeutsche Gedanke in der Weimarer Republik, in: Annali dell'Istituto storico italo-germanico in Trento IV (1978), S. 369-386.

JENA, KAI VON Polnische Ostpolitik nach dem Ersten Weltkrieg, Stuttgart 1980.

KERUSS, JANIS Themenmodul „Lettland in der Zwischenkriegszeit", in: Dokumente und Materialien zur ostmitteleuropäischen Geschichte, hg. vom Herder-Institut, URL: https://www.herder-institut.de/digitale-angebote/dokumente-und-materialien/themenmodule/modul/6/seite.html, 15.03.2024

KNUDSEN, OLAV F. The Foreign Policies of the Baltic States. Interwar Years and Restoration, in: Cooperation and Conflict 28 (1993) Heft 1, S. 47-72.

KREKELER, NORBERT Revisionsanspruch und geheime Ostpolitik der Weimarer Republik. Die Subventionierung der deutschen Minderheit in Polen 1919-1933, Stuttgart 1973.

KUSBER, JAN Ressentiment, Konflikt und Vernichtung. Osteuropa in der ersten Hälfte des 20. Jahrhunderts, in: Europäische Perspektiven im Geschichtsunterricht, hg. von BÄRBEL KUHN/ HOLGER SCHMENK/ ASTRID WINDUS, St. Ingbert 2011, S. 9-22.

KUSBER, JAN Überleben zwischen den Großmächten. Lettische Außenpolitik 1918-1940, in: Lettland 1918-2018. Ein Jahrhundert Staatlichkeit, hg. von IVARS ĪJABS/ JAN KUSBER/ ILGVARS MISĀNS/ ERWIN OBERLÄNDER, Paderborn 2018, S. 51-62.

KUSBER, JAN Wegscheide Krieg. Defekte Imperien, defekte Nationalstaaten, in: Osteuropa 64 (2014) Heft 2-4, S. 233-246.

LEHTI, MARKO Baltic League as a Construct of the New Europe. Envisioning a Baltic Region and Small State Sovereignty in the Aftermath of the First World War, Frankfurt am Main 1999.

LEHTI, MARKO The Dancing Conference of Bulduri. A Clash of Alternative Regional Futures, in: Forgotten Pages, in: Baltic History. Diversity And Inclusion, hg. von MARTIN HOUSDEN/ DAVID J. SMITH, Rodopi 2011, S. 71-94.

LEONHARD, JÖRN Der überforderte Frieden. Versailles und die Welt 1918-1923, München 2018.

MANELA, EREZ The Wilsonian Moment. Self-Determination and the International Origins of Anticolonial Nationalism, Oxford 2007.

MICHALUK, DOROTA/ PER ANDRES, RUDLING From the Grand Duchy of Lithuania to Belarusian Democratic Republic. The Idea of Belarusian Statehood, 1915-1919, in: The Journal of Belarussian Studies 7 (2014) Heft 2, S. 3-36

Minutes of the Conference held at Bulduri, Washington D.C. 1960

MYLLYNIEMI, SEPPO Die baltische Krise 1938-1941, München 1979.

Nichtangriffsvertrag zwischen Deutschland und der Union der Sozialistischen Sowjetrepubliken, 23. August 1939, Einführung von BIANCA PIETROW-ENNKER, http://www.1000dokumente.de/index.html?c=dokument_ru&dokument=0025_pak&l=de, 14.05.2017.

NIEDHART, GOTTFRIED Die Außenpolitik der Weimarer Republik, München 2006.

NITSCHE, PETER Der Reichstag und die Festlegung der deutsch-polnischen Grenze nach dem Ersten Weltkrieg, in: Historische Zeitschrift 216 (1973) Heft 2, S. 335-361.

Pakt o vzaimopomošči meždu SSSR i Latviej. http://www.hrono.ru/dokum/193_dok/19391005_lat.html, 31.08.2022.

RAUCH, GEORG VON Geschichte der baltischen Staaten, 2. Aufl. München 1990.

SCHIEMANN, PAUL Zum Tode von Meierowicz', in: Berliner Tageblatt, Nr. 400, 25.8.1925.

SENN, ALFRED ERICH The Great Powers, Lithuania and the Vilna Question 1920-1928, Leiden 1966.

SNYDER, TIMOTHY Bloodlands. Europa zwischen Hitler und Stalin, 5. Aufl. München 2015.

TAUBER, JOACHIM Die Memelfrage im Rahmen der deutsch-litauischen Beziehungen 1919-1939, in: Deutschland und Litauen. Bestandsaufnahmen und Aufgaben der historischen Forschung, hg. von NORBERT ANDERMANN/ JOACHIM TAUBER, Lüneburg 1995, S. 107-118.

THOMAS, LUDMILLA Georgi Tschitscherin – „Ich hatte die Revolution und Mozart“, Berlin 2012.

Treaty of Good Understanding and Co-operation, signed at Geneva, September 12th, 1934, and Declaration of the same Date, in: Dokumente und Materialien zur ostmitteleuropäischen Geschichte. Themenmodul „Estland in der Zwischenkriegszeit“, bearb. von KARSTEN BRÜGGEMANN/ RAIKO JÄÄRATS, URL: https://www.herder-institut.de/digitale-angebote/dokumente-und-materialien/themenmodule/modul/14/seite.html, 15.03.2024

WEBER, CLAUDIA Der Pakt. Stalin, Hitler und die Geschichte einer mörderischen Allianz 1939-1941, München 2019.

WESTENBERGER, HANS Die handelspolitischen und wirtschaftlichen Beziehungen Deutschlands und Lettlands bis zum Abschluß des deutschlettländischen Vertrages vom 28. Juni 1926, in: Osteuropa 11-12 (1926) Heft 1, S. 656-667.

Autorinnen und Autoren

Benecke, Werner, Dr. phil., Univ.-Prof. für Kultur und Geschichte Mittel- und Osteuropas, Europa-Universität Viadrina Frankfurt (Oder)

Bogojavlenska, Svetlana, Dr. phil., Wissenschaftliche Mitarbeiterin, Johannes Gutenberg-Universität Mainz

Brüggemann, Karsten, Dr. phil., Univ.-Prof. of Estonian and General History, Tallinn University

Conrad, Benjamin, Dr. phil., Wissenschaftlicher Mitarbeiter, Humboldt-Universität zu Berlin

Kusber, Jan, Dr. phil., Univ.-Prof. für Osteuropäische Geschichte, Johannes Gutenberg-Universität Mainz

Müller, Christian, M. Ed. / M. Sc., Boehringer Ingelheim

Nahler, Timo, M. A., Arolsen Archives

Niendorf, Mathias, Dr. phil., Univ.-Prof. für Osteuropäische Geschichte, Universität Greifswald

Tikka, Marko, Dr. phil., Tampere University

Index

Personen:

Orte:

www.ingramcontent.com/pod-product-compliance
Ingram Content Group UK Ltd.
Pitfield, Milton Keynes, MK11 3LW, UK
UKHW041824290926
8980IPUK00002B/38

9 783631 907740